The Commercial Revolution in Nineteenth-Century China

The Commercial Revolution in Nineteenth-Century China

*The Rise of Sino-Western
Mercantile Capitalism*

Yen-p'ing Hao

UNIVERSITY OF CALIFORNIA PRESS
Berkeley • *Los Angeles* • *London*

University of California Press
Berkeley and Los Angeles, California

University of California Press, Ltd.
London, England

1   2   3   4   5   6   7   8   9

Library of Congress Cataloging in Publication Data

Hao, Yen-p'ing, 1934–
   The commercial revolution in nineteenth-century China.

   Bibliography: p.
   Includes index.
   1. China—Commerce—History—19th century.   2. China—
Foreign economic relations.   3. Capitalism—China—
History—19th century.   I. Title.
HF3836.H26   1985   380.1'0951   85-1083
ISBN 0-520-05344-3

For My Teachers

Contents

Maps and Tables

Preface

The controversial term "capitalism" is ambiguous and loaded with contemporary and anachronistic connotations, but the fact remains that during the nineteenth century, for better or worse, capitalism fundamentally changed the world, including China. Capitalism in its commercial stage was a most vigorous and fascinating development in China, yet no other major area of modern Chinese economic history is more neglected by scholars than the commercial sector.

When I first worked in the archives of the large American and British "Old China" trading houses during the mid-1960s, I came to believe that China's economic relations with the West were much more vigorous and important than was generally assumed. With time, I was increasingly convinced of the validity of the central theme of this study: China's trade with the West during the nineteenth century gave impetus to a full-fledged mercantile capitalism that constituted a commercial revolution. Because there are no better substitutes, I have used the controversial terms "capitalism" and "revolution," and I hope this book will help stimulate further discussion of the subject.

After the late 1960s, scholars in the West became increasingly skeptical about the historical significance of the early Sino-Western contacts, concentrating instead on China's indigenous developments. Meanwhile, capitalism not only was blamed in America for her involvement in Vietnam, but became a cardinal sin in the People's Republic of China as the Cultural Revolution unfolded. However, after the late 1970s, private entrepreneurship and economic competition regained some of their luster in the United States, and China, too, launched her awesome "Great

Leap Outward"—an economic outreach to the West. It is now high time to put nineteenth-century Sino-Western commercial relations in the proper historical perspective.

In this book, I have not written an exhaustive examination of modern China's commercial revolution in general and Sino-Western economic relations in particular. Rather, I focus on the scope, intensity, and salient features of nineteenth-century Sino-Western commercial capitalism and evaluate its effect on the Chinese economy and society. I shed light, too, on three other related issues in modern Chinese history: "incipient capitalism," economic imperialism, and the historical role of the treaty ports in affecting China.

In preparing this book, I have benefited throughout the years from discussion and association with many teachers, friends, and colleagues. John K. Fairbank read the first draft of the manuscript and made elaborate, valuable comments. For stimulating and fruitful discussions, I am indebted to Kwang-Ching Liu who first introduced me to the historical study of the records of Western firms in late Ch'ing China. As an economist, Dwight Perkins read an early version of the manuscript and offered important suggestions in connection with China's economic history. Yeh-chien Wang read the revised version and made major contributions in both general concepts and historical details. I have similarly benefited from the valuable comments of the anonymous readers of the University of California Press. I am indebted to Wayne Farris, Jane Park Farris, and Richard Rice for frequent consultation on editorial matters and general historical issues. My wife, Pin-han, has been of enormous help throughout the preparation of the manuscript. I am grateful to all of them.

Through the goodwill of the late Sir John Keswick, Matheson and Company kindly permitted me to examine the historical archives of Jardine, Matheson and Company at the Cambridge University Library. Allan Reid of Matheson's read the first draft of the manuscript and made some suggestions regarding the company's activities in China. I am obliged to Dilip Basu, Sarah R. Blanshei, Ch'ü Shu-chen, LeRoy P. Graf, Robert G. Landen, Robert W. Lovett, John H. Morrow, Jr., Jack E. Reese, and Eugene Wu for their help and encouragement during various stages of research. The Department of History of the University of Tennessee, Knoxville, has been helpful in many ways, especially in typing several versions of the manuscript. I am also indebted to Nancy A. Blumenstock for meticulously editing the manuscript, and to Lowell Dittmer, Grant Barnes, Phyllis Killen, and Barbara D. Metcalf for facilitating publication of the book. For financial support, I am grateful to the American Council of Learned Societies, the American Philosophical Society, the Social Science Research Council, and the University of Tennessee, Knoxville.

For their assistance in various ways, I am grateful to the staffs of the Baker Library and the Harvard-Yenching Library, Harvard University; the China Trade Museum, Milton, Massachusetts; the Library of Congress; the Essex Institute; the Hoover Library; the Massachusetts Historical Society; the Haskins Library of the University of Tennessee, Knoxville; the Cambridge University Library, Cambridge, England; the Public Record Office, London; the School of Oriental and African Studies Library, University of London; the Library of the Institute of Modern History and the Fu Ssu-nien Library, Academia Sinica, Taipei; the Library of the Chinese Maritime Customs, Taipei; the Feng P'ing-shan Library, University of Hong Kong; and the Tōyō Bunko, Tokyo.

Yen-p'ing Hao

Knoxville, Tennessee

Abbreviations

BPP   British Parliamentary Papers (Blue Books).

BSP   Bryant and Sturgis Papers. Baker Library, Harvard University, Boston.

CP   John P. Cushing Papers. Baker Library, Harvard University, Boston.

DP   F. G. Dexter Papers. Massachusetts Historical Society, Boston.

FBF   Frank Blackwell Forbes's Letter Books. Baker Library, Harvard University, Boston.

FC   Forbes Collection. Baker Library, Harvard University, Boston.

FO   Great Britain, Foreign Office. Public Record Office, London.
FO 17: General Correspondence, China
FO 228: Embassy and Consular Archives, China
FO 405: Confidential Prints, China
FO 682: Chinese Language Materials

FP   Forbes Papers. China Trade Museum (formerly the Museum of American China Trade), Milton, Massachusetts.

HC   Heard Collection. Baker Library, Harvard University, Boston.

HC II   Heard Collection, Second Part. Baker Library, Harvard University, Boston.

HLB   Houqua Letter Book. China Trade Museum (formerly the Museum of American China Trade), Milton, Massachusetts.

IMC	China, Imperial Maritime Customs.
JMA	Jardine, Matheson & Company Archives. University Library, Cambridge University, Cambridge, England.
KH	Kuang-hsu.
NCH	*North-China Herald.*
PCP	Perkins and Company Papers. Baker Library, Harvard University, Boston.
PP	Perkins Papers. Massachusetts Historical Society, Boston.
RA	Russell and Company Archives. Baker Library, Harvard University, Boston.
RP	Russell Papers (Samuel Russell and Company). Library of Congress, Washington, D.C.
SP	John Swire and Sons Papers (parent firm of Butterfield & Swire). School of Oriental and African Studies Library, University of London, London.
TC	T'ung-chih.

CHAPTER ONE

Introduction

China's economic relations with the West gave impetus to a full-fledged mercantile capitalism that constituted a commercial revolution in the nineteenth century. The late eighteenth century witnessed the fermentation of new mercantile activities along the Chinese coast from which emerged a new economic formation. Between the 1820s and the 1880s, changes in market structure, in the financial aspects of commerce, in trading centers, in shipping, and in methods of conducting business were so numerous, so pronounced, and so rapid that the total effect seems to have been revolutionary. These were structural as well as functional changes, which resulted in an economic form markedly different from the commercial activities that had existed in traditional China for centuries. In this book I will examine the scope, intensity, and salient features of this commercial revolution and evaluate its effect on the Chinese economy and society.

The word "capitalism" is ambiguous and loaded with anachronistic and contemporary connotations. This modern expression (coined about 1870) in its broadest sense dates only from the beginning of the twentieth century. (Marx was virtually unaware of the word.) Since then it has been much used and much abused. Controversy notwithstanding, I will use the word "capitalism" because, first of all, certain sophisticated economic mechanisms occurring worldwide, especially after the sixteenth century, are crying out for a name all their own. Indeed, if the word is used so much, it is because there is a need for it or for a word serving the same purpose. Moreover, there is no substitute for this word. In fact, the best reason for using the word "capitalism" is that no one has found a better word.[1]

For my purpose, capitalism refers to an economic system that is characterized by private ownership of property, freedom of enterprise with its accompanying profits and competition, and freedom of choice by individual consumers. When this system is dominated by trade rather than industry, it is called "mercantile capitalism" or "commercial capitalism." Although capitalism has been criticized from the points of view of the economics of resource allocation and the economics of resource employment, it is generally conceded to be an effective mechanism of exchange and production. The criticism of capitalism usually proceeds from moral or cultural disapproval of such features of the system as waste, inequality, and the concentration of private economic power. Whatever its drawbacks, the capitalistic system has significantly changed the modern world.[2] How did Sino-Western trade facilitate the rise of commercial capitalism in China? What are the ramifications of the commercial revolution regarding China's economic development?

In a sense the word "revolution" is a misnomer here, because fundamental changes in trade along China's coast evolved gradually over a long period of time, being barely noticeable at the beginning. This commercial revolution was a product of the secular economic expansion in China and in the West. Domestically, China experienced a prolonged period of peace and prosperity after 1683 when the Manchus effectively unified the country. The Pax Sinica of the eighteenth century witnessed an extensive growth of the Chinese economy; the increase in population,

1. For a general discussion of this issue, see Fernand Braudel, *Capitalism and Material Life, 1400–1800,* tr. Miriam Kochan (New York, 1975), pp. xii–xiii; and *Afterthoughts on Material Civilization and Capitalism,* tr. Patricia Ranum (Baltimore, Md., 1977), pp. 45–48. Commenting on the usage of the word "capitalism" in its broadest sense, Braudel writes, "I could somewhat arbitrarily state that it was launched in 1902 when Werner Sombart published his well-known *Der moderne Kapitalismus"* (*Afterthoughts,* p. 46).

2. Social and economic inequality is a burning issue for many scholars who have criticized capitalism. For Braudel, "the basic inequality of partners that underlies the capitalistic process is visible on every level of social life" (*Afterthoughts,* p. 62). Immanuel Wallerstein writes that both kinds of world-system—the world-empire with a redistributive economy and the world-economy with a capitalistic market economy—"involve markedly unequal distribution of rewards" ("The Rise and Future Demise of the World Capitalist System," in his *The Capitalist World-Economy* [Cambridge, England, 1979], pp. 21–22). See also his edited volume, *World Inequality* (Montreal, 1975). The fact that the capitalistic system has led the way from an age of scarcity to an age of potential abundance was recognized by Karl Marx and Friedrich Engels who wrote in 1848 that this capital-based economic system in "scarce one hundred years has created more massive and more colossal productive forces than have all preceding generations together" (*The Communist Manifesto* [New York, 1964], p. 10). "Mercantile capitalism" and "commercial capitalism" are used interchangeably throughout this book.

the expansion of interregional trade, rapid urbanization, and the growth of handicraft industries are eloquent examples. In the West, capitalist Europe, after one and one-half centuries of economic contraction and consolidation, gathered momentum and started worldwide expansion around 1750. The eighteenth century in Europe was not only what Fernand Braudel calls "a century of general economic acceleration" but also the beginning of a significant, secular economic expansion.[3]

Scholars of nineteenth-century Chinese economic history have so far concentrated on industrial enterprises, especially the steamship, mining, cotton textile manufacturing, railroad, and armaments industries.[4] The commercial sector has been essentially ignored. Source materials on modern China's economic history include voluminous collections treating industry, agriculture, and handicrafts, but little on commerce.[5] Studies on Sino-Western commercial relations are primarily concerned with the period of the Canton system (1757–1842).[6] What accounts for the lack of studies on commercial development in the post–Opium War period?

3. After eight years of fighting, the rebellion of the Three Feudatories was put down by the K'ang-hsi Emperor of the Ch'ing dynasty in 1681, and two years later he also took Taiwan. From the unification of China in 1683 to the turn of the nineteenth century, China experienced virtually unprecedented economic expansion. For a general view, see Wang Yeh-chien, *Chung-kuo chin-tai huo-pi yü yin-hang ti yen-chin, 1644–1937* (Taipei, 1981), pp. 13–15; and Yeh-chien Wang, "Evolution of the Chinese Monetary System, 1644–1850," in Chi-ming Hou and Tzong-shian Yu, eds., *Modern Chinese Economic History* (Taipei, 1979), pp. 434–35. Liu Shih-chi, "Ch'ing-tai Chiang-nan shang-p'in ching-chi ti fa-chan yü shih-chen ti hsing-ch'i" (M.A. thesis, National Taiwan University, 1975), gives a detailed account of the rise of market towns, extensively using local histories. For the activities of the merchants, see Fu I-ling, *Ming-Ch'ing shih-tai shang-jen chi shang-yeh tzu-pen* (Peking, 1956). For secular trends of economic development of modern Europe, see Wallerstein, *The Modern World-System II* (New York, 1980), pp. 24–29, 130; and Braudel, *Capitalism and Material Life*, p. 27.

4. See, e.g., Kwang-Ching Liu, "Steamship Enterprise in Nineteenth Century China," *Journal of Asian Studies* 18:435–55 (Aug. 1959); Albert Feuerwerker, *China's Early Industrialization* (Cambridge, Mass., 1958); Ellsworth C. Carlson, *The Kaiping Mines, 1877–1912* (Cambridge, Mass., 1971); Yen Chung-p'ing, *Chung-kuo mien-fang-chih shih-kao* (Peking, 1955); Li Kuo-ch'i, *Chung-kuo tsao ch'i ti t'ieh-lu ching-ying* (Taipei, 1961); and Wang Erh-min, *Ch'ing-chi ping-kung-yeh ti hsing-ch'i* (Taipei, 1963).

5. Ch'en Chen and Yao Lo, comps., *Chung-kuo chin-tai kungp-yeh shih tzu-liao* (Peking, 1957–1961); Sun Yü-t'ang, comp., *Chung-kuo chin-tai kung-yeh shih tzu-liao ti-i chi, 1840–1895 nien* (Peking, 1957); Wang Ching-yü, comp., *Chung-kuo chin-tai kung-yeh shih tzu-liao ti-erh chi, 1895–1914 nien* (Peking, 1957); Li Wen-chih, comp., *Chung-kuo chin-tai nung-yeh shih tzu-liao ti-i, chi, 1840–1911* (Peking, 1957); P'eng Tse-i, comp., *Chung-kuo chin-tai shou-kung-yeh shih tzu-liao, 1840–1849* (Peking, 1957). One notable collection of source materials on commerce is *Shang-hai shih mien-pu shang-yeh* (Peking, 1979), which cannot be compared with the above-mentioned collections in length. Besides, it was published only recently.

6. H. B. Morse, *The Chronicles of the East India Company Trading to China, 1635–1843* (Oxford, England, 1926); Michael Greenberg, *British Trade and the Opening of China, 1800–1842* (Cambridge, England, 1951); Louis Dermigny, *La Chine et l'occident* (Paris, 1964); and Liang Chia-pin, *Kuang-tung shih-san hang k'ao* (T'ai-chung, Taiwan, 1960).

Part of the answer may be found in the way in which China's relations with the West are perceived. It is widely held that Sino-Western trade was the single most important component of the "opening" of China; thus, its historical significance diminished once China was actually "opened." And it is generally maintained that the key to economic development was industry, not commerce. I will show that Sino-Western trade continued to play an active role in China's relations with the West after the Opium War and that this trade remarkably enhanced China's economic development, both on its own account and as a springboard for industrialization.

Economic development aside, commerce is worth studying in its own right. If the historical significance of an event lies mainly in the number of people the event has affected, then it is commerce, and not industry, that was of paramount importance in nineteenth-century China. Business enterprises were still predominantly in the commercial stage, and the dominance of commercial activities over industrial enterprises was clear in terms of share of investment, numbers employed, value added, and share of income. Within the modern sector of the economy, the largest share of profits came from trade and finance rather than from manufacturing. And by far the largest part of goods in trade was obtained not from industry, but from the traditional sector (agriculture and craft work).

Trade expanded steadily in late Ch'ing China, in part because the population was increasing and wealth accumulating, but also because the process of specialization continued, drawing a greater proportion of the population into the commercial nexus. These trends were strongest along the coast (map 1) where, for several reasons, a period of burgeoning commercial capitalism dawned during the nineteenth century. Private property and the resulting inequalities of wealth and income were vigorously protected under the so-called "treaty system." The accumulation of capital was closely linked with both savings and profits from enterprise. The basic machinery for the exercise of credit functions—banks as agencies of deposits and loans—was established. Finally, the profit system was both socially and morally defensible, because the coastal area was far from the centers of China's Confucian society and readily accepted private fortunes.[7]

7. For a general discussion of the population of China, see Ping-ti Ho, *Studies on the Population of China, 1368–1953* (Cambridge, Mass., 1959). In the hierarchy of Confucian social values, merchants were at the bottom, artisans were a step higher but still below the peasants, and scholars were at the apex.

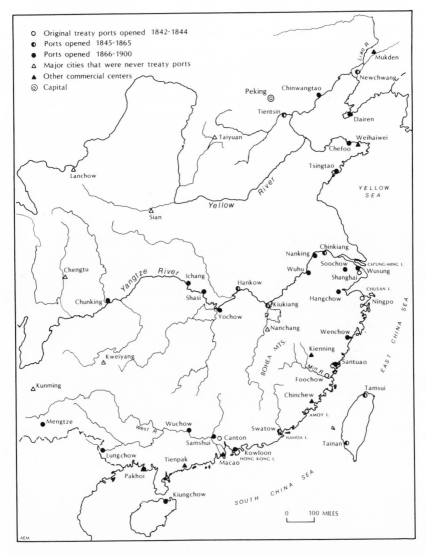

Map 1.   Major Commercial Centers in Nineteenth-Century China

Source: Adapted from the map, "The China Treaty Ports," in Murphey, *The Outsiders*, back endpaper.

The typical coastal businessman was a merchant who combined the functions of trader, banker, and speculator. His business was founded on the demands of the marketplace, and he was determined to supply the products that were most salable. The commodity market, rather than the labor market, was the main field of his activity, and his important contribution was not organization of the plant, but improvement of the exchange mechanism. Sino-Western commerce, stimulated by the liberal supply of money and easy, inexpensive credit, spearheaded the widening of the market and consequently intensified business risk and uncertainty. Meanwhile, competition was stiff. Capitalism thrived on the coast because of the expansion of the import, export, and shipping trade operations.

In many ways, I have departed in this book from the existing litera-ture on the treaty port commerce. First, it is a thematical study of com-mercial developments over a long period—from the late eighteenth cen-tury under the Canton system through the treaty period after 1842 to the end of the nineteenth century. In this sense, it is broader in scope than many previous studies on Sino-Western economic relations.[8] Further-more, I examine all the salient features of commercial capitalism along the coast. Free commerce is a major feature of capitalism; the generally accepted view of China's foreign trade in the old Canton days was that trade was limited to Canton and monopolized by the Cohong and the British India Company. In chapter 2, I question this view by exploring an important, but largely neglected, subject—the rise of the Chinese "shopmen" and the parallel phenomenon of the private traders from the West. Chapter 3 examines the introduction and spread of three new forms of money. The monetary function of opium is extensively dis-cussed, the total money supply estimated, and its economic ramifications evaluated. The novel mechanism of the "Soochow system," whereby Chinese merchants acting under the encouragement of Western traders brought opium from Shanghai to Soochow in order to procure silk, is also discussed in detail. In chapter 4, I examine how credit transactions in the treaty ports during the nineteenth century differed from traditional practices. I estimate the rates of interest along the coast, point out their trends, explain why the rates were remarkably low, and assess their overall economic impact on China.

8. Shigeta's study on tea is limited to Hunan, and Hatano's similar work, based largely on the Western literature of the nineteenth century on Chinese tea, deals only with the period prior to the Opium War. See Shigeta Atsushi, "Shimmatsu ni okeru Konan cha no seisan kōzō, gokō kaikō igo o chūshin to shite," *Jimbun kenkyū* 16.4:369–418; and Hatano Yoshihiro, "Chūgoku yushutsucha no seisan kōzō," *Nagoya daigaku bungakubu kenkyū ronshū, II, Shigaku* 1:183–210 (1952). Sherman Cochran, *Big Business in China* (Cambridge, Mass., 1980), discusses cigarette production and marketing, mainly in the twentieth century. I will not dwell on the silk trade, which has been carefully examined in Lillian M. Li, *China's Silk Trade* (Cambridge, Mass., 1981).

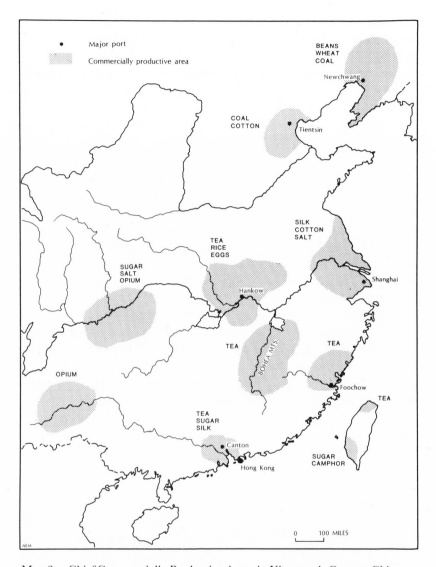

Map 2.   Chief Commercially Productive Areas in Nineteenth-Century China

Sources: Adapted from the map, "Major Ports and Chief Commercially Productive Areas in East Asia," in Murphey, *The Outsiders*, front endpaper; and the map, "Tea and Silk Areas of China in the Nineteenth Century," in Murphey, *Shanghai*, p. 105.

In chapters 5 and 6, I illustrate the widening of the market (map 2) with an extensive account of the trade of the most important commodities in import (opium) and export (tea). The expansion of the tea trade typifies the commercialization of agricultural products. In these chapters, I provide new, detailed accounts of the day-to-day operations of the opium trade and the upcountry purchase of tea and silk. I elucidate the optional trade, trade in futures, business based on contract, transactions through advances, and the introduction of new distribution networks and marketing techniques. There is no capitalism without competition.[9] Because the Western trading firms in China handled a considerable share of China's external trade and supposedly enjoyed oligopolistic power, it has often been asserted that they, having stifled competition, had an extremely restrictive effect on China's foreign trade. These exporting firms have been portrayed as manipulating prices at the expense of Chinese producers, with the result that low prices discouraged production. Similarly, it is suggested that importing firms depressed imports by charging higher prices than would result under pure competition. In chapter 7, I examine the extent to which these assertions are true and discuss whether foreign traders competed with one another in earnest. Whereas other scholars of Sino-Western relations have concentrated on the business rivalry between Chinese and foreigners,[10] I will stress competition in general among all coastal merchant-businessmen, native or foreign. My discussion of economic nationalism adds a new dimension to the study of Sino-Western economic competition in the nineteenth century.

Capitalism is an economic system based predominantly on private ownership and the use of accumulated wealth for the production and exchange of goods and services with the aim of earning a profit. In chapters 8 and 9, I investigate the ways in which the coastal merchants pursued profit. Although other scholars have briefly touched on the subject,[11] I will try to give a detailed, comprehensive account of the symbiotic relationship between Chinese and Western businessmen. By using archival materials, the practices of trading through joint accounts

9. That competition is an integral part of capitalism is controversial. Whereas most scholars recognize the importance of competition, Braudel stresses the role of monopoly (*Afterthoughts*, pp. 57, 111, 113).

10. E.g., Kwang-ching Liu, "British-Chinese Steamship Rivalry in China, 1873–1885," in C. D. Cowan, ed., *The Economic Development of China and Japan* (New York, 1964), pp. 49–78; Rhoads Murphey, *The Outsiders* (Ann Arbor, Mich., 1977); and Sherman Cochran, *Big Business*.

11. Wang Ching-yü's "Shih-chiu shih-chi wai-kuo ch'in Hua shih-yeh chung ti Hua-shang fu-ku huo-tung," *Li-shih yen-chiu* 4:39–74 (1965), is a careful study, but Wang has not used the records of the most important British and American firms in China. These records indicate that the *fu-ku* activities existed far more extensively and sophisticatedly than we have so far realized. G. C. Allen and Audrey G. Donnithorne, *Western Enterprise in Far Eastern Economic Development* (London, 1954) briefly mention the Chinese merchants' interest in such Western business practices as insurance.

and Chinese doing business under foreign names are elaborated. And the total amount of Chinese investment in foreign enterprises, as well as the rates of commercial profit returns, is estimated. Finally, I question the prevailing view that one crucial factor hindering China's economic development was the scarcity of capital.

Another salient feature of commercial capitalism is the ever-increasing business risks and uncertainties that are contingent on the expansion of the market, but scholars of modern Chinese economic history have not explored this wide-ranging subject in depth. Based primarily on the records of American and British firms in China, in chapters 10 and 11, I give an intimate account of market fluctuation, speculation, business losses, bankruptcies and financial crises, and endeavor to put these phenomena into a larger, socioeconomic context.

In examining Sino-Western trade in detail, I will throw light on the controversies of worldwide capitalism in general and on related issues of Chinese social and economic history in particular. The first controversy involves the historical transition from feudalism to capitalism, which was vigorously debated among Western Marxists in the mid-1950s.[12] China was affected, but a more relevant concern for her in this connection was not so much the timing and nature of such a transition as the issue of indigenous sprouts of capitalism in China. Was there in China the possibility of a spontaneous development toward capitalism, especially in handicraft industries and agricultural products, before she had established close trade relations with the West?

Many Chinese on the mainland assert that an incipient form of capitalism, which began during the fifteenth and sixteenth centuries, was steadily growing throughout the Ch'ien-lung period (1736–1795). Handicraft workshops of considerable number and size—especially in weaving, porcelain, and traditional mining—sprang up, and the commercialization of agricultural products was evident. Given the early domestic development of protocapitalism, they conclude that, even in the absence of intensified Western trade in the nineteenth century, China would have gone capitalist by herself.[13] Unfortunately, their

12. This debate was sparked by Maurice H. Dobb's study on the development of capitalism in Western Europe. For different viewpoints, see Rodney Hilton, ed., *The Transition from Feudalism to Capitalism* (London, 1976). For a recent perspective stressing the nature of transition, see Wallerstein, "From Feudalism to Capitalism: Transition or Transitions?" in his *The Capitalist World-Economy*, pp. 138–51.

13. Historians and political leaders in China have discussed this issue extensively since the 1950s. See Mao Tse-tung, *Mao Tse-tung hsuan-chi* (Peking, 1963), II, 620; and Chung-

discussions are limited to the period before 1800, and they pay little attention to the actual role that the indigenous elements played in instigating full-fledged capitalism in China. I will give a detailed account of the function of Chinese economic institutions in facilitating Sino-Western commercial capitalism during the nineteenth century and try to put the issue in proper historical perspective.

The second controversy concerns economic imperialism, which has attracted considerable attention, because it bears on the approaches to the study of Chinese history and on international relations throughout the world today. The theories of developmentalism and modernization have dominated the Western academe during the past several decades. These scholars see the process of economic change as a series of stages through which each country has to proceed. One may then examine what it takes to move from one stage to another, and why some countries take longer than others to modernize.[14] In these theories, economic development or underdevelopment is seen as being determined by the particular social, political, and cultural factors of traditional societies, and the primary influence of the West on the nonindustrial nations is seen as promoting development. This traditional-society approach has frequently been used in explaining modern China's slow development and in contrasting it with Japan's successful industrialization.[15]

After the mid-1960s, some neo-Marxist themes concerning the consequences of international capitalism reappeared.[16] A vigorous one is the "dependency theory," which maintains that the capitalist West has

---

kuo jen-min ta-hsueh Chung-kuo li-shih chiao-yen-shih, ed., *Chung-kuo tzu-pen-chu-i meng-ya wen-t'i t'ao-lun chi* (Peking, 1957–1960). For a discussion on the Chinese debates, see Albert Feuerwerker, "Chinese History in Marxian Dress," *American Historical Review* 66:327–30 (Jan. 1961).

14. W. W. Rostow, *The Process of Economic Growth* (New York, 1962), represents the developmentalist approach. The modernization theory is advanced by, among others, C. E. Black, *The Dynamics of Modernization* (New York, 1966); and S. N. Eisenstadt, *Modernization* (Englewood Cliffs, N.J., 1966).

15. See, e.g., John K. Fairbank, Edwin O. Reischauer, and Albert M. Craig, *East Asia* (Boston, 1965).

16. Earlier, the Singer-Prebisch-Myrdal "absorption" thesis, developed from 1949 to 1959, contended that underdeveloped countries have not benefited from commerical contact with rich countries. The export development that resulted in the poor countries may have absorbed what little native entrepreneurial initiative and domestic investment there was and thereby prevented the countries from developing what are called "growing points." After the late 1950s, classical scholars criticized this thesis in general. Chi-ming Hou, *Foreign Investment and Economic Development in China, 1840–1937* (Cambridge, Mass., 1965), maintains that it is not applicable to modern China. (The term "developing countries" has recently replaced the older, distasteful "underdeveloped countries.")

forcibly turned the Third World countries into economic satellites and dependencies; that within the global metropolis-satellite structure the former is destined to development, but the latter to underdevelopment; and that the degree of underdevelopment of the satellites is proportional to the extent of their contact with the Western metropolis in the past. Underdevelopment, therefore, is neither original nor traditional, because it is capitalism that has created underdevelopment.[17]

Since the mid-1970s, the "world-economy" approach has gained momentum.[18] To challenge modernization theory, Immanuel Wallerstein starts with the radical assumption that we all live in one world—a capitalist world. We do not live in a modernizing world, he argues, but in a capitalist world. What makes this world tick is not the need for achievement, but the need for profit.[19] Following Braudel's model, Wallerstein's world-economy has three concentric zones: the core, the periphery, and the semiperiphery in between. He maintains that the modern world-system took the form of a capitalist world-economy that had its genesis in Europe in the sixteenth century. Since then the capitalist nations of Europe have drawn successive areas of the world into the orbit of their economies, until by the nineteenth century much of the non-European world occupied a peripheral status in relation to Europe.[20] Among Western students of China, there are many Waller-

17. For the "dependency theory," see James D. Cockcroft, Andre Gunder Frank, and Dale L. Johnson, eds., *Dependence and Underdevelopment* (Garden City, N.Y., 1972); Andre Gunder Frank, *Capitalism and Underdevelopment in Latin America* (New York, 1967), *Latin America* (New York, 1969), and *Dependent Accumulation and Underdevelopment* (London, 1978); and Fernando Henrique Cardoso and Enzo Faletto, *Dependency and Development in Latin America* (Berkeley, Calif., 1979).

18. Braudel first coined the term "world-economy": "By world-economy—a word I forged on the pattern of the German word *Weltwirtschaft*—I mean the economy of only one portion of our planet, to the degree that it forms an economic *whole*" (*Afterthoughts*, p. 81). Wallerstein later defines a "world-system" as a unit with a single division of labor and multiple cultural systems. There can be two varieties of such world-systems, one with a common political system and one without; the former is called "world-empires," and the latter, "world-economies." In other words, a world-economy refers to a single division of labor but multiple polities and cultures. See Wallerstein's "The Rise and Future Demise," pp. 5–6.

19. Wallerstein, "Modernization: Requiescat in Pace," in his *The Capitalist World-Economy*, p. 133.

20. Wallerstein's structuralist challenge to modernization theory comes at an opportune moment, and "Wallersteinism" is becoming something of an academic growth industry. His *The Modern World-System* (New York, 1974) and *The Modern World-System II* are the first two in a projected four-volume series. His *The Capitalist World-Economy* (Cambridge, England, 1979) is a collection of essays. He is the editor of *World Inequality* (Montreal, 1975) and a coeditor (with Terence K. Hopkins) of *Processes of the World-System* (Beverly Hills, Calif., 1980). For reviews of his writings and works by his followers, see Angus McDonald, Jr., "Wallerstein's World-Economy: How Seriously Should We Take It?" *Journal of Asian Studies* 38.3:535–40 (May 1979).

stein followers.[21] But to what extent are the dependency theory and the world-economy theory applicable to modern China? Did foreign merchants in effect have insurmountable advantages over their Chinese rivals? Did they exploit China economically? By singling out the specific categories where economic imperialism was absent or conspicuous in China, I hope to refine our understanding of modern imperialism.

Finally, I will illuminate the important role of the treaty ports in modern China, through the study of commerce. The history of modern China is often viewed as a process of China's response to the West.[22] However, many scholars have started to emphasize China's indigenous forces, and the role of the treaty ports has been reassessed. A case in point is *The Cambridge History of China*, which, for the late Ch'ing period, adopts a new approach by looking at the Ch'ing empire from the perspective of Peking. Instead of following the conventional wisdom of discussing Sino-Western relations first, it begins by examining Ch'ing Inner Asia around 1800.[23] By the same token, Rhoads Murphey argues that, although India was remade in the image of Calcutta and although Japan pursued its own reactive path to modernization, China consistently resisted the Western goals. In the end it rejected in an indigenous revolutionary wave the model of development that the treaty ports symbolized and advocated.[24]

Trade expansion and technological advances led to fundamental changes in the structure of Chinese society and institutions. Indeed, Marxists and many others use the word "capitalism" to denote a particular institutional order, carrying with it a strong political-moral tinge. I will avoid such usage and try to adhere to the economic sense of the word. This book concentrates on the rise and vitality of Sino-Western commercial capitalism and is not intended to be an exhaustive

21. Frances V. Moulder's *Japan, China and the Modern World Economy* (Cambridge, England, 1977) is a general and controversial study. McDonald's "Wallerstein's World-Economy" assesses Wallerstein's theory and its applicability to China. Other specific studies include Dilip K. Basu, "The Peripheralization of China," in W. Goldfrank, ed., *The World System of Capitalism* (Beverly Hills, Calif., 1979), pp. 171–87; Edward Friedman, "Maoist Conceptualizations of the Capitalist World-System," in Terence K. Hopkins and Immanuel Wallerstein, eds., *Processes of the World-System* (Beverly Hills, Calif., 1980), pp. 181–223; and Alvin Yiu-cheong So, "Development Inside the Capitalist World-System," *Journal of Asian Culture* 5:33–56 (1981).

22. See Ssu-yü Teng and John K. Fairbank, *China's Response to the West* (Cambridge, Mass., 1954).

23. John K. Fairbank, ed., *The Cambridge History of China*, vol. 10, *Late Ch'ing, 1800–1911, Part 1* (Cambridge, England, 1978), chaps. 1, 2.

24. Murphey, *Outsiders*, chaps. 1, 12.

analysis of China's economic development in general and coastal commerce in particular. Nor will it elaborate the noneconomic aspects of commercial capitalism, although any study of commercial development cannot be entirely separated from the socioeconomic setting in which it occurs.

China's invaders from the West in the modern period left a more extensive record than anything we are as yet aware of from the Chinese side. Although exploits and impressions on the expanding frontier of the international trading world were recorded by Western diplomats, merchants, and others in a flood of correspondence, articles, and books, the Chinese who worked with foreigners were not accustomed to writing down their views and experiences for posterity. Thus, it is not surprising that Chinese source materials are much fewer than Western ones.

This book is based in large part on the Western records, especially on correspondence files in the Jardine, Matheson & Co. Archives in Cambridge, England; the Forbes, Russell and Heard collections at the Harvard Business School; the Houqua Letter Book available at the China Trade Museum, Milton, Massachusetts; and the British official correspondence in the Public Record Office, London. This is a minutely and specifically based study of China's trade with the West with reference to its expansion and mechanisms of operation. Details of these commercial activities are examined in the larger context of economic development. The theme is modern China's commercial revolution as seen in the form of Sino-Western commercial capitalism, and new market systems, economic organizations, and social relationships are identified. I also shed new light on such important issues as indigenous sprouts of capitalism, economic imperialism, and the important role of the treaty ports in modern China.

CHAPTER TWO

Free Trade
Along the Coast

Free trade is an important element in commercial capitalism. The generally accepted view of China's foreign trade in the Canton system days (1757–1842), however, is that it was limited to Canton and that this Canton system of trade constituted a rigid monopoly in sharp contrast to the laissez-faire spirit prevailing in the West at the same time. It is also generally thought that this Canton system of monopoly was enforced by both Chinese and British governments, and was accepted by merchants.[1] But a closer look, especially through the study of the archives of important British and American mercantile houses, indicates that these assertions are not necessarily true.

BEYOND CANTON AND THE COHONG

The Cohong was in charge of China's thriving trade with the West in Canton, which, according to a number of Western traders, became one of the best ports in the world in providing facilities for international trade in the 1820s and the 1830s. But China's external trade was not limited to Canton, nor was it entirely monopolized by the Cohong, which was not strictly a monopolistic company in the first place.

---

1. H. B. Morse, *The International Relations of the Chinese Empire*, vol. 1, *The Period of Conflict, 1834–1860* (Shanghai, 1910), p. 166. For a detailed account of the Canton system and its international ramifications, see Dermigny, *La Chine et l'occident*.

FREE TRADE OUTSIDE CANTON

China's foreign trade, inhibited at first by internal disorder during the early Ch'ing period, was actually conducted on a free trade basis as early as the lifting of the imperial ban on sea intercourse in 1684, one year after the pacification of Taiwan. For the next seventy-five years, European merchants traded freely at China's coastal ports, and Canton was but one of them. Even during the Canton system period, from 1757 to 1842, when the trade was nominally confined to Canton, this city by no means held a monopoly of China's foreign trade.

For one thing, after 1557 Macao, a small peninsula at the entrance of the Pearl River estuary, was a Portuguese settlement,[2] where they traded with the Chinese.[3] Although other foreigners were legally prohibited from trading at Macao, the Jardine, Matheson and Company's archives indicate that this gigantic British firm did a substantial trade there. Its agent at Macao for many years was a Portuguese named B. Barretto, who handled business for the firm on a commission basis.[4] Macao was also used extensively for social and residential purposes by other Western merchants who escaped from Canton during the slack summer season. When the illegal opium trade bloomed in the early nineteenth century, Macao carried even more of China's foreign trade by virtue of being an important opium disposal port. Foreign merchants were so deeply involved in this trade that a fiscal war developed between the British and Portuguese opium interests at Macao in the 1820s.[5]

Besides Macao, Chinese and foreign merchants were also engaged in trade at Amoy on the Fukien coast, especially with India and Southeast Asia. Legally, Amoy was only open to Spanish trade, but the Spaniards did not fully take advantage of their right, because Cantonese and Fukienese junks could carry on trade with the Philippines more economically. Although the Spanish did not trade at Amoy frequently (only one Spanish ship visited the port between 1810 and 1830),[6] the Jardine archives indicate that many British private traders, with the cooperation of the Cantonese merchants, did business at Amoy under Spanish colors.

2. China granted Macao to Portugal as a reward for its assistance in suppressing pirates, and the Portuguese did not assert full sovereignty over Macao until the mid-nineteenth century. For the rise of Macao, see T'ien-tse Chang, *Sino-Portuguese Trade from 1514 to 1644* (Leyden, 1934), chap. 5.

3. *Canton Register and Price Current*, Mar. 24, 1833.

4. Papers of Payva and Company, JMA.

5. Michael Greenberg, *British Trade and the Opening of China, 1800–42* (Cambridge, England, 1951), chap. 6.

6. BPP, *First and Second Report from the Select Committee of the House of Commons on the Affairs of the East India Company* 1830, pp. 170, 389.

For instance, Beale and Magniac, forerunners of Jardine, Matheson & Company,[7] chartered the ship *Anna Felix* in November 1806 to carry a cargo of Indian raw cotton to Amoy on joint account with a Cantonese merchant.[8] In like manner, James Matheson, who started his fortune as junior partner in the Spanish firm of Yrissari & Co., in 1823 sent the opium ship *San Sebastian* to Amoy where she stayed for four days.[9] Working under the shadow of the opium trade, the energetic young Matheson also tried hard to put the nonopium trade between Amoy and Manila on a regular basis.[10]

A new smuggling complex was formed on China's coast after 1821 when the Canton authorities were successful in driving the illegal trade of opium from Whampoa. The British private traders then removed their opium vessels to the islands of Lintin, Cumsingmoon (Kumsingmoon), and Hong Kong. Centering on these islands, the opium trade gradually spread northward on the coast. In time, Lintin Island became the most important station for smuggling opium and saltpeter to Canton. Meanwhile, sycee (silver bullion) and other rare metals (such as tutenag, a kind of Chinese zinc) were smuggled out of mainland China to Lintin. In addition to the contraband articles, legal commodities were often smuggled via Lintin to avoid the duties at Canton.[11]

It is thus evident that Canton did not monopolize China's foreign trade prior to 1842. We are not sure of the volume of trade in Macao and Amoy, but the trade at the smuggling center of Lintin certainly reflected the extent to which China's foreign trade was conducted outside the official, nominally monopolistic Canton system. In the 1832 season, for instance, the contraband article of opium constituted more than one-half of the value of foreign imports into Canton.[12] The *Canton Register* listed thirty-eight "country" ships, including several noted opium clippers, that came to China in 1832, but went no farther upriver than Lintin. Besides, there were several "hulks," such as the *Hercules*, that remained anchored at Lintin year after year.[13]

7. John K. Fairbank, *Trade and Diplomacy on the China Coast* (Cambridge, Mass., 1953), II, 56.

8. India Letter Books, Nov. 11, 1806, JMA.

9. Letter Books of Yrissari & Co., Sept. 2, 1823, JMA.

10. The plan fell through because of Matheson's preoccupation with the opium business (Letter Books of Yrissari & Co., 1821–1827, JMA).

11. India Letter Books, 1821–1839, passim, JMA.

12. The total import figure was $28,046,736, of which opium constituted $14,109,600 (H. B. Morse, *The Chronicles of the East India Company Trading to China, 1635–1834* [Oxford, 1926], IV, 339).

13. *Canton Register*, Feb. 11, 1834.

LIMITATIONS OF THE COHONG AS A MONOPOLY

Although the Cohong acted jointly in certain respects, it was not strictly a monopolistic company, as was the British East India Company.[14] The hong merchants were loosely organized and held together mainly by three collective actions. First, they acted as a group in carrying out the practice of *pao-hsiao*, that is, contributing money to the Ch'ing government. Second, if any one of them became insolvent due to losses in trade, the Cohong would assume collective responsibility for the repayment of foreign creditors out of their Consoo (club) fund. Third, all of them agreed to take the responsibility for supervision and control of foreign merchants. However, these collective activities had limitations. For example, the hong merchants could not always make satisfactory arrangements as to how much money each member would contribute to the *pao-hsiao* quota. Besides, their Consoo fund was not used automatically for all insolvent cases but had to be sanctioned each time. More importantly, they acted jointly in controlling the foreign merchant's behavior but not necessarily in doing business with him.

Except for these collective activities, which were conducted on a limited scale, the Cohong was neither a guild merchant nor a "regulated company" in the Western sense. It had no joint stock because each hong merchant traded not only on his own account and for his own firm, but also with his own capital and for his own profit. It seldom conducted corporate bargaining in spite of an imperial decree of 1780 ordering it to do so. On the contrary, for most of the time price competition existed among the hong merchants. In the final analysis, the Cohong system was instituted by the Ch'ing government not so much to enforce a commercial monopoly as to increase monetary gains and control foreign merchants. As long as the system accomplished these dual goals of the government, it enjoyed the various opportunities of free trade.

Furthermore, the hong merchants did not monopolize China's foreign trade at Canton because they did not obtain the exclusive possession of all trade. In fact, free trade prevailed outside the Cohong in a greater degree, both legally and illegally. The hong merchants handled the staple articles, but the "outside merchants" (also called "shopmen") were allowed by law to engage in the trade of such things as were necessary for the personal use of foreign residents in China. The Canton authorities frequently reminded them of this restriction and even enumerated the commodities, such as clothing, fans, umbrellas, and straw hats. But in

14. Greenberg, pp. 51–57.

practice they also traded more important articles, and their transactions were on an immense scale. Sometimes the volume of the trade of the shopmen was so large that it had to be conducted under the names of the hong merchants who were responsible for customs duties on cargoes.

Although a couple of the wealthy hong merchants had little to do with the shopmen, some of their impoverished colleagues were willing to lend their names and facilities to these outside merchants for a fee. For the British private traders at Canton in the early 1800s, it had been "a long and universal custom" to purchase from the shopmen such goods as rhubarb, cassia, and camphor, collectively known as "drugs."[15] The British also bought chinaware directly from "the China-Street people." In 1804 they concluded a cotton contract with a shopman "of considerable property and respectability."[16] James Matheson's close connections with certain shopmen from Chinchew (Ch'üan-chou of Fukien) at Canton in the late 1800s provided him with additional channels from which to buy various commodities, and William Jardine, when he first arrived at Canton in the 1820s, bought more goods from the shopmen than he did from the hong merchants.[17]

The shopmen also conducted illegal business. They often violated the rights of the hong merchants by trading in staple articles, such as tea, silk, and nankeen (a firm, durable, brownish-yellow fabric, made from a natural-colored Chinese cotton). They were able to undersell the hong merchants because they were not subject to as many financial impositions as the latter. Their highly competitive market prices were further helped by the changing business pattern as American merchants began to import British manufactures, which they conveniently bartered with the shopmen for tea and silk.

Consequently, while the agents of the East India Company honored the privileges of the hong merchants, the private British traders, as well as American merchants, found it more profitable to deal with shopmen than with the hong merchants in staple goods. For example, in the silk trade during the 1820s, when some British free traders wanted to purchase more silk than the official Ch'ing export quota allowed, they bought it from the shopmen and smuggled it out by the Lintin ships. Magniac & Co. was in an advantageous position in this regard, because it had "special connections with the outside shopmen" in the 1820s.[18] In the mean-

15. Letter Books, Nov. 6, 1801, JMA.
16. Letter Books, Nov. 14, 1804, JMA.
17. Letter Books, 1804–1806, JMA.
18. India Letter Books, 1825–1828, passim, JMA.

time, American merchants also dealt "very extensively" with the outside merchants.[19] The Boston firm of Perkins & Co. had a sizable business in silk piece goods with an "outside man" named Yeshing in the late 1820s and early 1830s.[20] As traders or manufacturers of silk, nankeen, floor matting, and many other less important articles, many shopmen amassed substantial wealth.[21]

This free trade outside the Cohong flourished with time. Determined not to be outdone by their fellow British and American traders, the East India Company began to intervene. In March 1828 the Committee of Supercargoes took up the issue of the illegal trade on the part of the shopmen, and an agreement with the hong merchants was soon reached. Both parties agreed that, with the supervision of the Hoppo (the superintendent of customs for Kwangtung province), any hong merchant who was proved guilty of covering a shopman by his name would be punished by forfeiting one of his shares in the company's business. But the profits were irresistible. Although illegal, the free trade was so lucrative to the private British traders, American merchants, Chinese shopmen, and the less wealthy hong merchants that "the agreement was at once broken."[22]

The "outside" trade of the shopmen also survived the intervention of the Canton authorities. In 1817 the governor-general closed down over 200 "outside" shops and confiscated their goods. According to James Matheson, however, a compromise was reached in 1820 whereby these shopmen would be permitted to engage in business that the hong merchants regarded as too insignificant to handle.[23] Official restrictions on the shopmen were further liberalized in July 1828. With pressure from both the American and the private English, the Ch'ing government changed the existing law. Hong merchants were to retain their theoretical monopoly of most of the leading articles of foreign trade, while the shopmen could legally trade more articles, including Chinese silk piece goods and imported cotton goods.

Meanwhile, a thriving Chinese junk trade existed; the junk trade to Southeast Asia and along the coast to Manchuria, from Amoy south and Ningpo north, was an important part of Chinese commerce along the coast. A case in point was the Sino-Siamese trade conducted under the

19. India Letter Books, July 26, 1830, JMA.
20. Box 1, PCP.
21. William C. Hunter, The "Fan Kwae" at Canton Before Treaty Days, 1825–1844 (London, 1882), p. 35.
22. Morse, Chronicles, IV, 168–69.
23. Greenberg, p. 55.

tribute system, especially in rice, from Bangkok to China.[24] Foreign
traders either took a major part in the junk trade or gave it stimulus.

THE COUNTRY TRADE AND
THE BRITISH PRIVATE TRADERS

Similarly, on the Western side, the British East India Company,
though it dominated the external trade of China, did not control it. In
time, the dominant position of the company was undermined by the
"country" trade and the private traders.

THE RISE OF THE COUNTRY TRADE

The country trade was the trade conducted by private businessmen
within the commercial domain of the various East India companies'
charters, which generally included all the Indian Ocean and Asia from
the Cape of Good Hope eastward. It lasted from the end of the seventeenth century to the advent of steamships in the middle of the nineteenth.[25] This trade at first centered in India but later expanded to
China in search for higher profit.

The rise of both the country trade and the British private traders was
beyond the control of the British East India Company. Admittedly, the
Honorable Company did enjoy special commercial privileges in the
East. For one thing, at least for British subjects, it legally monopolized
the China trade until 1834. The Charter Act of 1813 put an end to the
company's monopoly of the India trade, but the Court of Directors,
which controlled the company's business from London, carefully guarded
its monopoly of the Canton trade. It persisted in denying the right of
private Englishmen to take up residence in China. But the truth of the
matter is that there was a considerable discrepancy between legality and
reality. Various new factors had given rise to both the country trade and
the free merchants, and a certain degree of free trade existed even within
the company itself. At first the company allowed its supercargoes to engage in private trade either on their own account or as agents for others.
The large amount of this trade can be seen by the fact that W. H. Pigou,
a supercargo, paid into the company's treasury 77,367 taels (tls.) in 1776

---

24. For a recent study of the junk trade, see Sarasin Viraphol, *Sino-Siamese Trade, 1652–
1853* (Cambridge, Mass., 1976).

25. For a general account of the country trade, see W. H. Coates, *The Old Country Trade*
(New York, 1911).

and 235,539 taels in 1777 against bills on London in favor of his nominees.[26]

British purchase of China's products increased by leaps and bounds during the second half of the eighteenth century; the East India Company's tea shipment out of Canton rose from 2.6 million pounds in 1761 to 23.3 million pounds in 1800.[27] As a result of these mounting exports of tea and silk from Canton, the need for cargoes to sell to China became the most powerful economic factor at Canton. However, there was little demand for British goods on the part of the Chinese, and something more than British woolens was required in the tropical climate of Canton to balance the trade. Meanwhile, in sharp contrast to their unfavorable balance of trade with China, the East India Company exported a great deal to India from England. Especially after the opening of the India trade to private British merchants in 1813, India, for centuries an exporter of textiles, was flooded with Manchester cotton goods.

The country trade came to the rescue of this unbalanced British trade with China and India. By bringing, at first, raw cotton and, then, opium from India to Canton, it provided the vital link in the triangular commercial relations between China, England, and India. The importance of the country trade in this international trade can be seen from its increasing magnitude. In 1833, for instance, the annual England-China trade was about $11,000,000, but the trade between India and China soared to $32,000,000. In the seventeen years from 1817 to the end of the East India Company's monopoly in 1834, the country trade constituted about three-quarters of the total British imports at Canton.[28]

Thus, we have a circular trade: China exported tea and silk to England, England exported cotton goods to India, and India exported raw cotton and opium to China. This circular trade was one-way, because Canton did not need British cotton goods, and England did not want opium from India. India hardly bought any Chinese tea, which was by and large handled by the East India Company, and other Chinese goods were likewise unprofitable in India. Under these circumstances, some financial arrangements had to be made in order to perpetuate the triangular trade.

---

26. Morse, *Chronicles*, II, 26. For the relationship between the supercargoes and the merchants, see ibid., 83–93. "Ts." or "Tls." refers to the monetary tael, i.e., a tael-weight of silver.

27. Fairbank, *Trade and Diplomacy*, I, 59.

28. For a general estimate of China's foreign trade at this time, see J. Phipps, *A Practical Treatise on the China Trade* (New York, 1895).

Much of the East India Company's Canton trade was on an Indian account, which was provided by the growing magnitude of the country trade. The basic method of sustaining the Indian account was to pay the proceeds of the country trade into the company's Canton treasury in return for company bills in the Court of Directors or the India presidencies. However, this method became inadequate for the needs of the private merchants when their country trade outdistanced the requirements of the company's tea and silk investment. Consequently, they sought other ways of effecting remittance, such as the short-term loan called "respondentia bond," the purchase of the East India Company's certificates, and credit arrangements with the American China traders. But the most desirable means for the country traders was to ship Chinese sycee, the shoe-shaped ingots of pure silver. China prohibited the exportation of silver, but the country traders managed to buy silver with opium in the lower Canton estuary.[29] By providing a channel of remittance from India to England, the country trade thus became an indispensable link in the triangular trade between China, England, and India.

THE BRITISH PRIVATE TRADERS: AGENCY HOUSES

The private traders were a new element at Canton. To avoid the control of the British East India Company, enterprising British subjects as early as the 1780s began to remain at Canton as nominal representatives of other European governments. Here they formed "agency houses," acting mainly as agents for merchants in London or India, from whom they received cargoes on consignment to be sold on a commission basis. An agency house in the China trade might invest in the shipment itself, but it acted mainly as a middleman, providing all the necessary services of commercial exchange on behalf of its constituents, charting vessels, handling freight, furnishing warehouses, insuring cargoes, remitting funds, recovering debts, and charging a commission or fee for every service. By 1800 more than forty agency houses were set up, and they began to acquire fleets, form insurance companies, and carry on banking operations.[30] It was in the 1820s that the agency houses grew prominent, including the establishment in 1824 of Magniac & Co., which became the noted Jardine, Matheson & Co. in 1832.

Up until the mid-eighteenth century the British East India Company

29. Greenberg, pp. 157–59.
30. Fairbank, *Trade and Diplomacy*, I, 61.

also engaged in the trade between India and China, but the country trade became increasingly a private one.[31] The private merchants were, in theory, only licensees of the company, but "here was a chink in the wall of monopoly."[32] The Charter Act of 1813, by abolishing the Honorable Company's monopoly of the East India trade, opened up immense opportunities for British private traders, who naturally hastened to establish agency houses in India.[33] Consequently, private merchants in Canton became more active, and in 1827 they started the *Canton Register and Price Current*, which was their organ in China. The increase of the country trade was so rapid that by 1828 the private trade was practically all country trade.[34] The private merchants began to challenge the authority of the East India Company in 1830 in spite of the fact that they were theoretically only its licensees. They strongly resented the company's control of the rate of exchange between China, India, and England; furthermore, they demanded stronger political support than the Honorable Company could give. In December 1830, forty-seven private British subjects living in China drew up a petition to the House of Commons in which they complained of the inefficiency of the hong merchants, suggested establishment of a permanent residence at Peking for a British representative, and requested "the acquisition of an insular possession near the coast of China."[35] All in all, the private merchants were seeking a freer trade in China, especially after the 1820s.

Private merchants became more important for several reasons. First, their sale of cotton and opium was essential to the East India Company which, thanks to tea purchases, had an unfavorable balance of trade with China. To draw their proceeds into its service, the company made several arrangements—to purchase at a fixed rate of exchange, to grant "transfers in the treasury" at Canton, and to accept specie from them.[36] Second, the company could not control the country trade effectively after the establishment of Singapore as a free port in 1819. It had been illegal for private British subjects to ship goods from China to England prior to the 1820s, but, with the establishment of Singapore, a technique of transshipping was devised. Chinese goods were landed first at the free port of Singapore. Fresh bills of lading were then made out to London consign-

31. For trade figures in the 1817–1833 period, see Greenberg, p. 217.
32. Ibid., pp. 10–11.
33. For a general account of the British agency houses in India, see S. B. Singh, *European Agency Houses in Bengal, 1783–1833* (Calcutta, 1966).
34. Greenberg, pp. 13–14.
35. *Canton Register*, Dec. 24, 1830.
36. Greenberg, pp. 11–12.

ees, and the cargo was again taken aboard the same ship, which then proceeded to England. By 1831 there were four British free traders per season plying between Canton and London, all "transshipping" their cargoes at Singapore.[37] Their number increased with the passage of time. Thus, private traders, by using a legal technicality, made serious inroads into the Honorable Company's monopoly of the Anglo-Chinese trade.

Third, the private traders, thanks to the rise of American merchants in China, acquired a certain degree of financial independence from the East India Company. They had relied on the company to remit their proceeds of cotton and opium at Canton to London. From 1778 to the 1830s, for example, they asked the company to make credit arrangements to this effect.[38] With the advent of more American merchants in Canton after the 1820s, however, they resorted increasingly to the American bills or drafts on London instead of those of the company.

Another strength of the private traders lay in their strong sense of belonging and responsibility due to close kinship ties. Indeed, the Eastern commerce was developed by closely knit family and clan groups, whether they were Parsee merchants or traders from Great Britain. For the latter, intermarriage among the families of the principal partners made kinship ties even more pervasive than their names would suggest. For instance, the partners of Jardine, Matheson & Co., which epitomized the growth of private trade, included seven nephews of the founders.[39]

Finally, the power of the British private traders was strengthened by the nature of the trade that developed in both China and England; pressure against the East India Company's monopoly came from Canton as well as Manchester. With the expansion of machine-powered industry, the Manchester manufacturers regarded the East India Company's monopoly as an obstacle to continuous development of the new export market. They launched campaigns against the monopoly by promoting public meetings, distributing propaganda materials, and submitting petitions. Starting in 1813 and intensifying in 1829, these campaigns persisted until the abolition of the monopoly in 1834.[40]

37. Ibid., pp. 98–99.
38. Ibid., pp. 11–12.
39. See "The Jardine Family" and "Partners and Directors," in Maggie Keswick, ed., *The Thistle and the Jade* (London, 1982), pp. 262–65; and Fairbank, *Trade and Diplomacy*, II, 56–57.
40. Greenberg, pp. 179–84. To a lesser extent, pressure against the company's monopoly also came from India.

On the Chinese end, it was the development of the opium trade that, more than anything else, unleashed the British private traders from the company's control. Many of them, such as Hollingworth Magniac, W. S. Davidson, James Matheson, and William Jardine, engaged in this trade, and it quickly led them to fortune. After 1817, when the Ch'ing government reiterated its prohibition policy, the British East India Company refrained from engaging in the opium trade directly but encouraged its licensees, the private merchants, to trade. At first the company and these merchants cooperated at Canton and Whampoa, but after 1821, when the drug traffic was driven out of the inner Pearl River, most opium shipments were smuggled into and disposed of at the "outer anchorages," including Lintin Island. Thus, opium trade was conducted without even coming within observation range of the company's "factory" at Canton.

Two dominant British agency houses, Jardine, Matheson & Co. and Dent & Co., exemplify the private merchants' active opium trade on the coast. Jardine's at first acted mainly as an agent for owners of opium in India, charging a commission of 3 percent on sales, but after 1832 it built up a considerable opium fleet of its own. No sooner had James Matheson opened up a traffic in 1824 on the east coast than other private traders followed, causing a decline in prices. In order to test new markets, William Jardine had a six months' exploratory voyage in 1832 on board the new clipper *Sylph* to Shanghai and Tientsin. Successful experiments were likewise made in Foochow and Chinchew Bay. By 1836 Jardine's had a fleet of a dozen ships of almost every description, and the coastal trade was established as "a regular system."[41] Dent & Co. underwent a similar process of establishment and rapid growth.[42] In 1826 this company chartered the *Nile*, a Perkins & Co. vessel, with Robert B. Forbes as the captain, for the purpose of delivering opium at Lintin. With this opium-carrying vessel, anchoring on the high seas between Hong Kong and Lintin in late December 1826, Dent & Co. did business with some prominent Cantonese opium brokers. To compete with Jardine, the *Nile* joined Dent's other ships the next year in selling opium up the coast, a practice known as the "coastal system."[43]

The quantity of the total opium trade grew astonishingly until 1839. It was about $10 million annually when the Honorable Company came

41. Ibid., pp. 138–41. I discuss the opium trade in detail in chap. 5.
42. For a general account of Dent's opium trade, see Basil Lubbock, *The Opium Clippers* (Boston, 1933), which uses the company's papers.
43. James B. Connolly, *Canton Captain* (Garden City, N.Y., 1942), pp. 164–65.

to an end in 1834.[44] By 1838 many of the foreign merchants at Canton, English, American, and others, had no hesitation or moral scruples in receiving consignments and in selling as many chests as they could. Some of those who did not engage in the opium trade were refraining only "because they had not sufficient capital or trading credit to secure consignments of it for sale."[45]

In contrast to the regulated trade pattern of the company, the private merchants relied more on free competition on the market. Admittedly, they both shared some common commercial practices at Canton, such as trading and contracting goods with hong merchants without written agreement. But in some respects their ways of doing business were remarkably different. For one thing, they treated the hong merchants differently. The company tended to treat the Cohong as a unit, apportioning its tea contracts among the hong merchants according to their seniority and fixing the same price for all. The private merchants, on the other hand, dealt separately for each ship's cargo with whichever hong merchant would give them the best price. Jardine archives show that many private traders in India consigned their goods to different agents in Canton who were free to sell these consignments to any of the hong merchants. The security merchant did receive a sum of $700 for his expenses and risks in securing a ship but was not necessarily able to profit from its cargoes.[46] H. B. Morse was thus mistaken when he stated that foreign consignees could sell only to the hong merchants who "secured" the ship.[47]

The private traders also differed from the Honorable Company in their actual business transactions. The company usually "sold in truck" by bartering its British and Indian imports for tea and silk, that is, the prices that a hong merchant would pay for the imported goods were determined by the prices the Company paid him for his tea or silk. This practice of "trucking" can be found frequently in Morse's *Chronicles*, whereby "woollens and teas were sold together."[48] Because the private merchants did not buy tea, they as a rule sold their imports, mainly opium, for cash at the highest price on the market.

44. For the rise of the opium trade, see Hsin-pao Chang, *Commissioner Lin and the Opium War* (Cambridge, Mass., 1964), pp. 16–50, esp. p. 23.
45. Morse, *Conflict*, p. 206.
46. India Letter Book, Jan. 5, 1825–July 2, 1832, JMA.
47. *Conflict*, pp. 66, 75–76.
48. I, 263; II, 28, 97, 298; III, 60, 105, 244; IV, 123.

OTHER FREE MERCHANTS

The monopoly of the Honorable Company was applicable only to British subjects, and other non-British merchants in China were free traders in their own right. From the late eighteenth century, in addition to the British vessels, ships of Denmark, Portugal, and Germany also came to China. Meanwhile, attracted by greater freedom from the interference of the British East India Company in trading, some British merchants traded under non-British colors. Under this arrangement, several private English at Canton shipped tea to such European cities as Lisbon, Hamburg, Bordeaux, and Copenhagen between 1828 and 1834.[49] Among the non-British foreign merchants in Canton during the late eighteenth and early nineteenth centuries, the American traders were the most important.

THE AMERICAN COMMISSION HOUSES AS FREE TRADERS

Although Sino-American trade commenced in the late eighteenth century, it was not until the 1820s that the American commission houses, like their British counterparts (the agency houses), became prominent. Russell & Co., the largest American house in China, was established in 1824, and Olyphant & Co., the second largest, followed suit four years later. Sino-American direct trade started with the *Empress of China*, which sailed from New York to Canton in 1784 and returned home in May 1785. It was followed shortly by the *Pallas*, with a cargo of $50,000 worth of tea taken by Thomas Randall. With the increase in trade, Salem, Boston, Providence, New York, and Philadelphia became leading China trade ports.[50] The Pacific route, around the Horn and across the Pacific to China, was often used. This was preferred by fur traders, by merchants of South America, and occasionally by "out of season" vessels in the direct trade with Canton.[51]

Admittedly, American trade with China was not always the most profitable nor did it constitute a large proportion of total American foreign trade.[52] Besides, the American government, in contrast to its British counterpart, was a passive observer in East Asia, a fitful participant in

49. India Letter Book, July 10, 1828, Aug. 23, 1831, June 5, 1834, JMA.
50. Tyler Dennett, *Americans in Eastern Asia* (New York, 1963), pp. 6–10. For a detailed record of an early American China trade house, see RP.
51. Dennett, p. 34.
52. In the 1780s, American trade with Ile de France (Mauritius) was more profitable

events. But, thanks to various favorable factors, American China trade
advanced by leaps and bounds after 1784, and American merchants
soon assumed second place in the commercial world of Canton. In the
first place, the neutrality of the United States during the long
Napoleonic wars significantly helped American traders. Second, the enterprise and shrewdness of American seamen and merchants played an
important role. Sailors, such as Robert B. Forbes, and traders, such as
John P. Cushing and John M. Forbes, were undoubtedly first-rate tal-
ents in their time. They came mainly from the Boston–New York area,
the headquarters of American foreign trade. Until 1842 American China
trade was in the hands of a few prominent and enterprising commission
houses, such as Perkins & Co., Russell & Co., Augustine Heard & Co.,
Olyphant & Co., and W. S. Wetmore & Co.

But the most important factor was that American merchants were
bona fide free traders who were not restricted by a privileged incorporated monopoly. In contrast, their British counterparts were handicapped by the monopoly of the East India Company. For example, the British merchants trading in furs with the American Northwest coast were
allowed to do so only by special permission of the company and were
required to bring their cargoes back to China and exchange them, not for
Chinese produce, but for specie that had to be deposited with the company. For this specie the company would issue bills on London at twelve
months' sight. On the other hand, the Americans, by barter at Canton,
could get about 20 percent more for their pelts and were free to carry
their cargoes wherever they pleased. They usually took Chinese produce
to Europe and made a second turnover before returning to the United
States. Thus, the restrictions of the Honorable Company served to
eliminate the British traders from this competition.

The first American merchants went to China not so much to sell as to
buy, because the China trade developed mainly out of a desire to secure
certain commodities for the United States. Their cargoes from China
consisted mainly of tea and nankeen, and they also bought chinaware,
straw mats and matting, sugar, and drugs. In return, they exported certain articles to China. Ginseng and sandalwood were not good trading

---

than its China trade, and it is probable that before 1790 the total American tonnage in the
Indian ports exceeded that at Canton. From 1821 to 1897, American trade with all Asia
constituted only about 6.5 percent of the total American foreign trade. The value of its
China trade dropped steadily from 3 percent in 1860 to less than 2 percent in 1897 in terms
of total American trade. See Dennett, pp. 24–27, 580.

articles at Canton, as had been anticipated, but fur pelts quickly became important. As the supply of furs was adequate and the cost of collection was slight, furs met the pressing need of Americans for an article of barter. The total American fur trade with Canton from its beginning until its end in the early 1830s may be placed between $15,000,000 and $20,000,000 (U.S. dollars).[53] Around 1830 there developed a trade in bêche-de-mer, a sea slug much prized by the Chinese as an article of food. Four years later the consul reported that American-manufactured goods of coarse texture had begun to come into Manila by way of China.[54] The China trade, however, gradually encountered difficulties, because the Americans did not have enough goods to send. The supply of Hawaiian sandalwood was exhausted, and the trade in ginseng and bêche-de-mer was limited. Northwestern furs, going out of fashion, diminished in export after 1820. Meanwhile, the American cotton trade was in its infancy. On the other hand, American demand for tea and silk persisted, and the trade continued to be largely one-way.

Under these circumstances, it was only natural that the American merchants had to export specie to Canton. The largest China merchant in New York in 1824 stated that out of his total exports (U.S. dollars) to China of $1,311,057 for that year, nearly $900,000 was in the form of specie. His other items of export were British manufactured goods, valued at $356,407, and American produce, mainly furs and ginseng, worth only $60,000. It was asserted in 1852 that the United States had shipped $180,000,000 (U.S.) of silver to China since 1784, and the American port records show nearly $70,000,000 (U.S.) to have been shipped between 1805 and 1818.[55]

AMERICAN MERCHANTS AND THE OPIUM TRADE

The continuous export of specie, together with the one-way trade, could not last long. American merchants were in need of a commodity salable to China, and they found it in the opium trade.[56] They directly benefited from the trade, which, by virtue of the system of exchange initiated in the 1820s and further developed later, reduced the necessity

53. Ibid., pp. 21, 36, 41.
54. Ibid., p. 34.
55. Ibid., pp. 20–21.
56. For a general account of American merchants' role in the opium trade, see Jacques M. Downs, "American Merchants and the China Opium Trade, 1800–1840," *Business History Review* 42:418–42 (Winter 1968).

for the importation of specie by the substitution of bills on London.[57]
Compared with the British, the American merchants were far less involved with the opium business on China's coast. Starting to trade as
early as 1805, they nevertheless generally remained indirect and unim-
portant during the first two decades of the nineteenth century, conducting only about one-tenth of the total trade.[58] It had always been difficult
for them to participate directly in the lucrative opium import business,
because they not only lacked important connections with the British-
controlled opium market in India, but also did not have Britain's traditional close ties with the Parsee houses that dominated much of the production and trade. Besides, they did not command the extensive banking
and shipping resources necessary to pioneer opium shipments in the early days of the trade.

The American merchants were nevertheless the most active non-
British Western merchants who traded in opium in China in the early
nineteenth century. H. H. Lindsay, a British subject in China, observed:
"I will here add a few words to correct a very prevalent impression that
the Americans have had but little to do with the opium trade. On the
contrary, with one or two exceptions, every American house in China
was engaged in the trade. There were American depot ships at Lintin
and on the coast."[59] The Rev. W. H. Medhurst shared this view by
remarking that "both English and American houses in China trade in
the drug, each to the full extent of their means."[60] In fact, American
merchants helped British private traders to usher in Indian opium and
oust Turkish opium. The reasons for the diminishing demand for
Turkish opium in China are not entirely clear, though most likely, as
evidenced by the records of American trading firms, the primary
reason was a drastic increase in the supply of Indian opium, a generally
superior product. Turkish opium virtually disappeared from the Chinese
market after the spring of 1838, when the British started to allow
American ships to buy opium in India.[61]

Except for a few firms like Olyphant & Co., most American houses,
including the largest ones of Russell's and Heard's, traded in opium.

57. Ibid., p. 70.
58. Fairbank, *Trade and Diplomacy*, I, 226.
59. H. H. Lindsay, *Is the War with China a Just One?* (London, 1840), p. 14.
60. Medhurst added: "American citizens are fully as much implicated in this affair in
China as the subjects of Great Britain" (*NCH*, Nov. 3, 1855, p. 2).
61. Letter from Russell & Co. to J. M. Forbes, Mar. 7, 1838, File 12, FC.

Russell & Co.'s involvement in the trade can be traced back to the days of its forerunner, Perkins & Co. Although the partners' agreement of the latter firm forbade its members to engage in the trade, Captain Robert B. Forbes's ship engaged in it at Lintin Island in the early 1820s.[62] Russell & Co. also dealt extensively in opium. It set up its own network of clippers and receiving ships soon after its establishment. The *Rose*, one of its opium vessels, was frequently engaged in the sale of opium on China's northeastern coast during the mid-1830s.[63] Russell's opium trade was especially resented by public opinion at home, led by Protestant missionaries who were strongly opposed to the opium trade. It was a general practice in the treaty ports for prominent foreign merchants to serve concurrently as consuls. The fact that American consuls were no longer consistently appointed from Russell & Co. after 1854 was mainly due to the fact that Paul S. Forbes, consul and head of that house, extensively dealt in opium.[64]

Augustine Heard & Co., another big American house, traded in opium from its beginning. Its source of profit first came from opium trade and later from shipping. In the early 1830s it mainly traded Turkish opium but soon shifted to Indian opium.[65] Its trade in opium greatly increased in 1840 when it acted as the opium agent for the gigantic British firm of Jardine, Matheson & Co. during the Sino-British conflict over opium.[66] Four years later it chartered the schooner *Don Juan* at $1,000 a month to distribute 286 chests of superior Malwa opium along the east coast, hoping to get $820 a chest there instead of the $750 offered at Canton.[67] From 1846 to 1854 the firm's clipper *Lady Hayes* conducted opium business at Cumsingmoon station off Hong Kong.[68] Thus, both Russell's and Heard's acted either as agents for Parsee houses in India or as independent merchants in their own right, receiving, storing, transshipping, and marketing the drug in China.[69]

62. For Perkins & Co., see PCP and PP. For Samuel Russell & Co., see letters of Samuel Russell, especially those in the early 1820s, RP.

63. Case 4, RA.

64. Stephen C. Lockwood, *Augustine Heard and Company, 1858–1862* (Cambridge, Mass., 1971), p. 27.

65. Case 19, HC II.

66. Fairbank, *Trade and Diplomacy*, I, 226.

67. John Heard, Jr., to Augustine Heard, Sept. 1, 1844, EM-4, HC. Unless otherwise specified, the sign "$" refers to Mexican silver dollars.

68. "Cumsingmoon Opium Returns," Case 19, HC II.

69. S. C. Lockwood, pp. 26–27.

TABLE 1.   THE INCREASE OF CANTON TRADE, 1831–1837
(IN MEXICAN DOLLARS)

		English	American	Total
Imports	1831–1832	20,520,027	2,383,685	22,903,712
Imports	1836–1837	34,435,622	3,214,726	37,650,348
	Increase	13,915,595	831,041	14,746,636
Exports	1831–1832	13,216,483	5,999,732	19,216,215
Exports	1836–1837	25,339,284	9,527,139	34,866,423
	Increase	12,122,801	3,527,407	15,650,208

Source: H. B. Morse, *Conflict*, p. 168.

FREE TRADERS AFTER 1834

After the abolition of the East India Company's monopoly in 1834, all foreign merchants enjoyed complete freedom of trade on the foreign side. Consequently, the commerce of Canton was considerably expanded.[70] The export of tea rose from 335,697 piculs (1 picul equals 133.33 lbs.) in 1832 to 442,609 piculs five years later, and the shipment of silk increased from an annual amount of 21,727 bales in 1830–1833 to 49,988 bales in 1837. The opium import also increased from $13,000,000 in 1832 to $20,000,000 in 1837. All in all, the increase of both exports and imports in the 1831–1837 period was considerable (table 1).

At the same time, there was a sudden growth of foreign "free" merchants in Canton after 1834, as shown in table 2. These private traders constituted a dynamic force in the Eastern commerce, because it was they, not the British East India Company, who constantly sought fresh opportunities and explored new possibilities in the East. They were not content with semi-free trade; in fact, their eagerness to institute completely free trade with China was so great that they accelerated the abolition of the Honorable Company's "monopoly" in 1834 and precipitated the Opium War of 1839–1842.

70. The tempo of trade expansion in Canton after 1834, however, was not extremely fast, as might have been expected, partly because considerable private trade already existed. Robert B. Forbes argues that the year 1834 did not have great commercial effects on Canton. For a general discussion of trade at Canton during this period, see Robert B. Forbes, *Remarks on China and the China Trade* (Boston, 1844).

TABLE 2.   NUMBER OF FOREIGN MERCHANTS IN CANTON,
1826, 1831, AND 1837

| | British | | | | | Total | No. of |
	EIC[a]	Free	Total	American	Other	merchants	firms
1826	20	5	25	19	32	76	4
1831	20	12	32	21	30	83	6
1837	0	158	158	44	11	213	18

Sources: Morse, *Chronicles*, IV, 128–254; and *Chinese Repository*, V, 426.
a. Merchants connected with the British East India Company.

The 1820s played an important role in the process of liberalizing trade, because the British and the Americans in this period established their most powerful mercantile houses in the China trade, and the Manchester manufacturers intensified their campaign for a freer trade. On the Chinese side, in addition to the shopmen who made the Canton system much more flexible, the rapid increase of Western merchants gave rise to the house comprador. In contrast to the old-style ship comprador (a ship chandler who furnished provisions for foreign ships), the house comprador was the Chinese treasurer and business assistant in the Western agency house. With the assistance of his own staff, whom he was soon permitted to hire,[71] the house comprador in a great measure promoted free trade at Canton before the "treaty system" of 1842.

Behind the growth of trade along China's coast, which was considerably free in nature, lay the basic fact that both the British demand for tea and the Chinese demand for opium increased by leaps and bounds after the late eighteenth century. However, this commercial expansion could hardly sustain itself unless China's monetary system was improved and its credit mechanisms made more sophisticated.

71. For the origins of the comprador, see Yen-p'ing Hao, *The Comprador in Nineteenth Century China* (Cambridge, Mass., 1970), pp. 45–48.

CHAPTER THREE

New Forms of Money

The general economic expansion in China and in the West during the eighteenth century[1] called for the use of money more regularly and on a larger scale than ever before, but China in the mid-Ch'ing period still lacked an effective medium of exchange. The existing bimetallic monetary system of silver (mainly in the form of bullion or sycee) and copper "cash" (round coins with square holes) had a number of defects. First, the volume of money depended largely on the availability of the two kinds of metal, over which the government did not exert effective control. It was thus a poor system that lacked the flexibility of adjusting money supply to market demand for circulating media. Second, the (ideal) relationship between these two kinds of money was fixed by the government at the parity of one tael of silver to one thousand copper coins, but the actual exchange rate between silver and copper cash in the market fluctuated so much that it generated risks and uncertainties in business transactions.

Third, the traditional bimetallism lacked uniformity. Because silver circulated in bullion without standardization, its value was determined by its weight and fineness. The latter standard called for the expertise of a money-changer, but there was no standard concerning the former. Thus, hundreds of units of account appeared with varying degrees of weight and fineness. By the same token, the copper cash consisted of a variety of coins, uneven in weight and quality. Consequently, the monetary world was filled with different sorts of tael and coins, together with

1. I have discussed this topic in chap. 1; see n. 3.

great fluctuations of exchange rates between them. Finally, both kinds of money were cumbersome and costly to move when a large amount was involved.[2] As a consequence, three new kinds of money—in the form of silver, paper, and a special commodity—were introduced and increasingly used, first on the coast and then in the interior.

THE INTRODUCTION OF SILVER DOLLARS

Spanish silver dollars were introduced into China through trade as early as the sixteenth century, but they were either melted into silver (for hoarding or jewelry) or put into circulation by weight. It was not until after the late eighteenth century, when tea drinking became increasingly popular in the West, that the import of silver dollars increased substantially. Coins were not necessarily better than bullion in all aspects of China's monetary sector, but, in contrast to China's complicated bimetallic system, the imported silver dollars were standardized in form, weight, and fineness. Hence they proved to be far more convenient as media of exchange than the traditional silver ingots or pieces. The nineteenth century witnessed the widespread use of silver coins in place of silver bullion as media of exchange and, to a lesser extent, in place of the tael as a unit of account. There were many kinds of dollars in circulation in China, but for the period before the mid-1850s the Spanish dollar and, following it, the Mexican dollar may be considered standard coins.

THE SPANISH DOLLARS

Europe received large amounts of gold and silver from the Americas in the sixteenth and seventeenth centuries. It kept gold but reexported silver to Asia. The Spanish silver dollars, known to the Chinese as the *peng-yang* (standard dollar), were introduced into China in the second half of the sixteenth century from the Philippine Islands, which were conquered by Spain in 1565. The coins used in this period were piastres (pieces of eight).[3] A brisk and long-lasting trade, especially in silk, be-

---

2. Wang Yeh-chien, *Huo-pi*, pp. 5–12; Yeh-chien Wang, "Evolution," pp. 425–33; and Frank H. H. King, *Money and Monetary Policy in China, 1845–1895* (Cambridge, Mass., 1965), pp. 39–42, 46–47. The silver was usually in the form of sycee (silver "shoes") bearing the maker's chop. Copper coins were strung on strings.

3. Wallerstein, *Modern World-System II*, p. 108; and Braudel, *Capitalism and Material Life*, p. 342.

tween Manila and South China soon followed, and the volume of trade was much higher than what is generally believed.[4] Meanwhile, in the seventeenth century and early half of the eighteenth century, Europe had an unfavorable balance of trade with Asia. As European traders, especially Dutch and English, heavily bought silk, tea, and chinoiserie (lacquer, porcelain, etc.), more Spanish dollars went to China via India and the East Indies.[5] At the turn of the eighteenth century, they were commonly accepted as media of exchange in Kwangtung and Fukien. Thereafter, their circulation expanded northward to Chekiang and Kiangsu. One century later, China experienced a massive influx of Carolus dollars (struck in the reigns of Charles III, 1759–1788, and Charles IV, 1788–1808). They remained the standard coins in Canton until 1853 and in Shanghai until 1857. When the Spanish stopped minting these coins in the early 1840s and the Chinese continued to hoard them, their monetary role was replaced by the Mexican dollar after the 1850s.[6]

When the Spanish dollars were first introduced into China, they were accepted because of their weight and quality.[7] By the late eighteenth century, they were widely circulated along the coast from Kwangtung to Kiangsu.[8] In the first quarter of the nineteenth century, the Carolus dollar was "the basic circulating coin in foreign commerce at Canton"[9] and also in circulation in the provinces on or close to the coast, such as Kwangsi, Kweichow, Kiangsu, Chekiang, and Chihli.[10] By 1830, because of its convenience and its reputation for consistency, the dollar coin was used in the domestic commerce as well as accepted for tax payments in certain areas.[11] After the Treaty of Nanking, dollar coins

4. Ch'üan Han-sheng, "Ming Ch'ing chien Mei-chou pai-yin ti shu-ju Chung-kuo," in his *Chung-kuo ching-chi shih lun-ts'ung* (Hong Kong, 1972), I, 435–50; and William S. Atwell, "Notes on Silver, Foreign Trade, and the late Ming Economy," *Ch'ing-shih wen-t'i*, III.8:1–2 (Dec. 1977).

5. K. N. Chaudhuri has written on this topic extensively. See his "The East India Company and the Export of Treasure in the Early Seventeenth Century," *Economic History Review* 16:23–38 (Aug. 1963); "Treasure and Trade Balance," *Economic History Review* 21:480–502 (Dec. 1968); and "The Economic and Monetary Problem of European Trade with Asia during the Seventeenth and Eighteenth Centuries," *Journal of European Economic History* 4:325 (Fall 1975).

6. King, *Money*, pp. 86–87, 169–74; *Shang-hai ch'ien-chuang*, p. 23; and Yang Tuan-liu, *Ch'ing-tai huo-pi chin-yung shih-kao* (Peking, 1962), p. 269.

7. Yang Tuan-liu, *Huo-pi*, p. 273.

8. Ou Pao-san, Feng Tse, and Wu Ch'ao-lin, comps., *Chung-kuo chin-tai ching-chi ssu-hsiang yü ching-chi cheng-ts'e tzu-liao hsuan-chi* (Peking, 1959), p. 38; and *Chung-kuo chin-tai huo-pi shih tzu-liao*, Chung-kuo jen-min yin-hang, comp. (Peking, 1964), I, 54.

9. Greenberg, p. vii.

10. Liang Chia-pin, *Kuang-tung shih-san hang k'ao* (T'ai-chung, 1960), pp. 122, 128; King, *Money*, p. 272.

11. Yang Tuan-liu, *Huo-pi*, pp. 272, 273.

were more widely accepted as media of exchange in China, as many British merchants testified.[12]

Although both Carolus and Mexican dollars were in circulation, merchants decidedly preferred the former in the 1850s.[13] Augustine Heard, Jr., a leading American merchant, also noted the popularity of the Carolus dollars in Shanghai and in the country's inland regions during the first two decades of the treaty system.[14] The dollars were especially popular in Chekiang because the authorities there often insisted on the use of dollar coins for tax payments.[15]

Because the Carolus dollars were popular in Shanghai, foreign trading firms vied in using them to promote business. Alexander Perceval of Jardine's made note of this on August 11, 1856: "As a rule I have been well supplied with funds but there are times when it would be very advantageous had I had a discretionary power to have in any one month to the extent of £30,000 or so. Smith Kennedy & Co., who always pay *hard dollars*, are difficult people to oppose, and even Gilman Bowman & Co. get the preference" of the Chinese merchants by using dollar coins.[16] Despite the rising popularity of the dollar coins in Shanghai, they remained more valuable in southern China. For this reason, dollars were shipped from Shanghai to Canton from time to time.[17]

In fact, the Carolus dollars were so popular that local acceptance of them at a premium over their silver content was well established in Canton during the eighteenth century. This situation remained unchanged in 1815, when the British East India Company's records indicate that the price of sycee was very low, a 7 or 8 percent discount in terms of the dollar. As the purity of sycee was generally considered to be 8 percent better than dollars, this would mean a difference of 15 or 16 percent between sycee and dollars when one purchased sycee at Canton

12. BPP, *Report from the Select Committee on Commercial Relations with China, Minutes of Evidence*, vol. 5, pp. 24–25.

13. In a letter to Thomas Hunt at Whampoa, Joseph Jardine recorded this fact from Hong Kong in 1853: "My comprador desires me to tell you that he has sent seventy sovereigns to Janneson Lifford and Co.'s comprador—the price of which is $294 Spanish, or $4.20 each. He says if you haven't got Spanish Dollars, Mexicans will do, altho' 'Spanish more better'" (Apr. 17, 1853, JMA).

14. "The Carolus dollar, unchopped, was current [in Shanghai]. It was accepted in the interior silk districts, and the great development of the silk trade about 1853 and later sent up its value enormously" ("Old China and New," p. 33, GQ-2, HC).

15. Yang Tuan-liu, *Huo-pi*, p. 274.

16. Perceval (Shanghai) to Joseph Jardine (Hong Kong), Aug. 11, 1856, JMA.

17. James Macandrew of Jardine's noted one such cargo on May 30, 1851: "There are a good many Carolus dollars going down to Canton just now, which may tend to reduce their value there, so that I should be glad to know if you still wish remittances in that form" (Macandrew [Shanghai] to Jardine, Matheson & Co. [Hong Kong], JMA).

and shipped it to Calcutta for sale.[18] Actually, quoting prices in numbers of dollars as opposed to weight did result in some export of sycee in exchange for the dollar. To prevent the exporting of sycee the Tao-kuang emperor in 1829 prohibited the importation of silver dollars and decreed that prices not be quoted in numbers of dollars but only by weight and fineness.[19] Yet the unchopped dollars continued to pass at a premium relative to their silver content.

The Carolus dollars also commanded a high premium in the interior of China. They had been accepted by dealers in raw silk from central China for a long time, which enhanced their value from 10 to 15 percent. In one season during the 1830s, Russell & Co. sold $60,000 to a hong merchant at a premium of 30 percent,[20] and this situation continued through the ensuing decades. During the first half of the nineteenth century, around 400 thousand unchopped Carolus dollars were in circulation in Wuhu, Anhwei.[21]

The premium for silver dollars largely accounted for the warm affection of the hong merchants toward the American traders, because a high proportion of American imports consisted of silver dollars—Spanish, Mexican, and South American. The senior hong merchant Houqua (Wu Ping-chien) sold Carolus dollars from time to time for John P. Cushing of Boston.[22] The increase in value of the Carolus dollars is evidenced by the exchange rate between dollar and cash coin, as indicated by the following figures:[23]

18. Morse, *Chronicles*, III, 230.
19. BPP, *Correspondence Relating to China*, vol. 36, p. 180; and Kuo T'ing-i, *Chin-tai Chung-kuo shih-shih jih chih* (Taipei, 1963), I, 36.
20. Hunter, pp. 58–59.
21. Morse, *The Trade and Administration of China* (New York, 1921), pp. 164–65.
22. One shipment arrived during the beginning of the Opium War, and Houqua later wrote:

> The dollars arrived at the time the difficulties with the opium trade commenced, when there was no demand for them outside, or they could not be sold except on a credit to persons whom I then did not think it prudent to trust. For these reasons they were brought [from Whampoa] to Canton. When landed here I did not deem it judicious to force them on the market at once, hoping to obtain a better rate by waiting a demand for them, and in this way they remained on hand several months in Russell & Co.'s treasury, but finally they were sold at the best price that could be had for them (Houqua [Canton] to J. P. Cushing [Boston], Dec. 17, 1840, HLB).

23. *Shang-hai yen-chiu tzu-liao* (Shanghai, 1936), pp 289–91. The depreciation of copper cash was due also to the debasement during the period of the Taiping uprising, especially in the 1850s. The dollars' increase in value, of course, could have reflected the changing value of silver as well. For a thorough study of changes in the ratio between silver and copper cash in the Ch'ing period, see Ch'en Chao-nan, *Yung-cheng Ch'ien-lung nien-chien ti yin-ch'ien pi-chia pien-tung* (Taipei, 1966).

Date	Cash coins per dollar
Jan. 4, 1851	1,320
May 9, 1851	1,470
Sept. 19, 1851	1,500
March 26, 1852	1,520
May 14, 1852	1,500
Apr. 7, 1855	1,800
June 1, 1855	1,859
June 27, 1855	1,900

In other words, from 1851 through June 1855, the dollar-cash exchange rate increased 44 percent in favor of the dollar.

The popularity of the Carolus dollar can also be seen in the foreign exchange rates. The intrinsic value of one Carolus dollar was 4s. 2d. Up to the end of 1852, the usual exchange rate at which exporters could buy six-month bills on London was from 4s. 6d. to 4s. 10d. for the Carolus dollar, which thus had a premium of 8 to 16 percent. Impressive as the premium was, it remained moderate, because this period was a peaceful one. In time of war or money stringency, exorbitant premiums ensued. From 1853 to 1856, for instance, when Shanghai was threatened by the Taiping invasion and disturbed by the insurrection of the Small Sword Society, the exchange rate in that port fluctuated between 6s. and 7s. 9d., representing a 44 to 86 percent premium above the intrinsic value of the coinage.[24] The Carolus dollar still overshadowed the Mexican dollar in popularity, despite the latter's gaining ground in southern China by the mid-1850s. Although both coins had identical intrinsic value (416 grains and .900 fineness), different quotations existed simultaneously, the Carolus dollar being valued higher. Whereas one Carolus dollar was quoted at 7s. 9d. in Shanghai on September 15, 1856, one Mexican dollar was worth only 4s. 11d. in Canton on September 27.[25]

Because of the scarcity of the Carolus dollars and the extraordinary premium paid for them, the tael replaced the dollar as the standard unit of account in Shanghai in the spring of 1857. By 1863 the Carolus dollars were "quoted in proportion to the tael," but, because of their convenience in trade and ease of carrying them into the upcountry, they always

24. Morse, *Conflict*, pp. 468–69. One must, however, bear in mind that fluctuations in the rate between dollars and pound sterling were also related to price changes between gold and silver in the world market.

25. Ibid., p. 469.

carried a premium, sometimes as high as 15 percent above their value as mere silver.[26]

THE MEXICAN DOLLARS

Having become independent from Spain in 1821, Mexico started to mint silver dollars of its own in 1824. They were gradually imported into China where they were known as the *ying-yang* (eagle dollars). In terms of quantity, they overshadowed the Carolus dollars in China's monetary sector after the fifties.[27] Although the Mexican dollar became the standard coin in Hong Kong as early as 1842, its wholehearted acceptance in China was relatively late. The American merchant Augustine Heard, Jr., recalled that during the first decade of the treaty system, "the Mexican dollar came very slowly into use—and only at a discount."[28] After 1853, however, when the Mexican dollar replaced the Spanish dollar as the standard coin in Canton, it was widely accepted along the coast, and its value relative to that of the Spanish dollar increased.[29]

In support of his proposal to mint the Hong Kong silver dollar, Sir Hercules Robinson, governor of that colony, pointed out in 1863 that the Mexican dollars were not only the sole legal tender of payment in Hong Kong but were also in wide circulation in China. They passed current in large quantities in Canton as well as in Shanghai, and "in the silk districts of central China payments had to be made in undefaced Mexican dollars which were at a high premium."[30] This statement was borne out by the personal observation of the American missionary-diplomat, S. Wells Williams. Commenting on the monetary situation in Shanghai in 1863, he wrote: "The former fancy of the natives for Carolus dollars has passed over to clean [i.e., undefaced] Mexican dollars, which now bear a high price."[31] Meanwhile, the silver dollars were used in some coastal areas, particularly Chekiang, for tax payments.[32]

The Mexican dollars were so popular in the tea and silk districts that both Chinese and foreign merchants used sycee to buy silver dollars in the treaty ports and then transported them to the interior for upcountry purchases. F. B. Johnson of Jardine's Shanghai office in March 1868

26. S. Wells Williams, *The Chinese Commercial Guide* (Hong Kong, 1863), p. 199.
27. *Shang-hai ch'ien-chuang*, p. 23; and Yang Tuan-liu, *Huo-pi*, pp. 269, 278–79.
28. "Old China," p. 33.
29. Yang Tuan-liu, *Huo-pi*, p. 279.
30. E. J. Eitel, *Europe in China* (London, 1895), p. 35.
31. *Commercial Guide*, p. 199.
32. Yang Tuan-liu, *Huo-pi*, p. 274.

made advance to Acum in the amount of "Tls. 10,000 for the purchase of Dollars to be sent into the Moyune Country" and to Aleet "for the purchase of Ningchow Congous." Because of these activities, "cash is said to be cheaper in the interior than at the River ports."[33] In another report on the purchase of silk, Johnson indicated that in 1869 the price of silk in the silk districts was "definitely fixed in Mexican Dollars."[34]

The Mexican dollars were also used to pay for cotton in the interior after the 1870s. Because these coins were so useful upcountry, they were bought in large amounts immediately before the beginning of the tea, silk, and cotton seasons by speculators in the treaty ports in anticipation of their rise in value.[35] This was also the case in times of political disturbances, and the speculators usually ended up with handsome profits.[36] By 1887, the Mexican dollars were circulating not only in the treaty ports, but also in such littoral areas as Kwangtung, Kwangsi, Fukien, Taiwan, Shantung, and Chihli. They were also used in many inland provinces, including those on the northeastern frontier.[37] By the end of the nineteenth century, these coins were accepted more freely in China, especially in areas where upcountry purchases proceeded vigorously.[38]

Like the Carolus dollar, the Mexican dollar also enjoyed a premium. The latter was quoted almost at par with the former during the early fifties when the Mexican became the standard coin in Canton.[39] Many people bought silver dollars at a high premium over their silver content in the late fifties and early sixties when the Taiping uprising spread.[40] The premium of the Mexican dollar was higher in South China than in the Yangtze Valley. This difference prompted A. G. Dallas of Jardine's to buy these coins in Shanghai from time to time and transport them to Canton and Hong Kong for sale.[41] Mexican dollars became scarce in China after the mid-sixties, because they were increasingly used by

---

33. Aleet was Jardine's comprador at Shanghai in the 1850s, and Acum, also referred to as Ee Loong, was the firm's comprador from 1860 to 1863 (Johnson [Shanghai] to William Keswick [Hong Kong], Mar. 10, 1868, JMA).

34. Ibid., July 10, 1869.

35. The dollar-sycee exchange rate in Shanghai was usually in favor of the dollar in April, May, and August (*Shang-hai ch'ien-chuang*, pp. 593–94).

36. Ibid., pp. 26, 39.

37. King, *Money*, p. 225.

38. Heard, Jr., "Old China," p. 33.

39. Yang Tuan-liu, *Huo-pi*, p. 279.

40. *Shang-hai ch'ien-chuang*, p. 26.

41. Dallas wrote in 1851: "I hear of nothing doing in Exchange, but Bills are wanted. Please keep me advised of the value of Mexican dollars, as I may occasionally pick them up, & I am now offered 20,000 [dollars] by [the British] Gov't" (Dallas [Shanghai] to David Jardine [Hong Kong], May 3, 1851, JMA).

Western traders to pay for silk in Yokohama, Japan. This new circulation in Japan affected the dollar-sycee exchange rate in China, usually to
the advantage of the Mexican dollar.[42]

OTHER DOLLARS

The Carolus and Mexican dollars were the major silver coins in China
during the nineteenth century, but other types of dollars were at one
time or another introduced into China with varying degrees of success.
One of these was the Hong Kong dollar. Governor Hercules Robinson of
Hong Kong had proposed the establishment of a mint on that island,
and in 1863 the proposal was approved. The Royal Mint of Hong Kong
began producing dollar coins on May 1, 1866. Although high costs
forced it to close in 1868, it coined about 2 million Hong Kong dollars in
the two years of its operation.[43] The Japanese bought the machinery for
$60,000 and established a mint in Osaka. This mint issued the Japanese
silver yen, which was in circulation along the Chinese coast, in Hong
Kong, and in Southeast Asia. Between 1871 and 1897, more than 165
million silver yen were coined, of which over 110 million were shipped
abroad.[44]

The design of the Mexican dollar was changed in 1868, following the
restoration of the Republic. The new dollars were officially assayed in
Shanghai in 1872 and found to contain 1.5 percent more silver than the
old.[45] At the end of 1875, the Imperial Maritime Customs (IMC)
approved the use of the new Mexican dollars for the payment of duties.[46]

The so-called Saigon dollar (piastre de commerce) was issued in 1885.
Although 13 million of them were minted during the following decade,
the coin did not have an important monetary role in China, because its
heavy weight (420 grains with 378 grains of pure silver) caused it either
to be hoarded or melted. The piastre's weight was finally reduced in
1895.[47]

42. William Keswick had this to report from Shanghai in 1864: "Mexican Dollars
declined on the arrival of the Yokohama steamer, and touched as low as Ts. 728 [per 1000
dollars] but today they are dearer, say Ts. 735, and I expect to see them go considerably
higher on receipt of intelligence that Silk is obtainable at Yokohama, and I think it probable next advice from Japan will be to that effect" (Keswick [Shanghai] to James Whittall
[Hong Kong], Oct. 7, 1864, JMA).
    43. Eitel, pp. 375, 453.
    44. King, *Money*, p. 179.
    45. Ibid.
    46. Circular No. 48, Dec. 31, 1875, IMC, *Documents Illustrative of the Origin, Develop-
ment, and Activities of the Chinese Customs Service* (Shanghai, 1937), I, 350.
    47. King, *Money*, p. 179.

Compared with the Saigon dollar, the American trade dollar was more important for China's coastal economy. This coin, authorized by Congress in 1873, was intended to provide a use for America's surplus silver production. The United States tried to use this coin on the Chinese market to compete with the Mexican dollar, because the American dollar was slightly superior in weight and workmanship. It was originally intended that the cost of laying down the American trade dollar in China would be covered by the margin provided by the 8 percent export duty the Mexican government levied on silver. A joint Congressional resolution in 1876 specified that this coin was not legal tender in the United States and was issued for export only. The San Francisco mint was reported to have coined the trade dollars at the rate of some 20,000 daily. Even though it is not possible to determine their eventual destination, a considerable amount reached China's coast where their reception was encouraging. They passed at a significant premium, sometimes even over that of the Mexican. This dollar received the customary official Chinese sanction, following an official assay. The authorities of Kwangtung, Kwangsi, Fukien, and Chekiang made proclamations in the mid-seventies to protect this coin against counterfeiting. Conflict over the status of the trade dollar arose in the United States, however, and the coin was withdrawn in 1887. The coins remaining in China were soon melted down. Thus, American trade dollars disappeared from China by the end of the nineteenth century.[48]

In addition to foreign silver dollars, there were various foreign subsidiary coins in the treaty ports. English shillings and sixpences were passing current in Amoy in 1843, though they passed by weight. In 1868, however, shillings were passing at 25 cents of a Mexican dollar. Hong Kong 10-cent pieces were sold at eight or nine to the dollar, and francs were accepted at 20 cents but paid out at 25.[49]

The expansion of trade prompted the Chinese to coin silver dollars of their own after the end of the eighteenth century. Although some Chinese silver coins were minted in the interior, the most vigorous silver-coining activities took place in the coastal area, and the majority of them involved counterfeiting of foreign dollars. These imitation dollars usually were made and used in Kwangtung, Fukien, Chekiang, and Kiangsu, especially after the 1830s.[50] By the 1890s, the British, Dutch, and

48. Ibid., pp. 179–80, 273–74.
49. Ibid., p. 114.
50. Yang Tuan-liu, *Huo-pi*, pp. 285–86. An edict issued by the Tao-kuang Emperor in 1843 prohibited counterfeiting foreign silver dollars (Kuo T'ing-yi, *Jih-chih*, I, 51).

Japanese ministers in Peking complained to the Tsungli Yamen that counterfeits of the coins of their respective nations or of their colonies were manufactured in China and exported abroad. The Maritime Customs had to make new regulations in 1896 in order to stop this traffic.[51]

Existing side by side with foreign dollar imitations were Chinese official silver dollar coins. Lin Tse-hsu minted heavy dollar coins in Kiangsu when he was the governor (1832–1837),[52] and dollar coins were known to have been cast in Fukien during the Tao-kuang period (1821–1850). Similar coins were minted on the coast, particularly in Taiwan in 1827, 1845, and 1853. The Wenchow customs officer reported in 1878 that dollars had been minted at T'ai-chou and Wenchow, and the Wenchow dollar was used as the basis for the formula in which customs duties were paid. These early official silver dollars, few in number and doubtful in reliability, passed at a discount in terms of the better known foreign dollars.[53]

The minting of the Chinese silver dollar on a large scale by modern machinery began in Kwangtung. Chang Chih-tung, governor-general of Kwangtung and Kwangsi, memorialized in 1887 that he was setting up a cash mint in line with the imperial edict, but he also requested permission to mint silver dollars. Imperial approval was granted, and the Canton mint issued its first coins in 1889. The mint, reportedly capable of producing 2 million cash per day with an additional capacity for 100,000 silver pieces, was one of the largest mints in the world. It was operated efficiently after its establishment, and the Canton dollar was soon declared legal tender for the payment of customs duties. Besides dollars, the mint also produced silver subsidiary coins of four denominations, which were in enthusiastic demand along the coast.[54]

SILVER DOLLARS AS A UNIT OF ACCOUNT

Not only did silver dollars become widely accepted as media of exchange in China, but they gradually established themselves as a unit of account in competition with the tael system. The unit of account in China was the monetary tael, the dollar coin being only one of many

51. In a circular dated June 27, 1896, Robert Hart, the inspector-general of the Chinese Maritime Customs, instructed the customs commissioners that treasure and money would be placed on the same footing as ordinary merchandise. They "shall be required to take out landing and shipping permits; and if landed or shipped without permit, they shall be liable to confiscation" (Circular No. 723, IMC, *Inspector General's Circulars* [Shanghai, 1879–1910], VII, 310).

52. Yang Tuan-liu, *Huo-pi*, pp. 285–86.

53. King, *Money*, p. 224.

54. Ibid., pp. 212, 225–26.

types of money in the monetary system. Some retail prices might be quoted in terms of dollars (*yuan*), but the seller had to take the exchange risk. For larger transactions, quotations were generally in tael, and dollars were accepted at the rate of the day. Under this system, the dollar played a subsidiary role to sycee, although it was common tender and generally accepted at market rates quoted in the newspapers and at banks. The dollar, however, was never simply a subsidiary coin, taking a fractional value of the tael in accordance either with an arbitrary decision or with its metallic content. Rather, the dollar entered China's monetary system because it was preferred to sycee for payments in general.

There existed several categories of dollar units of account on the coast during the late Ch'ing period. The simplest was the standard dollar system in which the unit of account was payable at par by a standard coin that existed in sufficient quantity to be considered normal tender. A fictitious dollar system sometimes developed when the standard dollars became scarce and were used so rarely that they hardly performed the function of money. A case in point was Shanghai immediately before 1857. In extreme cases, sycee was not available in the community, and dollars were the only silver money. The tael, in which prices were normally quoted, was then purely imaginary money, and all payments in silver involved an exchange transaction. In the retail sector, however, it was customary to quote a price in the dollar unit of account.[55]

The use of the dollar unit of account in interregional payments was mainly confined to the treaty ports, but dollars were also transported to the interior in the upcountry purchase of tea and silk. This was why the dollar received a high premium in the treaty ports during the tea and silk seasons. For local transactions, the dollar coin was largely used in southern China, particularly in coastal regions.[56] In certain cities of southern China, the supply of the dollar was so abundant that it caused the use of a dollar unit of account, monetary bullion being quoted in terms of dollar. In other places where prices were in tael, dollars were accepted in payment at rates that varied with the supply or demand for the coin.

In Soochow the prices of commodities were, as noted by a local scholar, gradually expressed in silver dollars instead of tael from the 1780s on. Along the Fukien coast, as the governor-general of Fukien and Che-

---

55. Ibid., pp. 81–82. Actually, there were four major categories of dollar units of account: the imaginary dollar system, the standard dollar system, the bank money dollar system, and the dollar bullion system (ibid., p. 116).

56. *Shang-hai ch'ien-chuang*, p. 556. Although dollars were known in the north of China, Shanghai marked the northern limit of their use as the standard of payment and of the use of a dollar unit of account.

kiang memorialized in 1789, freight was sometimes quoted in dollars. In 1828, Pao Shih-ch'en wrote that various kinds of trade in Kiangsu and Chekiang were all conducted in similar manner.[57] After the Treaty of Nanking in 1842, this practice became more widespread, as George T. Braine of Dent & Co. testified in 1846 concerning the trade of opium and silk along the coast: "The dollar is always employed as the means of fixing the value in all transactions whether for cash or barter."[58] Meanwhile, as a British official noted, native bank notes in dollar denominations "were freely circulated" in Foochow in 1845. By the same token, the *North-China Herald* reported in 1856 that silver notes in circulation in Shanghai were mostly expressed in dollars. It added that in that city most businessmen in retail trade had adopted the silver dollar as the unit of account, while those in wholesale business still adhered to the traditional tael.[59]

A fact that unmistakably testifies to the importance of the dollar unit account was that in the mid-nineteenth century it was used beyond the commercial world: taxes and stipends of lower officers, soldiers, and sailors were stipulated in dollars in the coastal provinces from Kwangtung to Kiangsu. Partly for this purpose, paper notes in dollar denominations were issued first by various local government banks in the late nineteenth century and later by the Hu-pu Bank in 1906.[60] Nevertheless, the tael still held sway as a unit of account over large parts of China, and the century-long struggle between the two units of account—tael and dollar—continued. The imperial edict of May 27, 1910, finally abolished the tael as the official unit of account. At the same time, the dollar coin of 0.72 Kuping liang weight and .900 fineness was adopted as the basis of the silver standard.[61] In that year the celebrated series of official reports on finance, the *Ts'ai-cheng shuo-ming shu*, used the dollar (*yuan*) as the unit of account.[62] The dollar unit of account was used throughout state budgetary documents in 1911.[63]

57. *Chung-kuo chin-tai huo-pi shih tzu-liao*, p. 54; P'eng Hsin-wei, *Huo-pi*, p. 811; and Yeh-chien Wang, "Evolution," p. 438.

58. BPP, *Report from the Select Committee on Commercial Relations with China, Minutes of Evidence*, vol. 5, pp. 24–25.

59. BPP, *Returns of Trade*, vol. 40, pp. 5–6. The *NCH* report is cited in *Chung-kuo chin-tai huo-pi shih tzu-liao*, p. 57.

60. Yeh-chien Wang, "Evolution," p. 438; and P'eng Hsin-wei, *Huo-pi*, pp. 811–12.

61. Circular No. 1701, June 23, 1910, IMC, *Circulars*, XI, 341.

62. See, e.g., Anhwei, sui-ju pu, ts'ao-liang section, esp. p. 29. Some financial reports, however, still used the tael as the unit of account.

63. The budget, prepared for 1912, called for a revenue of $350,777,408 and an expenditure of $356,361,607 (Chia Shih-i, *Min-kuo ts'ai-cheng shih* [Taipei, 1950], I, 32). Budgetary planning was never implemented because of the Republican revolution of 1911.

THE USE OF PAPER NOTES
AND BANK MONEY

Paper money has a long history in China, but its volume and circulation were greatly limited. It declined rapidly after the thirteenth century and virtually disappeared after the sixteenth.[64] However, paper currency revived at the turn of the nineteenth century, becoming a significant sector of the Ch'ing monetary system. In contrast to the time-honored practice whereby the government monopolized the paper notes, in the nineteenth century it was mainly the private, old-style banks and firms that issued silver notes and cash notes for circulation.

The first half of the Ch'ing period marked the apogee of bimetallism in Chinese monetary system, which was similar to what is known as parallel standard. The circulating media consisted of silver and copper cash. Private concerns rarely or never issued paper notes. Although the newly established Manchu government issued paper money, the amount was insignificant, and its circulation lasted for only a decade from 1651 to 1661.[65] By the early nineteenth century, however, silver notes and cash notes issued by private concerns were widespread, and the traditional bimetallic regime had been transformed without government participation into a troika of silver, copper cash, and paper notes. Meanwhile, foreign mercantile houses and banks also played an important role in the supply of paper money in China. Modern-style Chinese banks, however, were not established until 1897.

CHINESE PRIVATE NOTES

Ssu-p'iao (private notes) were paper notes issued by Chinese private business establishments. Issued mainly in the form of silver notes (*yin-p'iao*) and "cash" notes (*ch'ien-p'iao*) by native banks, pawnshops, and some established grocery stores for circulation in lieu of silver and cash, these private notes were increasingly used at the turn of the nineteenth century. It is interesting to note that when the government later issued paper notes in 1853, it called them *yin-p'iao* and *ch'ien-p'iao*, the same names as the notes previously issued by the private concerns.

In sharp contrast to the public sector of the economy, private notes

---

It was not until 1933 that the Nationalist government finally brought the old regime of tael to an end in the commercial world as well.

64. King, *Money*, p. 103; and Lien-sheng Yang, *Money*, p. 62.

65. Yeh-chien Wang, "Evolution," pp. 425–26.

played a crucial role in facilitating China's commercial revolution. The importance of *ssu-p'iao* in modern China's monetary system is evidenced by the fact that the paper money issued by the Ch'ing government failed to perform satisfactorily. In times of military emergency, the central government printed paper notes, but these experiments were short-lived. Meanwhile, a number of provincial banks (*kuan yin ch'ien hao*) circulated convertible notes in their provinces, but only during the later part of the nineteenth century, and the amount was insignificant when compared with that of the private notes. And the paper notes issued by the Chinese governmental modern-type banks did not materialize until 1899.[66]

The origin of the use of these paper notes was not much different from what had happened in Europe in early modern times. At the beginning paper notes were issued like warehouse receipts by local banks or money shops for the deposit of silver and cash from their customers. Money shops served as custodians of the treasures entrusted; customers could withdraw part or all of their deposit any time upon the presentation of the receipt issued. Soon these receipts were circulating in the market because they, in contrast to hard currencies, made the monetary system less unwieldly. The silver notes or cash notes thus became representative full-bodied money, because they were fully backed by metallic money in the safe of money shops. These local bankers soon discovered that they needed to keep only a fraction of the deposits to meet the demand for withdrawal from customers and that they could safely lend the rest to earn interest. Finally, many local banks and other shops simply issued their own notes for circulation because they knew that it was unlikely that all of their notes would be presented for redemption at the same time. Accordingly, these paper notes turned into credit money, some being promissory notes in nature and others like demand deposits.[67]

The privately issued notes, especially cash notes, were probably used by the end of the eighteenth century, but it was not until the early nineteenth century that their circulation became widespread. In general, cash notes were mostly used in the north, while silver notes dominated in the south. In Peking, cash notes were common as early as 1810, and by 1852 native bank notes were used in this capital city to settle business

66. For the military campaigns at the beginning of the dynasty, the Ch'ing government printed paper notes in the modest amount of 128,000 strings annually from 1650 to 1661 (P'eng Hsin-wei, *Huo-pi*, p. 808). During the Taiping uprising, the short-lived experiment from 1853 to 1862 was a failure, because the value of the notes dropped sharply due to their inconvertibility (Lien-sheng Yang, *Money*, p. 68). For other types of government banks, see ibid., p. 70.

67. Yeh-chien Wang, "Evolution," pp. 436–37.

transactions that amounted to 500 cash or more. In the 1820s well-established businessmen from Shansi and Shensi issued paper notes that circulated for two or three decades without the need to pay out any cash. In Szechuan the widespread use of private notes prompted the governor-general to memorialize banning them.[68]

In Southeast China, trade along the coast facilitated the use of private notes. In Shanghai, for example, a notice from the magistrate office in 1841 indicated that trade in beans, wheat, cotton, and cloth all relied on silver notes as exchange media. In Foochow, two British officials noted that in 1845 this port had about 100 native banks and that their notes of three types—cash notes, sycee notes, and dollar notes—were freely circulated. In fact, the notes were so popular that they commended a premium over coin.[69] This observation was borne out by a report of the governor-general who noted in 1853 that, though people in Fukien had used silver, cash, and cash notes in their business transactions, "in recent years 80–90 percent of trade has been settled by cash notes alone."[70] Meanwhile, Western traders also used the native bank notes as a means of payment. For instance, David Sasoon & Co. in 1859 used these notes to pay for the gold that the firm purchased.[71] One foreign insurance company in 1862 was willing to accept notes issued by native banks for the payment of its policy premiums.[72]

By the 1860s the privately issued notes were widely used in many parts of China. Actually, those issued by well-established native banks were so popular that they sometimes commanded a premium over coin.[73] Inasmuch as a 100 percent of reserve was not used, the issue of paper notes also strengthened the lending power of the issuing body. As a consequence, native banks were usually profitable. A British trader testified in the mid-nineteenth century that "there had been an inclination on the part of the Chinese to establish banks."[74]

Thanks to the rapid expansion of China's foreign trade after the 1860s, native banks in the treaty ports grew by leaps and bounds in both number and capitalization. In Canton, for example, their number in-

68. Ibid., pp. 437–40; and Yang Tuan-liu, p. 147.

69. *Shang-hai ch'ien-chuang*, p. 12; and BPP, *Returns of Trade*, vol. 40, pp. 5–6.

70. *Chung-kuo chin-tai huo-pi shih*, p. 237, cited in Yeh-chien Wang, "Evolution," p. 437.

71. *NCH*, Sept. 17, 1859, p. 17.

72. *NCH*, Mar. 1, 1862, p. 34.

73. BPP, *Returns of Trade*, vol. 40, pp. 5–6; and Sir Harry Parkes, "An Account of the Paper Currency and Banking System of Fuchowfoo [Foochow]," *Journal of the Royal Asiatic Society* 13:179–90 (1852).

74. BPP, *Report from the Select Committee*, vol. 5, p. 86.

creased from 68 in 1873 to 120 in 1930. There were 100 native banks in
Tientsin in 1867; 40 of these had a capital of around Tls. 10,000 each, and
another 40, Tls. 4,000 each. The remaining 20 were small ones, each
having a capital of Tls. 2,000.[75] The native banks in that port reached
their golden period in 1899, when the total number reached an all-time
high of more than 300.[76] Hankow was another treaty port where native
banking thrived. There were some 20 Shansi banks and 50 money shops
in that port during the late seventies,[77] and 40 of these banks were large
ones by the early eighties.[78] In Shanghai, the largest treaty port, over
forty-five years (1858–1903), the average capital of a native bank tripled,
and the total capital of the native banks quadrupled. Because of their
close relationship with foreign trade, the great majority of them operated
in the foreign settlement (table 3). A similar trend existed in Tientsin.[79]

The native banks had sophisticated devices to prevent successful
counterfeiting of their notes. They used solid blocks of brass for engrav-
ing purposes, and filled in, with a brush pen, the value of a bill, date of
issue, and words to facilitate the detection of a counterfeit. Stamps of
various shapes and sizes, some elaborately engraved, were impressed on
different parts of the bill, using red or black ink. The use made of the
margin was the greatest security against counterfeiting: on it were
written various phrases before the bill was cut and put in circulation.[80]

WESTERN PAPER NOTES

Western trading establishments and banks in China likewise issued
notes for circulation. Actually, all agency houses, as noted in chapter 2,
carried some form of banking operations after they established themselves at Canton at the turn of the nineteenth century. Because there
were no professional Western bankers in China before 1848, foreign merchants also had to be financiers. The houses thus accepted deposits,
made loans, remitted funds, and did various exchange business. In addition, these firms undertook many of the ancillary services of a modern
bank, granting letters of credit to travelers and acting as trustees, execu-

75. *NCH*, Oct. 19, 1867, p. 311.
76. Yang Yin-p'u, *Chin-yung*, pp. 274–75.
77. Ibid., p. 312.
78. IMC, *Decennial Report, 1882–1891* (Shanghai, 1892), p. 44.
79. Wang Yeh-chien, *Huo-pi*, p. 68. There were three major groups of native banks in
Tientsin at the turn of the century: those in the eastern part of the port; those in the western
part of the port; and those in the foreign settlements (Yang Yin-piu, *Chin-yung*, p. 275).
80. Lien-sheng Yang, *Money*, p. 69.

TABLE 3. THE NUMBER OF NATIVE BANKS IN SHANGHAI, 1858–1911

	Chinese Section		Foreign settlement		
	Number	*Percent*	*Number*	*Percent*	Total number
1858	—	—	—	—	120
1873	80	44	103	56	183
1874	30	38	48	62	78
1876	42	40	63	60	105
1883	23	40	35	60	58
1886	31	55	25	45	56
1888	25	40	37	60	62
1903	23	28	59	72	82
1904	26	30	62	70	88
1905	30	29	72	71	102
1906	33	29	80	71	113
1907	35	32	76	68	111
1908	37	32	78	68	115
1909	23	23	77	77	100
1910	17	19	74	81	91
1911	14	27	37	73	51
Average	31.3	33.7	61.7	66.3	94.7

Sources: *NCH*, June 12, 1858, p. 182; and *Shang-hai ch'ien-chuang*, pp. 30, 32, and 94. Calculations are mine.

tors, and investment bankers. British officers, for example, banked with Jardine, Matheson & Co. during the Opium War.[81] A prominent American merchant later recalled that "in the very early days every House was its own Bank, and it sought no facilities outside of its own resources." Consequently, "the old House with large capital had a practical monopoly of the business" of the American China trade without resorting to financial assistance from bankers at home.[82]

Under the treaty system, virtually all of the Western agency houses continued to offer some measure of banking services. Jardine's, for example, issued dollar notes in both Chinese and English that circulated

81. Greenberg, pp. 152–53; and Maggie Keswick, *The Thistle*, p. 74.
82. Augustine Heard, Jr., "Old China," p. 38, GQ-2, HC.

locally, though deposit and remittance facilities were more common.[83]
The leading merchant houses, by acting as private bankers, at first provided a formidable barrier to the entry of smaller houses into the China
trade. Edward Cunningham of Russell & Co. recalled this situation in
1873:

Twenty to twenty-five years ago [1848–1853] the prominent houses, including one American, did a flourishing exchange business. They acted as interme-
diaries between less known houses and British capital by buying drafts on the
former on London and giving them currency by their endorsement and then
selling them to the holders of British hard currency. One English bank had less
business than some one of the mercantile houses.[84]

The thriving economic activities along China's coast after 1842 created a demand for the establishment of specialized financial institutions
to finance imports and exports. In response to this situation, Western
banks started to operate in the treaty ports. In 1848 the British-
chartered Oriental Banking Corporation opened a branch in Shanghai,
having established a branch in Hong Kong in 1843, and was the first
foreign bank to operate in China. It was soon overshadowed by the
Mercantile Bank of India (established 1854), the Chartered Bank of
India, Australia, and China (established 1857), and the Hongkong and
Shanghai Banking Corporation (established 1864 in Hong Kong and
1865 in Shanghai). From 1848 to 1872, a dozen Western banks set up
branches in Shanghai. In the opinion of a leading American trader, the
rise of modern banks substantially changed the business pattern of the
China trade:

There was but one Bank in China (prior to 1854), and that one [was] most
conservative, and exercising really but little influence. Afterwards there came a
great number of them—12 were established in Shanghai in 1864—and these . . .
were the most potent instruments in revolutionizing business. . . . For instance, a
few Houses could never have maintained so long their monopoly at Foochow [for
the purchase of upcountry tea] if banks had been ready, as they were afterwards,
to lend assistance to those less strong.[85]

The rise of Western banks in China dealt a severe blow to the banking
business of the agency houses. By the early 1850s, the Oriental Banking
Corporation, for example, dealt mostly with foreign bills of exchange, a
fact that prompted a foreign trader to criticize in 1852: "They [Oriental
Banking Corporation] do not exercise [in Shanghai] the functions or

83. Keswick, *The Thistle*, p. 175.
84. *NCH*, July 26, 1873, p. 75.
85. Augustine Heard, Jr., "Old China, " pp. 2, 38–39, GQ-2, HC.

carry on the business of bankers properly so called. They are simply dealers in Foreign Bills of Exchange which is the legitimate business of a *merchant* exclusively, and is nowhere the business of a *banker*."[86] Furthermore, Chinese and foreign deposits, an important source of capital of the agency houses, deserted the trading houses for the more reliable banks. Heard's, for example, lost the business of some $70,000 in deposits in the spring of 1862.[87] In June of that year Edward Cunningham of Russell's noted that it was necessary to give 8 instead of 6 percent annual rate of interest on deposits in order to compete with the banks. This rate shot up to a dazzling 12 percent for a short period in 1865.[88]

The resources of Western banks in China were several. First, they raised their capital outside of China. Second, they had deposits in China. Besides receiving private deposits, most of the foreign banks acted as treasury agents for their respective governments and handled the Chinese customs and salt receipts that had been pledged as security against foreign loans. Such deposits must have been large, because the Hongkong and Shanghai Banking Corporation alone received deposits amounting to $6 million during the sixties and $22 million during the seventies.[89] The final financial resource of foreign banks was the issue of bank notes, which were widely circulated along the coast during the last decades of the Ch'ing period. It is true that foreign banks in China had to observe the regulations of their own countries regarding the issue of bank notes and thus had to put up gold or silver as reserve, but, inasmuch as a 100 percent reserve was not required, issuing bank notes not only strengthened their lending power but also greatly increased the supply of money in China.

After Western bank notes were issued in Hong Kong and Shanghai, denominated in dollars and taels, they generally found acceptance along the coast. In Fukien in 1852, people used them side by side with Chinese private notes. They were widely circulated in Chekiang, Kiangsu, and other southern provinces by the late seventies and were freely accepted at face value in the mid-Yangtze port of Hankow during the eighties. In fact, the bank notes were so popular that those issued at Hong Kong were at a premium of 0.75 to 0.8 percent in 1876, and the Western banks requested a raise in the limit on their note issue.[90] By the end of the

86. *NCH*, Aug. 7, 1852, p. 3.
87. John Heard, III (Shanghai) to Augustine Heard, Sr. (Boston), May 12, 1862, EM-7, HC.
88. S. C. Lockwood, p. 108.
89. *NCH*, Feb. 28, 1879.
90. Yang Tuan-liu, p. 236; IMC, *Decennial Report, 1882–1891*, p. 177; and King, *Money*, pp. 104–5, 191–92.

nineteenth century, foreign bank notes were an important element in
China's currency system.

BANK MONEY: CURRENT ACCOUNTS
AND TRANSFER ACCOUNTS

Native and Western banks provided two forms of bank money, which
gave a certain flexibility to the money supply and made monetary payments more convenient by minimizing the complexities of the bimetallic
system. The first form was the bank note which we have just discussed.
The second was the current of demand accounts. These accounts could
arise from a tender of coin or bullion, from a transfer from another bank,
or from the granting of a loan to a customer. They fulfilled the requirements of money and were generally accepted as a means of payment
through two ways.

First, bank checks were used. This was common practice by customers of modern Chinese and foreign banks, and sometimes the *yin-
p'iao* (silver notes) issued by Chinese traditional credit institutions performed a similar function.[91] Western agency houses developed similar
practices. After the 1860s these houses continued to perform the function
of banks, though on a limited scale, and the funds of the house were
usually entrusted to the comprador. Cash payment was not necessarily
used in day-to-day business transactions, for "orders, or cheques, were
drawn on him, precisely as on a modern bank."[92] This order or cheque
was called a "comprador order" and was used by all the foreign houses.
The order was usually paid on demand but was occasionally in the form
of a promissory note at three days' sight. Nor was it necessary for the
house to pay hard currency to its foreign employees, because their salary
was paid by a check drawn on the comprador, who held the funds
against which the employee wrote "chits" (memoranda), acknowledging
debts for retail transactions. These "chits" were accepted by shopkeepers and passed for collection to the firm's comprador.[93] The need for the
chit system was minimized after 1889 when bank notes denominated in
dollars became popular in Shanghai.

Second, other transfer arrangements could be made, such as the one
developed at Ningpo. This Ningpo transfer account system was the most

91. P'eng Hsin-wei, pp. 944–45, 951.
92. Augustine Heard, Jr., FP-4, p. 9, HC.
93. For a fuller discussion of the comprador's order, see Yen-p'ing Hao, *Comprador*,
pp. 72–73, 259.

advanced type of credit instrument in China before the Opium War. Under this system, business transactions could be carried out and payment made with current accounts, that is, through book transfer of accounts, which were maintained at a local bank by its customers. The transfer of money from one customer's account to that of another was usually made on instructions from both parties involved without the use of checks.[94] Under the treaty system, the transfer account practice was also used in Newchwang, the center of bean trade along the coast, where, with the consent of the bankers, there existed what we would call overdrawn accounts.[95] This kind of scriptural money, not unlike the German *buchgeld* (book money),[96] was especially convenient for large business transactions.

THE MONETARY FUNCTION OF OPIUM

The third new form of money was opium. In theory, any commodity is eligible as money if it is used as a medium of exchange or is generally acceptable as a means of payment. In practice, however, only a few commodities qualify, and convenience is an important criterion. Strictly speaking, opium was a commodity, not money, especially during the early nineteenth century. But later it was so widely used as a means of payment and a medium of exchange, especially in the purchase of tea and silk, along the coast as well as in the interior, that it may be considered money in a broad sense.

OPIUM AS MONEY

Opium was widely used as a means of payment in late Ch'ing China because there was a real and constant demand for it. Indeed, it was the one commodity for which there was always either a ready cash market or a bartering opportunity. Its importance to China's foreign trade was reflected in a report to the British Foreign Office by W. H. Mitchell, a local official at Hong Kong, in 1852: "We bring the Chinese nothing that is really popular among them.... Opium is the only 'open sesame' to their stony hearts."[97] This was particularly true for travelers who found

---

94. *Chung-kuo chin-tai huo-pi shih tzu-liao*, pp. 141–42. See also Susan Mann Jones, "Finance in Ningpo: The 'Ch'ien-chuang,' 1780–1880," in W. E. Willmott, ed., *Economic Organization in Chinese Society* (Stanford, Calif., 1972), pp. 47–77; and King, *Money*, p. 115.

95. King, *Money*, p. 115; and Yang Tuan-liu, p. 88. For a technical account of the transfer tael system in Ningpo and Newchwang, see King, *Money*, pp. 106–9.

96. Braudel, *Capitalism and Material Life*, p. 360.

97. To Sir George Bonham, Hong Kong, Mar. 15, 1852, FO 405/2, p. 410.

that opium was a desirable article to carry. A look at homicide cases in the late Ch'ing shows that travelers were often murdered because their boatmen or bearers had guessed from the weight of their baggage that they were carrying silver bullion. Even though opium was worth less by unit of weight than silver, it was far lighter than a copper cash equivalent, and its bulk and weight distribution could confuse the prospective murderer.[98] Consequently, veteran travelers carried opium with them. Numerous traveling merchants in southern China had opium with them and used it as a substitute for silver during the seventies and eighties.[99] The monetary function of opium was also attested to by the fact that even students traveling to Peking to take the civil examinations would carry opium with them to pay their expenses along the way.[100]

Opium was likewise used as a major means of payment by the Chinese shopkeepers, artisans, and coolies in Hong Kong around 1850. In that year W. H. Mitchell, at the governor's request, drew up a memorandum in which he described how opium, as its supply increased in the port, was used as the chief mode of remitting funds to the mainland: "The capital upon which the shopkeeper is trading here is probably borrowed at interest in his native village, and in paying up either the interest or principal, he remits opium instead of money."[101] This was also the case for other Chinese working classes in Hong Kong. In the same vein, Augustine Heard & Co. used opium "principally as a means of transferring money from one port to another" during the fifties.[102]

Opium was not only used as money, but opium orders also from time to time were regarded as currency. A British merchant testified to this fact during the late forties: "Opium order forms a temporary paper currency, by means of which given amounts of money are represented, to be finally realized not in cash but in opium."[103] The use of the order as a means of payment remained unchanged during the fifties. A case in point was Shanghai where foreigners frequently used the Malwa opium orders to pay for their debts to the Chinese from whom they bought tea and silk.[104]

Nothing testifies more eloquently to the monetary function of opium

98. Jonathan Spence, "Opium Smoking in Ch'ing China," in Frederic E. Wakeman, Jr., and Carolyn Grant, eds. *Conflict and Control in Late Imperial China* (Berkeley, Calif., 1975), p. 168.

99. For southern China, especially Yunnan and Kweichow, see Archibald R. Colquhoun, *Across Chryse* (London, 1883), I, 24.

100. Spence, p. 168.

101. Memorandum, Nov, 1, 1850, FO 17/183.

102. John Heard to Augustine Heard, Sr., Apr. 12, 1858, EM-1, HC.

103. BPP, *Returns of Trade*, vol. 39, p. 74.

104. A. G. Dallas (Shanghai) to David Jardine (Hong Kong), Jan. 13, 1852, JMA.

than the fact that opium was used as a medium of exchange in China's commerce, both on the coast and in the interior. As the greatest bulk of opium was transported from south to north by way of coastal shipment, foreign traders found it convenient to use opium in exchange for tea and silk in the coastal treaty ports. For instance, trade was sluggish in Shanghai during the early fifties because of the Taiping movement, but the foreign merchants dealing in opium, such as Jardine's, Dent's, and Lindsay's, were still able to pay for their teas with opium. Under these circumstances, the opium houses dominated the market. A British official had this observation to make in 1853: "The holders of opium and rich capitalists being the only parties able to purchase produce this year, few, if any, of the Manchester firms, who made consignments to China, will share in the export business."[105]

Through its representatives at Foochow, Thomas Larken and V. W. Fisher, Jardine's used opium to pay for its tea purchases at that port from 1855. This operation went smoothly, though not without hitches from time to time. For instance, it was difficult for Larken in late summer of 1856.[106] At the end of August he acquired 138 chests of Chunn King Congou at Tls. 9.2 per chest, 324 chests of Lau Fock Congou at Tls. 13.5, and 150 chests of Wo Fat Congou at Tls. 12.5. He added: "Against which I have placed 6 chests [of] Malwa Opium at $520 per pecul [picul]."[107] Jardine's expanded this kind of operation after 1860 when M. A. Macleod, an aggressive businessman, became its new representative at Foochow.[108]

The correspondence files of A. G. Dallas, the Jardine representative at Shanghai, testify that opium was also used in exchange for silk in that port during the fifties.[109] Dallas, however, occasionally encountered difficulties in this kind of transaction when the general demand for opium was weak, as he experienced in July 1852.[110] Under this condition, some

---

105. Quoted in Fairbank, *Trade and Diplomacy*, I, 406.

106. Larken mentioned this problem on July 13, 1856: "I have not been enabled to work off any large quantity of drug [opium] at present in barter for Teas, as the Teamen have been anxious to receive cash in payment in order to send the same into the country for further purchases. Later in the season I fancy the operations will be much easier" (to Joseph Jardine [Hong Kong], JMA). Larken's prediction proved to be correct.

107. Ibid., Aug. 29, 1856.

108. Macleod to Alexander Perceval (Hong Kong), May 11, 1861, JMA.

109. E.g., Dallas had this to report: "I this afternoon paid away to a Silk man my remaining stock [of opium], viz., 5¢ [chests] low numbers at $550 and 55¢ [chests] high numbers at $510" (to David Jardine [Hong Kong], Dec. 18, 1851, JMA).

110. Dallas made note of this on July 21, 1852: "The opium market is quiet and I am with difficulty making some sales [of Malwa opium] at $490 to $500 [per chest] in Silk payment" (ibid.).

Chinese merchants were forced into the opium trade when tea and silk could be paid for in no other way.

OPIUM IN THE INTERIOR

Opium was used as a medium of exchange in the interior. Though the Western merchants were still restricted to the treaty ports, they sent their compradors or other purchasing agents inland with large stocks of opium that could be exchanged for upcountry tea, silk, and other commodities. Tea overshadowed all other produce in terms of quantity before the eighties, and Shanghai was the port where such upcountry purchases were arranged. For this purpose, A. G. Dallas often made advances to Takee (Yang Fang, the firm's comprador) in the form of opium during the late forties and early fifties.[111] At the same time, Dent, Beale & Co. at Shanghai advanced the Cantonese teaman Coekeye opium for the purchase of upcountry tea. Coekeye frequently received opium from the company's opium ship, the *Emily Jane*, anchoring at Woosung in 1850 and 1851. The opium advance must have been of considerable quantity, because it was advanced for "large shipments of tea on account of Coekeye" in 1851.[112]

The foreign traders' practice of advancing opium to the Chinese for purchasing upcountry tea continued during the sixties. James Whittall, Jardine's partner residing at Shanghai, made advances, in the form of "money and opium," to a Chinese merchant in 1863 in order to "contract to buy [tea] at a fixed price." Because this merchant was a relatively new acquaintance to Jardine's, Whittall was reluctant to made advances on a large scale.[113] It was a different story, however, when Whittall dealt with Yowloong (Yu-lung), "an old native friend." During the spring of 1863, Whittall advanced Yowloong and his brother opium on such a grand scale that it drove up the tea prices in the interior.[114] By the same token, Gilman's, Russell's, and Heard's all advanced opium to the Chinese tea merchants during the fifties and sixties.[115]

Paying partly in opium, foreign merchants carried on extensive upcountry tea purchases from Foochow, about 300 miles away from the

---

111. Ibid., May 3, 1851.

112. Ibid., Dec. 18, 1851.

113. Whittall to Alexander Perceval (Hong Kong), Apr. 9, 1863, JMA.

114. "The idea generally among Chinese is that prices will open high" in the tea districts (ibid.).

115. Most of the tea merchants were Cantonese, e.g., Yowloong and Ehing (James Jardine [Canton] to David Jardine [Hong Kong], Jan. 7, 1855, JMA). For the operation in the sixties, see James Whittall (Shanghai) to David Jardine (Hong Kong), Apr. 9, 1863, JMA.

Bohea (Wu-i) tea districts of Fukien and Kiangsi. This was particularly true after 1854 when Foochow started to export tea. The American merchant Augustine Heard, Jr., had this observation to make regarding the dispatch of opium from Foochow to the interior: "Years after the Hong [Cohong] system had ceased to exist, foreigners were in the habit of sending large sums, both in the shape of money and opium, into the country districts from Foochow for the purchase of tea."[116]

It was in this fashion that Jardine's secured, after 1854 and throughout the sixties, a great amount of tea through its comprador, Acum, along with its teamen, Ahee, Taising, Yuntai, and Tonghing.[117] In 1855, for instance, "the amount of treasure that Ahee had with him in the country . . . including Drug [opium], was $440,065."[118] The next year Jardine's again entrusted a large amount of opium to another Chinese teaman named Awy, who in turn advanced a portion of the opium, valued at $10,000, to some smaller local tea merchants in the Bohea tea districts of Fukien and Kiangsi.[119]

Under the supervision of M. A. Macleod, Jardine's stepped up its operation after 1860 by sending opium into the tea-producing areas of northwestern Fukien in exchange for tea. Macleod channeled his operation largely through the Cantonese merchants, especially Ahee and Taising, who were particularly good in the tea business. When opium was in heavy demand in the interior, Macleod would dispose of his opium in highly favorable terms. He wrote to Hong Kong on May 11, 1861, that he "had charged them [Ahee and Taising] a very full figure, considering the state of the market at the moment."[120] Macleod reported to Jardine's head office in Hong Kong that the opium trade at Foochow thrived suddenly after April 6, 1861, when it was legalized with a tax of 30 taels per chest.[121] With the increase in the opium supply, however, the purchasing power of opium in the interior weakened.[122]

116. "Diary," p. 34, FP-4, HC.
117. *NCH*, Oct. 13, 1860, Supplement. For teamen, see M. A. Macleod (Foochow) to Alexander Perceval (Hong Kong), Apr. 8, 1861, JMA.
118. George V. W. Fisher (Foochow) to Joseph Jardine (Hong Kong), May 1, 1855, JMA.
119. Ibid., May 4, 1856.
120. Macleod (Foochow) to Alexander Perceval (Hong Kong), JMA.
121. Macleod made note of this when he reported to the head office in Hong Kong two days later: "There was a good deal of business done in Malwa owing to the new Custom House regulation coming into force on the 6th inst., about 200 chests having changed hands at from $820 to 840 per pecul." He added: "Pray observe that the old local squeeze of Ts. 57 & 6 mace per chest will continue to be exacted as heretofore" (ibid., Apr. 8, 1861).
122. Teaman Taising wrote from the interior: "Opium is going off upcountry more easily, but there is no improvement to notice in price" (Taising [Sueykut, Fukien] to M. A. Macleod [Foochow], Aug. 29, 1861, JMA).

In contrast to the augmented supply of opium at Foochow, demand for it in the interior decreased because of political disturbances. The Taiping uprising, which gained momentum during the late fifties, expanded its activity by 1861 to the mountainous, tea-producing area of Bohea. Teaman Taising noted in the interior on September 9 that it was difficult to use opium in payment of tea purchase.[123] Taising again commented from upcountry on the deterioration of the opium business eighteen days later.[124]

THE SOOCHOW SYSTEM

Around 1850 Chinese and foreign merchants at Shanghai developed the so-called "Soochow system" by which Chinese merchants brought opium from Shanghai to the silk-producing region of Soochow to pay for silk. This system was developed from the practice of opium trade at Woosung during the forties. The Chinese opium dealers at Shanghai, for example, would first pay the local silk merchants, from whom Jardine's bought silk, and then accept Jardine's opium delivery at Woosung. By using opium as the medium of exchange, both Chinese and foreign merchants dealing in silk and opium could save shroffage (money-changing) and other miscellaneous charges. Because many Chinese opium and silk merchants belonged to the same professional guild or geographical association, this practice of mixing legal (silk) with illegal (opium) trade was carried on smoothly before opium imports were legalized and taxed under the treaty settlement of 1858–1860.

The Soochow system of exchanging opium for silk was begun in the late forties by Yungkee, a Cantonese merchant at Shanghai, who then served as the comprador to Dent, Beale & Co.[125] In a letter from Shanghai to Jardine's head office at Hong Kong dated April 4, 1851, A. G. Dallas described how this system worked: "It is not usual to send more than five chests [of opium] in one boat, so the risk is divided. The arrangement will be to take delivery of the opium at Woosung, settle weight and quality there, and [settle] the price at Soochow. The pro-

---

123. "Opium had improved in value a little, Malwa being worth equivalent to $770 to 780 [per picul] at Foochow, but there was not much doing" (ibid., Sept. 9, 1861).
124. "The opium market is very quiet.... The rebels continue about Hohow as before, so there is nothing to be done in that quarter" (ibid., Sept. 27, 1861).
125. Hsu Jung-ts'un, known to the foreign community as Yungkee, was the uncle of Hsu Jun, a prominent merchant at Shanghai (Hsu Jun, *Hsu Yü-chai tzu-hsu nien-p'u* [1927], pp. 4b, 18; and Hsu Jun et al., *Kuang-tung Hsiang-shan Hsu-shih tsung-p'u* [1882], 7, 64).

ceeds to be paid here cash in a fortnight, or transferred to accounts if produce is being purchased."[126]

One reason for the foreign merchants to send opium to Soochow was that occasionally they could not easily use opium to pay for silk at Shanghai. James Macandrew of Jardine's noted in February 1851 the "difficulty of getting the [Chinese] silkmen to take Malwa for which there is little demand" at Shanghai.[127] Dent's initial exploration of the Soochow system must have been successful, because other foreign merchants, such as the Parsees and Lindsay & Co., soon followed suit.[128] Because Jardine's was also engaged in the opium trade at Woosung, Dallas was tempted to adopt this new way of doing business. He wrote: "The Honan men [Cantonese] and other large [opium] dealers resort to Soo-choo [Soochow] to make their purchases [of silk], I see nothing for it but to adopt the system cautiously."[129]

Determined to use opium as a medium of exchange for silk at Soochow, Dallas tried to cooperate with Takee, a renowned merchant from Ningpo who was heavily engaged in the silk business at Shanghai. Dallas had this to report on April 3, 1851, regarding their preliminary talk: "Takee has been here anxiously waiting my arrival with the view of continuing his old business [of silk], and I have just had a long and satisfactory conversation with him regarding which I will write you tomorrow."[130] The next day Dallas wrote enthusiastically about Takee. According to Dallas, even though "hitherto or rather at first he was not an opium man," Takee, because of his experience in the silk trade and his excellent reputation as a businessman at Shanghai, was nevertheless a valuable merchant to work with. As a matter of fact, other foreign traders at Shanghai had approached him for the same purpose. Dallas continued: "Most [foreign] houses here have at various times made overtures to him, and several of them would go a great length to get his business or cooperation, but he has always stuck firmly to McKinzie & me."[131] Takee so deeply committed himself to work with Jardine's that he was willing to live in Jardine's establishment in the British Settlement.[132]

126. To David Jardine, JMA.
127. To Jardine, Matheson & Co. (Hong Kong), Feb. 18, 1851, JMA.
128. A. G. Dallas (Shanghai) to David Jardine (Hong Kong), Apr. 4, 1851, JMA.
129. Ibid.
130. Ibid.
131. Ibid.
132. "He will if I like come & live in our house—having of course his own family house in the [Chinese] City [of Shanghai]" (ibid.).

To use opium as a medium of exchange for silk must have become an irresistible trend by 1851. Takee had declined Dallas' invitation to engage in the Soochow system in early 1850: "He shook his head at proposals of mine last year to sell [opium] at Soo-choo [Soochow], as D. [Dent] B. [Beale] & Co.'s comprador does." But Takee changed his mind in April 1851, as Dallas continued: "With reference to my conversation yesterday with Takee, I have only now to advise you that he proposes confining himself entirely to do our business, or with others with my sanction. He has finally wound up & squared all his old accounts [with Jardine's]." According to Dallas, it was only natural for Takee to change his attitude, because the Soochow system offered the best opportunity for Takee to further develop his silk business. Dallas went on: "Now he says he is prepared to do this [Soochow system], & indeed it is the only method by which he can get on, as in the shipping season cash cannot be had for large transactions & the foreigner must pay opium or other produce."[133]

Under the Soochow system, Takee acted as an opium broker, and Jardine's had to take the business risk. Dallas remarked on Takee: "I have implicit confidence in his honesty & intelligence, & his lookout must be against thieves on the route, etc. All this however he says he will arrange."[134] Thus, Jardine's and Takee cooperated in launching a successful business to use opium to pay for silk. One month later, Takee was so confident in this operation that he started to take the risk on his own. Dallas had this to report on May 3, 1851:

Upon becoming further acquainted with matters here, I had come to the determination of not selling at Soo-choo, unless occasionally to try the market. When purchasing Produce largely most of my payments will go through Takee's hands, & as he has his arrangements now complete, it will be more satisfactory for us to settle prices here, & to let him send the Drug [opium] to Soo-choo at his own risk.[135]

As the Soochow system dealt with both opium and silk, sending opium from Shanghai to Soochow constituted only one way of the trade. For the purpose of purchasing silk, Takee revitalized his old silk firm, the Manfoong Hong, both at Shanghai and Soochow. The firm had an excellent reputation, as Dallas wrote from Shanghai: "It stands A-1 here, as does Takee himself."[136] The Manfoong Hong used 340 chests of Mal-

133. Ibid.
134. Ibid.
135. Ibid.
136. Ibid.

wa opium of Jardine's to pay for silk in Soochow at the end of April 1851, and it received another 103 chests from Dallas on May 3 for the same purpose. Four days later Dallas "settled with Takee" 195 bales of Soochow silk.[137] Takee's action unmistakably symbolized the trend of the increasing use of opium as a medium of exchange.

The pace of Takee's supply of silk to Jardine's had to be adjusted from time to time. In writing to David Jardine in Hong Kong, Dallas had this to report on July 25, 1851: "Takee had instructions & funds to buy about 500 Bs. [bales], but in consequence of the discouraging advices from time to time received from you I did not press him to buy quickly but rather told him to hang on, & he is now only beginning to bring me in a few Bales of the finest Chops—the prices of which are not exactly settled."[138] When Takee had surplus silk, he either sold it to the foreign traders in Shanghai or shipped it to Europe on his own account via Jardine's steamers.[139]

Takee was by no means the only person through whom Jardine's operated under the Soochow system. Dallas also asked Affo, a Cantonese merchant at Shanghai, to try the opium market at Soochow. Dallas wrote on August 20, 1851: "William Affo is here now living with his brother [Wu Chien-chang] who is acting Taotai. He says he cannot openly engage in trade, but still he seems inclined to engage in the transaction of opium to Soochow. He has, I believe, no means of his own, but yet I suppose I am safe in trusting him to sell for me to a smaller extent, merely to try the market."[140]

Takee continued to handle Jardine's opium and silk business between Woosung and Soochow in 1852.[141] In the spring of 1852, Dallas and Takee agreed to drastically expand the Soochow business, but this plan did not materialize due to Takee's illness. At the same time, Affo, preoccupied with his compradorial duties, could hardly concentrate on the opium-silk trade. In order to continue the Soochow system, Dallas started to cooperate with Aloong, a Cantonese merchant at Shanghai, after September 1852. Aloong took forty chests of Jardine's inferior Malwa from Shanghai to Soochow to pay for silk.[142] Meanwhile, Dallas also

137. I do not know the exact exchange ratio between opium and silk, but it is probable that the ratio was negotiable. Dallas added: "Besides these [silks] I may be able to pick up some more if the man [Takee] comes to my terms" (ibid.).
138. Ibid.
139. In one case, Takee shipped 139 bales of Soochow silk to England in May 1851 (ibid., May 7, 1851).
140. Ibid.
141. Ibid., Jan. 22, 1852.
142. Ibid., Sept. 15, 1852.

dealt with other Chinese silk merchants in order to operate the Soochow system.[143]

Jardine's was not alone; the American firm of Russell & Co. and the British firm of Lindsay & Co. also "sent opium to Soo-choo regularly" in the early fifties.[144] All of these operations, however, were dwarfed by that of Dent & Co., which started the Soochow system. For instance, during the month ending May 20, 1851, Dent's was reported to have committed large stocks of Malwa opium, valued about $200,000, for the purpose of exchanging silk at Soochow.[145] Commenting on the popularity of opium among the Chinese merchants at Shanghai, Dallas wrote on May 3, 1851: "Most of the other [Chinese] Hongs [besides Takee's Man-foong Hong] now I find are getting quite into the way of taking payment in Opium, & I do not think of asking for Cash."[146] Thus, the fact that opium played the role of money in the Soochow system was but a reflection of the general commercial practice in Shanghai during the fifties, when the Taiping uprising caused the temporary scarcity of other forms of money.

AMOUNT AND SIGNIFICANCE
OF THE NEW FORMS OF MONEY

Let us now examine the total amount of the silver coins. For the official silver dollar coins, the Canton mint produced $15,782,427 from 1889 to the end of 1909. During the same period, this mint also produced 228,568 pieces of half-dollar coins, 631,214,496 pieces of 20-cent coins, 119,494,896 pieces of 10-cent coins, and 2,616,000 pieces of 5-cent coins.[147] The total amount produced by the Canton mint was $154,219,894. Other kinds of official silver coins also existed, such as those in Hupei and Kiangnan, so the total amount of the official silver coins could well have been around $200,000,000. It is difficult to estimate the amount of silver dollars privately minted in China. Because the premium placed on the Carolus and Mexican dollars was high, numerous counterfeiters must have existed. In one case it was reported that the dies came from Europe and that over 100 workmen were employed in

143. Ibid., Dec. 18, 1851.
144. Ibid., May 3, 1851.
145. Takee's estimate (ibid., May 20, 1851).
146. Ibid.
147. Ts'ai-cheng shuo-ming-shu, 7, 50b.

this illegal enterprise.[148] Because the counterfeited coins were in circulation in large areas covering Kwangtung, Fukien, Chekiang, and Kiangsu, their total amount was probably over $40,000,000 by the end of the nineteenth century.

We do not know exactly how many foreign silver dollars existed in China during the late Ch'ing period, but the amount may be estimated according to the way in which they were imported. In the seventeenth and eighteenth centuries, the Spanish conquerors of the Philippine Islands had a brisk trade with Chinese merchants from Fukien and Kwangtung and, eventually, with the Portuguese in Macao. In this instance, the Spanish used silver from their fabulously rich mines in modern Bolivia, Peru, and Mexico to buy a wide variety of Chinese products. In a good year the amount of silver passing through Manila into Chinese hands totaled between 2 and 3 million pesos or approximately 2 million taels.[149] If the average annual import was $1,000,000 (Spanish), the total amount would be at least $200,000,000 by the early nineteenth century.[150] The second source of the importation of silver dollars was from Europe via India, mainly by the ships of the British East India Company and the free traders. As K. N. Chaudhuri's studies clearly show that there was a persistent outflow of bullion from Europe to Asia during the seventeenth and eighteenth centuries, it is likely that $500,000,000 were exported to China in this manner.[151]

Third, the American traders brought Spanish and American dollars to China. Based on J. Smith Homan's work on the foreign commerce of the United States, it seems reasonable to estimate that $150,000,000 were thus imported to China prior to the conclusion of the Treaty of Wanghia in 1844.[152] Fourth, large amounts of silver reached China from Japan and Macao,[153] mainly through Portuguese traders, which could have amounted to $150,000,000 by the 1840s. All these silver coins were

148. King, *Money*, p. 224.

149. Atwell, "Notes on Silver," pp. 1–2.

150. R. M. Martin, *China*, I.176, estimates the amount to be $100 million, and P'eng Hsin-wei, *Huo-pi*, accepts this figure. In light of recent scholarship, however, this estimate seems overconservative. Ch'üan Han-sheng, "Mei-chou pai-yin," p. 449, estimates that in the 1571–1821 period 400 million pesos were exported from America to the Philippines, and half of these were reshipped from the Philippines to China.

151. H. B. Morse made this estimate in a lecture given at Clark University, cited in P'eng Hsin-wei, *Huo-pi*, p. 892.

152. J. Smith Homan, *A Historical and Statistical Account of the Foreign Commerce of the United States* (New York, 1857), passim, esp. p. 181.

153. Atwell, pp. 1–2.

TABLE 4.   AMOUNT OF SILVER COINS IN CHINA, 1910
(MILLION MEXICAN DOLLARS)

Item		Amount
Chinese official coins		200
From the Canton mint	154	
Other coins	46	
Chinese private coins		40
Foreign silver dollars		900
From America via the Philippines	200	
From Europe via India	500	
From the United States	150	
From Japan and Mexico	150	
From worldwide sources after 1842	300	
Amount melted in China	(200)	
Amount exported for opium purchase	(200)	
Foreign subsidiary coins		180
Total		1,320

Sources: Atwell, "Notes on Silver," pp. 1–4; Ch'üan Han-sheng, "Mei-chou pai-yin," p. 449; P'eng Hsin-wei, *Huo-pi*, pp. 879–82; *Ts'ai-cheng shuo-ming-shu: Kuang-tung* 7:50b; and Yang Tuan-liu, *Huo-pi*, pp. 280–81. Calculations and other estimates are mine.

shipped to China before the Opium War. For the next seventy years from 1842 to the end of the Ch'ing period in 1912, it is probable that, based on the statistics of Chinese maritime customs, $300,000,000, including those from Mexico and Japan, reached China.[154]

The gross total is $1.3 billion. Out of these, about $100,000,000 were melted soon after their importation, $200,000,000 went out of China to pay for opium, and another $100,000,000 were melted during the late Ch'ing period.[155] The net total is $900,000,000. If for every such dollar there existed 20 cents of foreign subsidiary coins, the value of the latter would be about $180,000,000. The total value of foreign silver coins in China might have been $1,080,000,000. The grand total of Chinese and foreign silver coins in China at the end of the Ch'ing era was therefore about $1,320,000,000. (See table 4.) The new metallic money also involved the copper sector. The long tradition of copper cash was broken

154. P'eng Hsin-wei made this estimate. For customs figures, see Liang-lin Hsiao, *China's Foreign Trade Statistics, 1864–1949* (Cambridge, Mass., 1974).
155. P'eng Hsin-wei, *Huo-pi*, p. 881.

in 1898 when copper coins of a new model call *t'ung-yuan* were first minted in Kwangtung. The new coins were struck by machines and bore no holes. Most of them were made to represent 10 old copper cash, and other denominations ranged from 1 to 100 cash. By the end of the Ch'ing period, about 200 billion pieces existed, valued at $149,000,000.[156]

It is difficult to arrive at an accurate figure concerning the volume of paper money. With respect to the silver notes denominated in taels, P'eng Hsin-wei estimates that by the end of the Ch'ing period there existed around 20,000,000 taels. However, judging from Lien-sheng Yang's study on the situation at Ying-k'ou, Manchuria, I think the amount would be at least 30,000,000 taels. On the other hand, P'eng's appraisals seem reasonable that the amount of silver dollar notes in circulation was approximately $50,000,000, and that of copper cash and modern copper coins, 134 million strings, valued at $100,000,000.[157]

For the foreign notes circulating in China, we know that the Hongkong and Shanghai Banking Corporation issued dollar notes in the amount of $1,900,000 in 1875, $6,500,000 in 1890, $12,500,000 in 1900, and $24,800,000 in 1912. However, because many banks circulated their notes in China as well as in other countries but did not publish the Chinese portion separately, an assessment of the total amount in the late Ch'ing China is inevitably tentative. P'eng Hsin-wei's estimate is $100,000,000. Because his figure does not include the notes issued by commercial firms, such as Jardine's, the total could have been $110,000,000.[158] The two traditional sectors—silver bullion and copper cash—continued to perform monetary functions. By the turn of the twentieth century, there existed approximately 250,000,000 taels in silver bullion, valued at $347,000,000, and 500 billion copper cash, valued at $373,000,000.[159] Thus, by 1910 the grand total of money in China was around $2.5 billion, as shown in table 5.

This figure does not take into consideration opium whose monetary function was, after all, marginal. Table 6 shows that the quantity of opium that was shipped annually from India to China was valued at $4,600,000 in the 1810s, $9,700,000 in the 1820s, and $13,200,000 in the 1830s. In the several decades following the Treaty of Nanking, the annual consumption of opium in China grew from 15,000 to over 60,000

156. Lien-sheng Yang, *Money*, p. 26; and P'eng Hsin-wei, *Huo-pi*, pp. 882–83.
157. P'eng Hsin-wei, *Huo-pi*, p. 887; and Lien-sheng Yang, *Money*, p. 69.
158. Wang Yeh-chien, *Huo-pi*, p. 71; and P'eng Hsin-wei, *Huo-pi*, pp. 887–88.
159. P'eng Hsin-wei, *Huo-pi*, pp. 882–85.

TABLE 5.   FORMS AND QUANTITY OF MONEY IN CHINA, 1910
(IN MILLIONS)

Forms of money	Quantity	Value in dollars	Percent
New Forms of Money[a]		1,771	71
Silver Coins			
Chinese	240 dollars	240	9.6
Foreign	1,080 dollars	1,080	43.4
		1,320	53
Copper Money			
New copper coins	200,000 pieces	149	5.9
Paper Money			
Silver tael notes	30 taels	42	1.7
Silver dollar notes	50 dollars	50	2
Copper cash notes	134 strings	100	4
Foreign notes	110 dollars	110	4.4
		302	12.1
Old Forms of Money		720	29
Silver Bullion	250 taels	347	14
Copper Cash	500,000 pieces	373	15
		720	29
Total		2,491	100

Sources: Table 4; Atwell, "Notes on Silver," pp. 1–4; Homan, Statistical Account, passim; Liang-lin Hsiao, Statistics, p. 128; P'eng Hsin-wei, Huo-pi, pp. 879–97; Wang Yeh-chien, Huo-pi, pp. 12–22; and Lien-sheng Yang, Money, pp. 26, 69. Other estimates and calculations are mine.

[a]Does not include opium as money, whose value of annual consumption was around $51,000,000 in the 1880s.

chests, valued at $18,000,000 to $35,000,000.[160] In addition, the Chinese cultivation of opium sizably increased during the seventies. In a letter to the British Foreign Office concerning opium, Kuo Sung-tao, China's minister in London, admitted in 1877: "The Chinese people smoke it more and more each day; poppy cultivation also spreads daily more widely in recent years."[161] If we assume that the domestic opium consti-

160. Morse, Conflict, p. 556.
161. To the Earl of Derby, London, Aug. 24, 1877, FO 405/22, p. 71.

TABLE 6.   ANNUAL OPIUM CONSUMPTION IN CHINA,
1810s–1880s
(MILLION MEXICAN DOLLARS)

	Imported	Domestic	Total
1810s	4.6	0	4.6
1820s	9.7	0	9.7
1830s	13.2	0	13.2
1840s	18.0	0	18.0
1850s	30.0	3.0	33.0
1860s	35.0	8.0	43.0
1870s	36.0	13.0	49.0
1880s	34.0	17.0	51.0

Sources: Hsin-pao Chang, *Commissioner Lin*, p. 233; and Morse, *Conflict*, p. 556. Other estimates and calculations are mine.

tuted one-third of the imported, its value would be around $13,000,000 annually in the seventies.

By the early eighties opium cultivation became popular even in the coastal provinces, as is evidenced by several British consular reports. One of these summarized the situation in 1881 by stating that "the growth of native drug was increasing year by year."[162] If we assume that China produced one-half of the imported amount during the eighties, the value of the domestic opium that was produced annually would be about $17,000,000. It is thus clear that the annual consumption of opium in China steadily increased during the first three-quarters of the nineteenth century. Its value rose from less than $5,000,000 in the 1810s to more than $50,000,000 in the 1880s, representing an increase of more than elevenfold over a period of seventy years (table 6). Admittedly, not all opium in China performed monetary functions, but a considerable portion of it was used as a medium of exchange many times before its final consumption.

The monetary role of opium was all the more important, because not all commodities were readily acceptable as media of exchange. For example, during the fifties when Jardine's was occasionally out of opium stock in Foochow and Shanghai, the house tried to substitute British

162. FO 405/27.

piece goods for opium in exchange for tea in the Bohea districts as well as for silk in Soochow. No matter how hard M. A. Macleod strove in Foochow and A. G. Dallas endeavored in Shanghai, their efforts invariably ended in failure. The piece goods were too bulky for merchants to transport inland, especially to the mountainous tea-producing regions, and there was little demand for piece goods by the Chinese people in the interior. This situation was true even at Soochow in the early fifties when the Soochow system was burgeoning.[163] Against this background, the monetary function of opium is worth noting.

What are the implications of the stock of money in its multiple forms during the late Ch'ing period? First, the total amount of $2.5 billion dollars is unprecedentedly large, increasing nine times during the Ch'ing period of some two and one-half centuries.[164] Second, during the same period per capita monetary stock increased more than 17 percent from 4.6 dollars to 5.4 dollars.[165] This means that, during the Ch'ing period while the population growth was phenomenal, the increase in money supply was even more spectacular. Third, new forms of money constituted 71 percent of the total amount. Among them the sector of silver coins, valued at $1,320,000,000, is most conspicuous, making up more than half of the entire stock. On the average, each Chinese would have about three such coins. But dollars were not universally used in China; they were circulated largely in the coastal area and in the lower Yangtze Valley. If we assume that the population in these areas constituted about one-third of China's population, the population-dollar ratio would be about 1:9 in these highly commercialized regions.

The expansion of money in modern China has its strengths and weaknesses. From the late eighteenth century on, the financial sector, prompted by increasing commercial and industrial activities, exhibited fundamental changes, which pointed in the direction of a uniform and flexible monetary system. The first sign of this progressive trend was the imported silver dollars that spread from South China to North China

163. A. G. Dallas (Shanghai) to David Jardine (Hong Kong), May 16, 1851, JMA.

164. The monetary stock was about 200 million taels (approximately 278 million dollars) during the late Ming period in the mid-seventeenth century (P'eng Hsin-wei, *Huo-pi*, pp. 890–91).

165. Ping-ti Ho writes that China's population was around 430 million in 1850, and the reported figure was 583 million in 1953 (*Population*, p. 278). If we assume that in 1910 the population was about 460 million with a monetary stock of $2,491 million, then on average each Chinese would have 5.4 dollars. P'eng Hsin-wei suggests that at the end of the Ming period China had a population of 60 million with a monetary stock of 200 million taels (about $278 million) (*Huo-pi*, pp. 890–91). Per capita figure was thus 4.6 dollars.

and overshadowed bullion in business transactions. The accelerating degree with which these coins gained acceptance as exchange media and as units of account is unmistakably clear. The widespread use of Chinese private notes represented another forward step. During the early nineteenth century, the Chinese silver stockpile was dwindling due to the opium trade; at the same time Western bank notes, Chinese silver dollars, and modern-style copper coins had not yet appeared on the Chinese market. Under these circumstances, the success of Chinese private notes in the monetary sector was all the more impressive; they constituted possibly as high as one-third of the total volume of money in circulation.[166]

By the end of the Ch'ing period, however, although new forms of money made up a considerable portion of the monetary stock, most of them were in metallic form. This was because the major Western powers, after having adopted the gold standard, exported large quantities of silver to China.[167] And the time-honored bimetallism continued to function. Consequently, paper money constituted only a meager 12 percent of the entire stock of money, indicating the limitations of Chinese commercial capitalism. Also, foreign money, especially in the forms of silver coins and paper notes, made up a large portion of the supply of money in China, constituting almost 48 percent. By investigating these new forms of money, I have covered only a part of the monetary development, because the sector of credit remains unexamined. In reality, there is no absolute difference in nature between metallic money, substitute money, and instruments of credit.[168]

166. Yeh-chien Wang, "Evolution," pp. 425, 438.
167. China imported 88,769,000 silver dollars during the period from 1888 to 1900 (Liang-lin Hsiao, *Statistics*, p. 128).
168. If it is possible to argue that everything is money, as demonstrated by the mercantilistic perspective, then it is just as possible to claim that everything is, on the contrary, credit—promises, deferred reality. Joseph Schumpeter, for instance, writes that "currency . . . is nothing other than an instrument of credit, a title which gives access to the only means of definite payment, namely consumer goods" (quoted in Braudel, *Capitalism and Material Life*, pp. 363–64).

CHAPTER FOUR

The Expansion
of Credit

Credit expansion was a crucial factor, equal to that of an improved monetary system in modern China's commercial revolution. Modern capitalism, in Fernand Braudel's words, "deploys itself" in the domain of credit and can "find its tools here."[1] Generally speaking, credit refers to a transaction between two parties in which one (the creditor) supplies actual resources—goods, services, securities, or money—in return for a promised future payment by the other (the debtor). Even though the practices and principles of credit transaction had existed in traditional China, new factors regarding credit along the coast after the 1820s fundamentally changed business patterns.[2] With the sophistication of credit instruments, it became more convenient for coastal merchants to obtain credit. More importantly, the expansion of money and credit in this region led to a low rate of interest that was conducive to the expansion of business.

During the first two decades of the nineteenth century, a considerable portion of China's trade with the West was conducted on a cash basis. This was especially true of the opium trade on the coast. On the island of Lintin, for instance, "the consignee sold [opium] by sample for cash— never...on credit."[3] Similarly, opium merchants on the coast "dis-

1. *Capitalism and Material Life*, p. 363.
2. In his *Money and Credit in China*, Lien-sheng Yang details the practice of credit in traditional China. Modern lenders usually evaluate three basic factors, sometimes called the "three C's," of credit: the applicant's character, capacity, and collateral; these criteria were also used by lenders in traditional China.
3. Morse, *Conflict*, pp. 179–80.

posed of opium always for silver."[4] Cash was paid either on the spot or in Canton. Russell & Co. sometimes simply exchanged fur, Turkish opium, and gold for tea, silk, and floor matting, taking a commission on both sales and purchases. It extended credit neither to its fellow American traders nor to Chinese merchants. John P. Cushing, in his instructions to T. H. Forbes, emphasized the punctuality of payment in cash when the latter traded with the Chinese.[5] Under these circumstances, it is not surprising that foreign merchants kept large amounts of silver on hand.[6]

Although trading on credit was not an established practice along the coast during the last decades of the eighteenth century, it is abundantly clear that by the 1820s China's foreign trade was based increasingly on credit through the use of bills and notes instead of cash. Two reasons accounted for the change. First, the increase in the opium trade required a more convenient way of payment. Second, the London bill of exchange, being both convenient and fairly safe, fit the requirement nicely, thus making credit transactions easier. The British free traders, the American commission houses, and the hong merchants all used it. By 1860, it was virtually impossible to do meaningful business on the coast without resorting to some kind of credit.

BILLS, DRAFTS, AND CHOP LOANS

It was in the 1820s that the bills of exchange on London, which conveniently transferred capital from London to China's ports, made credit transactions along the coast easier. By the mid-century when more Western banks were established in the treaty ports, coastal merchants started to use drafts of these banks for the purpose of arranging credit. After the 1860s, Western banks or mercantile houses often granted short-term loans, known as "chop loans," to native banks.

BILLS OF EXCHANGE AND BANK DRAFTS

British old China hands point out that by the 1820s China's foreign trade was based increasingly on bills and notes instead of cash.[7] The

4. Nathan Allen, *The Opium Trade as Carried on in India and China* (Lowell, Mass., 1853), p. 15.
5. Connolly, *Canton*, p. 207; and Cushing to Forbes, Mar. 31, 1828, FC.
6. John Heard III wrote during the Opium War: "We had a large amount of treasure in the vaults, nearly $500,000, partly ours and partly J. M.'s [Jardine, Matheson & Co.'s]" ("Diary," 1841, p. 42, HC). The importance of cash payment on the coast partly accounted for the fact that the bonding warehouse was not established until 1880, although the idea was first suggested in 1844.
7. R. Montgomery Martin, *China; Political, Commercial, and Social; in an Official Report*

correspondence of Houqua also demonstrates that this Chinese merchant prince, thanks in part to the ingenuity of the American traders, started to use the new financial instrument of bills for credit arrangements in the late 1820s.[8]

During the first quarter of the nineteenth century, the United States had an unfavorable balance of trade with China. Few American merchants could afford to send their money to China and wait months or a year for returns, so a new means of financing American purchases was necessary, and the answer was bills on London. Beginning in 1827, at the request of some enterprising American traders, a few large London bankers, such as the Barings, the Browns, and the "three W's" (the houses of Wiggin, Wildes, and Wilson), issued credits and advanced them. The bankers sent the credits to the American commission houses in China to buy goods. The goods were then shipped to the American merchants who sold them and sent enough of the proceeds to London to pay off the principal and interest due on their bills. By now the bills on London were largely in the hands of the hong merchants who accepted them from the American commission houses in China as payment for their tea and silk. The hong merchants would then use these bills to purchase opium, woolens, and cotton goods from the British merchants who would finally cash in these bills in London. The American merchants brought nearly $9,000,000 of these bills of exchange to China during the period from 1827 to 1833.[9]

This kind of credit arrangement was expanded after the thirties. The commission house, in order to increase its business, began to receive bills on London directly from London on its own account. As early as 1828, for example, the ship *Danube* of Perkins & Company sailed from Boston to Canton carrying "a letter of credit on the Barings of London for sixty thousand pounds."[10] The commission house then advanced to the American clients a substantial share of the funds that their purchases required. Merchants in the United States, now having no longer to borrow from London on their accounts, had only to place their orders with the commission house and agree to pay the cost of the goods as well as in-

---

to Her Majesty's Government (London, 1847), I, 20; and Robert Fortune, *Three Years' Wanderings in the Northern Provinces of China* (London, 1847), p. 373.

8. Houqua (Canton) to Mahomed Ally Rogay (Bombay), Nov. 23, 1833, F-5, FC.

9. Duncan Yaggy, "John M. Forbes: A Biography" (Ph.D. dissertation, Brandeis University, 1972), discusses in detail how Forbes used bills on London. Also see Timothy Pitkin, *A Historical View of the Commerce of the United States of America* (New Haven, 1835), p. 303.

10. Connolly, *Canton*, p. 186. The ship was captained by F. B. Forbes.

terest and commission charges. The commission house drew a bill on London on behalf of their clients on terms that would allow the clients enough time to sell and recover proceeds of their goods. The clients then paid the commission house for the goods received plus interest and commission charges. Finally, the commission house cleared the bill drawn earlier for the purchase of the goods in China. Sometimes the clients paid the London banker principal and interest directly on behalf of the commission house. Under this system, the commission house assumed more risk but received more commission fees, and, at the same time, credit and trade were expanded.

With the expansion of trade under the treaty system, the American traders even more widely used bills on London to finance their purchases of tea and silk from China. In a letter to Donald Matheson in Hong Kong dated December 19, 1844, David Jardine recorded this situation at Canton: "I find some of the Yankees, including your friend Mr. [Edward] King [of Russell & Co.] are offering to sell their bills to Chinese whom they have been buying teas from."[11] During the fifties the London banking houses continued to work directly with the Western firms in China (the British agency houses and the American commission houses). They extended credits to such large American houses as Russell & Co. and Augustine Heard & Co. According to these credit arrangements, the American firms in China could draw bills for shipping to anyone of their choice.[12] The dependence of business on credit was illustrated by Heard's in 1860. Heard's purchases totaled more than $1,500,000 in that year; only 25 percent of this sum represented house funds, and the rest was obtained through credit.[13]

In time, it became no longer necessary even for some of the commission houses in China to apply for credit from the London bankers. As a few large British houses occasionally did not want to invest fully in a risky market, they made loans to other foreign traders who were in need of capital. A case in point was Jardine, Matheson & Co., which made loans to many Western firms to enable them to pay for their tea and silk during the forties and fifties. Some of the loans were repaid in Hong Kong, but most of the loans were settled by these firms' London representatives who would repay the loans to Matheson & Co., Jardine's representative in London, within ninety days.[14]

11. JMA.
12. John Heard III (Boston) to Augustine Heard, Jr. (Hong Kong), Dec. 12, 1858, EM-7, HC.
13. Cases 7, 8, 21, HC II.
14. Donald Matheson (Hong Kong) to A. G. Dallas (Shanghai), Sept. 7, 1847; David Jardine (Hong Kong) to Joseph Jardine (Canton), Feb. 5, 1852, JMA.

As more Western banks were established after the sixties, bank drafts were used more frequently than before. James J. Keswick at Shanghai sent a telegram of Jardine's Hankow representative in 1885, directing the Hankow comprador to "secure more favorable exchange for Mercantile Bank Shanghai drafts."[15] The Chinese merchants were willing to accept these bills and notes from the foreign merchant for the payment of their tea and silk. Takee, the Shanghai silk merchant mentioned in the previous chapter, for instance, received bills for $2,500 in early December 1851 from Turner & Co. in liquidation of an overdue balance. A. G. Dallas of Jardine's in Shanghai later purchased these bills.[16]

Many Chinese not only obtained loans from a Western house but also specifically requested that their loans be made in the form of bills or drafts in order to facilitate their businesses. One of them was Yowloong who in 1863 applied to Jardine's Canton office for a draft drawn on Shanghai in the amount of $40,000. In a letter to the head office in Hong Kong dated March 26, 1863, C. S. Matheson asked whether Yowloong's request could be granted.[17] William Keswick quickly approved the loan on Yowloong's terms. Jardine's made similar loans in the sixties and seventies, including those to Tong King-sing in Canton for Tls. 3,000 in 1868,[18] Yowloong in Hong Kong for Tls. 30,000 in 1870,[19] and Chi Jung Soon in Hong Kong for Tls. 10,000 in 1870.[20] As requested, all these

15. The Hankow representative responded: "I yesterday afternoon received your Telegram of the 26th . . . and I have spoken to [the comprador] Wun Hing on the matter. I understand from him that the small amount drawn for was done at the Exchange of the day on which the transaction took place, the rate being under 3% which I think must be considered good, as such a rate as this cannot be done since" (B. A. Clarke [Hankow] to Keswick, May 28, 1885, JMA).

16. Dallas reported to Hong Kong: "The Bills for $2,500 which I have just this moment purchased, were paid over by Turner & Co. to Takee in liquidation of a balance overdue" (to Jardine, Matheson & Co., Dec. 8, 1851, JMA).

17. "Yowloong wishes to place funds in Shanghai to the equivalent of $40,000 and will be glad to know whether you can give him a draft for the amount and on what terms" (Matheson [Canton] to Jardine, Matheson & Co. [Hong Kong], JMA).

18. S. I. Gower, Jardine's agent in Hankow, informed the Shanghai office: "I have drawn on you c 3D/S [at three days' sight] no. 24, in favour of Tong King-sing for Tls. 3000 c [at] 3% [per month] which please protect on presentation" (to Jardine, Matheson & Co., Apr. 11, 1868, JMA).

19. Similarly, Yowloong asked the firm's Hong Kong office for a loan, as Herbert Magniac wrote to Shanghai: "Yowloong also wants our drafts on you for Tls. 30,000 in the course of a short time. I have told him I will let him have them at 73¾—the Bank rate is 74 on demand—but I have not heard from him since as to the time about drawing. I tell you this in order that you may be prepared to meet them but regret I cannot be more explicit as to time" (to Francis Bulkeley Johnson, Jan. 7, 1870, JMA).

20. Magniac wrote: "I have drawn on you for Tls. 10,000 in favor of Chinaman Chi Jung Soon" (ibid.).

loans were made in the form of drafts on Shanghai, often at three days' sight.

Bills and drafts played an important role in promoting commercial activities not only in the treaty ports, but also in the interior. The bills on Hong Kong, for example, linked the trade between inland areas and the treaty ports during the second half of the nineteenth century. The southern merchants transported Yunnan produce, mainly opium and tea, overland to Wu-chou, Kwangsi, for sale. They took payment at Wu-chou in bills on Hong Kong, with which they purchased Lancashire cottons and yarn from Hong Kong. They then transported these imported goods to Wu-chou via Tongking.[21]

THE CHOP LOAN

The chop loan (*ch'e-fang* or *ch'e-k'uan*) was a short-term loan that a foreign bank or a foreign mercantile house granted to a native bank after the 1860s. On receipt of the loan, the native bank would give the firm a promissory note. The "chop" (seal) of the firm's comprador was always put on the note as his commitment to guarantee the loan, hence the name "chop loan." It was similar to the "call loan" in the United States and "call money" in Great Britain.[22] During the sixties and seventies, the period of such loans varied from two to ten days, and its annual interest rate ranged from 12 to 28 percent.[23] The chop loan was reminiscent of the way that Indian silver had been brought to Canton in the 1830s to earn high interest.

Thanks to the compradors, the chop loan was initiated by the Hongkong and Shanghai Banking Corporation in Shanghai in the late sixties.[24] Jardine's immediately followed suit and started to make investments in a few reputable and guaranteed native banks, or "money shops," which returned much higher interest than that obtainable within the Western business community. F. B. Johnson described his feelings about it in 1868: "I find that I can occasionally invest our Cash balances in Chinese Bankers' orders at short dates, say 3 c [to] 7 days, at rates of [annual] interest varying from 12% to 15% with, I think, perfect safety,

21. F. S. A. Bourne et al., *Report of the Mission to China of the Blackburn Chamber of Commerce, 1896–1897* (London, 1898), p. 89.
22. *Shang-hai ch'ien-chuang*, pp. 36, 38, 90.
23. The annual interest rate was 12 to 15 percent in 1868, and 15 to 28 percent in 1878 (F. B. Johnson [Shanghai] to William Keswick [Hong Kong], May 20, 1868, JMA; and *Shang-hai ch'ien-chuang*, p. 44).
24. *Shang-hai ch'ien-chuang*, pp. 28–29.

as I should not discount the paper on any one Bank to a greater extent than Tls. 10,000 or 15,000."[25] Johnson's initial investments must have been successful, because he showed more enthusiasm for the chop loan business as time progressed. He reported to Hong Kong on February 1, 1869: "I am inclined to believe that with caution and good judgment there is a good business to be done in these local transactions, especially in Banking business with the Chinese."[26] His conviction was confirmed by the fact that on May 10 he loaned "a further Tls. 50,000 among three Native Banks at 15% per annum for 10 days."[27]

A financial crisis for some of the prominent Chinese merchants in Shanghai in 1871 illustrates the benefits that they received from the Western traders' short-term loans. On May 29, 1871, when there was a run upon the three native banks in Shanghai that were operated by Acum, Aleet, and Tong King-sing, F. B. Johnson showed his concern by writing to William Keswick in Hong Kong: "You may hear reports as to difficulties among Native Banks in which Aleet and his friends are interested and there was I believe a run upon them today which was completely met. I will not fail to be careful as to our pecuniary position with the Cantonese about us though I have reason to believe that there is no cause for anxiety."[28]

On the next day, however, Tong Kong-sing applied to Johnson for assistance. Although Johnson found to his "surprise and dissatisfaction" that Tong, as comprador, had improperly used Tls. 80,000 of the firm's funds, he was obliged to help Tong. He wrote Keswick on June 1, 1871: "My first business was to investigate the pecuniary position of Tong King-sing & the Banks & having ascertained as fully as the nature of the case admitted that they were solvent, I saw that there was no alternative but to render whatever assistance might be necessary." He telegraphed Keswick, asking for the authority to do so. After getting such permission, he advanced Tls. 40,000 to Tong in addition to the Tls. 80,000 wrongfully appropriated.[29]

Tong King-sing's malpractice notwithstanding, Jardine's did not stop doing business in chop loans. The firm's account books of April 1874 show that it made chop loans to Chinese banks in Shanghai totaling Tls. 24,000 at 2.5 mace per tael per diem.[30] Jardine's decided to remain in the chop loan business with an eye to competing with the newly rising for-

25. (Shanghai) to William Keswick (Hong Kong), May 20, 1868, JMA.
26. Ibid.
27. Ibid.
28. Ibid.
29. Ibid.
30. Shanghai, Apr. 1874, Accounts, JMA.

eign banks.[31] Other foreign commercial houses also made frequent chop loans; the German firm of Renter, Brockelmann & Co., for example, was engaged in this kind of business through its comprador in the seventies.[32]

The total amount of the chop loans that the native banks in Shanghai received was over Tls. 3,000,000 in 1878, and it exceeded Tls. 10,000,000 at the end of the nineteenth century. Some big native banks received as much as Tls. 700,000 or 800,000 of chop loans in the early twentieth century.[33] By the last decade of the Ch'ing period, however, the influence of the chop loan had declined. Meanwhile, the loan period was generally limited to two days, and the foreign firms were entitled to call back the loan at any moment if they so desired.[34]

The chop loan system was dealt a severe blow in 1911 when the three native banks of Sheng-ta, Yen-ta, and Ta-ch'ing, operated by the family of Yeh Ch'eng-chung (1840–1899), a prominent merchant in Shanghai, went broke. Together, they owed more than Tls. 2,000,000 in chop loans.[35] Furthermore, many other native banks, going bankrupt in the liquidity squeeze resulting from the Republican Revolution on October 10, 1911, could not meet their chop loan responsibilities as well. Among them, six large banks owed Tls. 1,820,000 of chop loans to eight foreign banks (table 7), and on October 18, 1911, the total amount of the unpaid chop loan stood at Tls. 8,815,000. Although the amount was repaid gradually—and indeed it was reduced to Tls. 4,482,000 by November 11, 1911—it was not totally repaid until 1926.[36] These two incidents, coupled with the rise of the modern Chinese banks and the decline of the foreign firms in China due to World War I, severely limited the role of the chop loan in China's economy during the Republican period.[37]

Thus, the chop loan was a popular and influential means of easing the problem of fiscal fluidity on China's coast during the late Ch'ing period. The native banks in Shanghai, for instance, depended to a great extent on the chop loan for cash flow and business expansion. The average capital of a native bank at that time ranged from Tls. 20,000 to Tls. 40,000, but sometimes the bank could get as much as Tls. 1,000,000 on

31. Jardine, Matheson & Co. (Shanghai) to Jardine, Matheson & Co. (Hong Kong), Sept. 28, 1875, JMA.
32. *Shen pao*, Nov. 23, 1876, p. 3.
33. *Shang-hai ch'ien-chuang*, pp. 44, 60–61.
34. Ibid., p. 38.
35. For Yeh Ch'eng-chung, see Arnold Wright, ed. *Twentieth Century Impressions of Hongkong, Shanghai, and Other Treaty Ports of China* (London, 1908), p. 560. For the bankruptcy of the three native banks, see *Shang-hai ch'ien-chuang*, p. 61.
36. *Shang-hai ch'ien-chuang*, pp. 61, 90.
37. For a fuller account of the chop loan system, see ibid., pp. 8–10, 36, 38, 60, 90, and 490.

TABLE 7.   CHOP LOANS FROM EIGHT FOREIGN BANKS,
SHANGHAI, 1911
(TAELS)

Western name	Chinese name	Nationality	Amount[a]
Deutsch-Asiatische Bank	Te-Hua yin-hang	Germany	397,800
Yokohama Specie Bank	Cheng-chin yin-hang	Japan	305,400
National City Bank of New York	Hua-ch'i yin-hang	U.S.A	235,400
Banque de l'Indochine	Tung-fang hui-li yin-hang	France	233,000
Nederlandsche Handel-Maatschappij	Ho-lan yin-hang	Holland	184,300
Bank of Taiwan	Tai-wan yin-hang	Japan	182,000
Russo-Chinese Bank	Tao-sheng yin-hang	Russia	154,000
Banque Belge pour l'Etranger	Hua-pi yin-hang	Belgium	128,000
Total			1,820,000

Sources: Shang-hai ch'ien-chuang, p. 90; and Lien-sheng Yang, Money and Credit, p. 89.
[a] These figures represent only a part of the total chop loans, because they do not include those from the Shanghai and Hongkong Banking Corporation, the Chartered Bank of India, Australia and China, and the Mercantile Bank of India, all of which are known to have engaged heavily in chop loan business. See Shang-hai ch'ien-chuang, p. 38.

chop loan from the foreign firms. Consequently, the chop loan expanded the amount of credit available on the market.

NATIVE BANK ORDERS

The history of the native banks can be traced back to the eighteenth century, but their direct role in financing Sino-Western trade did not begin until after the mid-nineteenth century.[38] The growing volume of

38. Although the use of drafts existed in the seventeenth century, the oldest Shansi bank cannot be traced back earlier than about 1800 (Lien-sheng Yang, Money and Credit, p. 82). The notes of money shops were circulated in the market during the first half of the eighteenth century, and the association of money shops at Shanghai existed by 1776 (Shang-hai ch'ien-chuang, p. 3). For a careful study of the native banks in Shanghai and the role played by the Ningpo clique, see Susan Mann Jones, "The Ningpo Pang and Financial Power at Shanghai," in Mark Elvin and G. William Skinner, eds., The Chinese City Between Two Worlds (Stanford, Calif., 1974), pp. 73–95. For a general discussion of native bank orders, see Yang Yin-p'u, Yang-chu Chung-kuo chin-yung lun (Shanghai, 1932), p. 232; Yang Tuan-liu, Huo-pi, pp. 147–48; and Shang-hai ch'ien-chuang, pp. 18–19.

foreign trade after 1860 gave impetus to the development of native banks, especially in the treaty ports. There were two basic types of native banks—remittance and local. The former, known as *p'iao-chuang* (draft banks) or Shansi banks, transferred funds in large sums from one market to another through their drafts, which were important credit instruments.[39] The local banks were money shops, known as *ch'ien-chuang* (money-banking shops) in southern China and *yin-hao* (silver-banking shops) in northern China. The main functions of the money shops were to advance funds and to change money from one local currency standard to another. As noted in the previous chapter, they issued paper notes for circulation locally and sometimes handled transfer accounts, both of which were also instruments of credit. But it was their bank orders (*chuang-p'iao*) that were most active in facilitating Sino-Western commercial capitalism. These orders were like promissory notes, payable generally at five, ten, and twenty days' sight, issued on behalf of their customers for the purchase of goods.

DOMESTIC AND FOREIGN TRADE

A businessman frequently did not have enough ready cash at hand to pay for the goods he planned to purchase, but the seller might be unwilling to accept his promissory note. To deal with this impasse, some well-established native banks started in the eighteenth century to issue their customers bank orders as a means of payment. When the bank order was due, the seller would collect the money from the issuing bank. At the other end of the transaction, the buyer would repay the bank the principal and interest at a mutually arranged date.[40]

The bank orders issued by the money shops in Shanghai, called *Shen-p'iao* (Shanghai note), played an active role in instigating the commercial revolution during the mid-nineteenth century. The native banks extended much-needed credit to the local merchants who, armed with the *Shen-p'iao*, purchased tea and silk from southeastern China and hides from northwestern China after the 1860s. The merchants in the interior, especially those from Hunan, Szechwan, and Yunnan who specialized in imports, usually acquired these bank orders to be carried to Shanghai for purchasing Western goods. Merchants in other treaty ports similarly relied on this instrument of credit. In 1881, for instance, about 90 per-

39. For draft banks, see Ch'en Ch'i-t'ien, *Shan-hsi p'iao-chuang k'ao-lueh* (Shanghai, 1937).
40. Yeh-chien Wang, "Evolution," p. 436.

cent of the funds that tea merchants at Foochow borrowed came from local native banks.[41]

The native bank played a crucial role in China's foreign trade after the Opium War. Before 1842, because the foreign traders and the Chinese hong merchants knew one another quite well, credit arrangements among them were made on personal security or without any security. Things were different, however, in the treaty days, because creditors and debtors seldom knew one another. In business transactions, foreign traders, being ignorant of the Chinese market, would not accept promissory notes from Chinese purchasers. Instead, for several reasons they insisted on being paid through native bank orders. First, a native bank, being a financial institution, was by and large more reliable than individual traders. Second, the comprador, who guaranteed the native bank orders for his foreign employer, was more familiar with the native banks than with the exporters or importers.[42] Finally, the bank order served as double security, because, if the issuing body became insolvent, the foreigner could still collect the amount from the comprador as guarantor. It is not surprising, then, to find that as early as 1846 Western traders in Shanghai started to accept this important instrument of credit from their Chinese counterparts.[43] The company records of Jardine's and Heard's indicate that this practice gained gradual acceptance in the forties and fifties, becoming indispensable after 1860.

The pivotal role of the native bank orders in China's external trade was clearly demonstrated at Shanghai in 1853 when the Taiping movement led to money stringency at that port. An insufficient supply of Carolus dollars circulating in Shanghai early in that year "led to the universal adoption of Chinese banker's orders."[44] Several months later, however, the unavailability of these orders caused difficulties in the import and export businesses. On March 5, for instance, five of the leading British firms at Shanghai complained to their consul that "from the refusal of the native bankers to grant the usual facilities, it has become quite impossible to obtain payment of the Export and Import duties from the Chinese dealers, or to effect the sale of goods to meet those more directly due by the Foreign Merchants, thus leading to the detention of

41. Chang Kuo-hui, "Shih-chiu shih-chi hou-pan-ch'i Chung-kuo ch'ien-chuang ti mai-pan hua," *Li-shih yen-chiu* 6:92–97 (1963).
42. E.g., Tong King-sing received a "native draft for Taels 14,800" for Jardine's in May 1869 (F. B. Johnson [Shanghai] to Jardine, Matheson & Co. [Hong Kong], May 6, 1869, JMA).
43. Frederick E. Forbes, *Five Years in China, From 1842 to 1847* (London, 1848), p. 68.
44. *NCH*, May 7, 1853, p. 158.

several outward bound ships now ready for sea."[45] The native bank order played an increasingly important role in China's external trade during the last decades of the Ch'ing period.[46]

The native bank orders issued at Shanghai were frequently transferred from one port to another. Jardine's, for example, often used native drafts in remitting funds in this manner. S. I. Gower, the firm's representative at Hankow, wrote to the Shanghai office on April 4, 1868, acknowledging receipt of "Tls. 23,000 in native drafts." Gower must have anticipated that he would receive native bank orders from time to time, because he added: "To prevent any difficulty please have inserted in all future Bills sent me, 'payable in Kong Koo [kung-ku, publicly assayed] sycee,' as the Bill for Tls. 2,000 does not state this and may cause trouble and a difference of about 2% in value of sycee."[47] In the same manner, Jardine's remitted funds between Shanghai and Hong Kong during the 1870s.[48]

The growing volume of external trade, the long history of the native banks, and a partner's unlimited liability to his bank orders all accounted for the popularity of native bank notes during the nineteenth century. Lu Chao-lin estimated in 1919 that the native banks at Shanghai annually issued bank orders totaling around Tls. 1,700,000,000.[49] If Shanghai represented one-half of the orders issued in China, the total amount of orders would be Tls. 3,400,000,000. Taking into account the gradual expansion of native banks, we may say that the annual issuance of China's native bank orders was around 3 billion taels during the last decades of the Ch'ing period.

WESTERN TRADERS

The Western commercial houses frequently made loans to Chinese merchants. Because the houses regarded them as "native friends," credit was sometimes extended without obtaining substantial security except in the form of promissory notes of native banks. From the correspondence of Jardine's partners, we have glimpses of such credit arrangements. The

45. Quoted in R. Alcock to British community, Mar. 10, 1853, FO 17/204. See also Fairbank, Trade and Diplomacy, I, 403.
46. Shang-hai ch'ien-chuang, pp. 177–79, 184.
47. Gower (Hankow) to Jardine, Matheson & Co. (Shanghai), Apr. 4, 1868, JMA.
48. Jardine, Matheson & Co. (Shanghai) to Jardine, Matheson & Co. (Hong Kong), Jan. 18, 1879, JMA.
49. Shang-hai ch'ien-chuang, pp. 551–52.

house lent large sums to hong merchants before the treaty days but never committed such large amounts at one time in loans to Chinese merchants after 1842. Nevertheless, the firm continued to make loans to the Chinese. Actually, there were few seasons after the Opium War in which some of the firm's capital was not on loan to Chinese merchants. In the forties and fifties these loans, being usually made on a short-term basis, were advanced not only to opium dealers, but also to the firm's compradors and, through them, to provincial officials. In most cases Jardine's obtained native bank promissory notes for these loans.[50]

Loans made on the promissory note of an individual were much less safe than the funds advanced on the security of designated goods or bank orders. Jardine's Canton office, for example, made a loan to Yeckchong in 1862 on the latter's personal promissory notes. By January 1863, however, Jardine's office, after having written several letters "to his native village near Macao," was still unable to locate him.[51] Jardine's learned a lesson from this incident, and, after the mid-sixties, its loans to the Chinese were usually secured by the promissory notes of the native banks.

In January 1849, M. A. Macleod in Canton made note of his intention to give financial assistance to two Chinese merchants who were having difficulties.[52] In Hong Kong, a Chinese named Ayung borrowed considerable amounts of money from Jardine's head office during the fifties.[53] A more important port for credit transactions between Chinese and foreign traders was Shanghai. Aloong, a Cantonese in that port who bought opium and rice from Jardine's, and in return sold tea and silk to the firm, frequently received loans from the house during the forties and fifties.[54] This borrowing must have been common practice, because Aloong in September 1859 was still in debt to the house to the amount of Tls. 1,833.[55] In a similar fashion, Ahoy, another Chinese merchant dealing in tea, benefited from Jardine's liberal credit arrangements during

50. Shanghai, 1845–1859, Accounts and Cash Books, JMA.
51. The firm's representative reported this incident to Hong Kong: "Regarding Yeckchong's promissory note . . . Yeckchong's whereabouts is at present unknown to me. I caused several letters to be written to him, to his native village near Macao, but have not received any reply. He is thought to be either in Macao or in Hongkong" (C. S. Matheson [Canton] to Jardine, Matheson & Co. [Hong Kong], Jan. 24, 1863, JMA).
52. Macleod reported the pressing situation: "Both Ahoo and Yeng Coon are very hard pressed for money just now, and I think it will be necessary to give them a little assistance in a day or two" (to Joseph Jardine [Hong Kong], Jan. 4, 1849, JMA).
53. James Whittall (Shanghai) to Jardine, Matheson & Co. (Hong Kong), Mar. 1, 1859, JMA.
54. A. G. Dallas (Shanghai) to David Jardine (Hong Kong), Mar. 22, 1852, JMA.
55. Ibid., Sept. 3, 1859.

the fifties.[56] A Jardine's memorandum dated March 7, 1857, shows that the following Chinese owed a total of $106,900 to the house:[57]

Tongyu	$ 1,200
Yanetae	400
Looming	15,800
Cheyuen	13,300
Fatmow	8,400
Coongwo	8,000
Ahone	23,400
Kuitae	7,200
Aleet	18,700
Yengcoon	7,800
Atun	2,700

Compared with the previous decades, the 1860s witnessed rapid commercial development and credit expansion. Whereas, before the 1840s opium trade on the coast was as a rule on the basis of cash payment, in the 1850s Jardine's started to sell opium to the Chinese at Foochow against native bank orders. M. A. Macleod had this observation to make in 1861:

I take note of your further allusion to my sales of opium in January. . . . You would appear to be under the impression that Drug [opium] sold for cash is paid for at once. If so, you are mistaken. The money is not actually paid down on the delivery of the opium. On the contrary, it is always some days, and often even weeks before the Dollars can be all collected [from the native banks].[58]

In a letter to William Keswick dated January 31, 1868, F. B. Johnson of Jardine's wrote from Shanghai on the firm's loans: "By the last steamer I sent you down Ateong's accounts which show an amount owing by him on Green Tea operation of Tls. 813.7.7 and another on loan account of Tls. 2677.1.6, against which we have only the security of a native promissory note at a deferred date for Tls. 1000."[59] Ekee and other Cantonese joined Jardine's in operating a native bank during this period. He misused the bank's funds in 1867 and went broke at the end of that year.[60] By September 1868 he still owed the house a large sum of money,

56. Ibid., May 11, 1859.
57. Memorandum of Liabilities and Assets, Shanghai, Mar. 7, 1857, Memoranda, JMA.
58. Macleod (Foochow) to Alexander Perceval (Hong Kong), Feb. 18, 1861, JMA.
59. JMA.
60. Liu Kuang-ching, "T'ang T'ing-shu," p. 146.

totaling Tls. 206,058.[61] Concerning credit accounts with other Chinese, Johnson wrote to the Hong Kong office on September 11, 1868, stating that Acum and Tong King-sing "promised that some payments would shortly be made on their account." From June to September, Yakee also paid Tls. 3,000 for his account.[62] All these loans were made against the native bank orders.

Some Chinese merchants dealing in tea in the mid-Yangtze Valley applied to Jardine's Kiukiang office for an emergency loan to finance upcountry purchases in April 1869. Henry Beveridge, the firm's representative at that port, wrote to the Shanghai office for help. F. B. Johnson approved the credit and immediately remitted Tls. 50,000 in the form of native bank drafts.[63] At the same time, the firm's Foochow office requested a credit extension, and Johnson replied by sending $30,000 in native bank drafts, because foreign bank drafts were not readily available.[64]

Jardine's continued to make loans secured by native bank orders in the seventies to the Chinese merchants in Shanghai, especially Tucksing (Te-sheng), a prominent businessman from Swatow.[65] The trial balance sheet on April 30, 1875, indicated that the following Chinese owed a total of Tls. 138,084 to the house:[66]

Chow Wan Kee	Tls. 2,220
Tong King Sing	25,000
Te San	300
Him Shun Oan	40,000
Aleet	20,000
Hung Ching Kung	3,000
Cat Cheong	47,564

By the end of June, the firm had lent a total of Tls. 324,097 to the Chinese merchants in Shanghai.[67]

---

61. Johnson (Shanghai) to Jardine, Matheson & Co. (Hong Kong), Sept. 11, 1868, JMA.

62. Ibid. Tong's balance was Tls. 6,008.

63. Johnson (Shanghai) to William Keswick (Hong Kong), May 10, 1869, JMA.

64. "I cannot remit you as all the [Western] Banks decline to draw on Hongkong excepting at [a discount of] 23 c [to] 23½ [percent]. I have however sent $30,000 in native bills on Foochow to Mr. Hamilton" (ibid.).

65. William Keswick asked Johnson in Shanghai about Tucksing: "What is Tucksing doing and how does his indebtedness to us now stand?" (Aug. 8, 1871, JMA).

66. Trial Balance Sheet, Shanghai, Apr. 30, 1875, Memoranda, JMA.

67. Ibid., June 30, 1875.

Western houses made advances from time to time to their compradors to tide them over during financial difficulties. H. G. Bridges, Heard's representative at Kiukiang, asked A. F. Heard in 1866 to what extent he should advance credit to Seating, the comprador, "in [the] event of Seating making any bad debts."[68] Heard's answer, as Bridges had anticipated, was affirmative. This was also the case with Jardine's. As we will see shortly, Tong King-sing, the firm's comprador at Shanghai, received a large advance payment from the firm on June 1, 1871. In the early twentieth century, many Chinese merchants, especially the Cantonese with comprador background, were still able to use native bank orders to get loans from the foreign firms.[69]

CHINESE MERCHANTS

Using native bank orders to facilitate a fluid credit relationship between Chinese and foreigners was by no means one-way; Chinese with extra capital also frequently extended credit to foreigners. In 1818 several of the hong merchants were reported to have supplied the American traders credit on a large scale. Houqua, for instance, was at that time extensively involved in these transactions. In 1839 an American merchant in Canton, P. W. Snow, was in a difficult financial position, and Houqua voluntarily loaned him $80,000 without interest in 1840.[70] Another hong merchant, Consequa, who was reported to have lost $1,000,000 in credit transactions with Americans, even went so far as to address a memorandum to the President of the United States. According to him, he had been led, after years of extensive dealings with the Americans, to give them extended credit, although it was against the laws of the Ch'ing government. He further stated that some of the Americans had not only declined to pay, offering frivolous excuses, but had even applied the capital to other branches of their business.[71]

The Chinese merchants continued this practice after the Opium War. In 1844 Kingwo and Chinam, two Cantonese in Shanghai, sold tea to Jardine's on credit. They did not ask the firm to pay until April 1845.[72] The Chinese loans to Jardine's were repaid in various forms during the

---

68. May 9, 1866, HM-23, HC.

69. P'eng Yü-hsin, "K'ang Jih chan-cheng ch'ien Han-k'ou ti yang-hang ho mai-pan," *Li-lun chan-hsien* 11:29 (Feb. 1959).

70. Houqua (Canton) to J. P. Cushing (Boston), June 1, 1840, HLB.

71. Dennett, *Americans*, pp. 85–86.

72. A. G. Dallas (Shanghai) to Donald Matheson (Hong Kong), Apr. 11, 1845, JMA.

fifties—in cash, in opium, or "in drafts on Canton and Indian bills."[73] Jardine papers indicate that this relationship was "customary" throughout the fifties and the sixties.[74] Jardine's was one of the foreign firms that were noted for their fortunes. For those with less capital, Chinese credit was all the more important. Dallas commented on the financial situation of his fellow foreign traders in Shanghai on October 11, 1851: "Most of our neighbours appear to be very hard-pressed for funds and some of them are reported to be deeply indebted to the Chinese."[75] These firms included the sizable Lindsay & Co., which was "reported to be largely indebted to the Chinese, to the extent of three laks [$300,000]."[76]

Russell & Co. is known to have owed the astounding amount of about $400,000 to Chinese bankers, silk merchants, and tea merchants in 1856. Alexander Perceval wrote from Shanghai on June 5: "Several firms are now spoken of amongst the Chinese as being unable to meet their Liabilities and amongst others L. [Lindsay] & Co. and R. [Russell] & Co.!!! The latter it is said owe 2 lacs [$200,000] to Chinese Banks and about 2 lacs to Silk and Tea men."[77] After the 1860s, many Chinese made large investments in Russell's various enterprises.[78] Augustine Heard & Co. also borrowed heavily from the Chinese. Its head office in Canton received at least $140,000 worth of deposits through the comprador in 1855. In addition, it obtained from Tongmow a one-year loan for $45,000 on September and another for $45,000 in December. Similar loans existed throughout the late fifties and early sixties.[79] When the firm's office in Hong Kong was desperately in need of money in 1863, A. F. Heard wrote from that port: "I must say the comprador [See Yong] has come out like a brick. I can count upon . . . certain $23,000."[80] When he considered in 1861 a proposal at Shanghai to undertake the lucrative transportation of the tribute rice to Peking, he expected that, out of the $600,000 cash advance needed, he would get $100,000 from the Chinese

73. A. G. Dallas (Shanghai) to Jardine, Matheson & Co. (Hong Kong), Nov. 14, 1851, JMA.

74. James Whittall, e.g., wrote from Shanghai in 1859: "I am enclosing statements of accounts together with account sales of various parcels produce on account sundry Cantonese friends showing balance to their credit which I will adjust as customary" (to Jardine, Matheson & Co. [Hong Kong], June 14, 1859, JMA).

75. To Jardine, Matheson & Co. (Hong Kong), JMA.

76. Ibid., Oct. 14, 1851. The term "lak" (or "lac"), which was frequently used in the correspondence of Western merchants, refers to the amount of 100,000.

77. To Joseph Jardine (Hong Kong), JMA.

78. Yen-p'ing Hao, Comprador, p. 121.

79. Case 9, HC II.

80. Heard to John Heard (Hong Kong), Feb. 28, 1863, FM-4, HC.

merchants.[81] Heard's practice of borrowing money from the Chinese continued during the seventies.[82]

The native banks, through their bank orders, also facilitated credit relationships among Chinese merchants. After the 1840s wealthy Cantonese merchants occasionally made loans to their northern fellow countrymen from Amoy and nearby places. They usually did not charge more than one percent per month but were able to maintain partners on the coast so as to keep a lien on goods and otherwise represent their interest until their loans were repaid. Under this credit arrangement, Chinese capital, formerly concentrated at Canton, was gradually diffused to Amoy and Shanghai.[83]

More importantly, native bank orders were instrumental in facilitating the upcountry purchase of tea and silk, especially based in the large treaty ports. In Shanghai, for example, Acum, Aleet, and Tong Kingsing operated three native banks in the late sixties and the early seventies that "made large advances upon Tea in the Country."[84] Hsu Jun, one of the most prominent merchants in Shanghai, tried to resume his tea business in 1886, two years after his bankruptcy. He borrowed more than Tls. 200,000 from several native banks at Shanghai for a period of six months in order to engage in the upcountry tea purchase in Hunan and Hupei.[85]

Many native banks also existed in the second-rate treaty ports, such as Foochow and Hankow, which were close to the tea-producing districts. Compared with their counterparts in Shanghai, these banks were small in size. But, because of their proximity to the tea and silk districts, they were extremely helpful to the local tea and silk merchants. Many native banks at Hankow made loans to the local tea merchants in the form of native bank orders during the sixties and the seventies. Two of these banks, Kum Chun Me and Sin Cheong Tai, were particularly involved in this kind of business. The latter made a loan for the amount of Tls. 18,000 in May 1871[86] and another similar loan for Tls. 4,574 in

81. Heard (Shanghai) to John Heard (Hong Kong), Jan. 21, 1861; John Heard (Hong Kong) to A. F. Heard (Shanghai), Feb. 8, 1861, EA-1, HC.

82. E.g., G. B. Dixwell wrote from Shanghai: "Before I went down to Hong Kong I borrowed 15,000 taels of the comprador, as we were short. This sum he says he wants in a couple of months, and I think as a matter of policy we had better pay it up as soon as we can conveniently" (to Augustine Heard, Jr. [Hong Kong], Mar. 29, 1870, EM-14, HC).

83. Fairbank, *Trade and Diplomacy*, I, 288.

84. F. B. Johnson (Shanghai) to William Keswick (Hong Kong), June 1, 1871, JMA, quoted in Liu Kuang-ching, "T'ang T'ing-shu," p. 149.

85. *Nien-p'u*, 41b.

86. Robert Anderson (Kiukiang) to F. B. Johnson (Shanghai), May 28 and June 1, 1871, JMA.

March 1872.[87] In contrast to the previous two decades, the 1880s, witnessed more caution on the part of the native banks in making loans.[88]

MORTGAGES AND UPCOUNTRY ADVANCES

A merchant could not use his promissory notes to obtain loans on all occasions, because it was up to the lender to determine what security he would require in order to protect him if matters went awry. In fact, numerous loans were substantially secured in other ways. Some foreign firms required specific and valuable security, such as shares of stock or the title deeds of property in the treaty ports. When loans were made to facilitate the storage and shipment of goods, the security would consist of a first mortgage on the entire goods or cargoes, where the lender took possession in case of default. Meanwhile, the Western mercantile houses frequently made huge advances to Chinese merchants to purchase tea and silk in the interior after the fifties, tea and silk being the main resources pledged as security for these loans. The Chinese merchants would agree either to sell them to the house at a fixed price or to offer the house the privilege of "first refusal" to buy the produce at the market price.

MORTGAGES

During the 1850s, Jardine's often made loans, guaranteed by valuable securities, to the Chinese merchants in the treaty ports, particularly in Shanghai. In 1859 James Whittall made loans to Takee and Ateong in this fashion.[89] Appaey, a tea merchant in Amoy, was interested in obtaining a similar loan from Jardine's main office at Hong Kong in 1863. He applied for a loan for the amount of $10,000 for which he would "pay 1% a month interest and give security."[90] At the same time, James Whittall made an unusually large loan to Takee, a Ningpo merchant

87. Jardine, Matheson & Co. (Shanghai) to Jardine, Matheson & Co. (Hong Kong), March 22, 1872, JMA.

88. A British consul observed that, in Ningpo during 1881–1882, "native banks exercised the greatest caution in making advances to traders even of the best standing" (BPP, *Commercial Reports of Her Majesty's Consuls in China*, 1884, p. 82).

89. "The sums at the debits of Takee and Ateong are for amounts loaned them on interest—and under security, as explained to you some time since" (Whittall [Shanghai] to Jardine, Matheson & Co. [Hong Kong], July 26, 1860, JMA).

90. Jardine, Matheson & Co. (Amoy) to Jardine, Matheson & Co. (Hong Kong), Jan. 7, 1863, JMA.

who was active in Shanghai during the fifties. Jardine's made Takee's property security, because Whittall stated that all the property stood "in the firm's name and [is] worth very much more."[91] In Hankow, Yowloong, who regularly traded with Jardine's in the sixties and seventies, used valuable securities to obtain loans from the firm. According to F. B. Johnson, Jardine's "held full security for the debt" of Yowloong in 1868.[92] In the seventies Yowloong continued to borrow funds from Jardine's Shanghai office[93] and often requested the house to "settle his account" with the main office in Hong Kong.[94] If he was hard-pressed to repay the loan when it matured, he would continue to borrow the principal as well as the interest.[95]

In the late 1860s, Tong King-sing, Acum, and Aleet jointly operated tea hongs and native banks. Thanks to Tong's compradorship with Jardine's, these enterprises became increasingly prosperous by 1871. However, because of a rumor circulating in Shanghai in the spring of 1871 to the effect that Jardine's was to wind up its business soon, these Chinese merchants were financially hard-pressed. On May 30, 1871, Tong finally applied to F. B. Johnson, Jardine's manager in Shanghai, for assistance. On investigating Tong's account, Johnson found to his surprise that Tong had improperly discounted about Tls. 80,000 of native bank orders not due, which Jardine's had entrusted to his care. Johnson immediately telegraphed the head office in Hong Kong, asking William Keswick's permission to give Tong further assistance. After having cleared it with Keswick, Johnson granted Tong a substantial loan of Tls. 120,000.[96]

91. (Shanghai) to Jardine, Matheson & Co. (Hong Kong), Jan. 8, 1863, JMA.

92. Johnson wrote: "*Yowloong's a/c* [account]. I enclose Mr. Gower's statement of the position of this matter and a copy of his letter explanatory of the items. There had been I regret to say no change in the figures since the date of the account. I understand from [James] Whittall that he held full security for the debt or for so much of it as may be justly chargeable to Yowloong" ([Shanghai] to William Keswick [Hong Kong], Feb. 12, 1868, JMA).

93. Yowloong owed Tls. 3,809 to Jardine's by August 9, 1873, and continued to borrow this sum from that date to April 30, 1874 (Shanghai, Apr. 30, 1874, Memoranda, JMA).

94. In a letter to the head office in Hong Kong, the Shanghai branch office wrote: "We enclose a copy of Yowloong's account from 9th August last, up to which date a copy was sent you on 13th of same month, showing a balance due with interest to 30/4/74 [April 30, 1874] of Tls. 4,139.7.2. He promised to settle his account with you and we will be glad to know if we may transfer the account and interest since to your debit" (Jardine, Matheson & Co. [Shanghai] to Jardine, Matheson & Co. [Hong Kong], Aug. 25, 1874, JMA).

95. Yowloong continued to borrow the principal and interest of the above-mentioned loan until August 31, 1874, making his total indebtedness Tls. 4,305.28 (ibid., Aug. 31, 1874).

96. Johnson actually was prepared to make a loan to Tong for Tls. 130,000. He

For this loan, Jardine's obtained securities in various forms. In addition to the drafts on Hankow for Tls. 30,000 and the promissory notes of the native banks for Tls. 30,000, Johnson further received from Tong "sundry shares and title deeds of property" in Shanghai and Chinkiang for Tls. 50,000.[97] By October, these securities included the title deeds of property at Hongkew, Shanghai, which were valued at Tls. 15,000 and produced Tls. 2,000 per annum; the title deeds of property in Shanghai in the name of Mr. Gowei, which were valued at Tls. 6,000 and produced Tls. 900 per annum; the title deeds of property (land and houses) at Chinkiang in the name of James Whittall costing Tls. 14,000; shares of the steamer *Nanzing* worth Tls. 15,000; and sundry shares for Tls. 12,000. Tong King-sing mortgaged these securities, valued totally at Tls. 62,000 to Jardine's to secure advances of Tls. 45,000.[98]

Besides stock shares and the title deeds of real estates, the Western merchant obtained security in other forms. One of them was the goods of Chinese merchants who temporarily stored them in the foreigner's warehouses or wharves. In an agreement between Augustine Heard & Co. and some Chinese tea merchants at Shanghai in 1847, Heard's agreed "to advance to such teamen money sufficient for their personal expenses to any amount under one thousand dollars." The advance would be repaid when the tea was sold, with interest at the rate of one percent per month. Any time under fifteen days would be accounted as one-half a month, and over fifteen days, one month. Should the tea merchants require an advance amounting to, or exceeding, $1,000, the firm would, if convenient, provide it. When money was advanced, the tea had to be transferred to the company's name, but the tea merchants would be charged for the premium of the fire insurance at the rate of one-quarter of one percent per month. Whenever the advance exceeded $1,000, the money had to be repaid within three months, or the tea would be sold by the firm for cash. Under no circumstance would the company advance a greater amount than one-half of the value of the tea stored in the warehouse.[99]

---

spelled out the arrangement: "I advanced Tls. 30,000 [to Tong] in addition to the Tls. 80,000 wrongfully appropriated and engaged to find a further sum of Tls. 20,000 on the 21st, but of this only Tls. 10,000 were found requisite, making Tls. 120,000 in all" (to Keswick [Hong Kong], June 1, 1871, JMA).

97. Ibid. See also Liu Kuang-ching, "T'ang T'ing-shu," p. 149.

98. Johnson (Shanghai) to William Keswick (Hong Kong), Oct. 6, 1871, JMA. See also Liu Kuang-ching, "T'ang T'ing-shu," pp. 151–52.

99. EA-1, HC.

After the early sixties, as the number of warehouses increased with the development of shipping, Jardine's began a large business in advances on goods stored in its godowns.[100] In this connection, the house as a rule did business with its "old native friends," including Acum.[101] Its Amoy office advanced a sum to Akow in 1868 against his "best teas of the season" that were stored in the firm's warehouses. Jardine's was glad to extend the period of the advance because Akow would continue to pay interest and fire insurance premiums to the house.[102] This practice continued in the seventies. Jardine's Shanghai account books of April 1874 indicate that the firm advanced in that month a total of Tls. 65,000 at 20 percent annual interest to fifteen Chinese merchants who stored goods in the firm's Hunt's Wharf. At the same time, Jardine's also advanced "Hung Ching-kung Tls. 2,000 at 10 percent on security 100 packages of Nankins [nankeens] stored in Ewo West Godown."[103] In September 1875 Jardine's Shanghai office tried to "keep funds available in Shanghai for wharf advances" because, according to the manager of the office, he could easily get a high rate of interest. Besides, the loans would be pledged "with good security."[104]

Still another form of security was the cargo that the Chinese merchants shipped via foreign vessels. In the words of a British consul, these natives "avail themselves of European capital advanced to them in the shape of ships, for which they pay interest in the shape of freight." This form of credit in a large measure benefited the southern traders from Kwangtung and Fukien "who thoroughly understand the benefit and use of credit."[105] They soon turned out to be powerful competitors, as we will see in chapter 7. Jardine files of correspondence from Shanghai indicate that this kind of credit started as early as December 1844, one year after that port was actually opened to foreign trade. According to A. G. Dallas, the firm's representative at that port, these arrangements were especially conducive to attracting Chinese merchants' silk consignments

---

100. Edward LeFevour, *Western Enterprise in Late Ch'ing China* (Cambridge, Mass., 1968), p. 137.

101. Reporting on the "Chinamen's accounts," James Whittall wrote: "The amount at debit of Acum is for goods purchased on the market and still in our godowns" ([Shanghai] to Jardine, Matheson & Co. [Hong Kong], July 18, 1861, JMA).

102. Henry Smith, Jardine's representative at Amoy, reported: "Akow still holds his teas. I have them all stored in our godowns, and he pays fire insurance. As interest is going on, I think I would let him hold them as he certainly has the best teas of the season" (to William Keswick [Hong Kong] Sept. 26, 1868, JMA).

103. Shanghai, April 1874, Accounts, JMA.

104. Jardine, Matheson & Co. (Shanghai) to Jardine, Matheson & Co. (Hong Kong), Sept, 28, 1875, JMA.

105. BPP, *Reports from Her Majesty's Consuls in China, 1864*, vol. 71, 1866, p. 50.

to Hong Kong.[106] Many Chinese tea merchants contracted tea in the
interior in 1846–1847 but found that the tea market in the treaty ports
was sluggish. In order to attract them into entering the export trade on
their own account shipped via Jardine's vessels, the firm offered them
inexpensive credit, which enabled them to meet debts due on the customary settling dates.[107]

In 1860 Jardine's advanced Chun Yun Chang £2,000 on his silk shipment from Shanghai to London via one of the steamers of the firm. A
similar loan was made to Acum the following year for his silk shipment
to Lyons.[108] M. A. Macleod, Jardine's representative at Foochow, was
so interested in this type of loan that he tried hard "to persuade the
teamen to ship under advance." For this purpose, for instance, he
advanced Yun Tai $10,000 in 1861.[109] In September 1866, Jardine's
Kiukiang office advanced a sum to Ateong who shipped four chops of
Congou tea from Kiukiang to London. Edward Whittall made it clear
that, although Jardine's funds were involved, this shipment was entirely
on Ateong's account.[110] Tucksing, a prominent merchant at Shanghai,
frequently requested and received from Jardine's advances against his
shipments of native produce.[111] This kind of advance became more popular in the seventies. The firm's Shanghai office wrote in September 1875:
"There were numerous applications for advances at the wharves."[112]
Jardine archives indicate that this trend continued throughout the
eighties.[113]

106. Dallas wrote from Shanghai to Hong Kong in 1845 concerning this kind of credit:
"Alum often asks me regarding the 50 bales of Tuysaund silk shipped from here in December 1844 per 'Vixen,' and upon which I gave an advance of $8,000, viz., $200 per pecul.
Please let me have account sales of this as soon as you can, and let me know whether you
wish me to encourage such a mode of doing business, as I could now get consignments of
silk" (to Donald Matheson, Nov. 17, 1845, JMA).
107. Matheson & Co. (London) to Jardine, Matheson & Co. (Hong Kong), Aug. 23,
1847, JMA.
108. James Whittall (Shanghai) to Jardine, Matheson & Co. (Hong Kong), May 5,
1860, JMA; and Shanghai, 1861, Memoranda, JMA.
109. Macleod recorded this situation: "For some time past I have been endeavouring
to persuade the teamen to ship under advance, including Yun Tai. Alum is now trying to
do something in this way" (to Alexander Perceval [Hong Kong], Feb. 18, 1861, JMA).
110. Whittall wrote from Shanghai to the Kiukiang office: "Please inform him that we
cannot take them over, and in the event of their showing a loss on the advance made him,
we will look to him to make it good" (to Jardine, Matheson & Co., Sept. 29, 1866, JMA).
111. Tucksing wrote Jardine's: 'I beg to inform you that I have to return you many
thanks for your kind favor in advancing money to my Inspector of Opium against shipment
[of native produce] as in accordance to my last request" (to William Keswick [Hong
Kong], Jan. 15, 1868, JMA). In September, Jardine's made another loan for Tls. 15,000 to
Tucksing against his nankeen shipments (F. B. Johnson [Shanghai] to Jardine, Matheson
& Co. [Hong Kong], Sept. 11, 1868, JMA).
112. Jardine, Matheson & Co. to Jardine, Matheson & Co. (Hong Kong), Sept. 28,
1875, JMA.
113. B2, Boxes 176–183, Unbound Correspondence (Local), JMA.

ADVANCE PAYMENTS FOR UPCOUNTRY PURCHASES

Jardine's frequently made advances to the Chinese merchants at Shanghai for the purchase of tea. A. G. Dallas extended to Aloong in 1852 "a moderate" advance in the amount of $1,828. He also advanced money to the Manfoong hong that specialized in the tea trade at Shanghai.[114] In the early sixties, Kiukee replaced Aloong as the most important tea merchant to receive Jardine's advances. William Keswick wrote on October 7, 1864: "I have today made Kiukee an advance on 200 bars on the same terms as I wrote you I had done on his shipment per 'Carthage.' These are large and very important transactions and will I hope meet with due approval from you."[115] In January 1868, F. B. Johnson made an unusual advance to Atoong of Tls. 20,000. He explained the situation: "The loan of Tls. 20,000 was ostensibly required to make advances upon Teas to be consigned to us for sale here. The money was really employed to relieve his pecuniary embarrassment."[116] In March, Johnson advanced Acum Tls. 10,000 for the special purchase of Moyune tea.[117] Meanwhile, Johnson made three substantial advances to Aleet, totaling Tls. 45,000 and $20,000, as shown by the following figures:[118]

Date	Account Tun Kai	Account Ningchow	Account Moyune
March 17	Tls. 10,000	0	0
March 21	0	Tls. 20,000	$20,000
March 26	Tls. 10,000	0	Tls. 5,000

In September, Johnson again made advances to Aleet for the purchase of Tun Kai and Moyune teas.[119]

It was the American houses of Russell's and Heard's that started the practice of making advances for upcountry purchases of tea at Foochow in the mid-1850s. Augustine Heard, Jr., recalled: "Huge amounts of money went into the county . . . in February and March, and did not come back in the shape of teas till May. It was a great risk to run."[120]

114. To Jardine, Matheson & Co. (Hong Kong), Mar. 22, 1852, JMA.
115. To James Whittall (Hong Kong), JMA.
116. To William Keswick (Hong Kong), Jan. 31, 1868, JMA.
117. Ibid., Mar. 10, 1868.
118. Shanghai, Apr. 1, 1868, Memoranda, JMA.
119. Johnson (Shanghai) to Jardine, Matheson & Co. (Hong Kong), Sept. 11, 1868, JMA.
120. "Old China," p. 21, GQ-2, HC.

Jardine's followed suit, advancing $20,744 to Ahee in March 1859.[121] Two years later, M. A. Macleod, the firm's representative, advanced $24,000 to three teamen for the purchase of scented teas.[122] One of them was seriously ill one month later, a situation that caused Macleod "a great deal of anxiety."[123] H. G. Bridges, the representative of Heard's in Hankow, wrote in 1863 of Russell & Co.'s commitment on upcountry tea advances in that port: "They advance money to teamen and pay expenses of transport from the country, and when the teas arrive, it is placed in their hands for sale for which they get 4%."[124] For this purpose, Jardine's in 1866 made a substantial advancement in the amount of $25,000 to Yowloong.[125] To a lesser extent, during the sixties Jardine's also made advances to other Chinese, including Ahi.[126] Having received advances from the foreign trader, Chinese tea merchants went to the tea districts and made contracts with the tea growers and producers. The price was prearranged, and earnest money was paid accordingly.[127]

Foreign merchants also made advances to the Chinese merchants on silk. By doing so, they were able to secure silk of superior quality. Four years after Shanghai was opened to foreign trade, Jardine's A. G. Dallas started to report frequently to the firm's main office in Hong Kong concerning his practice of silk advances in Shanghai.[128] He later wanted to know whether he should vigorously pursue business on this line, and Donald Matheson strongly encouraged him to do so.[129]

121. N. R. Massion (Hong Kong) to Jardine, Matheson & Co. (Hong Kong), Mar. 25, 1859, JMA.

122. Macleod had this to report from Foochow: "*Scented Teas.* Shortly after last addressing you I completed my arrangements for obtaining a moderate supply of these, and enclosed you will find copies of the agreements entered into with Yuntai and with Mantai and Tonghing. . . . The amount advanced so far is $24,000 in all. They started for the interior on the 13th, so that I expect to hear from them very shortly" (to Alexander Perceval [Hong Kong], Apr. 8, 1861, JMA).

123. "Yuntai, our scented tea man, is causing me a great deal of anxiety just now, as he is said to be in great danger, and hardly expected to live any time" (ibid., May 5, 1861).

124. To William Dixwell (Shanghai), Oct. 15, 1863, HM-23, HC.

125. S. I. Gower (Hankow) to William Keswick (Shanghai), June 5 and 16, 1866, JMA.

126. Henry Smith, Jardine's representative, wrote: "Ahi has paid $1000 and promises $2000 more this month, and the remainder at Chinese New Year. His money is safe, I think, and I hope to get it in before I leave Amoy" ([Amoy] to Jardine, Matheson & Co. [Hong Kong], Jan. 7, 1863, JMA).

127. Robert Fortune, a British botanist who was commissioned by the East India Company to smuggle tea plants from China to India, observed the tea purchase in Chekiang in the late forties: "It sometimes happens that a [Chinese] merchant makes a contract with some of the tea growers before the season commences, in which case the price is arranged in the usual way, and generally a part paid in advance. This, I understand, is frequently to secure any particular kind of tea" (*Wanderings,* p. 213).

128. To Donald Matheson, Jan. 5, 1846, JMA.

129. Matheson to Dallas, Feb. 20, 1846, JMA.

As Dallas continued to receive encouragements from the Hong Kong office, he kept making advances for upcountry purchases of silk. Meanwhile, most of the Western houses in Shanghai gave such advances in 1851. Refusing to be outdone, Jardine's rapidly expanded credit along this line. Its loans were made on a large scale; Takee, for example, asked Dallas in 1851 for an astonishingly huge advance of $100,000. Dallas made note of this on April 7, 1851: "To assist in these operations Takee asks me for an advance to the extent of a lac of dollars [$100,000], against which I have the 140 Bs. [bales] of silk, worth about $40,000. Most of the houses here give such advances, and indeed without them it is impossible to get early Tea or Silk. A corresponding advantage in price ought also to be obtained."[130]

Dallas again learned in May that the gigantic British house of Dent, Beale & Co. had made upcountry advances totaling $300,000 in that year. Besides, Dallas added: "Takee also tells me of $80,000 advanced to an old purser of his by Messrs. Lindsay & Co. for a similar purpose." Meanwhile, Dallas planned to extend another $50,000 to Takee, as he continued: "In addition to the lak of dollars [$100,000] already advanced or promised [to Takee], I am giving him more funds by degrees to the extent of half a lak more."[131] Jardine's Shanghai office also occasionally made advances for the purchase of silkworm cocoons. It made advances to Chunsing, Kintai, Aleet, Cheyuen, and Fahmow in 1860 for this purpose,[132] and these accounts stood largely unchanged one year later.[133]

During the late sixties, Jardine's made large amounts of silk advances to Aleet, a Chinese merchant who did business with the house after the fifties. F. B. Johnson wrote from Shanghai in April 1868: "I have arranged with Aleet to advance $60,000 for the purchase of chop Tsat-lees & $20,000 for Red Peacocks in the Country so as to give us an interest in early operations on the best terms. It is probably that we shall have new silk shipped by the first mail of next month but if purchases can be staged it will be very satisfactory."[134] In September, Johnson

130. To David Jardine (Hong Kong), JMA.
131. Ibid., May 20, 1851.
132. "The sums at the debits of Chunsing, Kintai, Aleet, Cheyuen & Fahmow have been advanced them on account of cocoon purchases" (James Whittall [Shanghai] to Jardine, Matheson & Co. [Hong Kong], July 26, 1860, JMA).
133. "*Chinamen's Accounts.* The balance at debit of Chunsing and Kintai will appear settled or materially reduced in the June accounts. They consisted of advances for cocoons" (ibid., July 18, 1861).
134. To William Keswick (Hong Kong), Apr. 20, 1868, JMA. Tsatlee and Red Peacock are different kinds of silk.

advanced Aleet another $50,000 for "country silk purchases."[135] At the same time, Jardine's advanced Tucksing Tls. 15,000 for purchasing nankeen. In May 1869, Johnson planned further advances to Aleet: "Mr. Messer is now in the Country with $80,000 and I hope to add to his stake in Cocoons $30,000 worth through Aleet. I feel sanguine of success though I don't like to build too strong hopes on it. I shall further furnish Aleet with $30,000 for upcountry purchases of silk."[136] This plan was soon carried out.

In the 1860s, it was a common practice for Jardine's Shanghai office to advance Chinese merchants funds for the purchase of tea, silk, and cocoon at the same time. In July 1860, James Whittall made several advances to Aleet and Yakee for these purposes.[137] Three months later, through Capt. Patridge, he advanced Yakee's agent the sizable amount of Tls. 66,000 for tea and silk purchases.[138] In October, Whittall made a further advance to Yakee of Tls. 22,000.[139] Jardine's account on September 13, 1861, shows that the house made similar advances to many other Chinese, including Aleet, Aloong, Ateong, Acum, Takee, Chunsing, and Cheyuen.[140] Jardine's advanced Yakee sums of such a large scale in early 1863 that its treasury was "on the whole pretty low."[141]

Advances to the Chinese for upcountry purchases declined in the early 1870s because of the increasing risk involved for the foreign houses. F. B. Johnson wrote from Shanghai on the subject on June 1, 1871:

It is also clear to my mind that the system of advances to the Chinese for upcountry purchases must be finally abandoned for there is never any profit obtained upon them worth the risk. We encourage the Chinese middlemen to raise the prices of [tea] leaf against us in the Country, not only to the extent of our advances, but by promoting their credit outside, and however cautious we may be, we cannot avoid every now and then being made the subject of a heavy loss. We arrived at this conclusion last year and there cannot be a doubt on the subject in view of the present circumstances."[142]

Although "there were numerous applications for advances in silk, tea and opium" in the mid-seventies,[143] Jardine's seldom made advances in

135. Ibid., Sept. 11, 1868.
136. Ibid., May 10, 1869.
137. To Jardine, Matheson & Co. (Hong Kong), July 26, 1860, JMA.
138. Ibid., Oct. 5, 1861.
139. Ibid.
140. Ibid., Sept. 13, 1861.
141. "Our Treasury is on the whole pretty low just now, taking into consideration the advance to Yakee, payments of coal purchases and other liabilities" (Peter S. Lawrie [Shanghai] to Alexander Perceval [Hong Kong], Jan. 10, 1863, JMA).
142. To William Keswick (Hong Kong), JMA.
143. Jardine, Matheson & Co. (Shanghai) to Jardine, Matheson & Co. (Hong Kong), Sept. 28, 1875, JMA.

large amounts. The account books of April 1874 show that under the heading of "silk advances" the house had outstanding loans totaling only Tls. 11,000 on April 1.[144] The balance sheet on April 30, 1875, shows that Jardine's Shanghai office had advanced Tls. 40,000 for tea purchase.[145] This was a small amount compared to the similar loans in the previous two decades. By the 1880s, the firm's advances for the up-country purchases were minimal.[146]

Western firms made advances to the Chinese not only for purchasing tea and silk, but also for selling its imports of opium and piece goods. As we have seen in chapter 3, foreign merchants frequently advanced Chinese in the form of opium. Compared with the advance in cash, the advance in opium was much more profitable to the foreign trader and was therefore made "on liberal terms."[147] Soon after Shanghai was opened for foreign trade, Jardine's offered some Chinese inexpensive cre- • dit to ship tea to England for sale. In return, the Chinese merchants would use the proceeds of the tea in London to order piece goods from the firm.[148]

In the mid-forties, Chinese merchants occasionally extended credit to foreign houses in the form of tea and silk.[149] In the early fifties, such credit arrangements were common in Shanghai, as A. G. Dallas observed in 1851 that "our neighbours are all, with few exceptions, more or less indebted to the [Chinese] Tea and Silk men."[150] For Jardine's, Yakee was a large creditor in the fifties and sixties.[151] At the same time, Jardine's owed Acum the proceeds of nineteen bales of silk in addition to a "large amount short paid him."[152] The house in 1861 owed to Yow-loong some of his contract teas and the sizable amount of $40,000.[153]

144. These loans were at 15 percent annual interest (Shanghai, Apr. 1874, Accounts, JMA).

145. Shanghai Trial Balance Sheet, 1875, Memoranda, JMA.

146. F. B. Johnson (Shanghai) to James J. Keswick (Shanghai), Feb. 5, 1883, JMA.

147. F. B. Johnson (Shanghai) to William Keswick (Hong Kong), Jan. 31, 1868, JMA.

148. Jardine, Matheson & Co. (London) to Jardine, Matheson & Co. (Hong Kong), Aug. 23, 1847, JMA.

149. Concerning such credit, A. G. Dallas made a report from Shanghai on April 11, 1845: "Kingwo is dunning me about the old balance due him by Chinam's heirs on account of the teas and silk" (to Donald Matheson [Hong Kong], JMA). See also Dallas' letter of Feb. 18, 1845, JMA.

150. To Jardine, Matheson & Co. (Hong Kong), Oct. 18, 1851, JMA.

151. James Whittall (Shanghai) to Jardine, Matheson & Co. (Hong Kong), Feb. 19, 1859, JMA. Whittall later explained: "The large amounts which you mention as appearing in the Trial balance sheet are to be accounted for as follows—that at credit of Yakee, was for a large quantity of teas delivered by him, some of which being on contract, we had not yet come to a final settlement about" (ibid., May 5, 1860).

152. Shanghai, June 1, 1860, Memoranda, JMA.

153. T. S. Odell (Canton) to Jardine, Matheson & Co. (Hong Kong), June 22, 1861, JMA.

Nevertheless, throughout the second half of the nineteenth century, it was usually the foreign traders who made advance payments to Chinese merchants.

LIMITATIONS AND SIGNIFICANCE OF CREDIT

Credit transactions along the coast had their limitations in terms of duration, amount, volatility, competitiveness, and overexpansion. Nevertheless, credit was extremely important, because it was indispensable to trade. Besides, easy credit along the coast led to a low rate of interest, which in turn remarkably stimulated commercial capitalism.

LIMITATIONS

The role of credit in stimulating China's commerce was restricted for several reasons. First, the effect that foreign loans to Chinese merchants had on China's economy was limited, partly because many loans were still made on a short-term basis. A Western trader would usually ask for the repayment of the loans he made to a Chinese merchant as soon as the latter sold tea and silk on the market.[154] During the sixties and the early seventies, the terms of Jardine's advances were generally from six to eight weeks, as F. B. Johnson wrote in 1871: "We shall have to wait for about two months before our advances are closed, that is to say until the 14 Chops of Tea have been sold, but I am led to believe that the greater portion will be redeemed in the course of six weeks—in point of fact we are in exactly the same position as we used to be years ago when we made large advances."[155]

The duration of these loans ranged from several days to one year; the average period was about six weeks. Although the six-week period was considerably longer than the duration of traditional credit transactions, it was not long enough for the purpose of modern economic development. Commercial loans do not tend to be long-term in nature, but the average six-day period of chop loan during the sixties was no doubt extremely short. Longer-term loans might have accelerated the commercialization of Chinese economy more rapidly.

154. Jardine's Shanghai office wrote to the Hankow office in June 1869: "We have no advice of our advances to Yowloong and Chipqua having been repaid, and, as the Teas have now been sold, we shall be glad to know how these a/cs [accounts] stand. We beg your prompt attention to the statements of account with our Native friends" (Jardine, Matheson & Co. [Shanghai] to Henry Beveridge [Hankow], June 17, 1869, JMA).

155. (Shanghai) to William Keswick (Hong Kong), June 1, 1871, JMA.

Second, the amount of foreign loans was not large. Given the entire picture of modern China's economy, foreign borrowing by private Chinese individuals and firms remained negligible. As indicated above, the Ch'ing government likewise did not borrow heavily from the foreigner, and many such loans were used mainly for noneconomic purposes. During the 1861–1938 period, 44 percent of the foreign loans to the Chinese government, as expressed in constant prices, were for military and indemnity purposes, 31 percent for railroads, 20 percent for general administrative purposes, and 5 percent for industrial purposes.[156] None of these loans was particularly devoted to commercial development. In the meantime, direct foreign investment in modern China became increasingly important as time went on.

Third, many Chinese merchants along the coast depended heavily on international credit, which was often volatile. Exchange rates in the treaty ports, which reflected the worldwide monetary market, were considerably unstable. This fluctuation in exchange rates tended to discourage the circulation of bills of exchange as negotiable instruments of credit. The discounting and sale of these bills was, therefore, not a lively business. Fourth, although the credit market along the coast was more competitive than that of the interior, it remained restricted in some ways. For instance, Jardine's in 1874 only charged its "native friends" an annual rate of interest of 10 to 15 percent, but it charged 20 percent for a loan of Tls. 65,000 to fifteen Chinese merchants who did not frequently do business with the house.[157]

Finally, although credit transactions were indispensable to coastal commerce, they were not without risk, because the expansion of credit led to financial "bubbles" and "panics," in which the slowing or stoppage of a rapid rate of credit expansion would uncover many unsound loans and lead to financial or business collapses, or both.[158] A case in point was the Shanghai financial panic of 1883, which will be discussed in detail in chapter 11. In that year John Samuel Swire, founding partner of the British China-trade house of Butterfield & Swire, visited Shanghai and was surprised by the firm's lax credit policy, which had resulted in heavy losses to the house. He particularly blamed the two employees who were mainly responsible for the situation:

156. Chi-ming Hou, *Foreign Investment*, p. 212.
157. Shanghai, Apr. 1, 1874, Accounts, JMA.
158. The root causes of these financial collapses are monetary, and the credit aspects of the overinflation is only one of several symptoms of monetary malaise.

I must express how keenly I feel the negligence on both your parts, that resulted in the heavy loss of nearly a lac [100,000] of taels. I have always been uneasy about the credit system but each time . . . [Henry B.] Endicott has assured me that there was no danger. Now, he says that supervising the collection of freights was not his province. . . . To have simply taken his [the comprador's] own words that the accounts were outstanding, without asking him for a list of the hongs that were in arrear, was most extraordinary & culpable negligence. . . . [This is] just like watching a small hole in a birdcage, and not looking whether the door was shut. My resident partners are equally blameable.[159]

Another example is the financial crisis at Tientsin in 1908, which also resulted from extremely easy credit practices. As the comprador system gradually declined after the 1890s, foreign merchants extended credits directly to Chinese merchants without the guarantee of the comprador. In 1907 numerous Chinese dealers had large debts resulting from "the unsound state of affairs which has grown up in the import trade at this northern port." By November, liabilities amounting to more than Tls. 7,000,000 were outstanding against goods delivered to them on credit by the foreign merchants. A considerable proportion of that amount would prove to be irrecoverable unless further liabilities on a large scale were incurred. In other words, much of the Tls. 7,000,000 would only be paid out of proceeds of new deliveries.[160]

In a letter to the British consul-general at Shanghai in 1908, the chairman of the China Association, an organization of the British merchants connected with China trade, commented on this crisis:

The origin of the trouble has, of course, been the development of the system of delivering goods to Chinese on credit; that method of trading has long prevailed at Tientsin, but only in recent years has it developed into the large proportions which have now brought about a crisis. My committee is of opinion that extensive trading on this basis is unsound, as neither foreign firms nor foreign banks can follow their securities after the goods have passed into native hands. The financing of internal trade can only be done safely and efficiently by native banks who know their customers and who can follow the security.[161]

CREDIT AS INDISPENSABLE TO TRADE

Nothing testifies more clearly to the need for business credit than the failure of the cash payment movement at Hankow in the mid-1860s.

159. Swire (Shanghai) to H. B. Endicott and J. L. Brown (Tientsin), May 17, 1884, SP.
160. Chairman of the China Association (Shanghai) to Consul-General P. Warren (Shanghai), Dec. 11, 1908, FO 405/94, p. 10.
161. Ibid.

Although foreign traders often granted Chinese purchasers long-term credit during the fifties and the early sixties, by 1865 they were reluctant to do so at Hankow for several reasons. First, the native banks, through which business credit was arranged, were much more shaky and insecure at Hankow than at Shanghai. H. G. Bridges of Heard's had this to report from Hankow on June 28, 1866: "An opium shop or any other buyer of goods establishes what he calls a bank, so he can give one of these orders in payment of purchases."[162] Consequently, several native banks went bankrupt, and foreign traders were reported to have lost some Tls. 15,000 in the period from 1862 to 1867.[163]

Furthermore, realizing the seriousness of this financial crisis, some compradors were reluctant to secure native bank orders for foreign traders. Heard's Hankow comprador, Seating, argued: "A foreign bank is made of iron, and how can I secure a Chinese bank that is made of paper? If I sell your goods to a man who takes them to his shop up the back street and they burn up, I cannot say; I am not an insurance office."[164] Finally, those compradors who were willing to guarantee native bank orders were themselves engaged in speculative trade that frequently led to bankruptcy.

As a result, the foreign traders at Hankow held a meeting on September 4, 1865, in which they declared that "the late alarming failures amongst the compradors have rendered some change imperative." To be specific, they decided to "get rid of the ackowledged dangerous and pernicious system of delivering goods on receipt of native banks' chops at three weeks to two months date." They made a resolution that they would sell only for cash or for five-day banker's orders. Besides, "this resolution should also fully apply to all goods held by foreigners on native account." These merchants further agreed that a fine of Tls. 1,000 be imposed on any person who should later violate this agreement. Besides, they selected three participants of the meeting to solicit support from their colleagues in Shanghai for this new policy.[165] From that time on, they met frequently to implement the policy of cash payment.[166] The British consul at Hankow reported that this effort was at first generally

---

162. To A. F. Heard (Shanghai), HM-23, HC.
163. *NCH*, Aug. 5, 1867, p. 191.
164. H. G. Bridges (Hankow) to A. F. Heard (Shanghai), June 28, 1866, HM-23, HC.
165. *NCH*, Sept. 16, 1865, p. 146.
166. They met on September 4 and 21, and on October 23, 1865. The chairman of the last meeting reiterated that "the commercial firms of this port [Hankow] are anxious to put an end to a pernicious practice of accepting Chinese Bankers' orders at long dates in their import transactions" (*NCH*, Nov. 4, 1865, p. 175).

successful at that port.[167] Meanwhile, the leading foreign firms at Shanghai gave their support by promising to carry out the same policy of demanding cash payment from the Chinese.[168]

But the foreign merchants' insistence on cash payment did not last long. By the end of 1866, because the cash payment system "failed to produce the beneficial results so frequently anticipated," the old practice of extending credit to the Chinese was restored. The Chinese were "again enabled to purchase goods from foreign hongs on credit." More importantly, the requirement for granting credit to the Chinese was not as strict as before, because the orders of the hong—not necessarily those of the native banks—became acceptable to the foreign traders.[169]

One reason for the failure of the cash payment movement was the resistance on the part of the Chinese merchants. Actually, as soon as this system was introduced, it encountered serious difficulties, because the Chinese merchants waged "long, steady, and vigorous resistance."[170] They insisted that the cash payment system should be bilateral, and they demanded "ready-money" payment when they sold tea and silk to the foreign merchants.[171] The compradors, who had been deprived of the opportunity to make extra money through the handling of native bank orders, also "endeavored to throw every possible obstacle in the way" of the success of the cash payment system.[172] At the same time, the taotai (intendant of a circuit) of Shanghai insisted in November 1865 on making the system of cash payment applicable to purchases of imports as well as to sales of produce.[173] The local official of Hankow also issued a proclamation in July 1867, prohibiting the sale of all produce to foreign hongs except on immediate cash payment.[174]

The foreign traders had several difficulties with a cash payment system. First, there was no way to enforce the agreement, especially concerning the penalty. Second, the foreign traders were concerned that the Chinese merchants might import directly from abroad if the cash pay-

167. Consul W. H. Medhurst (Hankow) to Rutherford Alcock (Peking), Mar. 3, 1866, FO 17/456.
168. *NCH*, Nov. 4, 1865, p. 175.
169. "The hong orders of three weeks' date are accepted in payment" (*NCH*, Feb. 22, 1867, p. 376).
170. *NCH*, Sept. 16, 1865, p. 146.
171. *NCH*, June 15, 1867, p. 107.
172. Consul W. H. Medhurst (Hankow) to Rutherford Alcock (Peking), Mar. 3, 1866, FO 17/456. Some compradors were reported to have spread rumors (*NCH*, Nov. 4, 1865, p. 175). For the comprador's vested interest in handling the native bank orders, see Yen-p'ing Hao, *Comprador*, pp. 94–95.
173. *NCH*, Nov. 4, 1865, p. 175.
174. *NCH*, July 22, 1867, p. 167.

ment system was strictly carried out.[175] Finally, immediate gains were often too attractive to resist.[176] In the final analysis, it was the market forces that counted. During the initial period of the cash payment system, the *North-China Herald* commented on September 16, 1865: "Any sudden crisis in the market for imports will impell the foreign merchants to disregard the agreement into which they have entered."[177] This sharp observation was borne out by the British consul at Hankow who reported on March 3, 1866, that this system "had a stagnating effect upon the import trade by limiting the sale of goods."[178] Consequently, the foreign combination failed miserably in Hankow. This system did not fare well in Kiukiang either, because "as soon as it was commenced, trade forsook the hands of foreign hongs, and went into those of native traders. Eventually three-month credit was the rule adopted."[179] At any rate, the foreign traders finally realized that "there was apparently only the choice of not doing any business at all, or doing a risky one."[180]

Actually, the foreign traders' cooperation at Hankow in the summer of 1866 was neither the first attempt to introduce the cash payment system into that port, nor was it the last. But all such attempts "had always fallen through whenever a cause for pressing sales had presented itself."[181] In early 1864, for instance, the principal foreign firms at Hankow came to an agreement that no sales of opium or manufactured goods should be booked except on receipt of a banker's order, due within three weeks, for the full value of the merchandise. No party could extend his term of credit without first giving due notice to the other parties to the agreement of his intention of doing so. This system worked smoothly until the spring of 1865 when the termination of the American Civil War caused a depression in the market for cotton manufactures and made holders anxious to realize their stocks. The agreement was then broken by several firms, which gave two-month credit to the Chinese purchasers. But these firms failed to live up to their promise of giving notice to other houses, and as a result, the cash payment system soon collapsed

175. *NCH*, Sept. 16, 1865, p. 146.
176. The British consul at Hankow wrote on this aspect in 1867: "It was found impossible to prevent certain parties to the agreement from deliberately ignoring it, wherever they found it to their interest so to do" (Report of Consul W. H. Medhurst, Hankow, 1867, FO 17/482).
177. *NCH*, Sept. 16, 1865, p. 146.
178. Consul W. H. Medhurst (Hankow) to Rutherford Alcock (Peking), Mar. 3, 1866, FO 17/456.
179. *NCH*, Aug. 5, 1867, p. 191.
180. Ibid.
181. *NCH*, Sept. 16, 1865, p. 146.

completely.[182] A similar effort to abolish the role of native bank orders in China's foreign trade ended in failure in 1910.[183]

At the Chinese end, the native merchants' demand for cash payment for their produce did not succeed either. In the summer of 1873, the tea and silk guilds of Shanghai adopted the policy of cash payment.[184] Members of the guilds agreed that tea and silk should only be delivered to foreign traders on the payment of cash before the departure of the vessel conveying the goods. As was the case with the foreign traders at Hankow in 1865–1866, this cash payment system was ineffective when the members of the guilds encountered sales pressure. The guilds finally yielded to the market forces and voluntarily cancelled the new policy in October.[185] Commenting on the central role of credit in China's foreign trade, an English merchant aptly summarized in 1867: "If you do away with credit, you do away with trade."[186]

THE RATE OF INTEREST

The rate of interest on private loans in traditional China was high, the normal monthly rate being 4 to 6 percent and the highest rate about 8 percent. In the thirteenth century, a monthly rate of 3 to 5 percent was considered reasonable, and occasionally one might charge as high as 10 percent. In general, the rate of interest on private loans dropped from about 6 percent per month in the T'ang period to 3 to 5 percent in the Sung, Yuan, and Ming periods. In the Ch'ing era, the interest rate was lower than that of previous times, with the monthly interest rate in pawnbroking being about 3 percent in the eighteenth century and a little over 2 percent in the nineteenth. The low rate was mainly due to the rise of the Shansi banks in the eighteenth century. Their good faith attracted both large deposits from private individuals and money from government treasuries, which frequently totaled eight to twenty times their capital. As a result, the interest rates in large cities were lowered substantially in the first part of the nineteenth century.[187]

Along the coast, especially in the trading ports, the rate of interest was even lower. In Canton during the 1825–1844 period, the prevailing rate of interest "with the best security, was 1 percent per month on running

182. Ibid.
183. Yang Yin-p'u, *Chin-yung*, p. 233.
184. *Shen pao*, TC 12/5/16, June 10, 1873.
185. *NCH*, Oct. 30, 1873, p. 367.
186. *NCH*, Aug. 5, 1867, p. 191.
187. Lien-sheng Yang, *Money and Credit*, pp. 95–100.

account, while 2 to 3 percent on temporary loans per month was common."[188] The rate further declined during the second half of the nineteenth century. The interest rate on private loans between the foreign mercantile houses and the Chinese merchants was on the average 1 percent per month, or 10 to 15 percent per annum. At Canton Augustine Heard & Co. obtained from Tongmow a one-year loan in September 1855 for $45,000 at the monthly rate of interest of 0.9 percent. Three months later another loan for $50,000 was arranged at 0.8 percent. E. M. Smith, an American merchant, in 1862 borrowed through his comprador Tls. 78,940 from the Chinese for which he paid 1 percent per month interest.[189] Appaey, a Chinese tea merchant at Amoy, was willing to pay 1 percent per month for a loan from Jardine's in 1863. The firm's Amoy office specified: "Appaey goes to Hongkong by this steamer. He wishes to apply to you for assistance next season by a loan to his tea hong of $10,000 for which he will pay 1% a month interest and give security."[190]

In January 1863, James Whittall loaned to Takee $260,000 at a monthly rate of interest of 1 percent for a period of several months.[191] This rate of interest remained unchanged in 1865.[192] Jardine's made a loan of Tls. 25,000 to Ekee in 1868 and charged him an annual interest rate of 10 percent.[193] Meanwhile, F. B. Johnson made a loan to Yakee at an annual interest rate of 12 percent.[194] Jardine's accounts show that by August 9, 1873, Yowloong owed the house Tls. 3,809. Both parties agreed to extend the loan to April 30, 1874, at an annual interest rate of 12 percent.[195] The account books of the firm's Shanghai office indicate that by April 1, 1874, the office made "silk advances" totaling Tls. 11,000 to Chinese merchants at an annual interest rate of 15 percent.[196] The interest rates were low not only for the loans made by the Western mercantile houses, but also for the loans made by the foreign banks. In 1865 the Hongkong and Shanghai Banking Corporation allowed an

188. Hunter, *Fan Kwae*, pp. 39–40.
189. Case 9, HC II; and *NCH*, Feb. 19, 1880, p. 147.
190. Jardine, Matheson & Co. (Amoy) to Jardine, Matheson & Co. (Hong Kong), Jan. 7, 1863, JMA.
191. (Shanghai) to Jardine, Matheson & Co. (Hong Kong), Jan. 8, 1863, JMA.
192. William Keswick (Shanghai) to Jardine, Matheson & Co. (Hong Kong), June 22, 1865, JMA.
193. F. B. Johnson (Shanghai) to Jardine, Matheson & Co. (Hong Kong), Sept. 11, 1868, JMA.
194. "I have debited this account with interest at 12 percent [per annum] and recent payments made by him only part [partly] cover the arrears of this charge. We have received Tls. 3,000 since June" (ibid.).
195. Shanghai, Apr. 30, 1874, Memoranda, JMA.
196. Shanghai, Apr. 1, 1874, Accounts, JMA.

annual rate of interest of 2 percent for the deposits and charged around
10 percent for its loans.[197]

Under special circumstances interest rates were high. First, as we
have shown, foreign houses charged more interest to the Chinese who
did not do business frequently with them. Second, interest rates increased when the surplus capital could not meet suddenly rising loan
demands. Under this condition, Jardine's Shanghai office claimed that it
"could easily have got from twenty to thirty percent" annual interest in
early September 1875. The office hastened to add, however, that such a
high rate was exceptional.[198] Finally, when the loans were made in the
form of bills or drafts, a high rate of interest had to be paid. Tong King-
sing applied for a loan at Hankow in 1868 in the form of a draft on
Shanghai, for which he paid a monthly interest rate of 3 percent. This
rate was substantially higher than the rate of loans in cash. Compared
with the market rate of 3.75 percent, however, Tong got a better deal
because he was the firm's Shanghai comprador.[199]

Several factors accounted for the low rates of interest in the treaty
ports. First, as foreign businessmen competed in earnest to make loans to
the Chinese, the rates of interest tended to remain low. Prominent
houses such as Jardine's, Dent's, and Lindsay's rivaled with one another
in advancing funds for upcountry purchases. Furthermore, after the sixties these mercantile houses also had to compete with the newly rising
foreign banks in providing loans to the Chinese. One letter of Jardine's
Shanghai office recorded this situation on September 28, 1875: "During
the last ten weeks . . . there were numerous applications for advances
on silk, tea and opium and also for advances at the wharves. Banks are
anxious to get this business. We may lose it if we do not accommodate
people."[200] It was exactly such rivalry that led to Jardine's opposition to
the founding of the Hongkong and Shanghai Banking Corporation in the
early sixties. After the establishment of the bank, some members of Jardine's sat on its board. Nevertheless, Jardine's found itself in close competition with the bank for over thirty years.[201] For the foreign merchants,

197. The bank advertised: "The Bank has this day commenced business. . . . Current
accounts are kept and interest allowed at the rate of 2% per annum" (*NCH*, Apr. 15, 1865,
p. 58).

198. Jardine, Matheson & Co. (Shanghai) to Jardine, Matheson & Co. (Hong Kong),
Sept. 28, 1875, JMA.

199. S. I. Gower, Jardine's representative at Hankow, commented on Tong's loan: "I
fear I shall not be able to do any more at this rate as I understand that 3¾% is being
freely given" (to Jardine, Matheson & Co. [Shanghai], Apr. 11, 1868, JMA).

200. Jardine, Matheson & Co. (Shanghai) to Jardine, Matheson & Co. (Hong Kong),
JMA.

201. LeFevour, p. 140.

these loans not only provided a profitable outlet for their surplus capital but also cultivated the friendship of the Chinese merchants. William Keswick noted in 1864 that timely loans could favorably influence "prominent men among the natives" and increase chances of doing business with them.[202]

Second, low interest rates prevailed in the treaty ports because these were the places where capital was relatively secure. In fact, Jardine's in 1864 had more confidence in the coastal Chinese than in the local authorities of Nagasaki, Japan; the house usually loaned to the former at a monthly interest rate of 1 percent but charged the latter 1.5 to 2 percent. In addition, Keswick thought that a Japanese loan would be safe only "with the precaution taken of having it made officially through the English Consulate."[203]

The third reason for the low interest rate along the coast was the way in which the security was handled. In the interior, a part of the interest represented handling charges. In 1882, for example, the pawnbrokers in villages and small towns of Liangkiang complained that the government ceiling of 2 percent per month was not adequate because they frequently received agricultural implements as pledges, which were of small value but required much handling and storage space.[204] In contrast, the security of Jardine's loans to the Chinese merchants, such as stock shares and title deeds of property, required only simple handling. Even the security in the form of warehouse-stored goods and shipping cargoes did not call for extra handling because, as noted above, the Chinese merchants had paid storage fees, shipping charges, and even insurance premiums.

Finally, the Ch'ing government was not a heavy borrower on the financial market. Although the government began to borrow from foreigners as early as 1861, large-scale borrowing did not start until 1895. Most of the foreign loans were used for military, administrative, and indemnity purposes. Furthermore, the rate of interest on the foreign loans contracted by the Ch'ing government in the nineteenth century was moderate, because almost all such loans were secured loans. The annual rate of interest was 8 to 9 percent for 1864–1886, and 5.3 to 7.0

202. (Shanghai) to James Whittall (Hong Kong), Oct. 14, 1864, JMA.
203. "I imagine a loan to the Japanese Government at Nagasaki would be safe, with the precaution taken of having it made officially through the English Consulate, and properly registered; and I fancy a high rate of interest would be paid, say 1½ c [to] 2 p. [percent] p. [per] month. You would oblige me by giving me as early as possible your instructions in the matter that I may give an answer to Glover and Co." (Keswick [Shanghai] to James Whittall [Hong Kong], Oct. 7, 1864, JMA). Keswick's suggestion was later approved.
204. Lien-sheng Yang, *Money and Credit*, p. 99.

percent for 1886–1894.[205] Consequently, the low interest rates on the coast were an advantage to private business, which could find credit without having to compete with the government in paying high interest charges.

The low interest rates prevailing along the coast are especially noteworthy when we contrast them with the exorbitant rates in the interior where risks were high and the market was far from being perfect. During the late nineteenth century and the early twentieth century, an annual rate of 40 to 80 percent was common in the interior, while a rate of 150 to 200 percent was not unknown.[206] The prevailing rate in Hopei and Shantung was 36 percent in the eighteenth century, and this rate remained virtually the same (26 to 48 percent) as late as the 1930s.[207] From the 1730s to the 1930s, whereas the monthly rates calculated as an average for a year appear to have been quite constant in these two northern provinces,[208] the rate of interest tended to be lower on the southern coast as time progressed. Even though interest rates charged by modern Chinese banks were considerably lower than those prevailing in traditional China,[209] it was difficult for the peasants in the rural area to obtain bank loans, because they generally had to use land as collateral against their loans.[210]

In short, credit along China's coast was readily available in the nineteenth century, and the rate of interest was low. The prevailing annual rate of around 12 percent in the mid-century was somewhat higher than that of contemporary Europe (between 6 and 8 percent),[211] but it was conspicuously lower than rates in traditional China (usually 40 percent or more) and in China's interior in modern times (35 to 50 percent or more).

The development of credit along the coast meets Braudel's expecta-

---

205. Chi-ming Hou, *Foreign Investment*, pp. 211–12.
206. R. H. Tawney, *Land and Labour in China* (London, 1932), p. 62. Tawney goes so far as to say that "in reality, indeed, no market rate can be said to exist."
207. Ramon H. Myers, *The Chinese Peasant Economy* (Cambridge, Mass., 1970), pp. 243–44. The interest rates in the regions of the treaty ports were lower than those in other regions. Calculations are mine.
208. Ibid., p. 241.
209. Interest rates ranged from 12 to 15 percent per annum around 1910 (Wang Ching-yü, *Chung-kuo chin-tai kung-yeh shih tzu-liao, ti erh chi*, II, 101b).
210. In the early twentieth century, land was the principal form of security used by peasants in Hopei and Shantung to obtain credit, and, in some countries, nearly three-quarters of the peasants borrowed in this fashion (Myers, *Peasant Economy*, p. 241).
211. The rate of interest in Europe varied between 6 and 8 percent around the 1840s (Norman S. B. Gras, *Business and Capitalism* [New York, 1939], p. 148).

tions, because modern capitalism can indeed "find its tools" here. The leading instruments of credit, in order of their importance, were bills of exchange on London, promissory notes, letters of credit, bank notes, and checks for the Western traders on the one hand, and native bank orders, private paper notes, drafts, and transfer accounts for the Chinese merchants on the other. One of the most important economic consequences of the easy financial flows was the low rate of interest.

CHAPTER FIVE

The Widening
of the Market:
The Opium Trade

The flourishing import trade gave eloquent testimony to the widening of the market, and the leading commodity was opium—only referred to as "drug" in the correspondence files of British and American firms. The trade is highly significant for several reasons. The first was its sheer volume. It was no petty smuggling trade, but probably the world's largest commerce of the time in any single commodity. Second, the British government in India monopolized the sale and manufacture of opium in its dominions after 1797, and the monopoly came, in the next century, to yield one-seventh of the total revenue of British India. Third, after the 1820s opium was the most important staple of the country trade, which provided the much-needed funds for the East India Company to buy tea at Canton. Fourth, it was a private trade, giving rise to the Western merchant community in China. Fifth, it was an illegal trade conducted outside the Canton system. Finally, its increasingly detrimental effects on China economically and socially prompted sporadic anti-opium sentiments in the West (e.g., Donald Matheson resigned from Jardine's out of conscience over the opium trade) and strong anti-opium policy in China. Various aspects of the opium trade precipitated the Opium War (1839–1842), which symbolizes the beginning of modern China.[1]

1. In the introduction of *A Practical Treatise on the China and Eastern Trade* (London, 1836), J. Phipps, the contemporary compiler of commercial handbooks, held that the extent of the trade in opium "can scarcely be matched in any one article of consumption in any part of the world" (cited in Greenberg, pp. 104–5; see also pp. 106–7). After six years as a partner of Jardine, Matheson & Co., James Matheson's nephew Donald left the firm in 1849 (Keswick, *Thistle*, pp. 66–67, 264). For a detailed study of the opium trade and its effect on China, see Peter Ward Fay, *The Opium War, 1840–1842* (Chapel Hill, N.C., 1975).

Although the rise of the opium trade can be traced back to the eighteenth century, it assumed a new form in the 1820s. After 1821, the trade centered on Lintin Island as a consequence of an imperial edict that closed Macao and Whampoa to opium smuggling; this started the "outer anchorage" system. And the volume increased by leaps and bounds. The two "grand staples" of the country trade were Indian ràw cotton and opium, but after 1823 the value of opium imports consistently exceeded that of cotton, and opium became the single most important commodity. The increasing use of new money and the expansion of credit on the Kwangtung coast were, in part, responses to this new development.

Opium trade thrived on the coast in the late Ch'ing. Plentiful foreign supply and ready domestic demand reinforced each other, and preventive efforts were handicapped by two major factors. Geographically, eastern China, with its long, jagged coastline, was exposed to foreign smuggling from the sea. Administratively, the decline of the Ch'ing state manifested itself especially in the inefficiency of its bureaucracy and the prevailing social disorder. Although the foreign merchants were equipped with faster and better-armed ships, their Chinese counterparts were more numerous and better-financed. All of these factors made opium smuggling an easy business. Legalized after 1858, the trade continued to flourish, reaching its peak in the 1870s. Opium was first imported from Turkey, Persia, and India. Turkish opium was gradually replaced in China after the 1830s by Indian opium, which dominated the Chinese market from that time on. Malwa, Benares, and Patna (or Behar) were the principal localities in India in which poppy was cultivated, and every chest of drug exported from India bore one of these names.[2]

BUSINESS IN THE OLD CANTON DAYS

Macao was the first principal opium market, because the Portuguese were the first to import opium to China in any sizable quantity. Attempting to confine the trade solely to Macao, in 1764 the government of Goa ordered that Portuguese merchants not be allowed to buy any opium from foreign vessels stationed on the outskirts of Macao and prohibited their ships from taking any drugs belonging to other nationalities. As the

---

Frederic Wakeman, Jr., "The Canton Trade and the Opium War," in John K. Fairbank, ed., *The Cambridge History of China*, vol. 10, *Late Ch'ing, 1800–1911, Part 1* (Cambridge, England, 1978), pp. 163–212, is the latest authoritative treatment of the subject.

2. Allen, *Opium Trade*, p. 8.

Portuguese merchants were short of capital, the Chinese opium market was supplied by two other means. The first was the delivery of opium on the Kwangtung coast, to be picked up by the Cantonese merchants, on orders arranged at Macao. The second was the rise of Whampoa as an opium trade center as a result of efforts on the part of British merchants.[3]

The plan of sending opium from Bengal to China was first suggested in 1767 by a Mr. Watson to a council of representatives of the British East India Company held at Calcutta. The company launched a small experimental venture into the opium trade in 1773, and it proved successful. From that time on, Whampoa was a center of opium trade in China. After some initial problems, the company in 1794 stationed one of its opium ships there for one year and sold out her cargo. After the Ch'ing prohibition edict of 1796, the company refrained from taking a direct part in the opium trade, but its Select Committee actively assisted private traders.[4] During the first two decades of the nineteenth century, Whampoa outdistanced Macao as an opium market, though the trade encountered difficulties from pirates as well as from the Ch'ing authorities.

Partners of the predecessor firms of Jardine, Matheson & Co. engaged heavily in opium trade. Alexander Shank of Reid, Beale & Co. sold opium at Macao for $560 to $590 a chest in 1801. In that year Thomas Beale sold 20 chests to Manhop, a Cantonese merchant.[5] For the most part opium trade was conducted at Macao instead of Whampoa in order to avoid possible detention by Chinese officials.[6] For this reason opium was consigned to the British firms at Canton in Portuguese ships. When some inferior Malwa proved unsalable in Macao in 1805 it was brought up to Whampoa, which led to a dispute between the Portuguese authorities in Macao and the British East India Company.[7] The dispute, however, was short-lived, and Beale & Co. regularly employed Portuguese agents in the Macao opium market in the early 1810s.[8] William Jardine and James Matheson did virtually nothing but opium trade during their first years in China in the early 1820s.

---

3. Hsin-pao Chang, p. 18; Fairbank, *Trade and Diplomacy*, I, 66; and Dermigny, *La Chine et l'occident*, III, 937–70, 1252–74.

4. Allen, *Opium Trade*, p. 12; and Hsin-pao Chang, p. 18.

5. Letter Book, 1801, JMA.

6. Various letters from Charles Magniac, of Beale and Magniac (Canton), to Mackintosh & Co. (Calcutta), 1804, Letter Book, JMA.

7. Beale & Magniac (Canton) to Fairlie & Co. (Calcutta), Dec. 3, 1805, Letter Book, JMA.

8. Beale & Co. (Canton) to Fairlie & Co. (Calcutta), July 26, 1811, Letter Book, JMA.

Some hong merchants are known to have engaged secretly in the opium trade. Although an imperial edict was issued in 1780 prohibiting the consumption and sale of opium, two years later the hong merchant Sinqua, at the low price of $210 (Spanish) per chest, bought the entire cargo of 1,601 chests of Patna opium on board the *Nonsuch* of the East India Company. On April 13, 1820, the governor-general and the Hoppo issued an edict at Canton requiring the hong merchants to search all foreign ships for opium and to bear full responsibility for any ships they passed. The hong merchants then wrote to the Honorable Company asking it not to import opium through the official ships, but they still traded in opium occasionally. In 1821 the hong merchant Poonequa was fined $5,000 by the officials in Canton because opium was found in one of the British ships that he secured.[9]

ILLEGAL TRADING CENTERS AROUND CANTON

From 1821 to the Opium War in 1839, the opium trade was centered at Lintin Island in the bay at the mouth of the Pearl River. This can be traced back to 1820, when an imperial edict required hong merchants to certify that the foreign ships they secured carried no opium. Both Macao and Whampoa were thus closed to opium smuggling by the Canton authorities in 1821. Foreign merchants now had to discharge all opium into ships outside Chinese jurisdiction. Their ships then proceeded with the remaining cargo to Whampoa and Canton to engage in legitimate trade. Hence, large armed vessels reposed at anchor throughout the year and constituted a floating depot of storehouses for receiving opium in large quantities from ships bringing it from India and dealing it out in chests and cases to the Chinese junks. Foreign merchants gradually established permanent, stationary receiving hulks at Lintin Island in the outer seas of Macao during the northeastern monsoon from October to March, moving them for safety to Cumsingmoon near Hong Kong during the southwestern monsoon from April to September. For easy delivery, opium was repacked in mat bags with rattan lashings and marked with the new owner's private sign and the weight of the contents.[10]

9. David Edward Owen, *British Opium Policy in China and India* (New Haven, Conn., 1934), pp. 53, 56–58, 65; Hsin-pao Chang, p. 221; and Morse, *Chronicles*, III, 358 and IV, 16, 41, 49, 55.

10. Allen, *Opium Trade*, p. 12; Morse, *Conflict*, p. 178; Geoffrey Robley Sayer, *Hong Kong* (London, 1937), p. 12; and Connolly, pp. 164, 208.

There were about five opium vessels in Lintin in the early 1820s. This number increased to twenty-five after 1826 when official patrol boats were introduced by Governor-General Li Hung-pin. Because they received about 36,000 taels a month, the officials in charge of these boats tolerated opium smuggling. The opium ships stationed at Lintin in 1830 included the British ships *Merope, Samaranny,* and *Jannisena*; the American ships *Scatter-Good, Tartar, Lintin, Margaret Forbes,* and *Terrier*; the Portuguese ships *Don Manuel* and *Letitia*; the Danish brig *Dansborg* and the French ship *La Rose.* The whole business of the transport of opium between Lintin and Canton was smoothly managed in the 1830s, and the ships were seldom bothered.[11]

Opium-smuggling was attractive to the foreign merchants, because legitimate trade was loaded with arbitrary and irregular charges and with galling restrictions. Opium, being prohibited, could not be taxed. Then too, because opium vessels were forbidden from entering port, opium could not be paid for except by hard cash in advance or on delivery. Moreover, because of the demand for it, it commanded high prices. It presented, therefore, a tempting way of escape from the rigid Canton system. The importation of Indian opium continued to grow, and its consumption rate and value in China from 1821 to 1831 can be seen in table 8.

During the 1830s, the amount of opium-smuggling between Lintin and Canton increased, with many foreign vessels operating as "passenger boats." There were some fifty of a large size, from 30 to 300 tons, outside the Bogue, and about thirty inside the river. The *Chinese Repository*, a British newspaper in Canton, described the busy traffic on the Pearl River: "Almost every part of the river, from the Bogue on the east to Fati on the west of the city, is made the theatre of the traffic."[12] After the winter of 1836, when foreign ships were forbidden to anchor at Cumsingmoon and the prohibition was enforced by the erection of a shore battery guarded by a naval squadron, the opium ships were mainly confined to the station at Lintin until the Treaty of Nanking was signed.[13]

William Jardine arrived at Canton in 1822 and, as a free agent, began to sell opium for Magniac & Co., which he joined as a partner in 1825. This lucrative business with relative safety prompted him to write in 1830 to a friend in England, urging him to invest in opium, "the safest

11. Liang Chia-pin, *Shih-san hang,* p. xxv; Allen, *Opium Trade,* pp. 13–14.
12. June 1838, cited in Morse, *Conflict,* p. 183.
13. Eitel, p. 77.

TABLE 8.   AMOUNT AND VALUE OF INDIAN OPIUM
CONSUMED IN CHINA, 1821–1831
(MEXICAN DOLLARS)

Season	Bengal[a]		Malwa		Total	
	Chests	Value	Chests	Value	Chests	Value
1821–22	2,910	6,038,250	1,718	2,276,350	4,628	8,314,600
1822–23	1,822	2,828,930	4,000	5,160,000	5,822	7,988,930
1823–24	2,910	4,656,000	4,172	3,559,100	7,082	8,515,100
1824–25	2,655	3,119,625	6,000	4,500,000	8,655	7,619,625
1825–26	3,442	3,141,755	6,179	4,466,450	9,621	7,608,205
1826–27	3,661	3,667,565	6,308	5,921,520	9,969	9,610,085
1827–28	5,114	5,105,081	4,361	5,227,000	9,475	10,382,141
1828–29	5,960	5,604,235	7,171	6,928,880	13,132	12,533,115
1829–30	7,143	6,149,577	6,857	5,907,580	14,000	12,057,157
1830–31	6,660	4,789,794	12,100	7,110,237	18,760	12,900,031
Average	4,228	4,510,081	5,887	5,105,712	10,114	9,752,899

Source: Greenberg, British Trade and the Opening of China, p. 220. Calculations are mine.
[a] Includes Patna and Benares.

and most gentlemanlike speculation I am aware of."[14] He joined James
Matheson and formed Jardine, Matheson & Co. in 1832. The house was
considerably involved in opium trade during its early years, and in 1837
Jardine was delighted to note that "opium is the only ready money article
sold in China."[15]

The whole opium business was an international one. It was reported
in the late 1820s that "Chinese and Japanese buyers were holding ren-
dezvous with opium clippers in the passageways among the [Kwang-
tung] islands."[16] Meanwhile, the Western merchants were assisted by a
host of local people. For example, the business of unpacking, weighing,
and repacking the opium at Lintin was "attended to rapidly by expert
crews who were mostly lascars and Filipinos."[17] Many Chinese also
assisted the Western merchants; compradors, shroffs (money changers),
carpenters, cooks, and other servants were usually Cantonese.

14. Apr. 30, 1830, William Jardine Private Letter Book, JMA.
15. May 29, 1837, William Jardine Private Letter Book, JMA.
16. Connolly, p. 164.
17. Ibid., p. 208.

Some of the hong merchants continued to trade in opium during the 1820s and the 1830s. For example, Houqua, the chief hong merchant, occasionally engaged in this business with the American merchants, particularly with Perkins & Co. and Russell & Co.[18] But the hong merchants' involvement in the opium trade was minimal; those who occasionally engaged in the trade were exceptions. In response to Governor-General Li Hung-pin's inquiry, Wu Shou-ch'ang and Lu Wen-chin, two prominent hong merchants, stated in 1829 that all the ships they secured did not, and would not, carry opium and that they would be willing to accept any punishment if they did not live up to their promise. Indeed, the great majority of the Chinese smugglers were small traders who were not members of the Cohong.[19]

Until 1842 the haunts of the opium trade were Macao, Whampoa, Lintin, and Cumsingmoon, all in the neighborhood of Canton. It is not surprising, then, that Cantonese merchants dominated the trade. The formal transaction was mainly carried out at Canton in the foreign factories where local traders purchased from various foreign merchants. Because the opium was not stored at Canton, foreign merchants as a rule would give an order on an opium clipper or receiving ship waiting on the high seas or at various "outer anchorages." With these written orders (chops) for opium, the Chinese merchants would then pick up opium with their own ships. To ensure a safe trip, they were usually equipped with fast boats and modern weapons.[20] According to H. H. Lindsay's first-hand estimate, there were thirty to forty-five Chinese opium boats on the Pearl River in the 1820s, each pulling from thirty to fifty oars. After having bribed officials, these boats "piled up and down the river in open day, passing to and fro, in front of the forts and government cruisers, without any notice whatever being taken of them."[21]

THE COASTAL SYSTEM

Attracted by good profits, some enterprising Chinese merchants initiated a new distribution network in the early 1820s, known as the "coastal system," by which they sold opium up the east coast. Prior to

18. Forbes Papers, in the possession of Crosby Forbes, Milton, Mass.
19. Liang Chia-pin, *Shih-san hang*, pp. 10–11, 139.
20. J. B. Connolly writes: "Several buyers might go together by a smug boat, which would be a large, red-painted junk with sixty or seventy oarsmen and enormous mat sails. The smug boats were armed with swivel guns and muskets, and contained comfortable quarters for the buyers" (p. 207).
21. Lindsay, *War with China*, p. 10.

1821 a small number of Chinese merchants from Fukien, Chekiang, and Kiangsu went to Canton to buy opium and then shipped it back for sale. To compete with them, some Cantonese merchants first purchased opium from one of the smuggling centers near Canton and then transshipped it to coastal junks to be sailed north to Swatow or Amoy. By doing this, they not only avoided the official squeeze at Canton, but also were able to sell at higher prices than those prevailing near the source of supply in the south.[22]

James Matheson tried out the "East Coast of China," sailing for Chinchew (Ch'üan-chou, Fukien) in June 1823. As a consequence of this trip, he wrote that "a prospect was opened sufficiently encouraging to induce us to hazard a repetition."[23] Two opium cargoes of that year brought in $212,000. According to him, this was the first attempt to effect sales on the coast without prearrangement. Other British firms, such as Dent & Co., and Portuguese merchants from Macao soon followed the lead, causing keen competition to emerge.[24] Meanwhile, in the south around Canton, opium trade grew "into a complete system of delivering . . . to the dealers on credit" in 1822–1823.[25]

The coastal system became a regular practice in the 1830s. The East India Company adopted a new policy that remarkably increased the production of opium in 1831, and China was flooded with cheap opium. Jardine's responded by revitalizing the coastal trade on a large scale. In 1832 William Jardine first sent two small brigs up the East Coast, then sent large vessels: the *Jamesina* to Foochow, the *John Biggar* to Chinchow, and the *Sylph* farther north to Shanghai and Tientsin. The first two trips were singularly successful, and the partners put other vessels to work, both east and west of Canton. For this purpose, through purchasing and building, Jardine's quickly formed a fleet of ships, including the *Red Rover*, and the *Mor*, two of the celebrated opium clippers of the time. By 1838, in addition to the regular stations at Namoa (Nan-ao), Tungshan, Chinchow, and Foochow, Jardine's coastal system extended one step north, as James Matheson wrote: "The coast trade flourishes to a wish, and we have lately extended it to Chusan."[26] In the late thirties and early forties, every receiving ship of Jardine, Matheson and Co. had

22. Greenberg, pp. 136–41; LeFevour, p. 14; and Liang Chia-pin, p. xxv.
23. Matheson letter, Sept. 24, 1823, Yrissari & Co. Papers, JMA.
24. Ibid., Feb. 12, 1824.
25. Ibid., Sept. 24, 1823.
26. Matheson (Canton) to Alexander Grant (England), May 1, 1838, James Matheson Private Letter Book, JMA. For Jardine's coastal system, see William Jardine's letters in 1832–1833 (Private Letter Book, JMA).

an opium comprador and an interpreter-shroff, usually coming from
Kwangtung. The firm's head office in Hong Kong had a sizable Chinese
staff for the auxiliary services of the opium trade, such as ship repairs,
warehousing, and accounting.[27]

In 1832 Hugh Hamilton Lindsay conducted a market survey on behalf of the East India Company on the ship *Lord Amherst*. The coastal
system was so popular by then that, at every place where the ship
stopped, Chinese merchants expected opium to be aboard and could hardly
be convinced of the contrary.[28] A well-informed writer in the *Chinese
Repository* described the opium trade along the coast in 1838: "The Chinese
coast from Macao to Chusan is now the constant cruising ground of twenty
opium ships. The waters of Canton are converted into one grand rendez-
vous for more than thirty opium boats."[29] It was profitable for the foreign
merchants to sell opium in this way, because they could get much better
prices than could be had at Canton. The price difference was from $100 to
$150 per chest, and sometimes even higher.[30]

Many Chinese along the coast made a living by engaging in the
opium trade in one form or another. A case in point was the activity
around Macao in 1838, where, besides several foreign houses engaged in
the sale of opium on a large scale, fifty or sixty smaller dealers distributed it by the catty (cake). The preparation of the drug for smoking
and its introduction into the interior, under every ingenious cover, gave
employment to more than ten times that number of Chinese.[31] Another
example was Namoa, one of those coastal stations on the border between
Kwangtung and Fukien. Warehouse ships were naturally stationed there
to serve as a depot of supplies for the brigs and schooners. Soon the
American schooner *Rose*, one of Russell & Co.'s opium ships, came to
Namoa with 300 chests. Some of them had been sold at Canton for delivery at Namoa, others taken to try the market.[32] In 1838 one of the
Chinese junks at Namoa had an order on the *Rose* for $150,000 worth of
opium. The merchant who held that order "unfolded it from a cotton
handkerchief, passed it calmly over, smoked an unhurried pipeful of
tobacco, and drank a few cups of tea while the opium was being handed
up from the hold of the schooner to his waiting boats."[33]

27. June 4, 1844, Coastal Letter Book, JMA.
28. H. H. Lindsay, *Report of Proceedings on a Voyage to the Northern Ports of China in the Ship
Lord Amherst* (London, 1834).
29. Cited in Allen, p. 14.
30. Morse, *Conflict*, p. 183.
31. Allen, p. 14.
32. Hunter, *Fan kwae*, p. 66.
33. Connolly, p. 212.

Chinese opium merchants at Namoa traded not only on the high seas, but also on the land. The British traveler Robert Fortune gives a vivid account of how the Chinese followed the movements of the foreign receiving ships. In the early 1840s, some of these ships visited the port, and hundreds of local people gathered on the coast where they erected huts and markets for supplying the ships and purchasing opium: "Whenever the ships moved to any other anchorage in the vicinity, the whole of the inhabitants, houses, market, and all, moved along with them." When Fortune returned to the same place a few months afterward, he found that, as "the change of station had taken place, not a vestige of the little village remained: men, women, and children, with their huts, boats, and all that belonged to them, had followed the ships, and had again squatted opposite to them on the beach."[34]

The opium trade along the coast was thus, in the main, a collaboration among the Western and Chinese merchants. The active business on Lintin Island and at other "outer anchorages," together with the extensive coastal system, constantly augmented the imported quantity. Foreign opium shipments to China grew from 4,570 chests in the season 1800–1801 to 40,200 chests in the season 1838–1839, increasing approximately nine times in the period of thirty-nine years. This increase can be seen from the average annual imports (in chests) between 1800 and 1839:[35]

Period	Amount
1800–1809	3,871
1810–1819	4,568
1820–1829	10,311
1830–1839	23,941

ECONOMIC CONSEQUENCES:
DEFLATION AND RECESSION

As a result of the opium trade, by the late 1820s, China experienced an unfavorable balance of trade virtually for the first time in her history. This produced in turn a net flow of specie out of the country.[36]

34. *Wanderings*, pp. 31–32.
35. Greenberg, p. 221; calculations are mine. For similar but less comprehensive figures, see Morse, *Conflict*, p. 540.
36. China's trade deficit seems to have disappeared temporarily in the late 1840s, and the trade balance turned again in her favor for the next decade because of the rapid growth in the export of tea and silk (Yeh-chien Wang, "The Secular Trend of Prices during the Ch'ing Period, 1644–1911," *Journal of the Institute of Chinese Studies of the University of Hong Kong*, 5.2 [1972]).

Many scholars seem to have underestimated the amount of silver outflow.[37] According to a conservative estimate, there was a net inflow of $74,700,000 from 1801 to 1826, but a net outflow of $133,700,000 from 1827 to 1849.[38] Given the fact that China's silver stock was around 1 billion dollars in the early nineteenth century and that one-third of it was in circulation, the massive exodus of silver represents a sharp reduction in China's money supply.[39]

A consequence of the shortage of monetary stock was that prices, in terms of silver, collapsed. An index number of retail prices in terms of silver for twelve food and handicraft products in Chihli Province in the first half of the nineteenth century, shows a general and often precipitously downward movement. The index number was around the 100 level (the average price for 1801 being 100) from 1801 to 1815, but down to 92 in 1816, 85 in 1820, and 55 in 1850. In other words, the level of prices went down by about one-half from 1816 to 1850. Other large commercial centers, such as Soochow and Hankow, experienced similar price falls.[40]

A serious effect of deflation on the economy was the conspicuous contraction of business activities. The junk trade showed signs of weakness. Feng Kuei-fen, a scholar-reformer, depicted the business depression in southern Kiangsu in the 1840s: "All great and wealthy merchants have gone bankrupt, and businesses of all kinds have decreased by 50 to 60 percent."[41] The sagging demand in the commercial centers affected the rural economy. The well-informed scholar Pao Shin-ch'en noted in 1846 that "peasants incur losses though crops of mulberry trees and cotton are abundant. They suffer economic hardship because of slacking market demand. All these can be attributed to the rising value of silver which is in turn caused by the scarcity of silver."[42] Deflation also increased the

37. They include David Edward Owen, H. B. Morse, and John K. Fairbank. Michael Greenberg stresses the issue of trade balance; his *British Trade*, p. 142, states that, based on the British official documents, between 1829 and 1840 nearly $56 million went out of China while only $7.33 million of silver was imported. But these figures do not reflect the activities of the non-British (especially the Parsees and the Portuguese) in the opium trade. Moreover, taking advantage of the silver dollars' premium in China, some Western merchants made profits by shipping silver dollars into China in exchange for larger amounts of silver bullion for export (P'eng Hsin-wei, p. 502).

38. Yü Chieh-ch'iung, *I-ch'i-ling-ling i-chiu-san-ch'i nien Chung-kuo yin-huo shu ch'u ju ti i-ko ku-chi* (Changsha, 1940), pp. 18–24, cited in Yeh-chien Wang, "Prices," II, 1572.

39. These are Wang Yeh-chien's estimates; see his *Huo-pi yü yin-hang*, p. 27.

40. Yeh-chien Wang, "Prices," II, 1554–55, and "Evolution," pp. 444–45.

41. *Hsien-chih-t'ang chi* (1876), 11.30–35, cited in Yeh-chien Wang, *Land Taxation*, p. 115.

42. Pao Shih-ch'en, *An Wu ssu-chung* (1872 preface), 26.37b, cited in Yeh-chien Wang, "Evolution," p. 444.

hardship of taxation, because it compelled the peasants to relinquish more of their crops in order to pay the same amount of taxes as before.

Two factors exacerbated the situation. First, the appreciation of silver vis-à-vis copper cash drove much silver out of circulation into being hoarded. Second, the issuing of paper notes by private concerns without regulation by the monetary authorities had a debilitating effect on the economy. A change in basic or reserve money against note issue brought about multiple changes in the money supply. Consequently, the reduction in silver caused a sharp contraction of silver notes in circulation, which in turn aggravated the business recession. It is thus clear that the enormous outflow of silver that resulted from the opium trade dealt a heavy blow to China's economy as evidenced by falling prices and the recession during the second quarter of the nineteenth century. It was under these circumstances that the Taiping uprising erupted.[43]

OPIUM-SMUGGLING UNDER THE TREATY SYSTEM

China was defeated by Great Britain in the Opium War of 1839–1842, but the Treaty of Nanking in 1842 did not mention opium. Although the opium trade remained illegal, it thrived nonetheless.

EXPANSION OF TRADE

Generally, the opium trade encountered difficulties during the years between the Treaty of Nanking in 1842 and the legalization of opium in 1858. The social and economic chaos resulting from the Taiping uprising reduced the purchasing power of the Chinese, especially those of the coastal provinces, and the competition between Chinese guilds and Western firms made it difficult for them to cooperate. (This cooperation developed only after the 1860s.)

Nevertheless, due to various factors, opium trade thrived under the new system. First, on the part of the Ch'ing state, the government relaxed its prohibition policy after the war, and many officials continued to facilitate the trade through connivance or active participation.[44] Second,

43. Yeh-chien Wang argues that, because the business recession hurt South China most severely, the Taiping movement started in the south ("Evolution," p. 445).

44. Rev. V. M. Lowrie, an American missionary on China's coast, wrote on opium in late 1843: "The Chinese officers make no effort whatever to prevent its introduction, and I saw opium pipes openly exposed for sale in the streets. A few years ago, it would have been

the Chinese compradors also helped in the expansion of the opium trade. After 1842 the foreign merchants were allowed by law to employ a Chinese staff headed by the comprador. Most of the compradors were Cantonese and went with the foreign merchants to the newly opened treaty ports after 1842. They became essential to the Western agency houses for conducting business, including the opium business.[45]

The Chinese merchants' guilds, especially those of Canton and Swatow, also played an active role.[46] Finally and ironically, it was often safer for the foreign traders to smuggle than to trade legally. For example, in 1846, having occasion to reproach Ch'i-ying for the mobbing of the Canton factories in July, John F. Davis was able to contrast the insecurity of foreign merchants established legally at a treaty port with the complete immunity of smugglers at Namoa.[47] Under these circumstances, the imports of Indian opium to China increased from 15,619 chests in 1840 to 62,882 chests in 1859, and increase of more than fourfold in two decades. The average annual import also shows a steady increase during this period. It was 26,825 chests in 1840–1844 and 35,082 chests in 1845–1849, but it increased to 50,438 chests in 1850–1854 and 61,827 chests in 1855–1859.[48]

The number of opium-receiving ships continued to increase along the coast under the treaty system. They anchored at each of the treaty ports just outside the limits of the port, where, on delivering orders signed by foreign merchants, opium was openly transferred to Chinese craft and imported into China, as in the old Lintin days.[49] By the mid-forties, for example, one of the big foreign firms in Canton (probably Jardine, Matheson & Co.) employed about fifty various vessels, ships, barks, schooners, and brigs, while another house had about thirty.[50] Rev. W. M. Lowrie, an American missionary, wrote in his journal while sailing along the coast in 1843: "It is almost impossible to find a vessel going up the coast which does not carry opium."[51]

---

almost as much as a Chinaman's life was worth, to have been detected in the sale of anything used in consuming the prohibited article" (Allen, *Opium Trade*, p. 15).

45. Yen-p'ing Hao, *Comprador*, pp. 22–36, 48–54, 173–74.
46. LeFevour, p. 24.
47. Sayer, p. 159.
48. Morse, *Conflict*, p. 556. Calculations are mine.
49. Sayer, p. 158.
50. Allen, p. 15.
51. Ibid.

In the mid-forties the *Mazeppa*, a schooner of 130 tons, once carried on board $500,000, the proceeds of opium sold on the coast, from the northeastern coast to Hong Kong.[52] In a letter dated September 27, 1849, S. Wells Williams wrote from Canton: "The opium trade is thriving, and from fifteen to sixteen millions of dollars leave China annually for this drug alone."[53] The directories of the treaty ports of 1855 openly listed the names of the opium-receiving ships stationed on China's coast, the officers in charge, and the names of the firms to which they belonged.[54]

Jardine archives clearly demonstrate that the British, especially the two gigantic houses of Jardine, Matheson & Co. and Dent & Co., continued to play a leading role in the opium trade after 1842. In 1843 Jardine's had five clippers on the Indian run and six on the coast, with receiving ships at Whampoa, Namoa, Tienpak (Tien-pai, south of Macao), Chinchew, Amoy, Chusan, and Woosung.[55] Alexander Matheson, who became head of Jardine's when James Matheson returned home, wrote optimistically on July 31, 1843: "The drug trade continues to prosper."[56] In 1845 the house maintained fifteen receiving ships, with one at Hong Kong and fourteen along the coast. In addition, there were four clippers to carry supplies between them. This coastal system cost the firm annually between $250,000 to $300,000, an enormous amount at the time.[57] Jardine's coastal system was well institutionalized after 1845. The coast was divided into a southern station and an eastern station, each supplied with ten to fifteen receiving ships during the fifties and sixties.[58]

In 1846 there were about fifty foreign ships engaging exclusively in the opium trade; Jardine's and Dent's each had about fifteen. Other foreign firms had fewer ships: Russell's with seven; Burn, Macivar & Co. with six; Gilman's with three; and Pyver's with two. Of the fifteen ships that Jardine's owned, five were employed to convey opium between India and China, and a large receiving ship of 700 tons was anchored all the year round at Hong Kong. One each was stationed at Amoy, Namoa, Chimmo Bay, and Whampoa. The remaining five clippers were plying between Hong Kong and the coastal stations. The *Lanrick*, one of the five ships going between India and China, once carried 1,250 chests

52. R. M. Martin, II, 259.
53. Allen, p. 17.
54. Morse, *Conflict*, p. 541.
55. B-2, JMA.
56. Alexander Matheson Private Letter Book, JMA.
57. Mar. 5, 1846, Private Letter Book, JMA.
58. Hong Kong to coast, vols. 1–5, Coastal Letter Book, JMA.

of Bengal opium valued at £200,000.[59] In 1858 two British receiving ships moored in each of the outer harbors of Swatow, Amoy, Chimmo, Chinchew, Foochow, and Ningpo.[60]

The Americans started to ship Turkish opium to China in 1804. The year 1821 witnessed a turning point in Sino-American commercial relations, because after this year the American traders willingly followed the lead of the British private merchants. The main Boston firm, Russell & Co., led the American opium trade, and its share in Indian opium traffic considerably increased after the mid-thirties.[61] Heard papers indicate that this American firm, compared with Jardine's and Russell's, traded in opium on a much smaller scale. Heard's sometimes imported opium directly from India, and their largest opium dealings were with Jamsetjee Jeejeebhoy, one of the most important Parsee firms in India.[62] When the firm was not an agent in importing the drug from India, it often bought and sold opium as a commodity to take advantage of the market at different treaty ports. The firm also peddled opium along the coast in small boats.[63]

TRADING CENTERS ON THE COAST

Jardine papers indicate that the most important centers of opium trade were on the Kwangtung coast and that, after the Treaty of Nanking, Canton continued to be a major center. In time of heavy demand, foreign firms at Canton often bought opium from Cantonese brokers and then reshipped it to the interior or other treaty ports for sale. Joseph Jardine, for instance, wrote from Canton on January 7, 1855, that a merchant in Canton named Ehing had purchased Malwa from Sassoon's for Russell & Co. at $460 per chest, and that another Cantonese named Yowloong was also "in the market" for Augustine Heard & Co. and Gilman & Co. He concluded that "the whole must be intended for Foochow."[64] David Jardine replaced Joseph Jardine as Jardine's manager at Canton in 1856. Expecting "a good demand for Chinese after the

59. R. M. Martin, II, 258.
60. Morse, *Conflict*, p. 542.
61. Downs, "American Merchants," pp. 418–42.
62. A. F. Heard to John Heard, July 30, 1860, HL-16, HC.
63. Ibid., May 19, 1860; and A. F. Heard, "Diary," 1855, HP-1, HC.
64. "There is no change in opium. It is quite true that Ehing bought Malwa from Sassoons today at $460 which is now the current quotation. Yowloong has since also been in the market for Augustine Heard and Co. and Gilman and Co. for 80 chests at the same rate. Ehing's purchases are for Russell and Co. and I am inclined to think the whole must be intended for Foochow" (Joseph Jardine to David Jardine [Hong Kong], JMA).

[Chinese] new year," he asked Yowloong to buy opium in the market in early February. The demand was great, and he regretted that he could not buy enough through this Cantonese broker.[65] The purchase of opium through Cantonese brokers continued in the summer of 1856 when Jardine's bought 120 chests of opium through a Cantonese merchant named Etai.[66]

After Hong Kong was ceded to Great Britain in 1842, it soon became, due to its geographical location, a depot for opium and a center of active illegal trade.[67] As an island close to the Canton estuary, Hong Kong was advantageous for smuggling. The eastern entrance to the harbor is only 600 yards wide, and until 1899 its northern shore was under Chinese jurisdiction. It was extremely easy for ships to slip from British waters into Chinese waters along the northern side of the island. At first the British government tried to prevent this from happening. Captain Elliot, with the desire to conciliate the Ch'ing government, forbade ships with opium to anchor in the port of Hong Kong, then the only anchorage open to British ships. Lord Aberdeen in 1843 also gave instructions to "prevent the island of Hong Kong from being a resort and market for the British smuggler."[68] But, with the development of the free-port sentiment in the colony, this prohibition was ineffective, and, after the Treaty of Nanking came fully into force, Hong Kong was a free depot for opium as well as for other commodities.[69]

Heard papers clearly show that this American firm used Hong Kong as the major base for opium trade in the 1850s. It hired Charles Jameson, an opium broker, to assess, inspect, and sell the drug. In 1858 he sold at least 200 chests for the firm at Hong Kong. He also shipped opium to other treaty ports.[70] In the 1860s Heard's did an extensive opium business with Chinese firms at Hong Kong, mainly with the firms of Heng-feng and Yung-yuan. On February 10, 1865, Heard's sold 20 chests of opium to another Chinese broker at $619 per chest.[71]

65. "Yowloong has only obtained five Chests more Patna at $405 a few days . . . it is most unsatisfactory [for] my not having been able to buy more, but I have done my utmost. Yowloong expects a good demand for Chinese after the [Chinese] new year" (David Jardine to Joseph Jardine [Hong Kong], Feb. 6, 1856, JMA).

66. Ibid., June 2, 1856.

67. In addition to opium, salt was also smuggled. Salt was cheap in Hong Kong, but expensive in China as a result of the government monopoly (H. B. Morse, *The International Relations of the Chinese Empire*, vol. II, *The Period of Submission, 1861–1893* [London, 1918], p. 380).

68. Morse, *Conflict*, pp. 231–33, 669.

69. Ibid., pp. 314–15, 335–36, 542.

70. Case 19, HC II.

71. Opium Memos., Cases 9 and 19, HC II.

After 1842 foreign opium merchants, as a rule, stationed their ships outside the treaty ports so as to avoid the supervision of their own consuls. Opium ships were at first moored two or three miles below Whampoa in 1843, because the anchorages of Whampoa and Lintin were closed to them. Soon Cumsingmoon on the western side of the Canton estuary became a permanent station, where new houses and roads were built for this purpose. Four receiving ships belonging to British, Parsee, and American merchants were usually stationed there in the 1840s.[72] Augustine Heard & Co. constantly maintained vessels there in the 1840s and 1850s, including the *Frolic, Race Horse, Lady Hayes, Cama Family, Snipe,* and *Lady Mary Wood.*[73]

In time, Amoy and Foochow became new centers of opium trade along the Fukien coast. In 1843 nine opium ships were anchored near Amoy where many well-to-do residents smoked opium. At the end of the decade, there were up to one thousand opium shops in that city, where the drug could be easily obtained and where facilities were furnished for smoking.[74] There were three big opium depots between Hong Kong and Amoy: Namoa (Nan-ao), Tong-san (Tung-shan), and How-tow-san (Hu-t'ou shan). The opium dealers in Canton and Macao had ships constantly stationed at these places to keep supplies of opium readily available; smaller vessels then carried opium to different parts of the coast, where it was usually disposed of for silver.

Before the coastal system was institutionalized, some Fukienese merchants used to come down to the Pearl River every summer to purchase opium. But soon foreign opium ships, with the help of the Chinese, started to frequent the Fukien coast. In 1843 two Cantonese named A-ping and A-kwang helped a British ship to sell opium at Foochow.[75] By the mid-forties, so many Cantonese opium merchants were at Foochow that hostility between Cantonese and Fukienese developed. On March 28, 1846, a Cantonese servant of Capt. James Miln of the opium ship *Vixen* was assaulted, and a clash broke out in Nantai between these two provincial groups. The leaders of the Cantonese in Foochow were the shroff and linguist of a British opium merchant, and a certain Le, who understood English and ran the Eho shop for the secret sale of opium.[76]

72. Morse, *Conflict*, pp. 541–42.
73. BP-1 and EJ-2, HC.
74. Allen, pp. 15, 28.
75. Fairbank, *Trade and Diplomacy*, I, 223.
76. Ibid., 221–22.

It is estimated that in the late 1840s about $2.5 million worth of opium was imported annually into Foochow, whence it was distributed into the interior. There were at least 100 retail shops and as many smoking houses at Foochow in 1848. In the 1850s two receiving ships were constantly stationed at the mouth of the Min River, about thirty miles from the city of Foochow. Two clippers supplied these receiving ships monthly with fresh cargoes, and the native merchants purchased the drug and shipped it to Foochow in small boats.[77] Opium was shipped from Foochow northwestward on the Min River to the tea districts of the Bohea Mountains. Robert Fortune visited there in 1849 and found that opium was kept in all the inns for sale to the guests, "just as a London innkeeper retails tobacco."[78] As the Cantonese dominated both opium trade and tea export business, it was only natural that the drug distribution followed the main routes of the tea export trade.

Chusan and Woosung were the two leading centers on the Chekiang-Kiangsu coast. There were three or four opium-receiving vessels in Chusan in 1845, and more than 2,700 chests were reported to have been sold there annually, valued at about $2,000,000. A large number of Chinese smuggling boats transshipped the drug to numerous cities and towns on the mainland, including Ningpo, which had just been opened as a treaty port.[79] Some foreign merchants tried to smuggle opium directly to Ningpo. For example, an American merchant in 1845 used the British schooner *Owners Delight* for smuggling, and an English-speaking Chinese also took part.[80]

Prior to the 1850s, Shanghai was the terminal port for the coastal opium trade that started from the Kwangtung coast. Because the trade was not legalized until 1858, it was covered by a veil of secrecy; but at Shanghai it was carried on in a semipublic way and only a decent cloak of concealment was called for.[81] We do not know exactly when foreign merchants started to sell opium at Woosung, an outer port twelve miles down the Whangpoo River from Shanghai, but Jardine records clearly show that the drug traffic became active by the mid-1840s. A. G. Dallas, Jardines's agent at Shanghai, wrote in 1845 that Shanghai was swiftly outdistancing Chusan as the center of opium trade on the east coast.[82]

77. Allen, p. 16.
78. *A Journey to the Tea Countries of China; Including Sung-lo and the Bohea Hills* (London, 1852), chap. 3.
79. Allen, p. 15.
80. Fairbank, *Trade and Diplomacy*, I, 332.
81. Morse, *Conflict*, p. 358.
82. To Donald Matheson (Hong Kong), Aug. 6, 1845, JMA.

TABLE 9.　ESTIMATED ANNUAL OPIUM IMPORTATION AT
WOOSUNG, SHANGHAI, 1847–1858
(CHESTS)

	Malwa	Patna	Total
1847	—	—	16,500
1848	—	—	16,960
1849	—	—	22,981
1850	14,000	5,000	19,000
1851[a]	16,000	6,000	22,000
1853	17,000	3,000	20,000[b]
1854	16,000	8,000	24,000
1855	19,000	9,000	28,000
1856	23,000	10,000	33,000
1857	23,000	9,000	32,000
1858	26,000	11,000	37,000

Sources: Prices Current, Case 26, HC II; Morse, *Conflict*, pp. 358, 544; and *NCH* (1850–1858), passim. Figures for 1847–1849 are from Morse's *Conflict*, and the rest are from HC II. Similar figures can also be found in *NCH*, 1850–58.
[a]Data for 1852 are not available.
[b]Morse's estimation is 22,200 chests.

The growth of the trade was fast, rising from 16,500 chests in 1847 to 37,000 chests in 1858 (when the trade was legalized) (table 9). The circulars of Augustine Heard & Co. estimated that in the late fifties the five Western receiving ships at Woosung always carried between 1,500 and 4,500 chests of opium ready for sale.[83]

The number of receiving ships at Woosung differed from time to time, varying with the volume of trade. Of the ten ships in the spring of 1854, four were consigned to British houses, two to American merchants, and four to Parsee and other firms. H. B. Morse mistakenly stated that "in 1854 the two American ships were withdrawn from service."[84] Actually, Heard papers indicate that during the mid-fifties much of Heard's opium in its Hong Kong warehouse was transshipped to its receiving ship, the *Anne Walsh*, at Woosung, where Captain William Endicott, the opium agent for several firms, carried on a lively opium business with Parsee and Chinese opium brokers.[85]

83. Price Current, Case 26, HC II.
84. *Conflict*, p. 542.
85. Price Current, Case 19, HC II.

The Chinese merchants, as evidenced by Jardine correspondence files, played a leading role in the opium trade at Shanghai. Soon after Shanghai was opened for foreign trade on November 11, 1843, A. G. Dallas of Jardine's established a branch there and hired a comprador named Asam. Opium was shipped to Shanghai via Woosung. To supervise, Dallas was "up and down every week to Woosung" where Chinese staff handled the trade. In 1844 the firm rewarded two Chinese clerks for their service in completing a difficult barter arrangement in this outer port of Shanghai.[86] Jardine's opium business at Woosung was institutionalized by the mid-1850s. There were Cantonese compradors at Woosung, and one of them specialized in opium. He supervised payment for, and delivery of, large monthly sales.[87] Like all other compradors, he was fully responsible for the business conducted by himself and for the conduct of his staff, because the comprador system was based on the Chinese institution of "complete responsibility" (*pao*).[88] The Cantonese merchants and agents engaged with Jardine's in the opium trade were one nucleus of the modern Chinese business class. When China began to recover economically after the Taiping uprising, they moved into many positions in foreign trade formerly commanded by foreigners.[89]

Around 1850, some Chinese and Western merchants in Shanghai cooperated in starting the "Soochow system" by which the Chinese merchants brought opium from the Shanghai-Woosung area to the silk-producing region of Soochow in exchange for silk. The monetary aspects of this system are discussed in chapter 3; here I am mainly concerned with its influence on the trade in the Kiangsu-Chekiang region in general. The Soochow system exerted a paramount effect on the market of this area. In early 1852, for instance, opium was oversupplied at Shanghai. However, the easy marketability of opium in the southern Kiangsu area, thanks to the Soochow system, stimulated the demand for opium there.[90]

The rising demand for opium at Soochow even prompted A. G. Dallas, the Jardine agent at Shanghai, to sell inferior Malwa there in

86. Dallas to Donald Matheson (Hong Kong), June 4 and Aug. 16, 1844, JMA.
87. Jardine, Matheson & Co. (Hong Kong) to A. G. Dallas (Shanghai), Feb. 18, 1852, JMA.
88. For a discussion of the institution of "complete responsibility" and its relationship with the comprador system, see Yen-p'ing Hao, *Comprador*, pp. 151, 160, 168.
89. LeFevour, p. 24.
90. A. G. Dallas reported to Hong Kong: "Immediately on the arrival of the *Sphynx*, there being no demand among the dealers, I got Takee to go to Woosung & select 80 chests for transmission to Soo-choo [Soochow]. This he did, & I have been trying to get him to settle a price here, without waiting for the actual sales. The dealers however are so alarmed by the subsequent sales at Woosung, that he is afraid to settle a price. I am in hopes of being able finally to conclude the sale at $500 to $510, as there is a good demand now at Soo-choo" (to David Jardine, Jan. 22, 1852, JMA).

September. Commenting on the difficulty of selling it at Shanghai, Dallas wrote: "In a bare market inferior drug often sells well . . . but with large supplies among so many ships, the dealers are very particular in their selection. . . . I had more than once asked [Aloong] to take the remainder of our inferior opium, but he steadily refused." Dallas therefore tried to sell it at Soochow, as he continued: "There being a good deal on board that had been frequently rejected & reported by Captn. Jauncey to me as bad, I persuaded a broker here to go down himself & select 40 chests to sell for me at Soo-choo."[91] The experiment proved to be successful.

Meanwhile, because the supply of opium was plentiful and Western merchants were able to sell more opium to this region than ever before, they could afford to purchase more silk there.[92] In fact, China's silk export steadily increased for several decades after 1850. There were many reasons for this increase, and certainly the Soochow system was one of them.

TRADE AFTER LEGALIZATION

Legalized and taxed under the treaty settlement of 1858–1860, the opium trade continued to thrive. With respect to the imported opium, its volume peaked in 1879 when 83,000 piculs were imported. The Cantonese merchants, who traded opium from the very beginning, remained as powerful as ever. Opium trade, however, steadily decreased after the 1880s.

TREATY PORTS AS TRADING CENTERS

After its legalization, the opium trade shifted its centers from the outer water anchorages to the treaty ports. For one thing, the ports provided

91. Ibid., Sept. 15, 1852. Under these circumstances, dealers in inferior opium at Shanghai often suffered losses, as Dallas wrote: "The [inferior] opium has been assorted, boiled &c [etc.] in Shanghai, & Aloong says he thinks he will lose a little by the transaction. I have every confidence in what he says. . . . The dealers sustain occasional heavy losses" (ibid.).

92. Sometimes the silk demand was so strong that its price rose in the Kiangsu-Chekiang region, as Takee noted in 1852. Jardine's J. Macandrew reported from Shanghai: "The [silk] market is firm, & some of our neighbours are on the lookout for any desirable parcels offering. On receipt of the overland news, I at once got Takee to dispatch instructions into the interior to extend his purchases as much as possible, not exceeding the currency of Mr. [A. G.] Dallas' late purchases, & he expects to be able to do this, though I cannot say to what extent. The stock in the interior is small, & he has no expectation of purchasing cheaper than before" (to David Jardine [Hong Kong], Mar. 5, 1852, JMA).

better facilities and lively markets. Thus, at Amoy, a relatively minor opium market, Jardine's sales reached an all-time high of Tls. 190,000 in 1861.[93] An agreement was also reached between China and Britain in 1886–1887 to check the opium-smuggling between Hong Kong and the outer water anchorages along China's coast.[94] The shift of the trading centers to the treaty ports, in turn, stimulated demand in China for both foreign and domestic produce. The annual import of Indian opium, which was about 30,000 chests in the 1830s, reached a peak of some 87,000 chests in 1879. Malwa was selling at the highest price in twenty years at Tls. 840 per picul in 1861,[95] and Indian opium generally commanded steady prices during the first half of the sixties. Meanwhile, the opium produced in China became more refined and more widely circulated.

In the early 1860s, Foochow witnessed active opium transactions. In addition to the Cantonese and Fukienese merchants, foreigners included, among others, the English, Parsee, and American traders. Gilman's and Russell's were particularly active.[96] M. A. Macleod, Jardine's agent at that port, reported in 1861 that heavy transactions in opium took place shortly before April 6, because a new custom house regulation at Foochow specified that the opium owner would have to pay import duty of 30 taels per chest after that date.[97] To avoid paying this duty, on April 5 Macleod sold the remaining stock of Jardine's opium at Foochow and "had the whole of our opium (69 chests in all) brought up from the ship" (stationed at the mouth of the Min River) to the firm's establishment at Foochow.[98]

93. Ledgers, 1861, JMA.

94. This agreement benefited both Hong Kong and China in terms of tax revenue (Morse, *Submission*, pp. 385–86).

95. Capt. Alexander Morrison (Amoy) to Jardine, Matheson & Co. (Hong Kong), Sept. 13, 1861, JMA.

96. M. A. Macleod, Jardine's Foochow agent, reported to Hong Kong: "A day or two ago the Parsees sold some 20 chests of Malwa at $700 per picul . . . and today both Russell & Co. & Gilman & Co. have either sold, or are offering to sell, some 30 to 50 chests on similar terms. In Patna the brokers speak of $975 to 980 as the rate at which the market will probably open" (to Alexander Perceval, Feb. 18, 1861, JMA).

97. Macleod wrote to Alexander Perceval: "Shortly after writing to you by the [steamer] 'Manila' there was a good deal of business done in Malwa, owing to the new custom house regulation coming into force on the 6th inst., about 200 chests having changed hands at from $820 to 840 per picul." The sale of more expensive opium, however, remained sluggish, as Macleod continued: "In Bengal drug however scarcely any thing has been done, the only sale being by Russell & Co. of 2 chests at $1140 per chest for old Patna" (ibid., April 8, 1861).

98. Macleod stated that on April 5 he sold "five chests Malwa at $850 per pecul and five chests Patna at $1150 cash" and rightly admitted that "my own sales to date are small" (ibid.).

Similar to the role of Hong Kong in the south, Shanghai was an entre-
pôt for central and northern China. During the decade before its legalization (1847–1858), opium imports at Shanghai constituted almost
one-half of the total amount imported to China. The amount of opium
importation into China via Shanghai steadily increased during 1847 to
1860, as the following figures show (in chests):[99]

Year	Total amount	Via Shanghai	Percentage
1847	33,250	16,500	49.6
1848	38,000	16,960	44.6
1849	43,075	22,981	53.4
1853	54,574	24,200	44.3
1857	60,385	31,907	52.8
1858	61,966	33,069	53.4
1859	62,822	33,786	53.8
1860	47,681	28,438	59.6

As was the case elsewhere, large British agency houses played a leading role in the opium trade at Shanghai. C. E. Parker of Augustine
Heard & Co. wrote at the end of 1860 that most of the opium importa-
tion was handled by the large British agency houses of Jardine's, Dent's,
Lindsay's, and Sassoon's.[100] As a rule, the Shanghai offices of foreign
firms supervised the business of their agents at the treaty ports north of
Ningpo, including that in opium. These places included the ports on the
Yangtze, such as Chinkiang, Kiukiang, and Hankow, as well as those
on the eastern and northeastern coast, such as Ningpo, Chefoo, and
Tientsin.

Jardine's operation was a good example. In the 1860s the Shanghai
office was headed by its various partners, including William Keswick
and F. B. Johnson, who directed the firm's business at these central and
northern ports. Commenting on the generally undesirable commercial
condition at Ningpo, James Whittall reported to Perceval in 1863: "At
Ningpo the French from all accounts are robbing right and left, driving
the people away & ruining all trade."[101] But, thanks to the energetic
agent at Ningpo in the mid-1860s, William Keswick regarded that port

99. Morse, *Conflict*, passim; and Prices Current, Case 26, HC II. Calculations are
mine.
100. To A. F. Heard, Dec. 12, 1860, HM-47, HC.
101. (Shanghai) to Perceval (Hong Kong), Mar. 30, 1863, JMA.

as an important station for opium trade in 1864, as he reported to Perceval from Shanghai: "I think we shall find Ningpo become a more important station now that we have a higher class agent."[102] In October Keswick ordered temporary suspension of the trade at Ningpo in order to obtain a higher price, which did not materialize.[103]

Opium was transshipped from Shanghai to the Yangtze ports, with Chinkiang being the closest port to Shanghai and the most important opium market on the Yangtze. According to Tong Mow-chee (T'ang Mao-chih), a prominent Chinese merchant at Shanghai from the 1860s on, the British merchants did an extensive drug business in that port.[104] In the sixties Jardine's regularly sent opium to Chinkiang,[105] where the firm's annual sale reached 7,000 to 8,000 chests in the early sixties. This figure dropped to 4,000 to 5,000 chests in the late sixties and early seventies, and further declined to 1,000 in 1879. Dent & Co. had an annual sale of 6,000 chests in the sixties.[106] In the same fashion Jardine's Shanghai branch kept an eye on the opium business at Kiukiang, as testified by the reports of the branch to the firm's head office at Hong Kong,[107] and by Kiukiang agents' frequent requests to the Shanghai office for opium intelligence.[108] The Shanghai office also sent opium to Hankow in the 1860s.[109] Opium was similarly shipped from Shanghai to the northern ports. Writing in 1863 from Shanghai, William Whittall was optimistic about the opium trade at Tientsin when it was compared with the generally deteriorating commercial situation at Ningpo.[110] Jardine's also sent opium from Shanghai to Chefoo.[111] The firm, however, practically left the opium trade in the seventies when it endeavored to develop the steamship enterprise.

102. Keswick to Perceval (Hong Kong), Jan. 11, 1864, JMA.
103. (Shanghai) to James Whittall (Hong Kong), Oct. 7, 1864, JMA.
104. NCH, Oct. 17, 1879, p. 387.
105. William Keswick (Shanghai) to James Whittall (Hong Kong), Oct. 7, 1864, JMA.
106. NCH, Oct. 17, 1879, p. 387.
107. E.g., James Whittall reported in 1863: "For the 30 chests at Kewkeang [Kiukiang] also the demand is good, Mr. Styan having sold 22 of the 30 chests I lately sent him at Ts. 615 [per chest]" ([Shanghai] to Alexander Perceval [Hong Kong], Mar. 30, 1863, JMA).
108. In 1869, e.g., Robert Anderson, the firm's agent at Kiukiang, requested opium intelligence from F. B. Johnson at Shanghai: "I would suggest your sending my comprador regular advices as to the state of your [opium] market" (Feb. 7, 1869, JMA).
109. William Keswick to James Whittall (Hong Kong), Oct. 7, 1864, JMA.
110. "The accounts from Tientsin are more favourable. Malwa having advanced to Tls. 625 [per chest] at which Maclean was trying to sell the few chests remaining, and I hope he will obtain it" (to Alexander Perceval [Hong Kong], Mar. 30, 1863, JMA).
111. William Keswick (Shanghai) to James Whittall (Hong Kong), Oct. 7, 1864, JMA.

Because the Cantonese merchants participated in the opium trade from the very beginning, they, more than any other group, were versed in the trade. It is not surprising that they dominated the trade in various ways. In April 1859 the local officials at Foochow asked them to "farm the opium duties." Tong Loong-maw, an extremely capable and enterprising Cantonese comprador-merchant at Foochow, was at first chosen to do the work. Tong was busy with his own business and did not want to do it, so another Cantonese merchant, "Nelson's old comprador," replaced him. This merchant was financially secured by both Tong and Russell & Co.'s comprador, who was also a Cantonese. These two sureties shared a certain percentage of the profits resulting from the farming of opium duties. The farming contract was "to commence the first of next China month."[112] In this way the Cantonese merchants at Foochow would farm the opium duties "as a joint concern." Meanwhile, a Foochow merchant also applied for the job.[113]

The ambition of Cantonese merchants led them beyond farming opium duties on the local level. They also tried to monopolize opium importation to China as a whole. In 1882 a certain Mr. Samuel suggested in vain that all opium sold in India should be sold to him and that he would pay to the Chinese government the statutory duty and the likin (a commercial transit tax) on all that reached China.[114] The Cantonese merchants, however, had earlier tried the establishment of a company to monopolize opium trade from India to China. Ho Amei (Ho Hsien-ch'ih), a prominent Cantonese merchant in Hong Kong, proposed before 1881 under the sanction and control of the Chinese government, to fund a company with an initial paid-up capital of $20,000,000. It would monopolize the importation of Indian opium to China and enjoy the sole distribution rights in Chinese ports of the imported opium for fifty years. The company would gradually reduce the amount of im-

112. Heard's agent at Foochow wrote: "Since I last wrote you, I have heard reports that our comprador [Tong Loong-maw] is going to 'farm the opium duties.' Dunn, the American Consul, told me today that the Customs House informed him that it was true. Our comprador did not want to do it, so they say, but made him. As I understand from Dunn, Nelson's old comprador is to do the work while our comprador and R. [Russell] & Co.'s are security and divide the profit. The contract, I hear, is to commence the first of next China month" (G. F. Weller to John Heard, Apr. 16, 1859, FM-13, HC).

113. Ibid., May 7, 1859.

114. Morse, *Submission*, p. 385.

ported opium, which would be completely eliminated at the end of the monopoly period.[115]

Ho argued that this scheme would stop opium-smuggling, do away with the necessity for the numerous likin stations, and put an end to the prevailing evasion and misappropriation of likin duties in China. In return, he offered the Ch'ing government at least Tls. 3,000,000 in addition to the annual taxation. The scheme was approved by Li Hung-chang, who, seeking imperial sanction, memorialized to the throne in 1881:

I have heard that Ho Hsien-ch'ih and the others are very rich, and have long been doing business in the Kwangtung and Hong Kong area. They understand both Chinese and foreign business methods. Other rich merchants have heard of this and want to put up capital and get stock [ch'u-tzu fu-ku]; they all know that a company with a monopoly of the opium trade is bound to make a profit, and not to fail, so it is not hard to raise capital.[116]

Li Hung-chang sent Wu Han-t'ao and a certain Taotai Ma to Calcutta to negotiate directly with Lord Ripon. We are not sure whether an agreement was reached with the Indian authorities, but the plan was blocked in China by the Tsungli Yamen on the ground that it was morally improper.[117] At any rate, thanks largely to the substitution of domestic opium for foreign opium, imports of opium gradually but steadily decreased after 1888 and were legally abolished in 1917, symbolizing the end of this infamous trade.[118]

115. Cheng Kuan-ying, *Sheng-shih wei-yen tseng-ting hsin-pien* (preface 1892), 8:1b; and Spence, p. 165.

116. Quoted in Spence, "Opium Smoking."

117. Cheng Kuan-ying, *Tseng-ting*, 8:1b; and Eitel, 559. Cheng maintains that, "after a hot debate," an agreement had been reached with the Indian authorities. On the other hand, Eitel asserts that "the whole scheme failed because the Indian Government declined the Viceroy's proposal."

118. For the decline in opium imports after the 1880s, see Liang-lin Hsiao, *Statistics*, pp. 52–53. Lin Man-hung, "Ch'ing-mo pen-kuo ya-p'ien chih t'i-tai chin-k'ou ya-p'ien, 1858–1906," *Chung-yang yen-chiu yuan chin-tai shih yen-chiu so chi-k'an* 9:385–432 (July 1980), maintains that the domestic production of opium took up the slack. The considerable success of the opium suppression campaigns at the turn of the twentieth century resulted from both foreign and domestic factors. With new types of investments and new sources of revenue for India, the British government responded favorably to the Ch'ing request for cooperation in this great moral movement (FO 405/185; FO 405/186). Furthermore, by the early twentieth century the British had lost their dominant position in the Chinese opium market (Circular no. 1543, Aug. 6, 1908, IMC, *Circular*, X, 540). On the Chinese side, the campaign was coordinated by tough senior officials like Hsi-liang who used military force against domestic growers.

CHAPTER SIX

The Commercialization of Agricultural Products: The Upcountry Purchase of Tea

As the use of new forms of money gradually spread from the coastal regions to the interior, credit expansion followed. Meanwhile, opium was used as a means of payment for tea and silk, and its legalization gave a new dimension to the coastal trade. After 1842 the treaty system gave impetus to these developments by ushering in an era of free trade never witnessed before. Taken together, they precipitated fundamental changes in trade. China's commercial revolution gained further momentum in 1860 when the new, large-scale upcountry purchase of tea and silk became fully developed. This expansion was possible for two major reasons. First, after the Convention of Peking in 1860, the Western powers adopted a "cooperative" foreign policy toward China, which resulted in decades of stable Sino-Western commercial relations.[1] Second, the defeat of the Taiping uprising paved the way for a vigorous domestic trade, making the system of upcountry purchase a possibility.

The commercialization of agricultural products is a major feature of commercial capitalism, and nothing better testifies to this than the upcountry purchase of tea and silk. After the mid-nineteenth century, Chinese independent merchants as well as agents of Western traders proceeded from the treaty ports to the interior to buy tea and silk directly from peasants and producers. By the early 1860s this system of upcountry purchase was well-developed. I discuss the upcountry purchase of silk in chapter 3 and examine the competitive nature of the silk trade in

---

1. For the cooperative policy, see Mary Clabaugh Wright, *The Last Stand of Chinese Conservatism* (Stanford, Calif., 1957), pp. 21–42.

chapter 7. This chapter, based heavily on correspondence files in the Jardine archives, concentrates on the upcountry purchase of tea in the Bohea (Wu-i) Mountains of Fukien and Kiangsi.

THE EXPANSION OF THE TEA TRADE

One important reason for the commercialization of agricultural products was that Chinese tea was in ever-increasing demand on the European and American markets during the late Ch'ing period. In response, Chinese and foreign traders, motivated by competition, widened the market on the Chinese end. Tea was purchased in large-scale amounts and at a fast pace. Commercial centers in the interior, where tea was traded, rose to national prominence. Some ports noted for their export of tea, such as Foochow and Shanghai, enjoyed international fame.

WESTERN MARKETS

Before the mid-1850s, Bohea teas were transported to Canton and Shanghai for export to the European market. After Foochow was opened up for tea export, however, a considerable amount of the Bohea teas was shipped to America. It required special skills and expenses to develop the American market, such as giving the teas fancy brand names and special packaging. But, according to George V. W. Fisher, the Jardine agent in Foochow, the house was "more than compensated" by the high tea prices in America that resulted from "flowered and neat packages."[2] In addition to Russell's, another American house, Wetmore & Co., was a major exporter of Foochow tea to the United States. This house loaded two full ships of tea in mid-December of 1855. In early 1856, Fisher prepared a big shipment of tea to the United States, including 300 half-chests of elaborately packaged common Congou.[3] In August, the American firm of King & Co. fully loaded its vessel, the *Wild Duck*,

2. "I am preparing an invoice for America and know all about the marking &c for Teas for America, through the kindness of Mr. Forster. It cost 2 mace per picul having the chests painted, but it is more than compensated by the larger price [that] the flowered and neat packages bring" (to Joseph Jardine [Hong Kong], Nov. 15, 1855, JMA).
3. Ibid., Dec. 19, 1855. Fisher wrote to Hong Kong: "300 HF Cts [half-chests] of *Contract common Congou* has arrived [from upcountry] & as they are in handsome flowd. pkgs. [flowered packages]. I am keeping them to ship to America with the rest of the Teas I have for that quarter. Wetmores say now that it might be 2 or 3 weeks before the ship arrives to load for America. . . . However, if an earlier opportunity presents itself, I shall avail myself of it" (ibid., Jan. 2, 1856).

heading for New York. At the same time, on a grand scale, Gilman & Co. and Dent, Beale & Co. bought about 4,000 half-chests of old Sueykut Oolongs for shipping to the United States.[4]

Chinese merchants not only played a role in expanding the tea market in China, in both the interior and treaty ports, but also were involved in tea exporting to America. About 2,000 chests of Congou tea were settled on the Foochow market on August 22, 1856, and 700 chests of these were bought back by Chinese merchants for shipping to the United States on their own account. These merchants were closely associated with the American house of Russell & Co.[5]

Meanwhile, the Foochow tea also supplied the European market. Large mercantile houses, such as Jardine, Matheson & Co. and Dent & Co., had their own ships which regularly carried tea from Foochow to European, especially British, ports during the fifties and sixties. In November 1855 George Fisher reported from Foochow to Jardine's Hong Kong office that his first priority of tea business was to "load a vessel for London." Only then "the teas would be ready for shipment" to other markets.[6] Sometimes a firm would share a ship with others when more room for freight was available, for instance, Dent's invited Lindsay & Co. to ship tea to England on board S. S. *Lord of the Isles* in May 1856.[7] One month later, the steamer *Vision* of Jardine's, heading for Liverpool, also took tea from Gibb, Livingston & Co. Although Thomas Larken thought that the latter would probably ship about 50 tons, he offered Richard Gibb the "right of first refusal" of 100 tons in the vessel, for which Gibb's would pay £6 per ton.[8]

Just as it was important for the upcountry tea purchasers to transport tea quickly from the interior to the treaty ports, it was essential for the export merchants, Chinese and foreign alike, to ship their cargo to the foreign markets as fast as they could. Actually, the competition was so keen that the freight was determined by the speed of the vessel.

DOMESTIC MARKETS

Although Foochow was not very far from the Bohea tea districts, it was not a major port for exporting tea prior to 1854. After that year,

4. Thomas Larken (Foochow) to Joseph Jardine (Hong Kong), Aug. 29, 1856, JMA.
5. Larken wrote: "About *2,000* Chests of Congou have been settled during the week including one chop of *700* chests taken by Messrs. Russell & Co. to be shipped, it is presumed, on Chinese account" (ibid., Aug. 22, 1856).
6. Fisher to Joseph Jardine, Nov. 15, 1855, JMA.
7. Ibid., May 17, 1856.
8. Larken (Foochow) to Joseph Jardine (Hong Kong), June 27, 1856, JMA.

however, because the Taiping uprising disturbed the traditional tea routes to Shanghai and Canton, and simultaneously the commercial activities on the coast became increasingly active, Foochow became a prominent tea export center. Foreign houses bought tea on the Foochow market at first but soon sent their agents to the upper Min River to purchase tea directly from upcountry.

The flourishing business in upcountry tea purchases in Fukien in 1855 was evident in two ways. First, in addition to Foochow, other tea-purchasing ports emerged along the Fukien coast, such as Amoy. Jardine's, for example, vigorously expanded tea purchasing in this area in late 1855, asking Captain Compton at Amoy to send tea musters to Foochow for careful examination. Second, the demand for tea was so heavy that not only superior and common tea was sold out, but also some "rubbish" tea was shipped from Amoy to Hong Kong. Augustine Heard & Co. bought a large quantity of the low-quality tea for shipping to America, and George Fisher of Jardine's also tried to buy large amounts for the European market.[9]

Meanwhile, the native merchants who made contracts with foreign houses to provide them with tea (referred to as "teamen" in the correspondence of foreigners) went to the upper Min River to purchase tea directly from the growers. From 1857 to 1861, for instance, Ahee purchased large amounts of tea at Sinchune (Shun-ch'ang), a city on the Min River about 150 miles northwest of Foochow.[10] In 1861 he went farther westward to Kienning (Chien-ning), a district on the Fukien-Kiangsi border.[11] At the same time, Taising, another Chinese teaman, purchased tea from various towns and cities on the upper Min River, such as Sueykut (Shui-k'ou, 15 miles southwest of Shun-ch'ang) and Shung-oan (Ch'ung-an, in the heart of the Bohea districts).[12] Arriving at Shung-oan on September 24, 1861, he wrote M. A. Macleod at Foochow regarding his tea purchases: price, amount, variety, and days needed for shipping them to Foochow.[13] As was the case with all the teamen's letters, Taising's letter was summarized in English by Jardine's agent in Foochow and transmitted to the firm's main office at Hong Kong.

As the Bohea tea districts were situated in both Fukien and Kiangsi, some teamen went farther westward from Fukien to Kiangsi to buy tea. Aleet was such a teaman. In the late sixties, he proceeded to the eastern

9. Fisher (Foochow) to Joseph Jardine (Hong Kong), Nov. 15, 1855, JMA.

10. Ahee (Sinchune) to Thomas L. Larken (Foochow), July 30, 1857, and Sept. 22, 1861, JMA.

11. Ahee (Kienning) to M. A. Macleod (Foochow), May 20, 1861, JMA.

12. Taising (Sueykut) to M. A. Macleod (Foochow), Aug. 29, 1861, JMA.

13. Taising (Shung-oan) to M. A. Macleod (Foochow), Sept. 24, 1861, JMA.

part of Kiangsi for active tea purchasing. He was so involved in the local tea business that he finally settled down in Kiukiang, Kiangsi.[14] The Cantonese teamen were by no means the only tea merchants in the Bohea tea districts; other merchants from the north were also active. In a letter written from the Bohea districts in the spring of 1863, Taising alerted Jardine's that, because various groups of teamen were present in Sinchune competing with one another, he did not think that tea would be cheap in that district.[15]

Western agency houses, like the Chinese merchants, played a direct role in expanding the tea market in Fukien. In order to have a more efficient network for the purchasing of tea, some foreign traders personally went from Foochow to the interior. According to George V. W. Fisher of Jardine's, a certain Mr. Rusden of Gilman & Co. "proceeded to the Interior of the Tea districts" of Fukien in March 1856. Fisher himself was also anxious to go to see the various tea hongs of its teamen and the process of preparing the tea. Because foreigners were at first not permitted by law to go upcountry, they had to disguise themselves by dressing up like Chinese.[16] Under this guise, foreigners usually stayed in the interior for short periods of time, ranging from one week to a month.

Because the Chinese tea growers regarded the coming of a foreigner to the tea districts as a signal of potential tea purchases on a large scale, tea prices zoomed whenever they saw a foreign trader.[17] Foreigners' direct involvement in the upcountry purchase of tea was institutionalized by Jardine's when the company sent John Mayor from Foochow to the interior on a regular basis in the summer of 1869. This practice was immediately followed by other houses.[18] The commercialization of agricultural products was further hastened by the keen competition among foreign and Chinese merchants.

LARGE-SCALE PURCHASES

After the successful attempt of Russell & Co. to export tea from Foochow in 1854, the upcountry purchase of tea increased by leaps and

14. John Mayor (Suyeada) to F. B. Johnson (Foochow), June 7, 1869, JMA.
15. Taising (Sinchune) to Edward Whittall (Foochow), Apr. 24, 1863, JMA.
16. Fisher wrote in 1856: "In speaking to Ahee on the subject of my going into the country bye & bye, when I have finished everything, he says there would not be the slightest difficulty about it and that by dressing up like a Chinaman I could go about & see the different Hongs & the process of firing the Tea &c [etc.]" ([Foochow] to Joseph Jardine [Hong Kong], Mar. 30, 1856, JMA).
17. M. A. Macleod (Foochow) to Taising (Sueykut), Apr. 30, 1863, JMA.
18. Mayor (Suyeada) to F. B. Johnson (Foochow), June 7, 1869, JMA.

bounds. Dent, Beale & Co. is known to have acquired $400,000 worth of tea from the Bohea districts during the first four months of 1856.[19] Through Taising and Ahee, Jardine's also conspicuously expanded its purchases. Thomas Larken, for instance, reported from Foochow to Hong Kong on August 22, 1856, that he would "in a few days have about 1,000 tons of tea ready for shipment."[20] In the same letter, Larken also noted:

Messrs. Dent & Co. have, I believe, a full cargo for the [steamer] 'Lord Raglan' and also for the "Wynaud" for Holland and Mr. C. J. King has Teas enough to fill the "Tamora" for London (about 600 tons). The 'Virginia' has about 700 tons on board and the 'Walmer Castle' 600 tons and these, with the 1000 tons of your Teas in the godown, are about all the stock in Foochow with the 5000 chests on the Market.[21]

Sometimes the purchase of tea from upcountry was on so large a scale that Jardine's teamen, after having spent all the money they had brought with them into the interior, had to ask for more funds from the Western houses in Foochow. For instance, through Shunhee, his agent in Foochow, Jardine's teaman Ahee applied for, and received from, the house, an additional $49,368 in early March 1859.[22]

The amount of upcountry tea purchased from Foochow significantly increased from the mid-fifties to the early sixties. This development was arrested in 1861 when the mid-Yangtze ports of Hankow and Kiukiang were "opened" for foreign trade, and considerable amounts of Bohea tea were shipped to these ports for export. Nothing better testifies to this change in commercial gravity than the history of Dent, Beale & Co. This gigantic British house reduced the number of its upcountry tea purchasing agents in Fukien in 1861. There were six to seven of these teamen from 1855 to early 1861, but the house trimmed the number to two or three in February 1861. The rest went to Hankow where the purchase of upcountry tea from Hunan and Hupei was burgeoning.[23] By the same

19. George V. W. Fisher (Foochow) to Joseph Jardine (Hong Kong), May 1, 1856, JMA.
20. To Joseph Jardine, JMA.
21. Ibid.
22. N. R. Massion (Hong Kong) to Jardine, Matheson & Co. (Hong Kong), Mar. 25, 1859, JMA.
23. M. A. Macleod of Jardine's wrote from Foochow to Hong Kong in 1861: "Just while I am writing I learn that Dent & Co. are moving away from this place the principal portion of their native Staff. They go down by the [steamer] 'Chusan' & report says they are bound for Hangkow [Hankow]. Hitherto Dent and Co. have had some Six or Seven buying Agents in the Interior providing for their Foochow wants, but for the present Season they are to have two or three only" (to Alexander Perceval, Feb. 18, 1861, JMA).

token, some foreign employees of the Foochow branches also went to Hankow. A case in point was a certain Mr. Smith of Lindsay & Co.[24] Despite this unfavorable development, Macleod still believed that the export of tea from Foochow would be huge.[25]

The tea business in Foochow was generally on a grand scale; thus it was essential to have large sums of cash on reserve. "To have a good supply of [Mexican] dollars on hand" enabled a merchant to respond to the Foochow market quickly, especially during the opening of the tea market, as Jardine's M. A. Macleod often reminded Alexander Perceval.[26] Moreover, the purchase of tea from upcountry required additional money from time to time. Macleod, for example, stated that he would have to send teaman Ahee a "further lot of dollars for the purpose of the second crop cargoes" in 1861. Mainly for these reasons, Perceval instructed Macleod to hold his dollar reserve instead of remitting a portion of it to the Hongkong and Shanghai Banking Corporation as originally planned.[27] But, because the demand for money was high, Macleod reiterated that more money would be required from Hong Kong "ere very long," even though he already had a surprisingly large fund of $300,000.[28]

Jardine's purchase of tea from the interior was indeed extensive. The house bought 600,000 chests of upcountry tea from teaman Taising alone in 1860 to 1861. Taising estimated that he would buy at least 470,000 chests for the house during the next season, including 100,000 chests of good teas, 270,000 chests of middling teas, and 100,000 chests of common teas.[29] Taising wrote on September 27, 1861 that even in the small town of Sueykut he had purchased 5,000 chests of tea in the previous few days. They consisted of 3,600 chests of good Congou, including one chop of Kafat of 240 chests, one chop of Chinwo of 620 chests, and

24. Ibid.
25. "I see no reason to change my opinion with regard to the probable export. I still think it will be 85 Million lbs. under any circumstances" (ibid.).
26. Macleod wrote Perceval: "You will no doubt remember that on the opening of the market here at Foochow, it will be well to have a good supply of [Mexican] Dollars on hand for the chance of an opportunity offering of doing some good in the leaf" (May 11, 1861, JMA).
27. Another reason was that the dollar exchange rate was low (ibid.).
28. Ibid.
29. Taising's letter, as summarized by Macleod, reads: "He [Taising] thinks that the quantity named will prove to be very near the mark" ([Sueykut] to Macleod [Foochow], Sept. 9, 1861, JMA). Two weeks later, Taising estimated from the interior: "The total supply to Foochow for the present season [will be] at about 500,000 chests, showing a short coming on last year of about 100,000 chests" ([Shung-oan] to Macleod [Foochow], Sept. 24, 1861, JMA).

another chop of 500 chests. Taising added that he had shipped 2,200 chests of these good teas to Foochow, and the remaining 1,400 chests were in the process of packing. In addition, he also bought 1,400 chests of middle-quality tea. Half of these had been shipped to Foochow and the other half was "in course of preparation."[30] At the same time, Jardine's also bought tea from other teamen. One of them, Ahee, estimated in September 1861 that the house would get about 500,000 chests of upcountry tea in 1861 to 1862.[31]

Jardine's purchase of tea from the Bohea districts in northwestern Fukien continued on a large scale throughout the sixties. In the summer of 1869, the house even sent one of its British employees, John Mayor, to the upper Min River area to buy tea. His operation was in such grand style that he spent from $6,000 to $10,000 a day and employed more than 100 coolies when he was in the town of Suyeada in early June. This large-scale operation led to a 10 percent reduction in operation costs, and the quality of tea became better.[32] In fact, the purchase of tea went so well that Mayor asked for more funds from Foochow. He stated that, although he still had about $20,000 in his boat, he would need an additional $10,000 or more. As the tea business prospered, Mayor and his son worked extremely hard. He continued: "On the whole I am very happy of the help of my son here altho' I much regret the misfortune that sent him to me. We are both working off our legs almost."[33]

Upland tea from Fukien was purchased not only in large-scale amounts, but also at a fast pace. In spite of expanding its warehouse facilities, Jardine, Matheson & Co. did not have enough space in Foochow to accommodate the tea shipments that were pouring in from the interior. George V. W. Fisher had a sizable amount of tea ready for shipment to London in early 1856, and he was "very much pinched" for storage space.[34] Later he felt much relieved when the tea was loaded on one of Jardine's ships. Meanwhile, Jardine's was making vast purchases on the Foochow market. In this manner Thomas Larken bought more than 1,200 chests of Congou in less than two days in June 1856.[35] He also

30. Taising (Sueykut) to Macleod (Foochow), Sept. 27, 1861, JMA.
31. Ahee (Sinchune) to Macleod (Foochow), Sept. 22, 1861, JMA.
32. Mayor wrote Johnson: "With 100 coolies on an average, day & night as busy as can be, I have reduced the price abt [about] 10% while the quality has become better" ([Suyeada] to Johnson [Foochow], June 7, 1869, JMA).
33. Ibid.
34. "The cargo for London is quite ready & [I] shall be glad when a vessel comes to take it away, for I am very much pinched for room" ([Foochow] to Joseph Jardine [Hong Kong], Jan. 2, 1856, JMA).
35. Larken (Foochow) to Joseph Jardine (Hong Kong), June 27, 1856, JMA.

planned to make some "further suitable purchases" for one of the firm's steamers, the *Vision*.

The speed with which the tea merchants purchased tea in the interior was demonstrated by Taising, one of Jardine's aggressive teamen. He shipped two chops of tea from Sueykut to Foochow on August 20, 1861. One week later he dispatched another two chops to Foochow. One chop, Wyhung, consisted of 218 half-chests, costing Tls. 16 at Foochow. The other chop of Fowfat had 100 chests, costing Tls. 18 at Foochow. The third chop of tea was nearly finished by August 29, and the fourth chop was "just about coming out." Taising added: "Rain has fallen lately in the Interior, and therefore the 4th chop leaf will prove to be a little better than that of the 3d."[36]

Taising's purchase of tea continued at a rapid pace and on a large scale. He purchased 1,100 chests of middling and good teas from the Bohea districts in only five days between September 9 and 14, 1861.[37] This was also the case with Ahee, another of Jardine's teamen. In mid-September 1861, he was in the Sinchune neighborhood, at a place called Wong Kang, where he bought about 200 chests of good tea, "but at a very high price, the cost laid down at Foochow being about 23 taels." "He also purchased some 300 chests of good middling quality, the cost of which at Foochow would be 18 taels." He completed the transactions of these 500 chests of tea "in the course of four or five days."[38]

THE ROLE OF THE CHINESE

Many Chinese, including teamen, compradors, and shroffs, played important roles in the commercialization of tea in the Bohea districts. The purchase of tea by Jardine, Matheson & Co., for example, was significantly facilitated by the assistance of the Chinese, particularly the Cantonese. Although Jardine's ships frequented Foochow as early as the beginning of the nineteenth century, these ships did not anchor at Foochow on a regular basis until 1846, when Capt. Crawford became the firm's first agent. After Foochow became a significant port for exporting tea in 1854, Jardine's sent John Williams to Foochow to establish a branch office in that year. Both Crawford and Williams were helped by the Chinese shroff who was clerk and treasurer.[39] After replacing Wil-

---

36. (Sueykut) to M. A. Macleod (Foochow), Aug. 29, 1861, JMA.
37. Ibid., Sept. 9, 1861.
38. Ahee (Sinchune) to M. A. Macleod (Foochow), Sept. 22, 1861, JMA.
39. Williams to Jardine, Matheson & Co. (Hong Kong), Sept. 21, 1855, JMA.

liams in November 1855, Geroge V. W. Fisher started an extensive upcountry purchasing program. Under special arrangement, Chinese teamen would bring their tea to Fisher for possible purchase. But, in the
process of transporting, they had the full control of the tea, which was
shipped on their account.[40]

Realizing the importance of the teamen in the upcountry market, Jardine's agent tried hard to cultivate their friendship. One way was to
protect their legitimate interests. Fisher, for instance, in 1855 saw to it
that the teamen would not be unduly "squeezed" by the comprador; he
arranged to pay the teamen directly through Captain Crawford instead
of through the comprador's office.[41] Another way was to tide them over
their financial difficulties. Teaman Ahee owed a considerable amount of
money to Jardine's in 1863, and M. A. Macleod urged the firm's head
office that it would be in the best interest of the firm to permit Ahee to
pay his debt gradually:

Ahee I think could pay 50 percent of his debt in the course of a few months,
and if you were to encourage him by waiving the other 50 percent, I think you
would be gainer, for you would be sure of getting the half as he would stretch a
point, whereas at present he can only pay small installments & if anything happened to him in the meantime you could not receive anything and I doubt if his
property is worth much, for which I hold title Deeds.[42]

The role of the Chinese in Jardine's tea trade became even more important when Acum started to serve as the comprador to its Foochow
office in 1860.[43] The upcountry tea purchase was so prosperous in the
upper Min River area in the summer of 1869 that John Mayor asked
Jardine's Foochow office to send more funds. He cautioned F. B. Johnson
that a Chinese shroff, not an Englishman, should be relied on to ship the
Mexican silver dollars to the interior.[44] It is not surprising, then, that
foreign traders tried hard to cultivate the friendship of the Chinese.

40. "The stock of Congous continues to decrease which is now 41 full chops & if the
price of common keeps to what it is now I believe we shall have less than 10,000 Chest
down within the next 2 months, that is on a/c of the Chinese themselves" (Fisher
[Foochow] to Jardine Matheson & Co. [Hong Kong], Dec. 7, 1855, JMA).

41. Fisher tried to ensure that the teamen would get no less than what the house paid:
"I am now having all the teamen paid here at Captn. Crawfords which obviates the necessity of the money being taken to the other Hong, & by which plan there can be no doubt
of the Teamen getting the same that the house pays" ([Foochow] to Joseph Jardine [Hong
Kong], Dec. 29, 1855, JMA).

42. Macleod (Foochow) to Alexander Perceval (Hong Kong), Aug. 10, 1863, JMA.

43. NCH, Oct. 13, 1860, p. 2.

44. From Suyeada in the Fukien interior, Mayor wrote to the Foochow office: "Please
don't rely much on the protection that the Englishman who accompanies the boat affords

In the late fifties and early sixties, almost all of Jardine's contract tea was bought from Chinese teamen, especially from Ahee and Taising.[45] At the same time, there were many independent Cantonese merchants who purchased tea in the interior and sold it on the Foochow market of their own accord. Yunkee, a merchant of considerable wealth, frequently bought numerous chops of Moning tea in the Bohea districts and shipped them to Foochow for sale during the fifties.[46] Jardine's also bought tea from other Chinese teamen, such as Aleet and Yakee. Furthermore, these independent teamen also exported tea to the West on their own accounts. M. A. Macleod reported in 1860 that the firm "increased in the shipping off of the whole of Aleet's and Yakee's teas."[47]

Because of their early association with the foreign traders, some Cantonese became tea workers in the Western houses in Foochow. Jardine's hired many of them to work under Fisher in the fifties. However, after discovering that some of them were dishonest, Fisher had to send them back to Hong Kong in 1855 and tried to rain Foochow men to replace them.[48] But it was by no means easy to replace the Cantonese with Fukienese. In fact, when John Mayor went to the interior to purchase tea in the summer of 1869, he hired about 100 Cantonese to work on the upper Min River.[49]

TOWARD INSTITUTIONALIZATION

The upcountry purchase of tea was on a sporadic and experimental basis during 1854 and 1855 but quickly became institutionalized. By 1856 the mechanism of purchase and the network of communication were well-established, and the teamen's working schedule was by and large on a regular basis.

---

to the treasure you may send—they are little better than straw men—but kindly send a trustworthy shroff in charge" (to F. B. Johnson [Foochow], June 7, 1869, JMA).

45. B-2, vols. 50–55, JMA.

46. Ahee (Sinchune) to M. A. Macleod (Foochow), July 30, 1857, JMA.

47. (Foochow) to Jardine, Matheson & Co. (Hong Kong), Nov. 17, 1860, JMA.

48. In a letter to Jardine's head office, Fisher wrote: "I have been obliged to discharge 2 of the Canton Coolies for stealing Tea. I had 2 muster Chests in, & the next day wishing to look at them I found nearly a quarter of each Chest gone—this has been the case with several other chests also. I had threatened them several times before for sundry other offences & have at least been obliged to make an example of 2 of them. I want to get them out of the place so I told them what is due to them (2 mos. wages) will be paid at Hong Kong. If I can get them to go I shall send them down by the next trip of the 'Gazelle.' I shall not require any more Canton men in their place as the Foochow men will do as well with a little training. The two men are Aheen & Atchune" ([Foochow] to Jardine, Matheson & Co. [Hong Kong], Dec. 7, 1855, JMA).

49. (Suyeada) to F. B. Johnson (Foochow), July 7, 1869, JMA.

THE MECHANISM OF TEA PURCHASE

There were three major ways by which tea in the interior of Fukien and Kiangsi was collected and exported. First, the foreign house sent its comprador upcountry to purchase tea directly from the tea growers. Second, the foreign trader contracted with the Chinese teamen to purchase tea. Finally, he bought tea on the open market at Foochow that was supplied chiefly by independent Chinese merchants. Because the comprador's role in the upcountry purchase of tea is discussed elsewhere,[50] here I concentrate on the other two methods.

Under the "contract system," the foreign trader had special arrangements with the Chinese teamen who provided a fixed amount of tea for him in Foochow at certain specified prices. By doing so, he did not involve himself in too much risk in the upcountry purchase and yet at the same time avoided paying the high prices on the Foochow market. Augustine Heard, Jr., recalled that, after Foochow was opened for tea export in 1854, "the contract system, as it was called, was in full operation" throughout the sixties, except for a short period of interruption during the Taiping Rebellion.[51] In this manner, the Foochow branch of Jardine, Matheson & Co. purchased considerable amounts of tea from such teamen as Ahee, Alum, Mantai, Taising, Tonghing, and Yuntai in the late fifties and early sixties.

Meanwhile, other foreign houses also contracted with the Chinese to purchase tea in the interior of Fukien. The American house of Augustine Heard & Co., for instance, bought contract tea from a Cantonese teaman named Sickqua in the summer of 1863. The contract tea, consisting mainly of flowery Pekoes, was of such a large quantity that the firm was to "have a vessel coming to them to load for a Russian port."[52] In fact, to purchase contract tea from the Bohea districts was a common practice for all foreign houses in the mid-fifties. In the first half of 1856, for example, the gigantic British agency house of Dent, Beale & Co. purchased 13,800 packages, and the large American house of Russell & Co., 10,700 packages. Other well-established mercantile houses included Heard's, Gilman's, and Lindsay's. The two small firms of Gibbs & Co. and Moncrieff & Co. also participated, bringing the total amount to 52,920 packages.[53]

50. For a detailed discussion of the comprador's role, see Yen-p'ing Hao, *Comprador*, pp. 77–82.

51. "Old China and New," p. 30.

52. M. A. Macleod (Foochow) to Jardine, Matheson & Co. (Hong Kong), June 11, 1863, JMA.

53. Thomas Larken (Foochow) to Joseph Jardine (Hong Kong), July 13, 1856, JMA.

In entering into contracts with Chinese teamen, the foreign merchant relied heavily on the opinion of his teataster. Besides, the contracts were usually sent to the firm's head office in Hong Kong for approval. For instance, in April 1861, M. A. Macleod, Jardine's agent in Foochow, sent to Alexander Perceval contracts with Yuntai, Mantai, and Tonghing. Macleod wrote: "You will observe that the prices stipulated for show a considerable reduction on those of last Season, & Mr. [R. F.] Hamilton [the teataster] assures me that he is certain they are quite safe at these figures. I shall be glad to learn however that the arrangements meet with your approval."[54] In addition to the teatasters, foreign firms also hired Chinese teaboys who served as liaisons between the house and the teamen. The teaman and the teaboy usually worked closely together. Their failure to do so sometimes caused serious problems in the business of upcountry tea purchase; this happened to Jardine's at the end of 1855. Ahee, the teaman, and Awy, the teaboy, brought charges against each other. The whole matter was so serious that Fisher wanted to go to Hong Kong in order to explain it to Joseph Jardine in person. Fortunately for Jardine's, the dispute had a happy ending ten days later.[55]

For the teamen, the contract tea was mainly financed by the foreign houses in the form of advance payments. Jardine's, for instance, made a huge advance in the amount of $440,065 to Ahee in spring 1856. By May 1, Ahee had brought contract tea to Foochow valued at $432,372.[56] Jardine's continued to advance money to Ahee. In May 1861, M. A. Macleod expected to "send Ahee a further lot of Dollars for the purchase of the second crop cargoes." Macleod stated that, although he had $300,000 on hand, this amount was not enough, and more would be required.[57] In addition to Ahee, the house similarly made advances to

54. To Perceval (Hong Kong), Apr. 8, 1861, JMA.

55. Fisher reported to Hong Kong: "I am sorry to say that Ahee & Awy, the Tea boy, cannot agree & that the former has charged the latter with numerous offences which I am now investigating. . . . Some weeks ago Awy told me that the Teamen were complaining that this money they were paid, was much mixed with broken coin & that it was not the same that they, our Tea Hong, received from Captn. Crawford. . . . On asking Ahee about it he denies that the money was changed & has brought a series of countercharges against Awy." ([Foochow] to Joseph Jardine, Dec. 19, 1855, JMA). Fisher wrote again on Dec. 29: "The dispute which I mentioned in my last has been arranged. I had proved 2 of the charges to have been false [and], it appears that 1 of the Canton Coolies I had discharged for stealing Tea has been the principal man by whom the charges were brought against the Tea boy. I had not been able to prove any of them against him who after having made an explanation with Ahee appear to be friends again" (ibid.).

56. George Fisher reported: "The amount of treasure that Ahee had with him in the country last year, including Drug, was $440,065, and the contract Teas to hand amount to $432,372, leaving $7,693 to his debit" (ibid., May 1, 1856).

57. (Foochow) to Alexander Perceval (Hong Kong), May 11, 1861, JMA.

other teamen, such as Alum and Tonghing, though on a less grand scale. For example, M. A. Macleod advanced $3,000 to Tonghing in April 1861 for him to buy Congou at Tls. 22 per chest.[58]

Most of the advances were in the form of silver. Because silver was light in proportion to its value, many teamen took sycee and silver dollars with them to the tea districts. Regular silver dollars were welcome in the interior, but the debased ones, called "broken money," were often rejected.[59] The teamen also received commodities from the foreign merchant as a part of the advance. As pointed out in chapter 3, opium, because it was light, was frequently used in this connection. Opium was carried to the interior for sale, and the proceeds were used for purchasing tea. Thus, in their letters to the foreign agents in Foochow, teamen frequently mentioned the opium market in the upcountry. Taising, for instance, was glad to report from Sueykut that "opium is going off upcountry more easily,"[60] and, eleven days later, that "opium had improved in value a little."[61] He was discouraged, however, when he knew "the opium market is very quiet."[62] This practice continued in the sixties. Taising received ten chests of Malwa at $700 per picul on August 10, 1863, for the upcountry tea purchase.[63] Occasionally, the teamen also received piece goods as a part of the advance. As was the case with opium, the proceeds of the piece goods were used for purchasing tea.[64]

Teamen maintained many tea hongs in the interior. As the primary function of the tea hongs was to buy tea, they were also called "purchasing stations."[65] These stations were strategically situated warehouses, as Augustine Heard, Jr., described them: "Hongs, that is, warehouses, were taken in central situations from which buyers went out to the fairs

58. Ibid., Apr. 8, 1861.
59. George Fisher (Foochow) to Joseph Jardine (Hong Kong), Dec. 19, 1855, JMA.
60. ". . . but there is no improvement to notice in price, the rate obtainable being equivalent to about $750 [per picul] only (for Malwa) at Foochow" (Taising to M. A. Macleod [Foochow], Aug. 29, 1861, JMA).
61. ". . . Malwa being worth equivalent to $770 c [to] 780 at Foochow" (ibid., Sept. 9, 1861).
62. After a short period of rise in price, the opium market retreated and stagnated in the interior, as Taising again wrote: "The Opium market is very quiet, & Malwa being only equal to about $812 per picul at Foochow" (ibid., Sept. 27, 1861).
63. M. A. Macleod (Foochow) to Alexander Perceval (Hong Kong), Aug. 10, 1863, JMA.
64. Taising wrote in 1861: "For lead & piece goods there was no demand at the moment [because of the presence of the Taipings in the upper Min River]" (Taising [Sueykut] to M. A. Macleod [Foochow], Sept. 9, 1861, JMA).
65. For instance, after having received instructions from M. A. Macleod to buy teas of good quality, Taising gave instructions to his employees "at various stations to go in & purchase fine teas" (ibid., Aug. 29, 1861).

or markets held on different days in the surrounding villages and brought in the leaf. Here it was prepared for shipment."[66] One important step in preparation was tea firing, which involved the skillful knowledge of timing—a skill for which the Cantonese became famous.[67] The tea hongs then examined, sorted, packed, and marked the teas before shipment.[68]

After the tea was purchased, processed, and packed in the upper Min Valley, it invariably took about two weeks to ship it to Foochow.[69] In the spring of 1856, Thomas Larken replaced Fisher as Jardine's agent in Foochow, but the transportation mechanism remained unchanged.[70] It generally took two months to purchase, fire, pack, and transport the upcountry tea to Foochow. If the tea was purchased in packed form, it only took about one month. In time of emergency, the tea could be hurried down "in a fortnight or 3 weeks."[71] Foreign houses occasionally used steamers to transport tea from the inland to Foochow on the Min River. Jardine's, for instance, employed two of its river steamers, *Vision* and *Ringleaders*, to ship down the contract tea in early July 1856.[72] To handle the upcountry tea purchase at the Foochow end, the teamen, such as Ahee, also maintained a tea hong in the port. Its functions included the financing of the upcountry operations, the handling of teas when they arrived at Foochow, and the packing and marking of teas for export shipment. It was therefore necessary to have a responsible man to take charge of the hong. This was why in January 1856 Fisher felt uneasy because Ahee would be "up the country the greater part of the year" and therefore could not look after the Foochow tea hong.[73]

Jardine, Matheson & Co.'s purchase of the Bohea teas was so success-

66. "Old China and New," pp. 30–31, GQ-2, HC.

67. George Fisher (Foochow) to Joseph Jardine (Hong Kong), Mar. 30, 1856, JMA.

68. Fisher wrote: "Ahee says that the Chests & HF [Half] Chests I ordered him to pack in the country for the steamer 'Colonies' are finished" (ibid., Jan. 2, 1856). For other steps of preparation, see his letter of May 4, 1856, JMA.

69. George Fisher wrote in early 1856: "No further arrivals of Contract Monings &c have taken place since the list I sent you on 19th ultimo, but Ahee says he is quite sure that the whole will be down in a fortnight so that by that time I shall be ready for a ship for the 'Clyde'" (ibid., Jan. 2, 1856).

70. Reporting on the activities of Ahee, Larken wrote: "3,000 chests [of Congous] were to be sent down [to] Foochow with all despatch and may therefore be expected to arrive here in about a fortnight" (to Joseph Jardine [Hong Kong], June 27, 1856, JMA).

71. George Fisher (Foochow) to Joseph Jardine (Hong Kong), Nov. 15, 1855, and Jan. 2, 1856, JMA.

72. Thomas Larken (Foochow) to Joseph Jardine (Hong Kong), July 13, 1856, JMA.

73. "He [Ahee] was saying that he should like another man to take charge of the [tea] Hong, as he is up the country the greater part of the year & therefore cannot look after it himself. I should not be glad of it, for I feel the want of [a] responsible man when he is away" (Fisher [Foochow] to Joseph Jardine [Hong Kong], Jan. 2, 1856, JMA).

ful in 1854 and 1855 that, by the end of 1855, the house planned to extend the operation deeper into the interior provinces of Hunan and Hupei and to export the teas through Foochow. Ahee, however, was more cautious. He maintained that "the safest way of remitting funds into the Interior would be via Shanghai & that the Oonams, Oopacks &c could go there much easier" than to Foochow.[74] Ahee's view proved to be correct. Although considerable amounts of interior tea were exported via Foochow, a large quantity of tea from the Kiangsi and Hunan areas was shipped to the Shanghai market. When Ahee, for instance, proceeded farther to the interior and arrived at Hohow [Ho-k'ou] on July 30, 1857, he "made particular inquiries" and found to his surprise that a large amount of "fifty-three full chops of Moning tea had gone to Shanghai."[75]

Another way to obtain tea for a foreign trader was to purchase it on the Foochow market, because it was not always possible for him to conclude contracts with the teamen. M. A. Macleod made note of this when he became Jardine's new agent in Foochow in 1861: "For some time past I have been endeavouring to persuade the Teamen to ship under advance, but without avail as yet, except in the case of Yun Tai. . . . Alum is now trying to do something in this way, but I can hardly expect he will be successful."[76] Generally, once teas arrived at Foochow from the upcountry, they were quickly settled on the market. Chinese tea merchants as a rule resided in "tea hotels" (ch'a-chan), so the tea transactions conducted in this manner were called "hotel sales."[77] Occasionally, however, if the tea price on the hotel market was unreasonably high, the foreign merchant would not buy immediately.[78] If the price was reasonable, teas of superior quality would be settled first, "in consequence of their scarcity." At any rate, when purchasing tea upcountry, Western merchants watched closely its price in England.[79]

---

74. Ibid., Dec. 19, 1855.
75. These Moning (Ningchow) teas were "arriving daily at Hohow, and Ahee estimated that the total supply of them would amount to 200 full chops" (Ahee [Sinchune] to M. A. Macleod [Foochow], July 30, 1857, JMA, as summarized by Macleod).
76. To Alexander Perceval (Hong Kong), Feb. 18, 1861, JMA.
77. Memorandum of R. F. Hamilton, Foochow, July 2, 1863, JMA.
78. E.g., George Fisher, who wrote in late 1855: "I have not made any purchases [on the market] this week as I have seen nothing that would be desirable" ([Foochow] to Joseph Jardine [Hong Kong], Dec. 19, 1855, JMA).
79. "The settlement of Tea on the market have been to the extent of about 6,000 Chests during the past week, and the present stock remains as before, viz., 5,000 chests consisting chiefly of the low common kinds and of the grades slightly better which latter are held for Taels 8.5 or 10 but at these prices do not show any margin upon present London

On the whole, Western merchants obtained more tea by purchasing
on the Foochow market than by contracting with teamen. In June 1856,
in addition to Jardine's, eight British, American, and Russian firms
bought a total of 20,780 packages of tea in this manner.[80] Jardine's similarly bought large amounts of tea. From July 1 to August 29, the company purchased 66,000 chests of Congou, 49,000 half-chests of Oolong,
5,000 chests of Souchong, and 3,000 chests of Flowered Pekoe.[81] In the
first half-year of 1863, the firm obtained 43,010 chests of tea under contract but purchased 172,546 chests from the Foochow market.[82] The
foreign merchant could buy unprocessed tea relatively cheaply on the
market, and he would fire the tea himself.[83] He then had to take the
trouble of packing.[84]

WORKING SCHEDULE OF THE TEAMEN

There were several crops of tea from the Bohea districts each year,
and the teamen went to the interior accordingly. The first crop, on the
market in April, was the most important one. To purchase it, the teamen
as a rule started from Foochow in early March, though they occasionally
postponed the journey until the end of the month.[85] When they proceeded upcountry, they usually carried with them the Western firms'
advances in the form of opium or Mexican silver dollars—in foreign
merchants' parlance, "in drug and treasure."

However, if they did not start from Foochow by late March, it would
certainly be too late to purchase the first crop. M. A. Macleod wrote
Alexander Perceval on February 18, 1861, concerning two of Jardine's
enterprising teamen:

Quotations" (Thomas Larken [Foochow] to Joseph Jardine [Hong Kong], Aug. 29, 1856,
JMA).
    80. Dent & Co. led the list with a purchase of 6,670 packages (ibid., July 13, 1856).
    81. On July 1, 1856, Jardine's had on stock 5,000 chests of Congou, 2,400 chests of
Souchong, 9,000 half-chests of Oolong, and 300 chests of Flowered Pekoe (ibid., Aug. 29,
1856).
    82. Memorandum of teas in Foochow, R. F. Hamilton [Foochow], July 2, 1863, JMA.
Calculations mine.
    83. Fisher commented: "Instead of the new Pucksin Congous in an unfinished state
have been shown, they appear to have a good deal of flavor, but I shall be able to tell more
about them when properly fired" ([Foochow] to Joseph Jardine [Hong Kong], May 1,
1856).
    84. Fisher wrote: "They [upcountry teas] will be down in a fortnight or 3 weeks by
which time the boxes I am having packed here will be finished" (ibid., Jan. 2, 1856).
    85. Ahee, e.g., left for the interior on the morning of March 28, 1856, as Fisher wrote:
"Ahee left this [port] for the country the morning before last" ([Foochow] to Joseph Jardine [Hong Kong], Mar. 30, 1856, JMA).

Both Ahee & Taising ought be back here in the course of two or three weeks, and they ought to be on their way upcountry before the last of next month, otherwise they would be too late. Last year the first advances to Ahee & Taising, in Drug & Treasure, left this in the first week of March, so you may judge from this that there is no time to lose, more especially if there be any truth that the New Teas are likely to come forward earlier than usual this Season.[86]

As soon as Ahee and Taising reached Kienning [Chien-ning] on April 13, 1861, they immediately started to buy tea. They also wrote frequently to Macleod in Foochow.[87] When some of the teamen entered into contract with Jardine's on a late date, they had to start their purchases in the interior later than usual.[88]

The second crop was due in late June, and the teamen's purchasing program became very active at this time.[89] Indeed, they were so preoccupied that sometimes they did not even have time to report to the Western merchants at Foochow.[90] Occasionally, the second tea crop came to the Foochow market earlier than usual. In February 1861, for instance, two of Jardine's teamen, Alum and Tonghing, stated that they expected the "new teas" of the second crop to be available on the upcountry market in May instead of June.[91] The third crop was in August, and the fourth crop was in October.[92] In response to special circumstances, however, some merchants also purchased tea upcountry on a limited scale from early November to mid-December.[93]

Due to cold weather, from late December to late February of the next year was an off-season for the tea business in Fukien. Thus, Cantonese tea merchants as a rule returned to Canton by ship for a short stay.[94] On their way home, some of them paid Hong Kong a business trip. In December 1855, for instance, Ahee planned to go to Hong Kong by ship

---

86. Macleod (Foochow) to Perceval (Hong Kong), JMA.

87. Macleod reported on "new tea from Ahee and Taising." "The other day Ahee's first letter reached me, dated Kienningfoo [Chien-ning] the 13th April" (ibid., Apr. 23, 1861).

88. Yuntai, Mantai, and Tonghing, e.g., did not go upcountry until April 13, 1861 (ibid., Apr. 18, 1861).

89. Thomas Larken (Foochow) to Joseph Jardine (Hong Kong), June 27, 1856, JMA.

90. Larken reported to Joseph Jardine: "I have nothing further from Ahee than what I have already informed you of and am rather anxious to know what he has been doing" (ibid., July 13, 1856).

91. M. A. Macleod (Foochow) to Alexander Perceval (Hong Kong), Feb. 18, 1861, JMA.

92. Thomas Larken (Foochow) to Joseph Jardine (Hong Kong), Aug. 22, 1856, JMA.

93. Ahee, e.g., proceeded to the upper Min River from Foochow on Nov. 3, 1855, and Jardine's agent received Ahee's first letter from the interior on Nov. 13. After having stayed in the interior for one and a half months, he returned to Foochow on Dec. 19 (George Fisher [Foochow] to Joseph Jardine [Hong Kong], Nov. 15 and Dec. 19, 1855, JMA).

94. Ibid., Nov. 15, 1855.

to talk to Joseph Jardine on the subject of next season's tea operation in the interior.[95] But, as it happened, he unexpectedly went upcountry again, because several chops of tea were offered to him at bargain prices.[96] Since Ahee had been in the interior, he decided to proceed to Canton overland. After about three weeks' journey to Canton, he would then see Joseph Jardine in Hong Kong.[97] Meanwhile, after having shipped their tea, foreign agents also left the scene temporarily, going first to Hong Kong for consultation with senior partners, and then to Canton or Macao for a short vacation before a new, busy season would start.[98]

THE NETWORK OF COMMUNICATION

The importance of communication in the upcountry tea purchase in Fukien was demonstrated by the frequency with which teamen provided market intelligence to the foreign house in Foochow. After teamen Yuntai, Mantai, and Tonghing "started for the Interior on the 13th" of April, M. A. Macleod would "expect to hear from them very shortly."[99] These teamen reported regularly from the interior, usually once a week. George V. W. Fisher wrote Joseph Jardine in 1855 concerning Ahee's upcountry purchase: "I also told him I was extremely angry with him for not letting me hear sooner from him. I told him in a previous letter that he was to write regularly to me once a week whether he had anything to say or not & let me know how the state of things were up there."[100]

The teamen's reports dealt not only with the particular purchase programs of their own, but also with the upcountry market in general. Taising of Jardine's, for example, went to Shung-oan to purchase tea in late September 1861. In addition to the report on his own tea purchases for the house, he also provided intelligence concerning the tea business in the Shung-oan area. Having summarized Taising's report for Perceval's information, Macleod added: "He will continue his advices when he has anything fresh to communicate."[101]

95. Ibid., Dec. 19, 1855.

96. Ibid., Jan. 2, 1856.

97. "Ahee will proceed thence overland to Canton where he expects to arrive at the latter end of this month when he will proceed to Hong Kong to see you" (ibid.).

98. Fisher wrote Jardine: "I should like [to] speak to you on this [tea hong in Foochow] and other subjects connected with business here, if as I observed in a previous letter, you would allow me to come down after I have shipped off my Teas" (ibid.). His request was granted.

99. To Alexander Perceval (Hong Kong), Apr. 18, 1861, JMA.

100. (Foochow) to Jardine (Hong Kong), Nov. 15, 1855, JMA.

101. (Foochow) to Alexander Perceval (Hong Kong), Sept. 30, 1861. Macleod in-

For his part, the teaman took pains to gather market intelligence. Naturally, he had much first-hand information to report. In addition, he obtained "advices" from his own employees in the villages and small towns. In a letter to Macleod on August 29, 1861, Taising reported that he "received advices from Ah Yaw to the effect that prices for Oolongs had not declined much, quotation being for *fine* 18 Tls. & for middling quality 16 Tls.—laid down at Foochow of course."[102] It usually took one week for a teaman's letter to reach Foochow from the upper Min River, but it might be as fast as three days.[103]

When purchasing contract tea, both quantity and quality were usually approved in advance by the foreign agent. As a result, teamen frequently sent down musters of tea to Foochow. Geroge V. W. Fisher indicated on May 1, 1856, that he was "expecting musters of new Green Teas in the course of 2 or 3 days."[104] In the sixties, Ahee similarly sent down tea musters to M. A. Macleod. Ahee reported on September 22, 1861, that he was then "on the look for good teas," and that in the event of his being able to secure a quantity, he would send down the musters at once to inform Macleod.[105] As meaningful communication necessarily involved two parties, the teamen received letters from the foreign agent in Foochow on a regular basis. Taising showed his uneasiness in Sinchune on April 24, 1863, when he pointed out that he had "not yet received the letter which Mr. [Edward] Whittall promised to send to him relating the latest [tea] intelligence."[106]

Because a Western merchant kept correspondence with several teamen, he was well informed of various costs to prepare the tea. For instance, Edward Whittall, Jardine's agent at Foochow, wrote to Taising on April 30, 1863, that the latter "made an error in his last letter as regards the costs of Teas at Kingyong [Chien-yang] & other places," because Taising stated that the teas were to be bought at Tls. 37 c [to] 38 per picul laid down in Foochow. After careful calculation, however, Whittall dis-

---

cluded his summary of Taising's letter, which read in part: "Taising reports the arrival at Shung-oan of 2 c [to] 300 chs. [chests] of Green Tea, and it is said that 3 c 4,000 chs. more are expected to arrive there shortly, the whole being intended for the Foochow Market for sale" (Taising [Shung-oan] to Macleod [Foochow], Sept. 24, 1861, JMA).

102. (Sueykut) to Macleod (Foochow), JMA.

103. E.g., Taising wrote a letter from Sinchune to Edward Whittall in Foochow on April 24, 1863, and it was received and summarized in English on April 27 (Taising to Whittall, Apr. 24, 1863, encl. in Whittall to Jardine, Matheson & Co. [Hong Kong], Apr. 30, 1863, JMA).

104. (Foochow) to Joseph Jardine (Hong Kong), May 1, 1856, JMA.

105. (Sinchune) to Macleod (Foochow), Sept. 22, 1861, JMA.

106. To Whittall (Foochow), JMA, tr. by Whittall's comprador.

covered that the price was too high, because he knew that Taising paid Tls. 25 to 26 per picul of tea at Kingyong and its vicinities, and that it would cost 25 percent of the cost "to prepare the tea for shipment." In addition, one picul had to pay transit duty for Tls. 1.7. Thus, the total cost would "equal to Tls. 32.8 per picul." Noting that "surely the charge for coolies, rent of hongs &c [could] never amount to 7 taels per picul," Whittall concluded that Taising had overcharged the house.[107] Taising later admitted his mistakes and reduced the price of tea accordingly.

Keeping contact with the teamen was only one part of the responsibility of a foreign firm's resident agent in Foochow; he also had to report promptly to the head office in Hong Kong. M. A. Macleod of Jardine's regularly wrote to the Hong Kong office concerning the tea markets in Fukien. Meanwhile, R. F. Hamilton, Jardine's teataster in Foochow, also addressed Alexander Perceval in Hong Kong "at greater length" with respect to tea. Sometimes Macleod and Hamilton did not agree in their opinion as to the probable course of the tea market in Foochow, and they reported their assessments accordingly.[108] Foreign agents in Foochow also occasionally sent some of the tea musters to Hong Kong for further evaluation.[109]

The business correspondence concerning upcountry tea purchases was considerably detailed and specific, dwelling on the quality, availability, on-the-spot price, and laid-down-at-Foochow price.[110] The quality of tea was specifically divided into five categories—best, good (fine), middling, common, and inferior. The grade of tea had a prominent place in the business correspondence among Chinese and foreign merchants. Having heard that Augustine Heard & Co. had a cargo of inferior tea ready for the United States, George V. W. Fisher of Jardine's wrote on November 15, 1855:

Heard & Co. have also brought some [inferior tea] here to put in the 'Golden State' for America. I have not heard what they paid for it. It is not to be com-

107. (Foochow) to (Sinchune), Apr. 30, 1863, JMA.
108. Macleod admitted frankly to Perceval: "Enclosed are a few lines from Mr. [R. F.] Hamilton on the subject of Teas. On next occasion he will address you at greater length, & meanwhile you will observe that he and I do not quite agree in our opinion as to the probable course of the [tea] market here" (to Perceval [Hong Kong], Feb. 18, 1861, JMA).
109. Macleod wrote Perceval on May 20, 1861: "Yesterday I received a letter from [teaman] Ahee dated Kienningfoo 8th May informing me that he was just sending off to me a small chop, 210 chests, of the new season Congou, and at the same time forwarding per *Special Messenger* a small muster of the parcel in question, a portion of which I now pass on to you by the present conveyance, with Mr. Hamilton's character of it & valuation" (ibid.).
110. Taising (Sueykut) to Macleod (Foochow), Sept. 27, 1861, JMA.

pared in leaf with the Sueykut Oolong selling here at Ts. 9 short, nor is it nearly so good in water. I am trying to get some of these latter at Ts. 8 or under, as there is a large quantity here, which if procurable would be worth attention.[111]

The "common" teas were usually the late fall crop. Although it was difficult for the Western companies to sell them, their low price was certainly attractive. Thomas Larken reported to Joseph Jardine on August 22, 1856:

Ahee [Jardine's teaman] writes me that *good* Teas are very scarce. . . . He expects to be able to make purchases of common Congous at or under Taels 6.5 laid down in Foochow. The present price here is Taels 7 or 7.2. I have instructed Ahee to buy as many *sound, clean* common Congous as he can at the former price limit. With freight at £2 to £5 they would pay well at these prices.[112]

In the fifties and sixties, teamen often worried that the quantity of good tea was not enough. Ahee complained from Sinchune on July 30, 1857: "Good tea is very scarce, and the price too high."[113] In September 1861, Macleod specifically instructed Ahee to buy good quality tea from the interior. However, Ahee admitted on September 22 that, although he had tried his best, he still could not come up with a satisfactory amount of this grade. "Good teas were very, very scarce," and Ahee even reported that he would "not be able to procure any quantity at the moment."[114] Fortunately for Ahee, he wrote Macleod four days later that he had just bought 300 chests of good tea, costing substantially more than the common tea, to be shipped to Foochow in two days.[115]

Taising found that it was extremely difficult to obtain good teas in the Shung-oan area in the fall season of 1861: "In the market upcountry there is very little *Good* Tea on offer; but of middling & common quality there is a large supply available. Any good Tea now in course of preparation for Foochow was purchased last month."[116] When he went to Sueykut three days later, he found that, though fine and middling teas enjoyed good popularity, the common teas were not part of the active market.[117]

111. (Foochow) to Joseph Jardine (Hong Kong), JMA.
112. (Foochow) to Jardine (Hong Kong), JMA.
113. To M. A. Macleod (Foochow), JMA.
114. Ibid., Sept. 22, 1861.
115. Macleod wrote: "Ahee now forwards a muster of chop Yuenlee 300 chests, costing at Foochow Ts. 18½. In two days more he will have ready for dispatch a chop of *good* Tea, about 300 chests, costing at Foochow Ts. 21½" (ibid., Sept. 26, 1861).
116. (Shung-oan) to Macleod (Foochow), Sept. 27, 1861, JMA.
117. "In the present state of the market upcountry, *good* Tea costs laid down at Foochow 22 c [to] 23 Taels, and *middling* quality 15 c 16 Taels. *Common* descriptions continue entirely neglected" (Taising [Sueykut] to Macleod [Foochow], Sept. 30, 1861, JMA).

Teamen's letters also usually included a detailed description of the quality and price of tea. Writing to Macleod on August 29, 1861, Taising reported that the prices of good and fair teas were unusually high. He continued:

Besides, at Suyhow & Kyshow fine or good Tea is also very dear, costing 22 Tls. laid down at Foochow, quality a little different 18 c [to] 19 T., and middling quality 15 c 16 Taels. At Sueykut fine costs 19 c 20 Taels, quality a little different 16 c 17 Taels, & middling 14 c 15 Taels. At Hupyong & Younghow fine Tea costs 21 Taels, quality a little different 18 c 19, & middling 15 c 16 Taels.[118]

If Macleod wanted to purchase teas in these districts, Taising added, "such are the prices [that] must be paid."

In early April 1861, Macleod entered agreements with teamen Yuntai, Mantai, and Tonghing to obtain scented teas. The agreements were comprehensive and specific. They stipulated the kind of tea, price of tea, and time and place it would be delivered. They also specified the amounts of advance payment and the way in which they would be paid.[119] In his correspondence with the senior partners in Hong Kong, Macleod always tried to be as specific as possible. After having made a contract with Taising for buying the Oolong teas, Macleod wrote to Alexander Perceval on April 8, 1861: "For Oolongs my calculation is based on 30 cents for good Cargo kind just as you specify, and Taising promises to do his best in trying to secure a supply at about that figure."[120]

FLEXIBILITY

Even though the upcountry purchase of tea from Fukien was increasingly institutionalized, rules were not always unchangeable. In fact, the upcountry system was often very flexible and full of vitality. For example, a new way of purchasing tea was developed from the existing pattern in the early sixties—the "first refusal" arrangement. Under this system, a foreign house would extend loans to Chinese teamen, charging minimal interest. In contrast to the contract tea arrangement, the teamen were not to provide a specific amount of tea at a fixed price. Instead, when their tea arrived in Foochow, they were bound to offer it first to the firm at the market price. Only after the refusal of the firm were the

118. Ibid., Aug. 29, 1861.
119. Macleod (Foochow) to Alexander Perceval (Hong Kong), Apr. 8, 1861, JMA.
120. Ibid.

teamen free to sell their tea on the market. In other words, by extending loans to the teamen, a foreign firm enjoyed the right of "first refusal" to buy the tea before the teamen put it on the market for sale. M. A. Macleod of Jardine's obtained the right of "first refusal" from teaman Taising in 1863 by making an advance to the latter. He wrote to the firm's head office in Hong Kong: "I have advanced to Taising on Loan $45,000 at 1% per month interest and 10 chests Malwa at $700 per picul. All Teas that come down to him are to be offered first to Mr. Hamilton [our teataster] before being put on the market, & interest to be paid monthly."[121] Alexander Perceval wholeheartedly endorsed this plan.

A teaman was legally responsible for providing tea if he entered into contract with the foreign merchants. However, when the tea price was unexpectedly high in the interior, he would seek fresh instructions from the latter. Taising, for instance, wrote Macleod on August 29, 1861: "The market upcountry is in a very unsatisfactory state as regards buyers of good & fair teas, as they are advancing in price daily, all parties being anxious purchasers of these descriptions." Taising therefore asked for fresh instructions from Macleod regarding further purchases.[122] Generally, the foreign merchants were willing to make necessary changes in order to facilitate smooth business. In a letter to Joseph Jardine concerning the contract tea of Ahee, George V. W. Fisher wrote on November 15, 1855: "I . . . am sorry to say that he has not bought any common Congous, as he said they were so common that I should not like them. I am dispatching a letter to him this evening telling him to buy as good as he can for the money, & extending his limits to Ts. 7.5 short delivered in Foochow."[123]

Sometimes teamen were allowed to purchase tea within a reasonable price range. The exact price of the teas laid down in Foochow would depend on various factors, such as packing and shipping expenses. Jardine's Taising, for instance, bought 240 chests of good Congou at Hupyong, and 600 chests of middling quality at Sueykut in September 1861. Taising estimated that the former would cost at Foochow about Tls. 21 to 22 per chest, and the latter about Tls. 16 to 17. However, he could not give Macleod an exact figure, because the teas were in the process of being packed and shipped.[124] If the teaman still could not

121. Ibid., Aug. 10, 1863.
122. (Sueykut) to Macleod (Foochow), JMA.
123. (Foochow) to Jardine (Hong Kong), JMA.
124. "As soon as these Teas have been packed & shipped off to my address, he will advise me as to the exact cost" (Macleod [Foochow] to Perceval [Hong Kong], Sept. 9, 1861, JMA).

purchase tea in this manner, he had to temporarily keep the funds advanced to him and wait for instructions regarding them.[125]

Although teas were divided into different crops, many tea chops were composed of mixed teas of various crops. Because the quality of the tea depended partly on its freshness, many chops prepared in the summer consisted of mixed first and second crops. Thomas Larken, Jardine's agent, reported to Joseph Jardine in July 1856 that Ahee had purchased 2,500 chests of this kind, with prices ranging from Tls. 18 to 19.7 per picul.[126] It is true that certain crops of tea would arrive in Foochow on specific dates, but exceptions existed. Some kinds of new teas might reach the port earlier than usual, and contingency plans were devised in order to load these teas in time for Western markets.[127]

The net result of these activities was a rapid increase in the export of tea from China. It rose from an annual volume of 20,000,000 pounds at the beginning of the nineteenth century to a peak of 250,000,000 pounds in the 1880s, when tea represented three-fifths of China's exports and 88 percent of the world's exported tea.[128] As a well-institutionalized practice, the system of upcountry purchase typifies the commercialization of agricultural products. This system connected China's interior economy directly with the coastal economy and ultimately with the world market. With the enlargement of the market, littoral merchants encountered new challenges in the form of intense commercial competition.

125. Edward Whittall (Foochow) to Taising (Sinchune), Apr. 30, 1863, JMA.
126. "There are no true second crop Kaesows down here yet, although several chops of mixed first and second crop have been put on the market for which Taels 20 are being asked" ([Foochow] to Jardine [Hong Kong], July 13, 1856, JMA).
127. Macleod of Jardine's wrote to Perceval in Feb. 1861: "Alum & Tong Hing both tell me that the New Teas will probably be hurried forward earlier than usual this Season, & that they expect to see them arrive here *early in May*. Of course this is merely their opinion, and as they do not give reasons for it, perhaps it is not worth much. Still it may be as well to bear it in mind in order that the [steamer] 'Flying Spur' may be here in good time, if this be her destination" ([Foochow] to Perceval [Hong Kong], Feb. 18, 1861, JMA).
128. Yen Chung-p'ing et al., *T'ung-chi*, pp. 15, 82. Calculations are mine.

The Intensification
of Competition

Capitalism hardly exists without competition, and commercial rivalry in export, import, and the shipping trade intensified along the coast after 1860, which singularly enhanced China's commercial revolution.[1] This intense competition was possible only after a fundamental change in communication, which reoriented Sino-Western business patterns. By 1860 the era of the clipper ship had ended with the advancement of the much more efficient steamship, and in 1869 the Suez Canal halved the distance between Europe and China. Telegrams were first sent from Britain to China via intermediary agents at Gibraltar or Trieste, and the steady extension of telegraphic communication to China had a profound effect on the commission business. The improved facilities thus provided were not much relished by foreign merchants, because they accentuated the keenness of the competition. The leisure with which business was conducted in the time of monthly mails was supplanted by the ever-increasing high-pressure rate of communication with all parts of the world.[2]

Suddenly the agency houses in China had to face up to new challenges. Brokerage business became more competitive, and, as the houses were increasingly involved in taking risks on their own part, commercial competition spread to noncommission business as well. Intense and pro-

1. Most scholars agree that competition is an integral part of capitalism, but Fernand Braudel stresses the aspect of monopoly (*Afterthoughts*, pp. 57–58, 113–14).
2. Both Jardine archives and Heard papers indicate that business correspondence noticeably increased after 1860. British consular records show that similar trends existed in the British official correspondence, as testified by the bulky volume sent from Shanghai in 1861 (FO 228, vols. 310–12).

longed commercial competition was waged between the two largest British houses, Jardine, Matheson & Co. and Dent, Beale & Co., and between two of the most prominent American firms, Russell & Co. and Olyphant & Co. These relatively large houses also encountered fresh competitors, because new, small foreign firms mushroomed after 1860, thanks to the financial resources provided by the newly established Western banks—the Chartered Bank of India, Australia and China in 1857 and the Hongkong and Shanghai Banking Corporation in 1864.

Meanwhile, Chinese merchants quickly became a force to be reckoned with. Taking advantage of the auxiliary services provided by the agency houses, such as banking, shipping, and insurance, the Chinese participated in virtually all aspects of foreign trade. They pooled capital, were familiar with market conditions, and ran business with minimum overheads. By the late sixties, a thriving and wealthy Chinese community existed in the coastal ports, particularly Shanghai and Hong Kong. Many were dealing in volumes larger than those of Westerners and had their own network of branches in China and throughout Southeast Asia. The Western traders believed in laissez-faire, including the spirit of competition, but their Chinese counterparts were often motivated by economic nationalism—a strong desire to compete with foreign merchants—that gradually emerged after 1860.

THE SPIRIT OF COMPETITION

Armed with the belief of laissez-faire, not mercantilism, Western traders came to China at the turn of the nineteenth century. Behind the steamships and modern buildings along China's coast stood the business traditions of the Western world, and one critical element was the spirit of competition. Although there are no data available on the share of total trade handled by the largest Western firms, the coastal commerce did not even resemble that of an oligopoly, because the relatively large firms were too numerous. At the China end, because trade was the main reason for the Western presence, it is no surprise that Chinese nationalism, arising from trade relations, developed early in the treaty ports.

WESTERN LAISSEZ-FAIRE AND CHINESE ECONOMIC NATIONALISM

In the days of true merchant adventure, the "free traders" who sailed halfway around the globe to China were genuine followers of Adam

Smith. James Matheson, the founding partner of Jardine, Matheson & Co., wrote in 1836 on the China trade that the laws of nature oblige all peoples to mingle freely with each other, as Vattel the Swiss jurist had demonstrated, and that free trade would benefit everybody and bring prosperity to all.[3] Augustine Heard, Jr., partner of the American firm of Augustine Heard & Co., later vigorously argued that the steady decline of American mercantile houses in China after the 1860s was due more to stiff competition on China's coast in general than to the alleged "opposition of British interests." He recalled in 1894: "There was the same competition, and no more, between British and American firms that there was amongst the American firms themselves. Englishmen and Americans were partners in the same House and stockholders and directors in the same banks and public companies."[4] Indeed, many coastal business enterprises were invested and managed by various nationals, such as the Hongkong and Shanghai Banking Corporation and the British-American Tobacco Company.

On the subject of the steamship trade in China, Edward Cunningham of the American firm of Russell & Co., wrote in 1869 to F. B. Johnson, representative of the British house of Jardine's, that, because the competition applied equally to all merchants in China, there was no special struggle between Englishmen and Americans. In fact, all foreigners in China were in a sense considered cosmopolitans:

Also, the attempt to excite British feeling upon the subject is equally childish and absurd. There is no struggle between English and Americans, as English and Americans in this department, any more than in shipments of produce. We, for instance, as Russell & Co., are scarcely more American than English in our general status. There are many Englishmen, in England and out of it, that think upon all subjects as we do, as there are Americans who think as we do. We are, in truth, all cosmopolitans, more perhaps than most of us know.[5]

A new form of credit on the coast emerged in the mid-forties whereby Chinese merchants used their cargoes as security for shipping via Western vessels (chap. 4). A British consul reported from Chefoo that the southern merchants from Kwangtung and Fukien, who "thoroughly understood the benefit and use of credit," quickly took advantage of this new credit arrangement and developed a thriving shipping business in the three years from 1862 to 1864. The Westerners, however, soon realized that by extending such credit they invited keen competition from

3. *The Present Position and Prospects of the British Trade with China* (London, 1836), p. 1.
4. "Old China and New," p. 42, GQ-2, HC.
5. (Shanghai) to Johnson (Shanghai), May 31, 1869, JMA.

these southern Chinese. The consul continued: "By their industry and special knowledge of the country they have become the greatest competitors that the foreign merchants have to contend with in business." However, believing in the ultimate benefit of the free trade, the consul concluded: "As the permissive measure alluded to is in accordance with the principle of free trade, it must eventually produce beneficial results to all concerned."[6] Indeed, by the nineteenth century, for both the Western diplomats and merchants, laissez-faire replaced mercantilism as the guiding principle of doing business in China.

Chinese commercial nationalism gradually emerged as a response to Western economic encroachment on China. The enlightened high officials and patriotic merchants in the treaty ports began to talk of economic competition (*shang-chan*, lit., "commercial warfare") with the foreigners after the early sixties.[7] The term *shang-chan* appeared first in 1862 in a letter of Tseng Kuo-fan but was used only occasionally.[8] Ting Jih-ch'ang, as Shanghai taotai, promised in 1863 to reduce the tax on Chinese junks in order to compete with foreign ships in the Newchwang-Shanghai bean trade. He wrote Li Hung-chang the following year suggesting that Chinese merchants should be encouraged to buy and build steamships. Equipped with modern means of maritime transport, Chinese merchants would outcompete the foreign trader, because they were more familiar with the local markets. The motivation of the Westerner's coming to China, Ting continued, was mainly to seek profit. If he could not get profit, he would naturally leave China. In this way, it would not be necessary for China to expel foreigners by force.[9]

Among those who discussed the subject of *shang-chan*, Cheng Kuan-ying's treatment was the most vigorous, and he became the most important proponent of the concept. This distinguished coastal merchant contended that, because the strength of the West stemmed from wealth that in turn came from commerce and industry, it would be more useful for China to learn to wage economic warfare (*shang-chan*) than military confrontation (*ping-chan*). Cheng stated that a Western country not only used cannon as weapons, but also used trade as a weapon for colonization. In fact, China, with an unfavorable balance of trade, was severely

6. BPP, *Reports from Her Majesty's Consuls in China, 1864*, vol. 71, Chefoo, p. 50.

7. For the rise of China's economic nationalism in historical perspective, see Yen-p'ing Hao and Erh-min Wang, "Changing Chinese Views of Western Relations, 1840–1895," in John K. Fairbank and Kwang-Ching Liu, eds., *The Cambridge History of China*, vol. 11, *Late Ch'ing, 1800–1911, Part 2* (Cambridge, England, 1980), pp. 142–210.

8. Tseng Kuo-fan, *Tseng Wen-cheng kung shu-cha* (Shanghai, 1876), 17.44a–b.

9. Lü Shih-ch'iang, *Ting Jih-ch'ang yü tzu-ch'iang yün-tung* (Taipei, 1972), pp. 56–62.

harmed by her commercial relations with the West. To fight back commercially, the Ch'ing government needed to reform the tax system and abolish the likin tax on local trade. The basic approach, however, was the elevation of the merchant's social status. Cheng concluded that, if China's commerce could compete successfully with that of the West, the foreign merchants would lose money and would naturally go home. The world at this time, as Cheng saw it, was a world of commercial rivalry, and Cheng was one of the first reformers in modern China to advocate mercantile nationalism.[10]

China's efforts to establish steamship enterprises on the coast gave eloquent testimony to her spirit of commercial rivalry with the West. Yung Wing and Hsu Tao-shen, with this commercial nationalism in mind and supported by the Tsungli Yamen, tried to set up a joint-stock steamship company at Shanghai in 1868. Although this project aborted, the China Merchants' Steam Navigation Company was inaugurated in 1872. Governor-General Li Hung-chang, the promoter, declared that the aim of this enterprise was to rival the Western steamship companies. Tong King-sing (T'ang T'ing-shu) and Hsu Jun, the company's managing directors, were extremely conscious of *shang-chan*. Their report to the shareholders in 1874 mentioned three favorable factors vis-à-vis the Western shipping concerns. First, the Chinese company could rely on the imperial tribute rice for Peking as freight; second, its administrative costs were low; and third, it could easily get freight from the native merchants. In order to prevent foreigners from subscribing to shares in the company, it was stipulated that names of shareholders and their native towns be registered on the share certificates, which could not legally be sold to a foreigner.[11]

THE SENSITIVE AND COMPETITIVE
MARKET ON THE COAST

In contrast to the interior markets which tended to be slow in tempo, those on the coast responded quickly to the market mechanism of demand and supply. To keep business in an ever-competitive condition, foreign partners always kept an eye on their fellow traders. A. G. Dallas,

10. Yen-p'ing Hao, "Cheng Kuan-ying: The Comprador as Reformer," *Journal of Asian Studies* 29 (Nov. 1969), pp. 15–22; Liu Kuang-ching, "Cheng Kuan-ying *I-yen*: Kuang-hsu ch'u-nien chih pien-fa ssu-hsiang," *Ch'ing-hua hsueh-pao* 8.1–2 (1970), pp. 373–425; and Cheng Kuan-ying, *Sheng-shih wei-yen*, 2.34b–43, and *Sheng-shih wei-yen hou-pien*, 1.1, 2.37b, 4.56b–57, 7.19, 8.32, 8.53.

11. *Chiao-t'ung shih*, I. 139, 144, 147.

agent of Jardine's at Shanghai, frequently mentioned "our neighbours" in his correspondence to the firm's senior partners at Hong Kong in the late forties and early fifties.[12]

In his autobiography, Hsu Jun cites many instances in which merchants, Chinese and foreign alike, incurred losses because they failed to see the sensitive aspect of the market. For example, in 1860, a foreign merchant bought seventy-five barrels of fruit from Foochow and shipped via S. S. *Fukien* to Shanghai for sale. His profit was three times the amount of his investment. Thus encouraged, he shipped more to Shanghai. This time, however, he lost money becasue the Shanghai market had been overstocked with fruit from South China. This was also the case with other commodities, such as incense from Southeast Asia and seafoods from Japan.[13] Hsu's observation was borne out by the Jardine archives. Taking advantage of a strong market in Hong Kong, Elles & Co. at Amoy shipped some camphor to that port to be sold through Jardine's. When the camphor arrived in Hong Kong, it realized less than expected because Chinese merchants had already shipped a "considerable quantity" of camphor from Taiwan to Hong Kong.[14]

The Heard papers provide a detailed, interesting episode of the sensitive rice market in Peking-Tientsin in 1861. During the winter of 1860, the Ch'ing government was arranging a contract with American merchants to provide Peking with rice. A. F. Heard of Augustine Heard & Co. and Edward Cunningham of Russell & Co. were interested in this rice business. On January 20, 1861, the two American houses submitted a joint proposal to the Ch'ing government. The negotiations between Heard and Cunningham were carried on with the utmost secrecy so as to avoid a fall in the price of rice in Peking and the rise in freight charges that would result if news of such a proposal were to be made public. They did not even reveal their plans to Hsueh Huan, the imperial commissioner in charge of foreign affairs, who had been sent to call on Heard's by the Ch'ing government.[15] The American merchants feared

---

12. See Dallas letters to Donald Matheson and David Jardine, B2, vols. 134–37, JMA.

13. Hsu Jun, *Nien-p'u*, pp. 7–8.

14. Elles & Co. wrote to Jardine's: "Your sale of our camphor at $25.50 per picul— rather less than we expected it to realize—is satisfactory as we hear of considerable quantity going forward to your port from Tamsui on Chinese account" ([Amoy] to Jardine's [Hong Kong], June 11, 1868, JMA).

15. Arthur W. Hummel, ed., *Eminent Chinese of the Ch'ing Period, 1644–1912* (Washington, D.C., 1943–1944), II, 744.

that he might tip off his Chinese friends, especially those connected with Jardine, Matheson & Co., who were potential competitors.

In spite of the effort on the part of these two houses for secrecy, the price of rice in Peking fell considerably below that proposed by Heard and Cunningham. The two houses had offered to ship the rice to Tientsin at Tls. 3.86 per picul, including a 35 percent profit. The market price of the grain by late February in Peking was already under Tls. 2 per picul indicating that the market had apparently been flooded in response to the rumored shortage. Chinese concerns had shipped considerable quantities of domestic and foreign rice to Peking. Although the proposed rice contract was aborted, Heard, having investigated the rice trade thoroughly, decided to engage in the shipment of the rice and compete on the open market. The house imported large amounts of rice from Southeast Asia, including 160,000 piculs in April alone, but due to the keen competition Heard's finally lost money. A. F. Heard wrote on June 16, 1861: "Just our luck, instead of making a lot of money, we shall lose heavily as the market has gone down instead of up and everybody has been getting rice in."[16]

The relatively small group of well-capitalized Western agency houses along China's coast during the first half of the nineteenth century is described in the Customs Report: "In old times, business was done in Shanghai by men having command of large capital, who bought heavy consignments here and stored them till there was a chance for sale."[17] These agency houses also functioned as banks, issuing dollar notes and providing deposit and remittance facilities, as in the case of Jardine's. Edward Cunningham of Russell & Co. wrote in 1873: "Twenty to twenty-five years ago the prominent houses, including one American, did a flourishing exchange business. . . . One English bank had less business than one of the mercantile houses."[18]

By the mid-nineteenth century, however, foreign houses competed in earnest with one another on two fronts. One method was cutting commission rates in order to expand business. The official rates for commissions on sales or purchases dropped from 4 to 3 percent from 1850 to 1860. Actually, many houses probably charged even less, because the official rates were not universally observed, and rebates and "return commissions" were in common practice. Besides, American firms, be-

16. (Shanghai) to George W. Heard, Jr., HL-35, HC.
17. IMC, *Decennial Report, 1882–1891*, p. 322.
18. *NCH*, June 26, 1873, p. 75.

cause of their lack of authoritative reputation, generally charged less than their British counterparts. Augustine Heard & Co., for instance, tried to increase its silk business in 1859 by asking only 1 percent for inspecting and 1 percent for negotiating bills.[19] The second method was that, rather than doing safe business on the basis of commissions, foreign houses were increasingly involved in taking risks on their own part. Some clients at home requested the house to share risks and profits with them, but quite a few conservative partners resented this new trend of "merchanting," arguing that it would be too risky. Given their choice, most would probably have preferred to continue doing business as pure commission agents, but the competition was so intense that no firm, not even the conservative Russell & Co., was in a position to refuse their clients' request.

Mercantile competition became even more intense after the sixties as a result of the trade expansion, which gave rise to a new commercial milieu on the coast and saw the commission business drastically decreased. Edward Cunningham was alarmed by the "great change" in June 1861.[20] Four months later A. F. Heard similarly acknowledged the necessity of direct house investment.[21] The adaptability of foreign houses to this new trend of "merchanting," as opposed to pure commission business, was crucial to their commercial success. The firm that fared best was Jardine, Matheson & Co., which, by the end of the sixties, was engaged in various enterprises involving direct investments. Russell & Co. was forced to reorganize in 1872 to meet the challenge. A less successful firm was the American house of Augustine Heard & Co., which deteriorated drastically during the seventies. The least responsive big house of all was the British firm of Dent, Beale & Co., which wound up its business in 1867. Under these circumstances, any unnecessary expenses of the merchants on the coast, Chinese and foreign alike, had to be reduced. One case in point was the Western traders' luxurious lifestyle which, as an Englishman observed, "the trade could no longer bear when competition became keener after the Treaty of 1860."[22]

THE EXPORT TRADE

In contrast to the distribution of imported goods, which was mainly controlled by the Chinese, the export trade offered much more lucrative

19. Lockwood, pp. 35, 129.
20. Cunningham to P. S. Forbes, June 4, 1861, FC.
21. Heard to Augustine Heard, Jr., Oct. 22, 1861, HL-36, HC.
22. Bourne et al., p. 23.

opportunities for Western merchants. One reason for this was that foreigners had played active roles in the earlier development of the supply of such new exports as hog bristles, hides and leather, and eggs and egg products. In the nineteenth century, they competed vigorously in purchasing Chinese produce for export and paid competitive prices to Chinese merchants for tea and silk. The sizable, relatively risk-free profit accorded to the Chinese merchants was, according to the British consul at Canton in 1867, the only reason why the export trade had not passed into Chinese hands. The consul might have somewhat exaggerated the situation, but the spirit of commercial rivalry is confirmed by the Jardine archives, which unmistakably show that exporting in tea and silk became much more competitive and less profitable to the foreign trading firms in China after the 1860s.[23]

Competition was intense for the trade in tea and silk on the part of the foreign merchants and was carried on not only in China but also in Western markets. John Samuel Swire, founding partner of the British China-trade house Butterfield & Swire, wrote in 1884 from London to the firm's branch offices in Shanghai and Foochow concerning tea musters:

Importers [in London] complain that they cannot get tea musters from OSS [Ocean Steamship Company, for which Butterfield & Swire served as agents], as soon as by Glens and P. & O. [Peninsular and Oriental Steamship Company]. The Glens place musters from *all ports*, so that they can be discharged immediately on berthing, whether the steamer has filled up at Singapore or not. This is a very important matter, so please attend to it.[24]

Some Western traders incurred losses even if they purchased tea cheaply from China, as is seen in the experience of the London market during the 1870–1871 season. A memorandum of Jardine's on this unpleasant episode notes that the anxiety to sell "at one time partook of the nature of a panic."[25] The Chinese were by no means passive in the ex-

23. The sizable profit accorded to the Chinese merchants was, in the words of C. B. Robertson, British consul at Canton in 1867, "the only factor that militates against the export going in the same direction" as did the import trade. He went on: "The competition among foreigners for teas and silk pays the Chinese better and without risk than their exporting themselves these products would do. If it was to cease by [foreign] combination (an impossibility) or otherwise, even the export trade would pass into Chinese hands" (to Edward Hammond, Feb. 28, 1867, FO 17/481). For the Jardine records, see LeFevour, p. 152.

24. Swire to Butterfield & Swire (Shanghai and Foochow), Sept. 4, 1884, SP.

25. "The fears entertained by some [tea] buyers in China that we should not have enough tea, led them to pay a large advance in August and September [of 1870], also to ship rubbish which swelled the export figures, and caused on this [London] side an anxiety

port trade. They often shipped tea and silk to foreign markets on joint-accounts with Western traders after the mid-century. Their more active role can be seen from their rivalry with foreign traders in the direct export of tea. The British consul, C. B. Robertson, for example, pointed out in 1865 that whereas Western merchants lost money in the previous years, "the Chinese have come out well and even with a profit." After having noted that the distribution of imported goods fell increasingly into the hands of the Chinese merchants, he pessimistically concluded that the export trade might follow the same course.[26]

The competition in China's export trade was such that a London newspaper in 1867 called for Chinese merchants to engage in direct export to London more actively.[27] We do not know whether the Chinese responded to this encouragement directly, but a group of southern Chinese, led by Li Chao-min of Canton, set up an export firm, named "Chao-hsing," a few months later. The head office was in Canton, and it had a major branch office in London. Having failed to enlist the services of the noted comprador-merchant Cheng Kuan-ying, Li appointed another townsman, Liu Shu-t'ing (Seating), as the resident manager in London. Liu was selected because he had been a comprador to Augustine Heard & Co. at Hankow in the mid-sixties. Because of the lack of government support and the difficulty in raising the projected capital of Tls. 300,000, the firm terminated its business three years later.[28]

The purchase of tea and silk from the interior played an important role in China's export trade. This upcountry system, in time, created stiff competition in the interior as well as in the treaty ports.[29] Planning to

---

to sell which at one time partook of the nature of a panic. During which time the cheapest bought teas of the seasons were sold without a profit, even in some cases at a loss" (Memorandum for season 1870–1871, Memoranda, JMA).

26. "Nor is it at all improbable that the export trade may, to a great extent, follow the same course. Already at Foochow and elsewhere large shipments of teas have been made by Chinese firms on consignment to England, and the fact has appeared that whilst foreign merchants have been having losses on last year's transactions in the home markets, the Chinese have come out well and even with a profit" (Report of Consul C. B. Robertson, Canton, Mar. 30, 1865, FO 17/434).

27. "The Chinese should themselves take the initiative, and consign their produce direct to this country, without the intervention of middlemen or agents. There would then be a better chance of reaching the lowest possible cost compatible with a fair profit for the merchant" (Enclosure in C. B. Robertson [Canton] to Edward Hammond, Feb. 28, 1867, FO 17/481).

28. For the history of Chao-hsing, see Cheng Kuan-ying, *Tseng-ting*, 2:18–18b; and *Shen pao*, Mar. 18, 1876, p. 1. For Liu Shu-t'ing (Seating), see letter of H. G. Bridges (Hankow) to A. F. Heard (Shanghai), Apr. 11, 1866, HM-23, HC.

29. G. C. Allen and A. G. Donnithorne, *Western Enterprise in Far Eastern Economic De-*

embark on large-scale upcountry purchase of tea and silk in 1851, A. G. Dallas of Jardine's noticed that other foreign houses and Chinese merchants were trying to do exactly the same thing. In particular, Dent's and Lindsay's planned to commit $300,000 and $800,000, respectively, for this purpose. Dallas was determined not to be outdistanced by the competition and made advances totaling $150,000 to Takee. He wrote:

> Under all these circumstances I am as you may suppose very anxious to keep pace with my neighbours, & at the same time feel deeply the responsibility & anxiety attendant upon making advances, & often regret that we are so far separate on these occasions. Takee still is very confident that he will have the first Teas down, & I am encouraging him to contract freely in the interior at or about the prices named above. With this view, in addition to the lak of dollars [$100,000] already advanced or promised, I am giving him more funds by degrees to the extent of half a lak more.[30]

By the end of the sixties, however, the competition in export was so keen that Jardine's F. B. Johnson even toyed with the idea of abandoning export trade altogether in favor of banking business: "I am inclined to believe that . . . in banking business with the Chinese . . . we shall probably find a better account than in the hard driven competition for the export of Tea and Silk."[31]

It was the Chinese who first went to the upcountry where they purchased tea and transported it to the treaty ports for sale. Upcountry purchases offered many advantages to the Chinese merchants. Reporting from Shanghai in 1867, the foreign commissioner at the customs office observed that the upcountry trade might "eventually prove extremely dangerous" and tended "to throw all the advantages of trade into the hands of the Chinese."[32] After the abolition of the Cohong system in 1842, the upcountry purchase of tea originated in and was operated from

---

velopment (London, 1954), pp. 53–54, give a brief account of Western merchants' tea purchases without mentioning the competition among them.

30. (Shanghai) to David Jardine (Hong Kong), May 20, 1851, JMA. Dallas wrote about Dent's and Lindsay's: "Extensive purchases by Foreigners or Canton men may however alter the complexion of affairs. I mentioned to you before that Dent, Beale & Co. had sold their Bills to some extent last month at 4/9. The funds went into the interior & Takee tells me that the proceeds of Malwa to the extent of 200,000 sold at Soo-choo [Soochow] have been appropriated to the purchase of produce. This coincides with the general report which says that they have sent three laks [$300,000] into the interior. Takee also tells me of $80,000 advanced to an old purser of his by Messrs. Lindsay & Co. for a similar purpose" (ibid.).

31. (Shanghai) to William Keswick (Hong Kong), Feb. 1, 1869, JMA.

32. BPP, *Reports on Trade by the Foreign Commissioners at the Ports in China Open by Treaty to Foreign Trade for the Year 1866*, vol. 69, p. 20.

the three major treaty ports of Shanghai, Hankow, and Foochow. Shanghai dominated the tea districts of Kiangsu, Anhwei, and Chekiang; Hankow controlled the middle Yangtze Valley of Hupei, Hunan, and northern Kiangsi; and Foochow governed the Bohea area of Fukien and southern Kiangsi.

UPCOUNTRY TEA TO SHANGHAI AND HANKOW

The increase in tea export resulted in keen competition in the interior. Robert Fortune, a British traveler, gave an eyewitness account of the business in the tea districts of Chekiang in the late 1840s:

When the teas are ready for sale, the large tea merchants or their servants come out from the principal towns of the district, and take up their quarters in all the little inns or eating houses. . . . The tea growers bring their produce for inspection and sale. These little farmers or their labourers may now be seen hastening along the different roads, each with two baskets or chests slung across his shoulder on his bamboo pole. When they arrive at the merchants' abiding place the baskets are opened before him, and the quality of the tea inspected. [If the price was agreeable to both parties the transaction was made; however,] should the price offered appear too low, the baskets are immediately shouldered with the greatest apparent independence, and carried away to some opposition merchants.[33]

After Shanghai was opened to foreign trade in 1842, it became an outlet for a portion of the Bohea tea of Fukien and Kiangsi, which was traditionally sent to Canton for export. Jardine, Matheson & Co.'s Shanghai office sent a Chinese teaman named Mounsey to Fukien to buy tea in 1847. Meanwhile, A. G. Dallas, the firm's partner and earliest representative at Shanghai, was concerned about the competitive tea market on the coast. He was especially eager to know about the Canton market because, as he put it, "our neighbours have tea musters of most of the chops sold there."[34] In 1852 the extensive purchase of tea by Mackenzie Brothers & Co. at Shanghai sent the price so high that James Macandrew of Jardine's decided to halt purchases temporarily.[35] In

33. *Wanderings*, pp. 212–13.
34. To Jardine, Matheson & Co. (Hong Kong), July 19, 1847, JMA.
35. "The Tea market is now fairly opened, & a large business has been done, chiefly in Moning Teas at Ts. 15 & 17 (the best here Ts. 17½ or 18, which for the quality are considered high prices). The largest buyers by far are Mackenzie Bros. & Co., & their object is so little understood that a pretty general impression prevails [namely], they are merely acting as J. M. & Co.'s agents. Mr. Wills has so bad an opinion of all the new Teas yet showing but more particularly of the Hokows, that he thinks it inadvisable to meddle with them & that at present valuations all the settlements must lose money to some extent.

early 1861 Edward Cunningham of Russell's, tipped off by a reliable Chinese tea dealer, was prepared to compete with fellow Americans, Olyphant & Co., on the Shanghai market for the purchase of a sizable supply of green tea arriving from Ningpo.[36]

As noted in chapter 6, the foreign merchant generally had two ways to purchase tea. The easiest way was to buy on the market which was, of course, competitive. Another method was to make advances to Chinese teamen who would proceed to the upcountry to buy tea. These teamen performed two functions that allowed the foreign merchant to complete effectively with his "neighbours." First, the teaman was obliged to purchase tea at a reasonable price, the most effective way to assure this being to check the price of one teaman against that of another. James Whittall wrote from Shanghai to Jardine's head office at Hong Kong in July 1861: "On comparing teamen Yakee's and Aleet's accounts, both acting perfectly independent of each other, I find that they agree pretty well, and from what I hear of similar transactions on account of our neighbours, I am satisfied that ours are cheap in comparison."[37] This was not an isolated case, for William Keswick wrote on the subject again in October 1864: "Ateong's Teas have been quite as cheap as his neighbour bought in the interior at the same time. With Aleet the case is somewhat different, and I have refused to take his Tea, in two cases, & in another he has agreed to pay the equivalent of the difference in price in London between his Tea & what the best of Chops (reported a good one) sells for."[38]

The teaman's second major responsibility was that of providing the quickest possible transport of tea from upcountry to the ports. One of Jardine's teamen was Aleet, a southern merchant who was active at Shanghai. With respect to the possibility of buying contract tea from Aleet in the future, F. B. Johnson emphasized the importance of timing. He wrote William Keswick on February 12, 1868: "If you decide upon doing anything, we must impress upon him the importance of bringing

I have therefore made no purchases" (James Macandrew [Shanghai] to David Jardine [Hong Kong], July 14, 1852, JMA).

36. "10,000 half-chests of green teas from the Tychow district came into Ningpo last week. . . . The men who have given the information are among the most respectable and reliable of the green tea dealers. I shall incline to the opinion that a chance in Greens may occur, if a large quantity comes down together. Olyphant & Co. cannot hold on forever" (Cunningham [Shanghai] to F. G. Dexter [Hong Kong], Jan. 26, 1861, DP).

37. To Jardine, Matheson & Co., July 30, 1861, JMA.

38. (Shanghai) to James Whittall (Hong Kong), Oct. 7, 1864, JMA.

down his first chops at least as soon as those from any other Hong. Last season he was much behindhand & our Ring Sing's have lost their market in consequence."[39]

After Hankow was opened to foreign trade in 1860, it became a major center for purchasing tea from the middle Yangtze Valley, especially from northern Hunan. R. B. Davis, agent of Jardine's in Hankow, made an arrangement with Avung, a Chinese teaman, to buy tea from the interior. Avung was apparently an efficient merchant, and Davis was particularly pleased with Avung's reasonable prices.[40] Other Western traders in Hankow made similar arrangements with Chinese teamen. The second important port on the middle Yangtze was Kiukiang, where foreign houses competed for buying the upcountry tea. E. H. Kenney, Jardine's agent at Hankow, reported in 1885 that the firm was outcompeted by Anderson & Co. in Kiukiang: "Our Kiukiang business has not worked so satisfactorily. Mr. Campbell's Compradore is a man of no influence, while R. Anderson & Co.'s Compradore Tataksing is a very large owner of fine teas, Ningchow's especially, so that R. A. & Co. have a great advantage over Mr. Campbell in buying fine teas."[41]

In addition to the southern teamen working for the Western mercantile houses, some merchants from Shansi province also went to the mid-Yangtze Valley to purchase tea for the Russians. Early in the summer of 1866, these "Shansi men" were the "principal purchasers" in the tea districts of Hunan and competed with the Cantonese teamen, including Yowloong of Jardine's. William Affray, the firm's agent at Hankow, reported to William Keswick in June 1866 that five tea hongs—representing Reiss & Co., Gilman & Co., a certain Mr. Scholefield, and the Russians—were competing for the second crop teas in a small town of northern Hunan.[42] The purchasing activities of the Shansi merchants remained aggressive in the region throughout the sixties.

39. (Shanghai) to Keswick (Hong Kong), JMA.
40. "Avung has arrived down from the Tea districts & called upon me today. He has brought down a fourth chop of Tea costing Tls. 185 including Linking [likin] tolls, which I do not find dear in comparing with other parties' country purchases" (Davis to James Whittall [Shanghai], Sept. 4, 1861, JMA).
41. "They carried their advantage this season to the extent of preventing their Compradore from selling us teas, and we were debarred from doing business with his hong. Mr. McEvers has repeatedly complained of not being able to do any business in Tataksing's teas" (Kenney to J. J. Keswick [Shanghai], May 27, 1885, JMA).
42. "I wrote you yesterday. Youloong has since received letters from the interior, where the market for second crop teas has already opened, with 4 c [to] 5 hongs competing, whilst at Yong Low Toong [Yang lou tung] and Cheong Son Ken the rates opened at Tls. 30 c 32 [per chest], principal purchasers being Shansi men for the Russians" (Affray to Keswick [Shanghai], June 13, 1866, JMA).

The Russian merchants often stayed in the upper Yangtze ports to supervise the purchase of tea. Sometimes they were the most aggressive buyers among all foreign merchants, "taking all the fine chops they could buy."[43] Thus, when their steamers appeared on the upper Yangtze to purchase tea, Affray observed that "the teamen are beginning to bestir themselves."[44] Affray's preoccupation with the Russians is clearly evidenced by the frequency with which he dwelt on them in his correspondence with Jardine's Shanghai and Hong Kong offices.[45] Occasionally, Jardine's even resold some of their tea to Russian merchants at a relatively high price, hoping to purchase again shortly, because, as Jardine's agent pointed out, "no doubt after the departure of the Russian steamer we shall see lower rates."[46] The Russian purchase of tea in the mid-Yangtze Valley continued to be on a large scale in the mid-seventies.

UPCOUNTRY TEA TO FOOCHOW

The third upcountry purchase center was Foochow, the closest treaty port to the Bohea districts. It was the American firm of Russell & Co. that first explored the possibility of exporting Bohea tea from Foochow in 1854, and the Chinese merchant Ahone was the man who acted on behalf of Russell's.[47] Meanwhile, Augustine Heard & Co. established a branch office in Foochow in the same year for the purpose of purchasing upcountry tea, and its comprador, Tong Loong-maw, was a most enterprising tea merchant on the coast.[48]

As was the case with those in the Yangtze ports, Chinese and Western traders in Fukien kept an eye on one another. For instance, in his reports to Hong Kong, John Williams of Jardine's frequently mentioned the tea-

43. F. B. Johnson wrote: "The latest news from Hankow reports a quieter feeling excepting among Russian buyers who were taking all the fine chops they could buy up to 43½ taels, Hankow currency. English operators were generally holding aloof, and the steamers were not progressing with their engagements" ([Shanghai] to William Keswick [Hong Kong], May 29, 1871, JMA).
44. "Certain Russian buyers have instructed the Teamen to send them musters of fine chops only and I think that these will command full rates" ([Hankow] to Henry Murray [Shanghai], May 16, 1871, JMA).
45. Ten days later, for instance, he again wrote: "Messrs. Reiss and Co., Gilman and Co., and the Russians and Mr. Scholefield comprize the chief purchasers of tea" (to F. B. Johnson [Shanghai], May 26, 1871, JMA).
46. Robert Anderson reported to Shanghai: "I have resold some of the teas to a Russian buyer at Tls. 43 per picul" ([Kiukiang] to F. B. Johnson, May 28, 1871, JMA).
47. George Fisher (Foochow) to Joseph Jardine (Hong Kong), Mar. 30, 1856, JMA.
48. Case 9, HC II.

purchasing activities of the American house of Russell & Co. in the 1850s.[49] Again, when Russell's Ahone arrived at Foochow from Shanghai in March 1856, George V. W. Fisher of Jardine's was deeply concerned about his next move. He wrote Joseph Jardine on March 30, 1856: "Ahone, Russell & Co. man, who did all their business for them last year, arrived down in the 'Antelope,' but have not heard yet what his movements are likely to be. I suppose from his coming down that he is going into the Interior to buy Teas."[50] Similarly, Jardine's teaman Ahee, in the interior in 1857, was alarmed when he learned that Dent, Beal & Co. and Lindsay & Co. had shipped a considerable amount of tea, particularly Moning tea, from the Bohea districts to Foochow in 1856 and 1857.[51]

The vigorous tea trade in Foochow as well as in the interior was so routine that Chinese merchants simply took it for granted; in fact, the lack of it was regarded as abnormal. Because Jardine's and Russell's were the only two foreign houses that were consistently buying tea in the upcountry at the end of 1855, tea prices were low. Being accustomed to active trading and high prices, Chinese merchants, instead of selling under these circumstances, preferred to keep their tea packed up in the upcountry and wait for a expected rise in price.[52]

The competition among foreign merchants in the Fukien tea districts in the mid-century was reflected in several ways. In the first place, they increased competition in the interior, which was already frequently disrupted by heavy buying. George V. W. Fisher reported to Joseph Jardine on May 4, 1856, that the teamen of Jardine's, Dent's, and Gilman's were vigorous in purchasing upcountry tea, driving up the price by one to two taels per chest.[53] Three months later, Thomas Larken of Jardine's dwelt on how these three rival houses competed in the purchase of com-

---

49. "M. R. [Messrs. Russell] & Co. purchased yesterday a chop of old Congou at 8 Ts. [per chest] short. The tea is all out of condition and cannot be called good" (Williams [Foochow] to Jardine, Matheson & Co. [Hong Kong], July 30, 1854, JMA).

50. (Foochow) to Jardine (Hong Kong), JMA.

51. Ahee (Sinchune) to M. A. Macleod (Foochow), July 30, 1857, JMA.

52. George Fisher of Jardine's reported from Foochow on Dec. 7, 1855: "I understand Russell & Co. & ourselves are the only foreign houses that are buying at present in the country. I believe the former have about 4000 chests bought. If prices get up here, I dare say we shall have as much as we want but from what I can gather from the Chinese here, they intend keeping what is packed up in the country until next year if prices do not improve" (to Jardine, Matheson & Co. [Hong Kong], JMA).

53. Fisher wrote that, following the suit of Jardine's teamen and Dent and Co.'s shroff, the teamen of "Gilman's commenced buying whereupon all followed & prices were run up Ts. 1 c [to] 2., when after buying some little, all of them held off again for lower prices" ([Foochow] to Jardine [Hong Kong], JMA).

mon Congou tea in the upcountry. He reported that he had instructed Ahee "to purchase as many as he could buy of clean, good common," adding:

Messrs. Dent & Co. have also I hear sent orders to buy common Congou and Messrs. Gilman & Co. are sending money up the country, doubtless with the same object. Mr. Hudson of the latter firm came down from Shanghai in the [steamer] 'Confucius' the other day and I fancy that he is induced to operate largely in Teas this season, as a good many purchases have been made by them within the last week at somewhat advanced rates.[54]

Meanwhile, many leading American firms, such as Heard's and Russell's, were also engaged in this kind of upcountry purchase of tea.

Second, the foreign houses competed for the fastest transportation of upcountry tea to Foochow. Fisher reported to Hong Kong on May 1, 1856, that Dent, Beale & Co. purchased a large amount of tea in that year and tried "everything to get their Teas down first [to Foochow]."[55] Fisher wrote again three days later: "I mention to Ahee every time I write, the necessity of getting his Teas down as soon as, or sooner than, other people's & he tells me not to fear, but I am afraid of Dent & Co. & Gilmans, for they have bought more in the country by a long way than anybody else. I understand Gilman & Co. are going to try 2 small vessels this year, the 'Chrysolite' & 'Congo.'"[56]

The market intelligence of Ahee and Fisher proved to be correct. Although Fisher managed to beat his "neighbours" in transporting the upcountry tea to Foochow quickly, he paid a high price for it. For one thing, all the foreign houses wanted to ship their tea to Foochow as early as possible. In fact, Dent, Beale & Co. was so determined to see the early arrival of tea that the house paid high prices for it. In a letter to Joseph Jardine in 1856, Fisher dwelt on the rivalry. He reported that he received three musters of tea, including one of the finest chops, Tchuey Wane. He hastened to add: "But this latter is not so fine as others I have tested of Lindsay & Co. & Gilman & Co. . . . The reason for these high prices Ahee ascribes to the fact of all the foreign houses wishing to get their Tea down first & that Dent & Co. shroff was the principal cause of it, as he told his men to buy the first Teas without regard to price."[57]

Furthermore, the Bohea tea was subject to nationwide competition, because not only the teamen from Foochow, but also those from Canton

54. Larken (Foochow) to Joseph Jardine (Hong Kong), Aug. 29, 1856, JMA.
55. (Foochow) to Joseph Jardine, JMA.
56. Ibid., May 4, 1856.
57. Ibid., May 17, 1856.

and Shanghai, went to the interior of Fukien to buy tea. The price of tea rose by three to four taels per chest; consequently, according to Fisher, only two or three teamen from Foochow were able to buy the projected amount of tea in mid-May. But a soaring market could not last forever, as Fisher added: "Ahee says everybody has stopped buying now & prices must be cheaper."[58]

As in the mid-Yangtze Valley, the Shansi merchants also went to the Bohea districts to represent Russian firms in the purchase of tea to be transported to Russia. These "Shansi men" purchased large amounts of tea in 1854, and their return to Fukien the following year was regarded by Western merchants as a portent for a high market. George V. W. Fisher, Jardine's agent, commented from Foochow in 1855: "I expect there is a large quantity [of tea] taken into Russia overland, for the Sansi [Shansi] men have again returned to Sinchune to buy Tea. Some Teamen say they will take some 20,000 pkgs [packages]."[59] Taising, teaman of Jardine's in the Fukien upcountry during the sixties, noted in 1863 that the price of tea, starting at a normal price of about Tls. 25 per chest at the beginning of the year, reached a startling Tls. 33 in late April. This, he asserted, was solely because of the presence of the Shansi merchants who purchased tea for the Russians. He therefore thought that upcountry tea would not be cheap, especially in the district of Sinchune.[60] The Russian purchases made it impossible to buy at lower prices in the upcountry, even if the European market was sluggish.[61]

Of all grades of tea, the "good" and "fair" classifications were most popular in the West. They were thus more frequently subject to buying waves. Taising, for example, reported from the interior of Fukien in August 1861 that the market upcountry was "in a very unsatisfactory state," because good and fair teas "are advancing in price daily, all par-

58. "He [Ahee, Jardine's teaman] says prices are higher this year Ts. 3 c 4 above last & that the price being so high he had only bought 14 c 15 Chops & that 10 Chops would be down in a fortnight, so I hope you will be able to stop one ship if not too late as there has been scarcely anybody buying in the country except foreign houses, & I am given to understand there will not be above 5 or 6 Chops on the Market that is Teamen's Tea. Ahee says that as Teamen from either this [port], Canton, or Shanghai have gone to Kaison to buy this year, & I believe it is pretty nearly correct as I hear that only 2 or 3 men from this [port] have bought the quantity mentioned in a previous part of my letter" (ibid.).
59. Ibid., Dec. 29, 1855.
60. Taising (Sinchune) to M. A. Macleod (Foochow), Apr. 24, 1863, JMA. This is the English summary of a letter in Chinese that cannot be found in the Jardine archives.
61. M. A. Macleod of Jardine's observed in 1863: "I do not see any chance of prices receeding [sic] for some time to come unless the news from home should be very discouraging, and even then rates may be kept up as there are several firms here buying for Russia" ([Foochow] to Alexander Perceval [Hong Kong], June 11, 1863, JMA). His prediction proved to be correct.

ties being anxious purchasers of these descriptions."[62] Again, in a letter dated September 9, Taising complained that, due to the highly competitive prices in the tea districts, "good teas are very slow and difficult to be had."[63] Under these circumstances, tea merchants sometimes purposefully gave false information in order to mislead fellow competitors. As a gimmick, Ahee, Jardine's teaman in Fukien, gave two names—a real name and an assumed name—to the same chop [brand name] of his own tea in 1861. M. A. Macleod, the firm's agent at Foochow, thus cautioned Alexander Perceval in Hong Kong not to make any allusion to this chop to his fellow traders.[64]

The competition in the purchase of upcountry tea was also evidenced by the number of business firms that operated in Sueykut, a small town in the Bohea tea district that was strategically situated on the upper Min River on the border between Fukien and Kiangsi. According to Taising, there were as many as sixty houses in Sueykut "waiting to operate in the leaf" in late April 1863. Consequently, tea prices were higher than those of the previous year, and Taising concluded that the price would not have dropped even if a large quantity of tea arrived.[65] Being initially unaware of the situation upcountry, James Whittall, Jardine's partner in Hong Kong, instructed Taising to purchase tea at the low price of 25 to 27 taels per picul, which was some 5 or 6 taels under the probable price. This instruction deeply frustrated Taising who immediately wrote to Whittall from the inland on the evening of April 24, 1863, stating that he would not be able to "buy a leaf" under this condition.[66] Taising therefore asked for new instructions from Whittall who then permitted

62. (Sueykut) to M. A. Macleod (Foochow), Aug. 29, 1861, JMA.

63. Ibid., Sept. 9, 1861.

64. "For certain reasons, this chop is to be shown in the market, and will appear there under its *real* name of Shum-foong, its *assumed* name being Chong-hing. Please therefore not to make any allusion to this chop to any of your neighbours" (to Perceval, Oct. 10, 1861, JMA).

65. Taising's letter of April 24, 1863, as translated by Edward Whittall, read in part: "He [Taising] reached Sueykut 22nd April, and in the following day, a small quantity of Tea was brought at such a price as would lay it down in Foochow at Tls. 33 per Pecul [picul], or one Tael higher than last year. . . . This year there are as many as 60 houses in Sueykut waiting to operate in the leaf & he therefore thinks that the price cannot be low" (Taising [Sinchune] to Whittall [Foochow], Apr. 24, 1863, JMA).

66. Taising's letter was summarized in English by M. A. Macleod: "Taising has just received Mr. Whittall's letter informing him that the mail has brought adverse accounts of the Tea Market and that exchange has gone up very much, and that Tea ought to be purchased in the country from Tls 25 c [to] 27 [per picul]. . . . In reference to the Sydney Tea he will bear in mind Mr. Whittall's instructions but must finish his purchases for best Teas first & will then turn his attention to buying good Common Congou. He begs Mr. Whittall to note that his limits are some 5 c 6 Taels under the probable price in the Country, and he is certain at those prices he cannot buy a leaf " (ibid.).

him to purchase at a more flexible range of price.[67] The tea export
from Foochow was particularly encouraging in 1866. In that year at
least 79 "large tea ships" arrived at Foochow "to secure the heavy
freights of new season's teas for England, Australia and America." As
a result, "speculation was active . . . in the interior for the purchase of
the leaf."[68]

Indeed, at times the competition in the upcountry tea market was so
intense in Fukien and the market in Europe so sluggish that both Augustine Heard & Co. and Jardine's planned to withdraw entirely. A. F.
Heard wrote on April 1, 1863:

I look upon [tea] shipments [to Europe] as dangerous except at low rates....
People are preparing to go heavily into Contracts, and there is every prospect of
high prices in the Country, and I have determined to attempt none.... The
Foochow Comp. [comprador] says prices will be very high, and that there are as
many houses in the country *now* being prepared as last year, and this prospect
was in favor of active competition in the interior, so I think it safer to stand
aloof.[69]

THE VOLATILE FOOCHOW MARKET

Responding to keen competition, the Foochow tea market was very
sensitive to the mechanism of supply and demand. When the supply was
"very limited," the price was immediately "much firmer."[70] Green tea
became remarkably popular in the European market during the mid-
fifties, but its quantity was much more limited than that of black tea.
Consequently, the price of green tea zoomed on the Foochow market.
Larken reported in August 1856 that the prices of the "common" grade
of such green teas as Young Hyson and Twankay were so high that it
was impossible to purchase for the English market.[71] This situation
lasted for another season, as Ahee reported in July 1857: "This year, the

67. James Whittall, however, instructed Taising to purchase tea at a price not more
than Tls. 30 per picul (Macleod [Foochow] to Taising [Sueykut], Apr. 30, 1863, JMA).
68. Report of Consul Charles Sinclair, Foochow, Mar. 9, 1867, FO 17/483, p. 5.
69. (Shanghai) to John Heard, HL-38, HC. The Foochow comprador was Akit
(T'ang Ying-chai), an enterprising tea merchant (FL-6, pp. 136, 221, HC).
70. Thomas Larken of Jardine's reported from Foochow in 1856: "I have addressed
you, as the arrivals of Teas from the Country have been on a very limited scale and the
Teamen much firmer than before" (to Joseph Jardine [Hong Kong], Aug. 22, 1856, JMA).
71. "Of Green Teas the quantity offering has been small and of those I have seen the
proportion of the common kinds of Young Hyson and Twankay have preponderated to a
degree to render the purchase of the entire Chop for England impossible at the price asked.
And in those Chops that have been offered to me the Teamen have declined selling the
Gunpowders, Imperials, and Hysons apart from the other descriptions" (ibid., Aug. 29,
1856).

supply of tea being very small, the teamen do not like to sell their teas cheap. Now, no.-1 best tea, there is none."[72] As good teas were similarly scarce, their prices were also high.

Strong demand also quickly brought about a firm price. From time to time even a potential demand would stir up the market. At the end of 1855, for instance, as England reexported more common Congou than usual, George V. W. Fisher of Jardine's reported that the tea price in Foochow would be higher.[73] In times of aggressive purchasing, Western traders occasionally went upcountry to supervise. Thus, sometimes the mere presence of foreigners in the tea districts for sightseeing had the effect of stimulating the market, causing teamen to pay extreme rates.[74]

The rise in tea prices, however, had its limits. For one thing, Western traders would slow down their purchasing activities. Jardine's did this in April 1863 when James Whittall gave instructions to teaman Taising to limit his purchases to the districts of Maison, Sueyhow, and Sinchune where prices were low. Specifically, Taising "must not go higher than Tls. 30 c [to] 31 per picul laid down in Foochow for the finest chops, & Tls. 25 c 27 for other descriptions." Even at these prices Whittall was "not particularly anxious to do a very large business." Whittall also imposed other limitations regarding timeliness.[75]

The merchants also temporarily stopped buying tea altogether in some cases. In late April 1856, when the prices of tea in the interior were unreasonably high, George Fisher of Jardine's wrote about Ahee, the firm's teaman, that the latter "has not bought any yet as prices are too high, & that all with the exception of Dent & Co.'s shroff are holding off for lower prices."[76] Similar situations occurred the following year. Ahee wrote that "no one is buying at present, but are waiting for lower prices." Ahee was one of the teamen who "has therefore stopped buying,

72. Ahee (Sinchune) to M. A. Macleod (Foochow), July 30, 1857, JMA.
73. "The great increase in the export of common Congou at home should I think be in favor of higher prices, as it relieves the stock of a quantity of Tea, which, were it not for the Export demand, would only help to swell the stock, as the home consumption runs principally on Congous from 1/- to 1/4 [one shilling to one shilling and fourpence]" ([Foochow] to Joseph Jardine [Hong Kong], Dec. 29, 1855, JMA).
74. James Whittall, Jardine's partner at Hong Kong, "is surprised to hear that the few foreigners who went upcountry on pleasure should have caused the teamen to pay extreme rates" for the tea (M. A. Macleod [Foochow] to Taising [Sueykut], Apr. 30, 1863, JMA).
75. "If Taising succeeds in purchasing at Mr. Whittall's limits, he hopes to get down in time for the first ships at least 8000 chests, and they should all be in Foochow by the 22nd c 25th May" ([Foochow] to Taising [Sinchune], Apr. 30, 1863, JMA).
76. (Foochow) to Joseph Jardine (Hong Kong), May 1, 1856, JMA. Fisher added that Dent & Co.'s shroff "only bought some 200 piculs at present for which Ts. 20 c [to] 22 have been paid which would be about Ts. 2 higher than last year's."

but thinks that the market will come down again, when he will recommence buying." When Ahee stopped buying tea due to high prices in the Fukien interior in late July 1857, he went to Hohow (Ho-k'ou) of Kiangsi to buy tea. Although there was a supply of Moning tea, the prices were also very high; hence he did not purchase any. He calculated that in about a month there would be a large supply of Oonam (Hunan) and Oopak (Hupei) teas in Hohow, and the price would therefore be lower. Only then would he start to buy.[77]

In the same fashion, when tea prices at Foochow jumped from Tls. 25 to Tls. 37 in April 1863, James Whittall, Jardine's partner at Hong Kong, instructed Taising "not to touch a tea leaf" until the price rolled back to Tls. 30. This instruction was transmitted to Taising through M. A. Macleod who was the firm's agent in Foochow: "Mr. [James] Whittall regrets very much to learn the very extreme prices ruling for the new Teas at Kinyang [Chien-yang], Kinningfoo [Chien-ning], Chunghow [Cheng-ho], and Sueykut [Shui-k'ou]—at Tls. 37 c [to] 38 per picul laid down in Foochow for Teas from these districts. Mr. W. [Whittall] hopes Taising has not touched a leaf, as they will only leave a very heavy loss under any circumstances." Whittall believed that the Chinese tea merchants who were connected with foreigners "are the parties who influence the market most." He figured that, because these merchants were not buying tea for the moment due to the soaring market, prices probably would not increase in the near future.[78] Two months later, because of the "fabulous prices" of new tea, M. A. Macleod decided not to buy for a short period of time, especially the Souchongs, scented teas, and flowery Pekoes.[79]

Like the Western traders and their Chinese teamen, the Chinese independent tea merchants were from time to time forced to suspend their operations. In the fall of 1861, Taising, a teaman of Jardine's, reported from Sueykut that, because "the second and third crop teas prove to be failures for want of rain, good teas are slow and very dear." As a result, the Chinese "contract houses and the teamen generally have suspended operations for the present—for the reason assigned that if they did purchase they see no chance of doing any good in the market of

77. Ahee (Sinchune) to M. A. Macleod (Foochow), July 30, 1857, JMA. Ahee's letter was written in Chinese and was freely translated by Macleod into English.
78. Macleod (Foochow) to Taising (Sueykut), Apr. 30, 1863, JMA. This is the English summary of a Chinese letter that cannot be found in the Jardine archives.
79. "Souchongs have brought fabulous prices and nothing can be done in them. Scented Teas are very poor, being almost without scent, & Flowery Pekoes are likely to open high" (Macleod to Jardine, Matheson & Co. [Hong Kong], June 11, 1863, JMA).

Foochow."[80] The export of tea from Foochow showed a decline in the early sixties. The newly opened Yangtze ports of Hankow and Kiukiang figured prominently in the market, but the high price of tea in Fukien, especially that of the second-grade, was also a definite factor.[81]

Chinese tea gradually lost ground on the world market after the 1870s, when it encountered stiff competition from Indian and Japanese teas. China's tea exports virtually monopolized total world exports before the 1860s: Britain acquired her tea almost entirely from China, and the United States purchased about two-thirds. However, China steadily lost her American tea market to Japan and Ceylon after the mid-seventies, supplying less than 20 percent after 1915. On the British market, Chinese tea gave way to Indian and Ceylonese teas, providing only half of Britain's tea by the end of the eighties.[82] In a letter to Jardine's head office in Hong Kong, the Koenigsberg Commercial Association of London wrote on March 15, 1881: "It has been apparent for some time the Indian teas have shown better value than the China growths, also that the quantity shipped to this country has increased every year and that they have begun to drive the China teas out of the market."[83] Indeed, Indian and Ceylonese teas in large measure replaced Chinese teas after the turn of the century, with Russia remaining the only major importer of Chinese tea throughout the last decades of the Ch'ing period.[84]

UPCOUNTRY SILK

Foreign merchants also watched one another closely concerning silk purchases. In his report to Hong Kong in 1851, A. G. Dallas commented on the difficulties of purchasing contract silk in Shanghai. Besides the fact that "the silkmen are not willing to make contracts to any extent," a more disturbing factor was that "there are too many people on the alert to allow me [to] do much without attracting notice."[85] When Jardine's did make a contract with Takee to purchase silk upcountry on a large

80. To M. A. Macleod (Foochow), Sept. 9, 1861, JMA, as summarized by Macleod.
81. T. S. Odelly of Jardine's commented on the situation from Canton in June 1861: "I am surprised to hear of the opening rates at Foochow, taking the quality of the teas into consideration and the probability of very full supplies this season, I consider they are much too dear. The best chops will probably pay a fair profit owing to the scarcity of fine teas at home, but I cannot see how the Second Teas are to come out" (to Alexander Perceval [Hong Kong], June 8, 1861, JMA).
82. Chi-ming Hou, Foreign Investment, p. 201.
83. JMA.
84. Chi-ming Hou, Foreign Investment, p. 201.
85. (Shanghai) to Joseph Jardine (Hong Kong), Aug. 9, 1851, JMA.

scale in 1852, Gilman & Co. also made extensive purchases. James Macandrew of Jardine's reported on July 14 that Gilman's was "endeavouring to sell their bills on London" in order to pay for the 2,500 bales of silk that they had already contracted for. They also demanded that the Chinese merchants ship the silk quickly: "In several instances so much haste has been used in bringing down the Silk to market that the books have been badly got up, & the Silk arrived out of condition, which has occasioned the rejection of some parcels."[86]

Takee could not fulfill his silk contracts with Jardine's in 1852 because he was ill and because he was deceived by the local silk merchants in the interior. Nevertheless, A. G. Dallas insisted that, given the intense competition among the foreign firms, Takee was too good a silk merchant to be abandoned: "My confidence is a good deal shaken in his ability . . . to conduct such a large operation, but there are great allowances to be made for him. We have had tools to work with, with which we must do the best we can, & I still think him one of the best of them, & far too good to be thrown aside. He would be eagerly picked up by any other house."[87] Dallas was correct: other Western traders soon tried to enlist Takee's help in purchasing silk.

Partly because of stiff competition and partly because of "warlike apprehensions" in Europe, the foreign trading firms realized in 1866 that it was not profitable for them to do business in China in general or to trade in silk in particular.[88] Nevertheless, with the help of its comprador Tong King-Sing, Jardine's continued to be aggressive in the upcountry purchase of silk in 1867. F. B. Johnson assured James Whittall that he would "lose no opportunity if offered to effect a [silk] contract with responsible natives." If necessary, the house would enlist the help of the most prominent Chinese silk merchants, including Aleet and Choping, in upcountry purchases.[89] Meanwhile, many independent Chinese silk merchants were competing with the agents of foreign houses in the up-

---

86. (Shanghai) to David Jardine (Hong Kong), July 14, 1852, JMA.

87. (Shanghai) to David Jardine (Hong Kong), Sept. 27, 1852, JMA.

88. The commissioner of maritime customs in Shanghai reported to Robert Hart, the inspector-general, in 1867: "The year 1866 closed on a state of depression never before witnessed in the China trade. An entire want of confidence prevailed, and the most sinister rumours in regard to the stability of firms resident in China were current. Prepared by three years of continuous failure, the more respectable firms were anxious to profit by the lessons of caution and economy which their lessons had so dearly taught them" (BPP, *Report on Trade by the Foreign Commissioners at the Ports in China Open by Treaty to Foreign Trade for the Year 1866*, vol. 69, p. 104).

89. (Shanghai) to Whittall (Hong Kong), May 3, 1867, JMA.

country. When these Chinese became less active, the foreign traders were delighted. This happened in 1871 after a sagging market in Europe the previous year. Anticipating less aggressive activities from the Chinese side, F. B. Johnson gladly reported from Shanghai to Jardine's manager in Hong Kong on May 29, 1871: "I am pleased to report that there is an absence of all appearance of eagerness on the part of the Chinese to operate in the Country. Nothing has yet been done in the Nanzing districts, and at Liuhoo very few purchases are said to have been made."[90]

The rivalry in the upcountry market in China, however intense it might have been, was but a part of the world market, which became increasingly competitive. To improve cost efficiency, Jardine's made special arrangements with their "friends in Lyons" in 1881, whereby they would jointly handle the sale of silk in France and share the profit. F. B. Johnson wrote from Hong Kong on May 18: "As we shall have no commission to pay for credits, we ought to compete successfully with our neighbours."[91] Johnson's expectations soon materialized. Chinese silk lost ground in the world market during the last quarter of the nineteenth century, and in 1877 several large Chinese silk firms went broke. These failures severely affected the foreign houses; Jardine's complained that the silk business was precarious in the seventies and eighties and that profits for investors through these two decades were highly unsatisfactory.[92] Although in 1877–1878 raw silk from central China constituted 52 percent of the export of raw silk from the East, Japan rapidly overtook China and became the leading supplier of silk on the world market by the turn of the century.[93]

When Chinese tea and silk lost ground on the world market after the 1880s, the intense commercial rivalry on the coast started to abate accordingly. At any rate, by the end of the nineteenth century China's three leading ports for the export of tea remained Shanghai, Hankow, and Foochow. The marked fluctuations in tea prices indicate that com-

90. (Shanghai) to William Keswick (Hong Kong), JMA.

91. "I arranged with our Lyons friends to undertake the [silk] business on the best terms we could obtain so long as our security is undoubted & to divide with them the remuneration. Now that by means of W. Rooston's signature we are in a position to negotiate documentary bills, our risk will be nominal in such transactions provided you obtain adequate margins" (to James J. Keswick [Shanghai], May 18, 1881, JMA).

92. LeFevour, pp. 152–53.

93. In 1913 Japan furnished 44 percent of the total silk supplied to the Western world; China provided no more than 31 percent (Chi-ming Hou, *Foreign Investment*, p. 201). This percentage dropped even lower in the ensuing decades.

mercial competition in the China trade, which was on the decline, did not lose its glamour entirely.[94]

THE IMPORT TRADE

Compared with the export trade, Western merchants were in a poor position to deliver imported goods to China; nevertheless, they still competed in earnest. They also had to deal with the increasingly active Chinese merchants. These coastal merchants were intense rivals in the import business, especially concerning general merchandise and opium.

GENERAL MERCHANDISE

Western traders watched one another closely in the import trade. A. G. Dallas of Jardine's reported from Shanghai in 1848 concerning the import business of American counterparts that he was "pleased" to observe that his American "neighbour" had "great difficulty in disposing of American manufactures which are not in favor" in China.[95] Also, the market conditions were such that it was not possible for any firm to dominate one area of the market. This was evidenced in 1893 by the abortive effort of Jardine's to control the distribution of petroleum in China, when the house offered to become the agent for both Standard Oil and Tidewater throughout Asia. In return, Jardine's promised to cooperate with Standard in the development of that company's new Sumatra concession; for that purpose, the Standard Sumatra Company would be established. In reporting to the firm's headquarters in Hong Kong, Jardine's Shanghai office stated that the capital of the proposed company would be £250,000 in 50,000 shares of £5 each. Jardine's would be the permanent manager of the company in Sumatra. In addition, the firm would act as the permanent agent for the new company in East and Southeast Asia for a commission of 3 percent on all sales.[96]

However, the Standard Oil Company informed the firm in early 1894 that they had decided to set up their own marketing organization in Asia. William Keswick of Jardine's observed from London on March 31, 1894: "This squeezes us out of the trade unless we can become the representative of either the other American or the Russian combination."

94. Ibid., p. 52.
95. To Joseph Jardine (Hong Kong), Nov. 28, 1848, JMA.
96. Jardine, Matheson & Co. (Shanghai) to J. Macgregor (Hong Kong), Apr. 12, 1893, JMA.

Keswick's hope could hardly materialize, because American and Russian oil interests were already competing around the world. He continued: "American organization has in great measure destroyed the Russian Oil business in Western Europe and has a certain hold in India, China and Japan."[97] Thus, Jardine's efforts to dominate petroleum on the Chinese market ended in failure.

Although import trade was at first controlled by foreign trading firms, Chinese merchants gradually shared in its profits. The British consul at Canton reported in 1865 that the import trade had increased, but it was "being gradually absorbed by the Chinese merchants" in Canton, Hankow, and Tientsin.[98] His remark was borne out by the trade report of the customs commissioner at Hankow in the same year, which emphasized that the Chinese merchants forwarded foreign imports from Shanghai to Hankow where, because they had no expensive establishments to maintain, they could undersell the foreign merchants.[99] By 1870 from one-half to two-thirds of the imported manufactures passing through Hankow to the interior was being handled by the Chinese. An eyewitness report describes commerce at Hankow in 1870: "We found the depression of trade a universal subject of complaint among the [foreign] residents. The keen competition of the natives has reduced profits to a minimum."[100]

Thomas Knox, an American merchant in China, observed in 1878 that, even though Sino-Western commercial relations "were a splendid thing for us at the start, the Chinese are taking their revenge in a way quite unexpected to us." This Chinese rivalry "has grown to enormous proportions and is growing every year." For instance, the sugar trade of Amoy and Taiwan, which had been a source of handsome income to foreign houses, went "into Chinese hands entirely" by the late seventies. At the same time, nearly all the flour shipped from San Francisco to China was on Chinese account, and the rice trade between China and other countries was mainly in Chinese hands.[101] At the end of the nineteenth century, the delegates of the Blackburn Chamber of Com-

---

97. To G. L. Montgomery (New York), JMA.
98. Report of Consul C. B. Robertson, Canton, Mar. 30, 1865, FO 17/434. For Canton, he added: "The import trade for 1864 . . . in all probability has very largely increased—only it has changed hands, the Chinese doing that for themselves now which formerly the foreign merchant did for them."
99. IMC, *Reports on Trade, 1864* (Shanghai, 1865), Hankow, p. 12.
100. BPP, *Report of the Delegates of the Shanghai General Chamber of Commerce on the Trade of the Upper Yangtze River*, vol. 65, p. 8.
101. Knox, "John comprador," *Harper's New Monthly Magazine* 57:431 (1878). Rice was traditionally carried by Chinese junks.

merce found that the foreign cloth trade between Shasi (Sha-shih) and Yunnan-fu was "an old established trade in which competition is very keen."[102]

OPIUM

The major Western competitors in the opium trade in Chinese waters during the first quarter of the nineteenth century were the British and the Portuguese. Portugal attempted in 1815 to gain a monopoly on the opium trade at Macao, then the major center of distribution for the product. British trade was thus forced first to Whampoa and then to Lintin Island. Having realized the British commercial potential, the Portuguese in 1819 invited their British competitors to join them in forming a monopoly of Malwa opium trade, but this offer was refused. In 1822 when the Chinese officials successfully suppressed the opium trade at both Whampoa and Macao, the British East India Company did not invite the Portuguese to join them at Lintin. This move forced the Portuguese to give up their opium trade at Macao by 1827.[103]

James Matheson in 1823 pioneered the "coastal system" of selling opium directly up the east coast, as seen in chapter 5. Because this experiment was considerably profitable, other British, Portuguese, and American traders quickly followed the lead next year, causing stiff competition to emerge. Matheson bitterly complained on December 2, 1824: "We have reason to regret that, being the originators of the coastal system, the competition of our neighbours has permitted us to enjoy the advantages of its so little."[104] The competition was so keen that it later forced Matheson to discontinue the trade temporarily.[105]

Opium trade along the coast encountered some difficulties during the second quarter of the nineteenth century. For one thing, harassment by pirates caused an increase in insurance premiums and consequently decreased profits. Besides, small traders were forced out of business. Several big agency houses, such as Dent's and Jardine's, were in a more advantageous position for two reasons. First, being the major consignees of the

102. Bourne et al., p. 86.
103. Morse, *Chronicles*, III, 357–58; IV, 61–62. Morse wrote: "The Portuguese residents in Macao had lost the opium trade, on which the port had mainly subsisted, and they now lived largely on their monopoly of land-owning, through which they were enabled to provide with houses the increased number of English and American traders who spent there in between-season" (ibid., 152).
104. Letter of James Matheson, Yrissari and Company Papers, JMA.
105. Ibid., Dec. 10, 1825.

bulk of Indian opium, these houses, equipped with large capital assets, were able to decline virtually all offers at Lintin or Hong Kong and send entire shipments to the northern coast. By doing so, they partially commanded the market before their rivals could go north to compete. Second, whereas the merchants with moderate means were discouraged from shipping opium in unarmed vessels or in native junks due to fear of the widespread piracy, the large houses could afford to ship in heavily armed vessels.[106]

Again, competition was keen among the large houses. A. G. Dallas of Jardine's reported from Shanghai on November 5, 1850, that Dent, Beale & Co. and Lindsay & Co. had been selling Malwa "more freely" and the price was lower.[107] One month later, after having found that Dent, Beale & Co. also penetrated to the interior where it sold good opium at low prices, Dallas was alarmed.[108] To compete with these British, American, and Parsee opium merchants in the lower Yangtze Valley, Jardine's hired some Chinese after the mid-fifties to sell opium in the Shanghai area, and their comprador also helped.[109]

After the fifties, it was common practice for the junks that shipped tribute rice from the lower Yangtze Valley to Peking in the early spring of each year to carry opium from Shanghai for sale in the northern provinces. Foreign houses, particularly Jardine's and Dent's, seized this opportunity to sell opium. In reporting on January 13, 1852, A. G. Dallas described such competition:

In the meantime the low price of Malwa will I dare say cause a good consumption between this [date] & the [Chinese] New Year, & as there will in all likyhood [sic] be an extensive demand a couple of months hence for the grain junks, we must look out that Dent & co. do not get the command of the Market with the large accumulated stock which they must have on hand.[110]

As small foreign firms mushroomed along the coast after the sixties, it became more necessary for the foreign traders to drum up opium business. They thus started to give bonuses to the Chinese dealers. M. A. Macleod of Jardine's wrote from Foochow on February 18, 1861: "A day or two ago the Parsees sold some 20 chests of Malwa at $700 per picul

---

106. B2, vols. 134–38, JMA.

107. To Donald Matheson (Hong Kong), JMA.

108. "Dent, Beale & Co. have been sending Malwa into the country, and selling good drug [opium] very low" (to David Jardine [Hong Kong], Dec. 13, 1850, JMA).

109. Alexander Perceval (Shanghai) to Joseph Jardine (Hong Kong), July 15, 1856, JMA.

110. To David Jardine (Hong Kong), JMA.

(giving as is usual with almost all my neighbours here, 2 cakes over weight), and today both Russell & Co. & Gilman & Co. have either sold, or are offering to sell some 30 to 50 chests on similar terms."[111] To match the deeds of their American and Parsee competitors, one month later Jardine's also offered a premium—"in some cases with one cake allowance."[112]

Along the upper Yangtze, from the spring of 1863 on Western firms intensified their competition to sell opium in Hankow and Kiukiang. By June, G. H. Styan, agent of Jardine's, reported from Kiukiang that "the opium quarrel" continued and that "Messrs. Fletcher & Co. and Messrs. Gibb & Co.'s compradores are still able to undersell the other Houses." Other merchants, including Jardine's, were determined to fight back, and Styan vowed that "the matter will not be allowed to rest where it is."[113] And he kept his word. Augustine Heard & Co. similarly felt the pressure of competition. From the early 1860s on, the firm employed a Chinese agent named Tang Sun Chi to do business along the upper Yangtze. In a letter to G. B. Dixwell on July 13, 1863, Tang wrote from Kiukiang that he was not able to sell the firm's opium because, as he put it, "good drug has come in abundance and makes one difficult to move."[114]

Meanwhile, another competitive force to be reckoned with was the Chinese traders along the coast. Following the example of Jardine's, some enterprising Chinese bought opium at Lintin Island and sold it on the northern coast after the thirties. Many Chinese also purchased opium directly from the foreign vessels anchored at Woosung, the outer port of Shanghai, after Shanghai was opened to foreign trade in 1842. David Jardine of Jardine, Matheson & Co. admitted in 1848 that, in addition to their fellow Western competitors, "both Parsee and Chinese houses are watching us closely" regarding the opium trade.[115]

Amoy was a port where, beginning in the forties, Jardine's opium ships regularly visited.[116] To drum up business, the firm in 1852 dis-

111. To Alexander Perceval (Hong Kong), JMA.

112. James Whittall wrote: "I have only managed to sell 100 chests of Malwa at Ts. 565 per chest, in some cases with 1 cake allowance, & today I cannot get a bid even at T. 560" ([Shanghai] to Alexander Perceval [Hong Kong], Mar. 30, 1863, JMA).

113. To James Whittall (Shanghai), June 11, 1863, JMA.

114. "At present the price of the best opium is % to %7 a bag. That which I have is not sold—buyers not liking it" (Tang Sun Chi to G. B. Dixwell [Shanghai], HM-30, HC).

115. (Canton) to Alexander Matheson (Hong Kong), June 17, 1848, JMA.

116. Duncan Forbes wrote from Amoy in 1846: "I will keep W. Thompson as a 3d mate if you will allow me. He has a good knowledge of what is required, [and is] in charge of the opium on board here" (to Donald Matheson [Hong Kong], Oct. 13, 1846, JMA).

patched James Bellamy to that port as an agent in residence. On his arrival, as he indicated in his first letter to the Hong Kong office, he was immediately concerned that other houses had been selling the drug all along.[117] Meanwhile, the Chinese merchants who probably bought opium directly from Lintin, soon vigorously exploited the market.[118] In order to strengthen Jardine's competitive position in Amoy, Alexander Perceval, the firm's Head in East, assigned the enterprising Henry Smith as the new representative in that port in 1862. Smith's major responsibility was to drum up opium business, although he also dealt with the cotton trade.[119] As Jardine's agents in Amoy frequently complained, the strength of the Chinese merchants is evidenced by the fact that they often undersold their foreign competitors, even occasionally "selling opium under Hongkong rates."[120] Although these agents tried hard to "keep the Chinese out,"[121] the Chinese persistently stayed in the trade.

By the sixties, James Whittall of Jardine's found that Chinese opium dealers were a vital force on the central and northern coast as well as on the Yangtze; many of them purchased opium from foreign vessels at Woosung and reshipped it immediately to the northern and Yangtze ports. This trade was both vigorous and extensive, which made Whittall feel strongly that the company's opium business was seriously jeopardized, especially on the Yangtze. In a letter to Alexander Perceval, Whittall complained from Shanghai on March 30, 1863: "Hitherto a considerable business has been done by the Chinese [opium] speculators on the spot for reshipment to Tientsin, Hankow, etc. which seriously interfered with our trade at these ports, especially the Yangtze ones."[122] Whittall's concern was by no means without reason. F. B. Johnson, the

117. "I have to acquaint you of my safe arrival at this port. I am now trying to get a house. Meanwhile, I reside with Capt. MacMurds, and have commenced to make sales. Several ships here have drugs for sale" (Bellamy to Jardine, Matheson & Co. [Hong Kong], Sept. 25, 1852, JMA).

118. Capt. J. MacMurd (Amoy) to Jardine, Matheson & Co. (Hong Kong), Oct. 13, 1856, JMA.

119. Smith reported in July that besides opium, he also sold "400 bales of Shanghai cotton at $16.40 per bale" (to Jardine, Matheson & Co. [Hong Kong], July 17, 1862, JMA).

120. Henry Smith reported to Jardine's head office in 1868 regarding the opium market: "Everything very flat—Chinese selling opium under Hong Kong rates" (to William Keswick [Hong Kong], July 23, 1868, JMA). One month later, Elles & Co. at Amoy wrote to Jardine's: "We have sold on your account 1 chest Benares [opium] at $703 [per chest]—market very dull and Chinese selling at less" (to Jardine, Matheson & Co. [Hong Kong], Aug. 15, 1868, JMA).

121. Henry Smith (Amoy) to Jardine, Matheson & Co. (Hong Kong), Oct. 12, 1868, JMA.

122. Whittall to Perceval (Hong Kong), JMA.

firm's partner at Shanghai, soon pointed out that the Chinese continued
to undersell them on the coast in 1867. He added: "Moreover, advices
from the [Yangtze] river ports are almost equally bad, but I think that
our agents cannot successfully compete with the Chinese who are con-
tinuously underselling there & [our agent] Mr. [S. I.] Gower [at Han-
kow] goes so far as to say that he cannot get a trial."[123]

While the Chinese outcompeted Jardine's in Hankow, Chinkiang was
the one Yangtze port where Western traders felt least comfortable in
respect to opium. A British consular report from that port in 1869 indicated that, for some time in 1868, "the native dealers were doing a large
business, [whereas] foreign merchants were unable to sell a single
chest."[124] During the next decade, the Chinese merchants, under the
leadership of Tong Mow-chee and Li Kuan-chih, dominated the opium
market. One of the noted British houses dealing in opium, David Sassoon & Co., was forced out of business in that port in the late seventies
due to the loss of money, and it finally sold its establishments to the
Chinese. The foreigners' accusation in 1879 that the Chinese tried to set
up a monopoly in the opium trade at Chinkiang was, however,
groundless.[125] The fact is that foreigners, being unfamiliar with the local
market and squeezed by the Chinese middlemen, often sold opium at a
higher price than did their Chinese competitors.[126]

THE SHIPPING TRADE

With the advent of clipper ships as a means of commercial transportation, merchants, Chinese and Western alike, competed for the fastest
service. When modern steamships were introduced to China's coast in
the 1860s, the Western traders came to dominate the shipping trade, but
they faced stiff competition among themselves. Moreover, the Chinese
merchants, with their growing mastery of foreign methods and the
motivation of economic nationalism, gradually came to compete effectively with Western traders for the shipping trade.

THE WESTERN TRADERS

Western merchants tried everything they could to improve the speed
of their ocean vessels. In fact, competition among them in shipping

123. To James Whittall (Hong Kong), June 18, 1867, JMA.
124. Report of C. F. Allen, Chinkiang, May 20, 1869, FO 17/531.
125. *Shen pao*, Sept. 3, 1879, p. 3, and Oct. 11, 1879, p. 3.
126. For a recent illuminating study of the effectiveness of Chinese indigenous systems

China's tea and silk to the Western world was so intense that by the early nineteenth century there existed a "system of graduating rates of freight in proportion to the speed of the vessel."[127] That is, the faster a vessel went, the higher freight rates it would charge. The fastest ship charged the highest rate; an overloaded ship, being slow, charged less. This is why freight rates ranged from 30 shillings to £2 per ton between Foochow and London during the mid-fifties.[128]

"Ocean racing at dangerous speed" was "frequently indulged in between fast team steamers" after the sixties. The loss of the S. S. *Drummond Castle* on May 31, 1873, was "attributed to this previously rather popular practice." This rivalry in long-distance, water-borne trade between China and Europe was also evidenced in the acts of some steamship owners in London in 1879. At the beginning of that year, freight rates were so low that the ships could hardly make a profit. They considered laying up their ships temporarily. In September in order to improve the situation, many of them formed a "combination to regulate the tonnage on the berth, to prevent the accumulation of cargoes, and to protect each other from loss." However, three months later the combination aborted due to the "want of coherence among the signatories of these conference rules." As it turned out, the principle of free trade triumphed, and the line between China and England remained as highly competitive as ever.[129]

Besides speed, economy of operation was another consideration. The foreign houses took pains to choose the most economical way to export tea and silk from China without seriously compromising timeliness. Agents of Jardine's and Lindsay's, for instance, weighed these factors carefully in 1852 to choose between steamships and clippers.[130]

Competition in general intensified with the advent of steamships.

---

in resisting foreign economic erosion, see Rhoads Murphey, *The Outsiders* (Ann Arbor, Mich., 1977), chap. 10.

127. Eitel, p. 495.

128. Thomas Larken of Jardine's commented from Foochow on the freight situation in August 1856: "The 'Walmer Castle' and 'Virginia' are both engaged full for London at £2 per ton, and will sail in a few days. The 'Earl of Elington' is doing nothing at present and as she will carry such a large cargo, I should not be surprised to hear of her taking freight at 30/[shillings] per ton" (to Joseph Jardine [Hong Kong], Aug. 29, 1856, JMA).

129. Eitel, p. 550.

130. A. G. Dallas describes how Jardine's and Lindsay's sought to reduce the shipping cost from Shanghai in 1852: "As I see little chance of our being able to secure tonnage for any quantity of Silk by the first & second Steamers, it might be perhaps desirable to make an early shipment by a Clipper Ship. Messrs. Lindsay & Co. are reported to have contracted for a quantity of New Tea, no doubt with the view of dispatching the 'Challenger' among the first ships of the season" (to David Jardine [Hong Kong], May 26, 1852, JMA).

After 1859, for example, between Canton and Hong Kong Russell's and Heard's "vied with each other" in providing "roomy, spatial river-steamers which ran both night and day."[131] The foreign merchants also competed in earnest on other routes. Although the Shanghai Steam Navigation Co., organized by the American house of Russell & Co. in Shanghai in 1862, led the steamship trade in China's waters for about a decade, it was not strong enough to prevent the entry of new enterprises into the field. The British firm of Glover & Co. organized the Union Steam Navigation Co. in 1867, and a local joint-stock company, the North-China Steamer Company, operated steamers on the Yangtze River the following year.

A powerful competitor was Jardine, Matheson & Co. which, with two steamships, shared the steam traffic with Russell's on the Yangtze. William Keswick, the firm's partner at Shanghai, watched closely what his fellow merchants were doing regarding steamships along the coast and on the Yangtze. With reference to coastal shipping, he noted with indignation in 1866 that the American firm of Augustine Heard & Co. was endeavoring to lure away Tucksing, a principal shipper associated with Jardine's. At the same time, Keswick noticed that the Shanghai Steam Navigation Co. of Russell's commanded "much of the native trade on the [Yangtze] River."[132]

F. B. Johnson, the Jardine partner at Shanghai, argued in 1868 that the firm could beat its competitors by inaugurating a Shanghai-Foochow line. He added that larger and more efficient steamers would be more profitable, because no other companies had introduced them to the coastal shipping trade. He wrote:

No such steamers are now in China, and it is certain that a company or firm, *commanding the interest of Chinese shippers*, could run two suitable steamers to shew [show] a handsome profit. It would be impossible for any boat now in the trade to compete with others carrying much larger cargoes at almost the same expense for crew and stores, having greater speed, and consuming far less fuel per trip, besides having comfortable accommodations for native passengers.[133]

He accordingly suggested that two such ships be ordered from England for this purpose. In 1869 the firm decided to run two steamships regularly from Shanghai to two ports on the China coast.

---

131. Eitel, p. 389. These steamers included the *Kinshan* and the *White Cloud*.
132. Keswick to James Whittall (Hong Kong), Feb. 4, 1866, JMA. For Heard's effort to lure away Tucksing, see chap. 8.
133. Johnson, "Memo. Regarding the Carrying Trade between Foochow and Shanghai," Shanghai, 1868, JMA; and Kwang-Ching Liu, *Steamship Rivalry*, p. 112.

Jardine's competition with other foreign firms was evidenced by the steamer *Sin Nanzing*. In August 1868 the North-China Steamer Company ordered a new paddle steamer from England, the future *Sin Nanzing*. However, due to their deteriorating financial situation, the company mortgaged it to the Hongkong and Shanghai Banking Corporation in February 1871. By the fall of 1872, Jardine's planned to organize a new joint-stock steamship company. Believing that the house could gain control over the consignment steamers through this new company, F. B. Johnson recommended in 1872 that Jardine's make an advance of Tls. 90,000 to the North-China Company to enable the latter to maintain the mortgage on its two ships, which was still held by the Hongkong and Shanghai Banking Corp. The steamer *Sin Nanzing* thus came under the management of Jardine's. In January 1873, Jardine's reorganized the various steamers under its management into the China Coast Steam Navigation Company, with an initial paid-up capital of Tls. 325,000. This company mainly competed with Russell's for the coastal trade.[134]

In the late spring of 1870, Russell's outcompeted Jardine's by shipping some 600 tons of freight, mostly tea that belonged to the Russian firm of Okooloff & Tokinakoff from Hankow to Tientsin. In a letter to the Shanghai office, Henry Beveridge, Jardine's Hankow agent, reported that in June another Russian firm, Haminoff & Rodionoff, inquired about the rate of freight on teas to Tientsin. After Beveridge told them that the full rate was Tls. 7.25 per tons, he "heard nothing more about it" until he realized that "the teas went forward by the Shanghai S. N. Co.'s steamer" of Russell & Co., "so Russell & Co. must have offered to take it for less." He added: "Russell & Co.'s agent here had done his best to solicit shippers against your steamers." Beveridge suggested that, while he was cultivating the friendship of the Russian merchants Ivanoff and Obervin, it would be advisable for Johnson to write directly to other Russian firms at Hankow, stating "the lowest terms to take teas from Hankow to Tientsin."[135] When George de Baranoffsky, another Russian merchant, stayed in Hankow on his way from Kiukiang to Shanghai, Beveridge "showed him all the attention" he could.[136]

Jardine's refused to be outcompeted by Russell's, but it could not change the situation immediately. F. B. Johnson wrote to Hankow two

134. Kwang-Ching Liu, *Steamship Rivalry*, pp. 78–79, 112, 135, 144.
135. "These houses hearing from your good selves would have a good effect. Mr. Okooloff I believe was rather annoyed at having to wait so long for his money in the 'Glengyle' case when she damaged the Russian firms' teas in 1867, I think it was, and your writing might smooth matters over" (to F. B. Johnson [Shanghai], July 2, 1870, JMA).
136. Ibid.

years later: "Russell & Co. are taking all the cargo from us. . . . They obtain all or nearly all the [tung] oil freight and other cargo offering at Hankow, and they must now not be permitted to engross it any longer." Johnson then replaced Beveridge with a more enterprising agent. To help the new agency, he asked the entrepreneurial Tong King-sing, the firm's chief comprador at Shanghai, to "arrange for a Native broker to live upon the premises to assist in the management of our cargo."[137] Jardine's position generally improved after that.

Another competitor was the China Navigation Company, which was founded by the British house of Butterfield & Swire in spring 1872, powerful because of its liberal start-up financing in London. Its paid-up capital of Tls. 970,000 was the equivalent of that of the Shanghai S. N. Co. and three times that of the China Coast S. N. Co. The aim of this new concern was to compete with Russell's and Jardine's for all the steamship traffic in China's waters. An intense freight rate war on the Yangtze between the new company and the Shanghai S. N. Co. followed in 1873. John Samuel Swire, the moving spirit of the company, expressed his determination to compete vigorously, if necessary, when he wrote to William Lang in July 1875: "We don't want a fight if we can help it, but should we commence one, we must endeavour to carry it thro to a succesful end. . . . We shall come out second to none & a great future will be before us. . . . So we rely on you, *at all fronts*, to remit every dol. [dollar] that you can spare."[138] The frequent shipping advertisements in *Shen pao*, a leading Chinese newspaper in Shanghai, also reflected the rivalry of these Western steamship companies.[139]

Sometimes the keen rivalry ended in a temporary truce, but the parties involved remained suspicious. For instance, a freight-rate agreement between Jardine's and Russell's was reached in February 1871, but, considering the ambition of F. B. Johnson to expand Jardine's steamship enterprise, this agreement was feeble at best. In May 1873, F. B. Forbes of Russell's complained about Jardine's disregarding the agreement: "I have about given up all idea of ever working pleasantly or profitably with that firm. Frank Johnson is so vacillating, and I fear so tricky, that arrangements made with him are worthless."[140]

Besides the Americans and the British, some continental Europeans

137. Johnson (Shanghai) to R. Anderson (Hankow), June 18, 1872, JMA.
138. Swire (London) to Lang (Shanghai), July 2 and 8, 1875, SP. For the freight rate war on the Yangtze in 1873, see Kwang-Ching Liu, *Steamship Rivalry*, p. 112.
139. *Shen pao*, 1873, passim.
140. Forbes (Shanghai) to Edward Cunningham, May 26, 1873, FBF. See also Kwang-Ching Liu, *Steamship Rivalry*, p. 144.

also joined the rivalry. W. H. Medhurst, British consul at Shanghai, reported in 1870 that, among all of the foreigners in China, the Germans operated steamship enterprises most economically, a fact that British traders sought to emulate.[141] Jealous of the prosperous business of the German steamer *Sedan* on the coast, F. B. Johnson of Jardine's in 1871 wrote on her profitable business: "There seems a very large business doing between this [Shanghai] and Hong Kong. The [steamer] 'Sedan' came up and has discharged 19,000 piculs of cargo of which 15,000 piculs were engaged in Hong Kong. She will soon go to Swatow and thus gross about Tls. 6.5000 for the round which will pay her." He vowed in conclusion: "We ought not to be driven off the Coast by North Germans!"[142]

THE ROLE OF THE CHINESE BEFORE 1872

In addition to the foreigners, the Chinese on the coast also participated in the competition for the shipping trade. That the Chinese were capable of doing this is evidenced by the fact that in 1857 "vessels manned by Cantonese" helped the Ningpo people to oust a large fleet of lorchas under the Portuguese flag.[143] In fact, the Chinese junks provided competition for the foreign shippers even before the late sixties, when most of the Chinese had adopted steamships. M. A. Macleod, Jardine's agent at Foochow, reported in 1861 that, with possible exception at Ningpo, foreign steamers could not compete with native junks for freight on the coast.[144]

The modern facilities for the shipping trade on the coast were available to the Chinese, which made it possible for them to compete with the Western traders. The increased activity of Cantonese merchants in the trade of northern China was due mainly to the introduction of the steamship to this area of the coast. The British consular report from

141. W. H. Medhurst, "Trade Report for 1869," Shanghai, 1870, FO 17/558B, p. 84.

142. Johnson (Shanghai) to William Keswick (Hong Kong), Aug. 30, 1871, JMA.

143. Rutherford Alcock, British consul at Canton, wrote in a memorandum in 1857 when he was on leave in Britain: "Three months ago . . . [there was] a combined attack by the Ningpo people, who had called in the aid of vessels manned by Cantonese, on a large fleet of piratical lorchas under the Portuguese flag, and manned by Portuguese chiefly, who had long been the terror and the pest of the contiguous coast" (Memorandum of Alcock, Dec. 31, 1857, FO 405/2, p. 119). A lorcha was a vessel with Western hull and Chinese rig, widely used on the Chinese coast.

144. "*Tientsin.* For that quarter there is nothing offering here at present, a large fleet of junks being now here preparing to proceed north, and the whole of the cargo available has already been secured by them. At Ningpo, however, a steamer might do some good" (to Alexander Perceval [Hong Kong], Apr. 8, 1861, JMA).

TABLE 10.   CHINESE AND FOREIGN SHIPPERS OF MAJOR
COMMODITIES SHIPPED ON FOREIGN VESSELS BETWEEN
SHANGHAI AND KIUKIANG, 1866

Commodity	Unit	Chinese merchants		Foreign merchants		Total amount shipped
		Amount	Percent	Amount	Percent	
From Shanghai to Kiukiang						
Grey shirting	Piece	75,640	85	13,500	15	89,140
Long ell[a]	Piece	15,143	94	900	6	16,043
Lead	Picul	11,238	95	600	5	11,838
Malwa opium	Chest	1,765	73	650	27	2,415
From Kiukiang to Shanghai						
Black tea	Picul	59,239	65	32,376	35	91,615
Green tea	Picul	46,268	58	32,850	42	79,118

Source: IMC, *Reports on Trade, 1866* (Shanghai, 1867), p. 66. Calculations are mine.
[a]An ell was a measure of cloth, varying between the English ell (45″) and the old Dutch or Flemish ell (27″). The long ell was probably 45″.

Chefoo in 1864 indicates that before the sixties the junk owners and northern merchants, especially those from Shantung province, "had a monopoly of the northern trade." This was attributable to the prohibition, contained in the treaties of Tientsin, against exporting peas and beancake from northern ports in foreign vessels. After the suspension of the prohibition by the Ch'ing government in 1861, however, "the junks which formerly came from southern ports to Chefoo and other gulf ports for peas and beancake [had] almost entirely disappeared" by 1864. This resulted in "a remarkable change in the whole trade of the north of China. It . . . brought forward a new class of native merchants who previously had no share in this trade." This new class consisted mainly of Chinese from Kwangtung and Fukien "whose means did not permit them to own junks" but who were able to "obtain the use of European vessels at a moderate rate" by paying the freight at the end of the voyage.[145]

The British consul at Canton observed in 1865 that "some of the finest steamers on the coast have been chartered and loaded by Chinese firms without European intervention."[146] Although his estimation that

145. BPP, *Reports from Her Majesty's Consuls in China, 1864*, vol. 71, Chefoo, p. 50.
146. Report of Consul C. B. Robertson, Canton, Mar. 30, 1865, FO 17/434.

the Chinese would soon dominate "the whole of the coast carrying-trade" proved to be exaggerated, his general view was borne out by the commercial development in 1867 at Tientsin where the Chinese merchants, "having learnt to avail themselves of every facility—such as steamers, etc.—at the disposal of the foreigner" were "fast ousting him" from the market.[147] F. B. Johnson of Jardine's, in a memorandum entitled "Regarding the Carrying Trade between Foochow and Shanghai," observed in 1868 that "the steamship traffic between these ports are entirely in the hands of Chinese," who preferred chartering steamers to purchasing them.[148]

After the Yangtze was opened to foreign steamers in 1861, many Chinese shipped cargoes between Shanghai and other Yangtze ports. The customs commissioner at Kiukiang reported that in 1866 the shipping of commodities between Shanghai and Kiukiang on foreign vessels was dominated by the Chinese merchants (table 10). The commissioner added: "From these figures I find that a fair estimate of the value of the trade which has passed through the hands of the Foreign merchant during 1866 gives Tls. 2,457,429 . . . out of the total of Tls. 10,119,020 . . . or roughly estimated one-fourth to the Foreign, three-fourths to the Native dealer."[149] Chinese merchants, because they used the modern ships, "are able to undersell the British merchants" in the import and export trade on the Yangtze, especially in Hankow.[150]

That the strength of the Chinese merchants was not taken lightly is illustrated by Jardine's ambivalent attitude toward its Chinese friends. In 1872 F. B. Johnson was trying to organize a new joint-stock steamship company, to be managed by Jardine's at Shanghai. He strongly encouraged the Chinese to invest in the company, and it is clear that he wanted to cultivate their friendship. At the same time, he noticed that some Chinese were "in the market here for steamers to carry tribute Rice to the North" and thus were "very hot" to buy the steamer *Sin Nanzing*, which was under the management of Jardine's, for Tls. 120,000.[151] Johnson, however, refused to facilitate its sale immediately, because these Chinese were "really bent upon competition with foreigners" in the Shanghai-Tientsin carrying trade. Johnson was therefore "anxious to

147. William F. Mayers, N. B. Dennys, and Charles King, *The Treaty Ports of China and Japan* (London, 1867), p. 476.
148. Johnson, "Memo," Shanghai, 1868, JMA.
149. IMC, *Reports on Trade, 1866* (Shanghai, 1867), p. 66.
150. Report of Consul Charles Winchester, Shanghai, May 6, 1868, FO 17/503.
151. (Shanghai) to H. Magniac (Hong Kong), Oct. 26, 1872, JMA.

delay the negotiations" until Jardine's could get all the shares in its new company subscribed for.[152]

The intensity of the Sino-Western competition in shipping in Chinese waters is illustrated by the rise of the China Merchants' Steam Navigation Company during the 1870s. This company, under the efficient and aggressive management of Chinese merchants, successfully competed with Western companies for the support of Chinese investors and shippers. Around August 1872, Governor-General Li Hung-chang organized the China Merchants' Steam Navigation Company in order to compete commercially with foreigners in China. Li relied heavily on prefect Chu Ch'i-ang, a traditional gentry-merchant in charge of the transport of tribute rice by seagoing junks. As a junk owner and a commissioner of the Chekiang Bureau of Sea Transport, Chu was knowledgeable in the shipping business, but his knowledge of Chinese junks was of little avail when it came to judging steam vessels. He was also troubled by the difficulties of raising capital for the new company, and by the spring of 1873 it became apparent that he could not develop the steamship project successfully. In May, Li appointed Tong King-sing, a prominent Cantonese at Shanghai, to replace Chu in managing the steamship enterprise. Hsu Jun, another Cantonese merchant, joined Tong in September and became his deputy at Shanghai.

Under the able leadership of these two Cantonese, the Chinese company began to compete in earnest with the Western steamship companies, especially in soliciting the support of Chinese investors. Since Li Hung-chang sought to have private merchants bear part of the entrepreneurial risk, the Chinese company was organized as a joint-stock company. During late 1873 and early 1874, many foreign houses in Shanghai persuaded their Chinese friends and compradors not to invest in the newly established Chinese company.[153] Nonetheless, in 1873 and 1874 Tong and Hsu succeeded in raising a sizable capital of Tls. 476,000. By 1877, this total had increased to Tls. 751,000. Besides Tong and Hsu, other Chinese, such as Seating and Awei, are known to have bought shares.[154]

152. (Shanghai) to James Whittall (Hong Kong), Nov. 15, 1872, JMA.
153. Nieh Pao-chang, "Ts'ung Mei-shang Ch'i-ch'ang lun-ch'uan kung-ssu ti ch'uang-pan yü fa-chan k'an mai-pan ti tso-yung," Li-shih yen-chiu 2:110 (1964).
154. "I also knew that he [Awei] had shares in Chinese Company, and that the Han-

The advent of the Chinese steamers led to an era of low freight rates. Although the Shanghai S. N. Co. was able to enter into an agreement with its British rivals to observe uniform rates in Chinese waters, these rates were not maintained because of Chinese competition. In the three years from 1873 to 1876, the Chinese company confronted foreign steamship enterprises with strenuous competition, and the American and British companies were hard put to operate profitably. In March 1874, one month after the three Western companies decided to maintain higher rates on the Yangtze River and on the Shanghai-Tientsin route, the Chinese company began to cut rates on the river, initially charging some 30 percent less than the American and British charged. By mid-summer, the freight rates on the Shanghai-Hankow route had fallen to Tls. 2 per ton—less than half the rate that Russell & Co. and Butterfield & Swire had agreed upon. The rates on the Shanghai-Tientsin route likewise declined.[155] Thus, according to *Shen pao*, the Chinese company successfully outcompeted foreign firms in securing freight.[156]

Although Tong King-sing later accepted Jardine's proposal that the three major companies on the Shanghai-Tientsin route observe a uniform rate for commercial freight, the Chinese company often got around this agreement by offering greater returns to shippers. Moreover, because of Governor-General Li Hung-chang's influence, tea shippers on Chinese steamers were exempted from internal taxes when their cargo was transshipped through Chihli province.[157] This arrangement naturally boosted the business of the China Merchants' Company. More importantly, Li granted the Chinese company the privilege of transporting the "tribute rice"—a tax-in-kind shipped regularly from the Lower Yangtze to Peking to help solve the capital city's food supply problem. It was reputed that competition existed even on this score. In 1875 a rumor circulated in Shanghai to the effect that Russell & Co. would compete with the China Merchants' Co. in transporting tribute rice from South China to Peking. It was said that Edward Cunningham of Russell's offered to ship the rice for the Ch'ing government at 0.1 tael per picul compared to 0.6 tael per picul charged by the Chinese company. This

---

kow agency had been offered to him" (F. B. Forbes to Walter Scott Fits, July 31, 1873, FBF).

155. Kwang-Ching Liu, "British-Chinese Steamship Rivalry in China, 1873–1885," in C. D. Cowan, ed., *The Economic Development of China and Japan* (London, 1964), p. 57.

156. *Shen pao*, TC 13/4/28, June 12, 1874, p. 2.

157. Kwang-Ching Liu, "British-Chinese," pp. 57–58.

would save the Ch'ing government Tls. 300,000 per year for the annual tribute rice (an average of 600,000 piculs) to be shipped to Peking.[158] This rumor, however, did not materialize.

The operations of the China Merchants' Company had damaging effects on the British China Coast S. N. Company's earnings. In 1874, shortly after the Chinese company started, the rate of return of the British steamship company was 19.7 percent, and it paid a dividend of 10 percent. These figures declined by about half in the following year. In 1876 its rate of return was further reduced to 8.9 percent, and it paid no dividend at all. By September 1876 the company's shares (Tls. 100 par value) were selling at Tls. 56. The prospects were so dim that the Jardine partners thought it would be best if the Chinese company could be persuaded to buy the China Coast Company's fleet. In November 1876 the idea was, in fact, referred to and approved by Sir Robert Jardine in London.

Compared with the British firm, the rate of return of the American house of Shanghai Steam Navigation Company was even less satisfactory. It was a meager 8.3 percent in 1874 and 1875, and fell to 7.9 percent in 1876. From 1866 to 1873, the company paid an annual dividend of 12 percent. After encountering Chinese competition, it could afford to pay only 7 percent from 1874 to 1876. Meanwhile, it had to pay out of its reserves for the necessary renovations of its fleet.[159]

EXPANSION OF THE CHINESE COMPANY

Despite minor corruption, the China Merchants' Company expanded remarkably during the decade from 1873 to 1883. The competence of these Chinese merchants is attested to by the fact that they bought the entire fleet of the American-owned Shanghai S. N. Co. in 1877. After Tong King-sing and Hsu Jun were placed in charge of the China Merchants' Company in 1873, their daring policy of fleet expansion enabled the Chinese company to put on a bold front before its American and British competitors. By the fall of 1876, when the Shanghai S. N. Co.'s shares (Tls. 100 par value) had fallen to Tls. 70, the company decided to sell out to the Chinese. An overture to the Chinese managers was accordingly made in December 1876 to which they immediately responded. Tong was away from Shanghai, but his deputy, Hsu Jun, negotiated

158. *Shen pao*, KH 1/2/9, Mar. 16, 1875, p. 1.
159. Kwang-Ching Liu, "British-Chinese," pp. 58–60.

with Russell and Co. and agreed on the price of Tls. 2,220,000. It included Tls. 2,000,000 for the Shanghai S. N. Co.'s fleet and properties and Tls. 220,000 for Russell and Co.'s waterfront properties in Shanghai and three other ports.

Having secured a loan of Tls. 500,000 from Governor-General Shen Pao-chen at Nanking, Tong signed the final purchase agreement with Russell's in January 1877. On January 6, after having paid a bargain money of Tls. 25,000, the Chinese company formally possessed sixteen additional steamships, together with wharves and warehouses in various treaty ports, including Shanghai, Tientsin, Ningpo, and the mid-Yangtze ports.[160] The Chinese line thus became the biggest in the steamship business, employing thirty-one steamers on seven routes in Chinese waters. It also put one ship in service from South China ports to Singapore, mainly for the purpose of carrying Chinese emigrants. In contrast, the other two British companies had only fourteen ships on five routes.[161] (See table 11.) Tong and Hsu were so confident of their victory that they declared in the "Report of Directors of China Merchants' Co." in April 1877: "Our experience in business shows us that we can fight foreign merchants successfully."[162]

After the grandiose purchase of the American firm, the Chinese company faced financial problems. Consequently, Tong and Hsu were willing to make compromises and to enter into agreements with the British companies in order to raise rates. However, such a policy of reconciliation was by no means unconditional. Although Tong made arrangements with Jardine's in March 1877 to observe uniform rates on both the Shanghai-Tientsin and Shanghai-Foochow routes, the Chinese company waged a rate war against the China Navigation Co. of Butterfield & Swire on the Yangtze. At issue was the number of departures each company was to schedule on the river. Freight rates between Shanghai and Hankow fell below 1 tael per ton, and the freight war extended to the Shanghai-Ningpo route. In September 1877 John Swire himself journeyed from London to Shanghai to seek a settlement, and an agreement was reached in December whereby rates were raised to 5 taels per ton from Shanghai to Hankow.

On the other routes, where uniform rates were not observed, competition remained intense. On the Canton-Macao route, the China Merchants' Company competed with the Hongkong, Canton & Macao

160. Hsu Jun, *Nien-p'u*, pp. 24–24b.
161. Kwang-Ching Liu, "British-Chinese," p. 60.
162. *NCH*, Apr. 21, 1877, p. 400.

TABLE 11.   THE NUMBER OF STEAMSHIPS EMPLOYED BY
THE THREE MAJOR STEAMSHIP COMPANIES IN SHANGHAI,
1877

Route	China Navigation[a] (British)	China Coast S. N.[b] (British)	China Merchants' S. N. (Chinese)
Yangtze River	3	0	10
Shanghai-Chefoo-Tientsin	0	4	11
Shanghai-Ningpo	1	1	3
Shanghai-Foochow	0	1	1
Shanghai-Canton-Hong Kong	0	0	1
Swatow-Shanghai-Newchwang	4	0	0
Shanghai-Amoy-Swatow	0	0	2
Shanghai-Chefoo-Newchwang	0	0	1
Amoy-Canton-Singapore	0	0	1
Total	8	6	30

Source: Kwang-Ching Liu, "British-Chinese Steamship Rivalry," p. 61.
[a]Under the management of Butterfield & Swire.
[b]Under the management of Jardine, Matheson & Co.

Steamboat Co., an Anglo-American-Portuguese concern based in Hong Kong under the general management of Jardine's. The Chinese company in 1881 used one of its better steamers, the *Kiang Ping*, to oppose the foreign company's "old and ill-adapted" steamer, the *Spark*. According to F. B. Johnson, Jardine's partner at Hong Kong, though the Chinese steamer had "very little profit," it inflicted "great losses" to the Western firm. The latter, however, refused to be outcompeted and proposed as "a substitute for the 'Spark' their steamer 'White Cloud' which will introduce an effective opposition to the 'Kiang Ping.'" But before doing so, the company tried to buy up the opposition by offering to charter the Chinese steamship at $500 per month.[163]

163. Johnson wrote from Hong Kong to the firm's Shanghai manager: "Before doing so, they have made an offer to the Native Company to charter the 'Kiang Ping' at $500 per month. I enclose for your private information a memorandum drawn up by the Secretary

In a letter dated May 7, 1881, F. B. Johnson instructed James J. Keswick, the firm's manager at Shanghai, to exploit fully the Chinese connections of the house in order to reach an agreement. At that time, Tong King-sing, Jardine's comprador from 1863 to 1873, was the general manager of the Chinese steamship company, and his elder brother, Tong Mow-chee, was Jardine's comprador in Shanghai. Johnson wrote:

If Tong King Sing be in Shanghai, I shall feel obliged by your seeing him without delay & ascertaining if any & what terms can be arranged. Should Tong King Sing be absent please try Tong Mow Chee to interview the [deputy] manager of the C. M. [China Merchants'] S. N. Co. & sound them on the subject. You will observe that our Directors would probably be prepared to give $700 a month if absolutely necessary for the purpose of buying up the opposition. I shall be glad if you will exert all the influence you can bring to bear to promote an arrangement of terms.[164]

Apparently Keswick's effort was an abortive one, for Johnson wrote again on May 18: "I am obliged to you for your advices with regard to your former negotiation with the C. M. S. N. Co. about their opposition to the local line of boats between Canton and Macao. I fear from what I have already heard that if the question is one to be decided by the Canton Agency of the Native Company, no arrangement will be practicable."[165]

Although the Chinese company reached an agreement with Butterfield & Swire in observing uniform rates on the Yangtze, competition remained stiff on the coast, especially for the trade between Newchwang and Swatow. As early as 1874, Butterfield & Swire started the Newchwang-Swatow trade by founding a separate "Coast Boat Ownery." This trade involved the portage of bean products from the Manchurian port of Newchwang to the southern port of Swatow, where sugar was loaded for a return cargo to the north. In November 1874, John Swire bought two steamers from Britain, the *William Batters* and the *Teresa Batters*, which were ideally suited for the Newchwang-Swatow trade because of their low draft and large capacity. The two ships, renamed *Foochow* and *Swatow*, operated successfully on the route, being used mainly for the business of "chartered trade," that is, they were chartered a shipload at a time by Chinese merchants. They were so profitable that

---

of the H. C. & M. [Hongkong, Canton, & Macao Steamboat] Company which explains the position" (to James J. Keswick [Shanghai], May 7, 1881, JMA).
164. Ibid.
165. Ibid., May 18, 1881.

in the latter half of 1875 the company decided to make a further investment of £40,000, and ordered two more steamers for the trade.

By 1879, Butterfield & Swire had six ships in the trade, and these
ships were already the favorites of the Chinese charterers. The commissioner of customs at Swatow reported in January 1880: "The trade between Swatow and those ports of China [Newchwang and Chefoo] is
chiefly carried on by steamers of Messr. Butterfield and Swire. . . . They
are gradually driving away the sailing vessels, taking cargo at very moderate prices, and giving great facilities to the Chinese merchants, who
are beginning to charter them by the trip in the same manner as sailing
vessels."[166] The Newchwang-Swatow trade inspired John Swire's ship-
building program, which involved plans to build nine new ships. In
1881–1882, the China Navigation Company invested in five new vessels
designed primarily for the Newchwang-Swatow trade. While Butterfield
& Swire was congratulating itself for the profitable trade on this route,
the steamships of the Chinese company appeared on the scene. Tong
King-sing and Hsu Jun ordered three light-draft ships in 1881–1882 for
the purpose of providing regular service on this route. Statistics of the
Imperial Maritime Customs show that the China Merchants' Company's ships entered and departed from Swatow 47 times in 1881, 69
times in 1882, and 120 times in 1883.[167]

Tong King-sing and Hsu Jun in 1882 revived the plans for a line from
the southern ports of Amoy and Swatow to Saigon and Singapore for the
purpose of carrying Chinese emigrants abroad and bringing home rice.
To support these undertakings, the company floated a new issue of some
Tls. 200,000 between 1879 and 1881. The new subscribers were mainly
Chinese in Hawaii and the United States, because the company was
proposing to initiate a new line to Honolulu and San Francisco. In addition, the company borrowed increasingly large sums from private
sources. Meanwhile, Tong, Hsu, and their fellow Cantonese merchants
were willing to increase their investments in the company. Five new
steamships arrived from Britain in 1882, and two more were anticipated
in 1883. Consequently, the company expanded its operations on several
routes: the service between Shanghai and Hong Kong was made more
frequent, and a new line was established between Shanghai and Wenchow. Meanwhile, Tong and Hsu decided to increase the company's
capital stock to Tls. 2,000,000, the holder of each old share having the

166. IMC, *Reports on Trade at the Treaty Ports, 1879* (Shanghai, 1880), p. 205.
167. Kwang-Ching Liu, "British-Chinese," pp. 69–70.

option of buying a new one. The new capital in the amount of Tls. 1,000,000 was fully subscribed by February 1883.[168] Meanwhile, by the early eighties, modern steamships gradually replaced the traditional junks as the major means of shipping for the Chinese. The statistics of Tientsin in 1882 indicate that the Chinese employed the service of modern Chinese steamships almost as much as the foreigners used the foreign steamers.[169]

To compete more effectively in China's waters, Jardine's established the Indo-China Steam Navigation Company in 1881. Five ships former-ly operated by the China Coast Company and three of the Yangtze Steamer Co., all being under Jardine's management, were taken over at a generous premium. Meanwhile, the Chinese company's new wharves and warehouses in Shanghai were completed in 1882 and were widely admired by Chinese and foreigners alike. Feeling the pressure im-mediately, F. B. Johnson of Jardine's wrote from Hong Kong to Shang-hai on January 3, 1883:

I observe a notice in the papers of the fine wharf which the China Merchants' Co. have acquired on the French side. If this wharf will suffice for the berthing of the company's own boats, what is to prevent Tong King Sing from utilizing the company's lower wharf and the adjoining Ningpo Wharf for bonded godowns and the berthing of outside steamers? That some such scheme is contemplated is rendered more than probable from the terms of Sir. R. [Robert] Hart's note to me and in view of it I requested [John] Macgregor to sell Hong Kew Wharf shares whenever practical. Under these circumstances, I think it may be as well not to undertake any expense at Pootung until we know with some certainty what the bonding scheme is to be.[170]

Two months later Johnson realized that Tong King-sing was deter-mined to keep Jardine's from possessing a highly desirable wharf prop-erty in Shanghai. He wrote William Paterson on March 17, 1883:

I hope that by the mail boat due tomorrow I shall hear something more about the Ningpo Wharf. From what I gathered from you as to the communications you had with Tong King-sing last year, I am apprehensive that that astute individual is not desirous that we should become the possessors of the frontage and his action in putting the property up for tender confirms my apprehensions. We *must* buy the property for the security of our Wharfage interests and it is clear to me that we should take the Directors of the S. & W. Wharf more or less into our confidence in treating for it. That is to say, it would be in the last degree impolitic

168. Ibid.
169. BPP, *Commerical Reports of Her Majesty's Consuls in China*, 1882, Tientsin, p. 95.
170. To William Paterson, JMA.

for us to give rise to any suspicion on the part of the shareholders that we are looking after our interests at the expense of theirs.[171]

Nevertheless, Jardine's tried to purchase the property through negotiation, as Johnson continued:

If the China Merchants' [Company] insist upon selling by tender, I fear we shall lose the property and that by their policy they intend us to lose it. Rather than tender I would negotiate for the purchase privately and I need not say that every effort should be made to come to an understanding with the C. M. [China Merchants'] S. N. Co. I cannot find the advertisement in the newspapers. You will have heard from [John] Macgregor about Chan Faiting's mission here to raise 300,000 taels on Shanghai property.[172]

Johnson appeared more hopeful in April 1883: "I hope the pressure upon the C. M. S. N. Co. to find the Korean indemnity may induce Tong King Sing to accept easy terms for the Ningpo Wharf."[173]

In January 1883, the Chinese company and the other two British companies reached a pooling arrangement. The China Merchants' Company, with its large fleet and its firm hold on a large sector of shippers, was accorded the major share. The pool earnings on the Yangtze River and on the Shanghai-Tientsin route were divided on a percentage basis among the three companies as follows:[174]

Route	China Merchants' S. N. Co.	Swire's	Jardine's
Yangtze River	42	38	20
Shanghai-Tientsin	44	28	28

As a result of the pooling system, Jardine's earnings on the Yangtze improved, although they remained far from being satisfactory. F. B. Johnson wrote on February 24, 1883: "I am glad to see that Hankow freights have been pretty well paid up and that the interest account of the Indo-China Co. will now be greatly reduced. We have not yet arrived at the result of the December and annual working, but I am afraid it will be very unsatisfactory."[175] Through the good offices of a certain

171. Ibid., Mar. 17, 1883.
172. Ibid.
173. Ibid., Apr. 5, 1883.
174. Kwang-Ching Liu, "British-Chinese," p. 68.
175. (Hong Kong) to John Macgregor (Shanghai), JMA.

Mr. Emmett, the manager of Butterfield & Swire's shipping department in Chefoo, and Wang Say Chee, agent for the China Merchants' Company in that port, a combination was temporarily formed.[176]

But on the other routes where the pooling system was not applicable, competition remained intense. For instance, freight rates were quite low on the southern coast, as F. B. Johnson complained in February 1883: "Steamer freights on the southern coast are avowedly low and there are scarcely as yet any signs shown of lessened competition."[177] As a result, Chinese merchants along the coast benefited in a great measure from the steamship rivalry, as J. H. Scott of Butterfield & Swire reported to John Samuel Swire in 1885: "It is very certain that the low rates of freight . . . benefited no one but the Celestial."[178]

Foreign steamship companies not only encountered external Chinese competition on all fronts but were also "squeezed" internally by their Chinese compradors. In a letter to William Paterson dated June 11, 1883, F. B. Johnson complained that Chinese compradors were detrimental to foreign shipping interests in China:

I . . . note what you say about [the steamer] 'Poo Yang,' and the system of squeezing in force on board the Indo-China Company's ships. I am not at all sure that the Compradoric system is not pushed to an extreme. . . . It looks as if the commissions and exactions of the Chinese staff about us would stifle foreign shipping interests as they have driven foreigners out of the traffic in merchandise on the Coast.[179]

After its purchase of sixteen vessels from Russell's in 1877, the China Merchants' line boasted a total fleet of thirty-one steamers. Between 1878 and 1883, it disposed of or lost fourteen ships but purchased nine new vessels of modern model and larger tonnage. In 1883 it led its main competitors, Butterfield & Swire and Jardine's, in both numbers of ships and net tonnage. The Chinese company was the strongest on several routes, including that of the Yangtze. It was at this juncture of ambitious expansion that, as we will see in chapter 11, a financial crisis loomed large in Shanghai during the summer of 1883, and as a consequence the expansion of the China Merchants' Company was arrested.

176. Wright, *Impressions*, p. 570.
177. (Hong Kong) to John Macgregor (Shanghai), Feb. 17, 1883, JMA.
178. (Shanghai) to Swire (London), Sept. 19, 1885, SP.
179. (Hong Kong) to Paterson (Shanghai), JMA.

CHAPTER EIGHT

The Pursuit of Profit

Although the Sino-Western trade along China's coast bred intense, nerve-racking competition, at the same time it also provided profitable opportunities for businessmen to explore. Commercial capitalism is an economic system based on private ownership and use of wealth for the exchange of goods and services with the aim of earning a profit. Private profit seeking, though not a proper occupation for the Chinese gentry, was regarded as the legitimate calling of merchants in traditional China. It was probably through the merchant community that the expression *Kung-hsi fa-ts'ai* (May you became financially prosperous) has become a Chinese new year greeting. Indeed, in the nineteenth century, there were plenty of profit-making opportunities along the coast for those daring enough to explore them. For the coastal merchants, Chinese and foreign alike, the logical first step was by legitimate means. One way was through Sino-Western cooperation, whereby Chinese and Western merchants traded in joint accounts. Another way was that in which the Chinese coastal merchants, conducting business in their own right, diversified their commercial undertakings. Both these practices enhanced the chances of profit making.

SINO-WESTERN SYMBIOSIS

Chinese and Western merchants along the coast frequently cooperated legally in the pursuit of mutual profit. The Chinese merchants received financial assistance from large foreign firms and profited by the latter's modern facilities, and the Western mercantile houses received fine Chinese goods for export or manufacturing and benefited by the increase in shipping and insurance business. Small Western firms sometimes needed Chinese capital to start modern enterprises.

THE CANTON SYSTEM

The hong merchants in China's foreign trade were relatively insignificant in the first half of the eighteenth century. After 1775, however, with the rise of their British counterparts, the supercargoes, the native merchants' role became increasingly important. From that time on, hong merchants and Western traders cooperated closely in their commercial transactions in Canton.[1] This relationship of intimate cooperation was further strengthened in the nineteenth century for two reasons: both of them had to deal with the increasing official pressure when hong merchants were made jointly responsible for bankruptcies; and closer cooperation became possible with the death of the powerful and independent-minded hong merchant, Puankhequa, in 1788.

Hong merchants and Western traders provided each other with various useful services. On the one hand, hong merchants saw to it that tea and silk that had been returned from abroad due to bad quality were quickly replaced without charge.[2] They also gave timely advice to supercargoes and private merchants concerning the purchase of Chinese produce.[3] Jardine, Matheson & Co. was grateful for such assistance rendered by Young Tingqua.[4] On the other hand, the British East India Company, for example, tried its best to help the hong merchants financially. In 1809, for instance, when the company learned that two hong merchants, Pouqua and Gnewqua, were on the verge of bankruptcy, it purchased an unusually large amount of tea from them. Similarly, the company helped Conseequa, Exchin, Manhop, Poonequa, and Goqua in 1812.[5] Six years later, two other hong merchants were able to escape bankruptcy because of the goodwill and aid of several British merchants.[6]

In a sense, cases like the 1809 bail-out by the East India Company of Pouqua and Gnewqua may not be viewed as good examples of voluntary

1. Liang Chia-pin, p. 293.
2. Ibid., p. 294.
3. J. Coolidge (Canton) to Jardine Matheson (Macao), Jan. 4, 1842, JMA.
4. "Young Tingqua thinks tea will be short and recommends our buying now" (ibid.).
5. Liang Chia-pin, pp. 293, 309–312.
6. FO 682/287.

cooperation, because given the system of advances (the collateral for which was the continuing existence of the Cohong member), the British company had no choice but to rescue the merchants. But the fact of the matter is that the British company was not obliged to make advances to any particular hong merchants or to buy extra amounts of tea from them, because, if they had gone bankrupt, the Hoppo would have appointed other ordinary merchants to replace them as hong merchants, and business would have continued as usual.

In the same vein, hong merchants, particularly Houqua, Kingqua, Cheepqua, and Footae, maintained a cordial relationship with the American traders.[7] In reporting to the firm's constituents in America, Russell & Co. wrote from Canton in 1832: "In point of veracity we have no hesitation in saying that we hold Cheepqua quite as high as many of the individuals who took extraordinary pains to reduce difficulty on this business."[8] Houqua, the most powerful hong merchant in the early nineteenth century, had an unusually close relationship with the partners of Russell & Co., for examples, John P. Cushing, John Murray Forbes, and Robert B. Forbes. His help, coupled with the rice famine in Canton in 1825, enabled Cushing to get a reduction in the tonnage dues on vessels laden with rice coming to Canton. Whereas other ships had to pay the full tonnage tax, ranging from $3,000 to $6,000, Cushing's "rice ships" paid only about $1,150.[9]

Houqua and Russell's partners often jointly engaged in the trade between China and Europe. On December 22, 1833, Houqua started one of his largest adventures by engaging the 200-ton Prussian vessel, the *Princess Service,* to ship his cargo to Hamburg at $40 per ton. He offered a quarter-share in the trade to Cushing, who in turn would ship the cargo under his name and provide insurance in the amount of $50,000.[10] In March 1840 Houqua and Cushing reached an agreement to ship Houqua's tea to England. Houqua advanced to James P. Sturgis of Russell's the amount of $50,000, and the tea was then shipped to London on Sturgis' account by Russell's vessels. As to risks, Houqua wrote to Cushing:

7. BJ-17, HC.

8. Letter of Russell & Co. to home constituents, Aug. 21, 1832, BL-6, HC.

9. Dennett, *Americans,* pp. 91–92. These "rich ships" were exempt from import duties after 1833.

10. Houqua (Canton) to Cushing (Boston), Dec. 22, 1833, F-5, FC. We do not know whether this suggestion was accepted by Cushing, who was not particularly interested in the scheme. Augustine Heard encouraged Cushing to accept, pointing out that Houqua's accounts in Europe were large (Heard [Canton] to Cushing [Boston], Feb. 18, 1834, F-5, FC).

"Should there be any loss by bad debts, or bad management in England, I alone shall be held responsible, while you are to run the risk only of a bad market, the amount on which you will be responsible being to the extent of $15,000, according to the terms of your letter."[11] In other words, Houqua and Cushing would share the profits and risks of this shipment.

The most important factor that brought Houqua and Russell's together was that Houqua assigned the latter as his agent in handling his overseas trade. This arrangement benefited both parties. On the one hand, Houqua profited from the firm's expertise in international trade, and he was able to proceed with his huge overseas shipments without being detected and squeezed by Chinese officials. On the other hand, the partners of Russell's received handsome commissions from Houqua. More importantly, the way in which Houqua's proceeds of tea and silk were paid further benefited them, because the bills on Bengal, a convenient device for getting the proceeds from Europe, provided purchasing power in India for Houqua and Russell's. These bills on Bengal not only enabled Houqua to buy opium, cotton, pearls, and other goods from India[12] but also significantly financed Russell's purchase of opium from Bombay and Calcutta. For buying opium in India, Russell's employed the service of several American brokers in Calcutta in 1831, including J. Church, J. B. Higginson, and P. Dixwell. In addition, Augustine Heard, the firm's partner in Canton, did considerable opium business with the banian (a Hindu trader) office of Anshootos Day.[13] On the Chinese end, the *Lintin*, an opium ship with Robert B. Forbes as the captain, did good business for Russell's in Cantonese waters, especially on Lintin Island.[14] The house imported from Calcutta to China 3,981 chests of opium from April to August 1831.[15] Given the fact that the total amount of Indian opium brought to China was about 18,760 chests in 1831,[16] Russell's opium business was an impressive one during the early 1830s.

After the death of Houqua in 1843, his family continued to have cordial relations with Russell & Co. Soon after the house established a branch office in Shanghai, Wu Ch'ung-yueh (1810–1863), son of the celebrated Houqua, recommended a fellow-Cantonese named Ahyue in late 1858 to serve as Russell's comprador. His suggestion was accepted,

11. (Canton) to Cushing (Watertown, Mass.), Mar. 13, 1840, HLB.
12. HLB, passim.
13. J. Church (Calcutta) to Heard (Canton), Dec. 11, 1831, BM-6, HC.
14. There were 1,300 chests of Indian opium on board the *Lintin* on Feb. 10, 1832 (Forbes [Lintin] to Thomas Perkins [Boston], Feb. 10, 1832, E-4, FC).
15. Indian Opium Account, H-7, HC.
16. Robert B. Forbes, *China and China Trade*, p. 44.

and the partners of Russell's considered Ahyue honest and faithful.[17]
After the Treaty of Nanking of 1842, the Cohong was abolished as the
intermediary institution of China's foreign trade, but Wu Ch'ung-yueh
continued to invest large sums of money in Russell & Co.[18] Meanwhile,
this house had cordial relations with other Chinese merchants. Wu
Chien-chang, onetime hong merchant, invested in Russell's in the late
forties and early fifties and became one of the seven big investors of the
company.[19]

Augustine Heard & Co., another American mercantile house, maintained warm friendships with many hong merchants, particularly Houqua and Kingqua.[20] These cordial relationships led the partners to remember the old days of the Canton system with nostalgia after it was
abolished in 1842. Learning that the Treaty of Nanking had been signed,
John Heard III deplored the measure in his diary: "The old and
pleasant Hong system was abolished!"[21] The goodwill of American merchants toward their old Chinese friends, the former hong merchants, was
attested to in 1858 when the modern customs house was to be established in Canton. Heard's at first objected to this idea, fearing that the
British would dominate the new customs house. However, after having
considered the sufferings of the families of former hong merchants, the
firm finally welcomed the plan. During that time, the families of Houqua
and Samqua, their old friends who had passed away, were being
"squeezed" by local officials to contribute money to the provincial treasury for war indemnities. John Heard III figured that the new customs
house, being a regular source of income to pay the indemnities, would
relieve the plight of their Cantonese friends' families.[22] Not surprisingly,
his view was shared by William Beckwith of Russell & Co.[23] The customs house was finally established in Canton in 1859.[24] Admittedly,
both companies knew that they would profit to a certain degree by the
customs house, and it would be naive to disregard this financial factor
altogether. But the fact that, in their *private correspondence*, these American
merchants did take the interests of their Chinese friends into consideration is worth noting. At any rate, the cordial relationships between the

    17. Russell & Co. (per John M. Forbes, Jr., Canton) to E. M. King, U.S. Consul
(Canton), May 2, 1868, Case 26, RA; and Edward Cunningham (Shanghai) to John M.
Forbes, Jr. (Canton), June 4, 1868, Case 26, RA.
    18. Hsu K'o, *Ch'ing-pai lei-ch'ao*, ts'e 17:102–4.
    19. Nieh Pao-chang, "Ch'i-ch'ang," p. 93.
    20. BJ-17, HC.
    21. "Diary," FP-1, p. 36, HC.
    22. (Canton) to Augustine Heard, Sr., Jan. 26, 1850, EM-7, HC.
    23. To P. S. Forbes, Sept. 26, 1860, FC.
    24. IMC, *Circular*, X, 514.

hong merchants and American traders were more than just a matter of formality.

After the Treaty of Nanking of 1842, the role of the hong merchant in China's foreign trade was superseded by the comprador—the Chinese manager in a foreign firm. Relying on each other for making profits, the foreign merchant and his Chinese comprador had a symbiotic relationship. The former benefited from the services of the latter in three ways, because the comprador was at once the head of servants, the Chinese business manager, and the purchasing agent in the interior—all essential for a successful business. On the other hand, the comprador obtained economic rewards from his position, because he received a salary and a commission from his employer.

At the same time, a comprador was an independent merchant in his own right. On the one hand, his own business prospered mainly because of the fact that he had important foreign connections. On the other hand, his close ties with the Chinese business community benefited his foreign employer. One example was the native bank business. Many compradors, such as Takee, Hsu Jun, and Tong King-sing, were concurrently partners of native banks after the fifties. Houses with extra capital, such as Jardine's, could make money through the comprador by lending the "chop loan" to native banks. (See chapter 4.) For firms that were short of capital, such as Augustine Heard & Co., they could borrow money through the comprador from native banks at a reasonable interest rate.

Another example was the freight brokerage business on the Yangtze. Large amounts of native produce were shipped from the upper and middle Yangtze Valley to Shanghai for export after the seventies, and many Western firms, including Jardine's, Heard's, and Butterfield & Swire, helped their compradors to set up freight brokerage shops in the treaty ports on the Yangtze. The comprador received extra income from brokerage fees, and his foreign employer benefited from freight and insurance for this trade. As the firm became successful, so the fortunes of the comprador grew. In the same vein, if the comprador was efficient, the profits of the foreign firm increased.[25]

In much the same way, a symbiotic relationship also existed between Western houses and independent Chinese merchants. From the late 1840s on, Jardine's often provided inexpensive credit to Chinese mer-

25. Yen-p'ing Hao, *Comprador*, pp. 22–43, 89–99.

chants in exchange for commission and shipping, as we have seen in chapter 4. After 1860 the firm steadily shifted its business to noncommission fields. As a managing agent or an investor, the house showed more willingness to work closely with Chinese businessmen in order to expand its enterprises to match the opportunities available. Jardine archives contain numerous such cases, for example, the relationship between Tucksing and Jardine's. They cooperated in China's coastal trade for more than twenty years, especially in the sixties. Tucksing dispatched his assistant from Shanghai to Hong Kong to buy opium in 1867. For this purpose, he asked William Keswick, Jardine's partner at Hong Kong, to advance him money. In return for this favor, he bought opium from the firm, and, in transporting the opium from Hong Kong to Shanghai, the firm received income from shipping and insurance charges.[26]

Meanwhile, Tucksing often sold Jardine's nankeen cloth. In order to facilitate Tucksing's purchases of nankeen, Jardine's advanced him funds, for example, an advance of Tls. 15,000 in September 1868. Two years later, when F. B. Johnson planned to make another advance of Tls. 20,000 to Tucksing, William Keswick at Hong Kong made suggestions concerning the loan:

I have no objection to your authorizing Tucksing to borrow on our account to the extent in value of Ts. 20,000, but please not to advance the money in Shanghai but arrange with Tucksing to give him a letter of credit on Captain Vincent who will buy him such funds as may be necessary to Swatow on being placed in possession of the Bills of lading & invoice of the sugar. Probably Tucksing will object to this form of finance but unless you have the most undoubted confidence in his doing us justice & in his stability it is the only prudent course open to us.[27]

The house subsequently made many advances to Tucksing for the purpose of buying native produce and imported goods. Its account current in August 1871 showed that Tucksing still owed money to the house.[28]

26. Tucksing wrote from Shanghai to Keswick in Hong Kong on Dec. 24, 1867: "By this opportunity, my inspector of opium (Ah Chie) is proceeding down to your port per str. [steamer] 'Ganges,' who will reside in Ho Lee Hong for the purpose of purchasing opium there; now I will therefore respectfully beg you to advance him money against shipment on opium, which is to be shipped in your own steamer for Shanghai, also the same to be insured in your respective [respectable] Firm" (JMA). Keswick gladly granted his request.
27. Keswick to Johnson (Shanghai), Jan. 29, 1870, JMA. For Jardine's advance two years earlier, see Johnson (Shanghai) to Jardine, Matheson & Co. (Hong Kong), Sept. 11, 1868, JMA.
28. Keswick asked, "What is Tucksing doing & how does his indebtedness to us now stand?" (ibid., Aug. 8, 1871).

One of Tucksing's most important services was that of providing Jardine's with valuable market information. F. B. Johnson valued him highly in this capacity, regarding him as "the best-informed native" in Shanghai. During the latter part of 1867, Jardine's Shanghai office had several joint-account shipments with him for coastal trade. Sugar was shipped from Canton to the northern ports, and bean products were transported to South China from Newchwang. In Johnson's view, the reasons for engaging in joint accounts with Tucksing were that this coastal trade would yield 15 to 20 percent profit, and the house would in this way "keep best informed." In fact, gaining market information from Tucksing was the "principal object" for cooperating with him, as Johnson frankly admitted to Keswick in 1867.[29]

Tucksing was most helpful in facilitating Jardine's plan to launch a steamship line between Shanghai and Foochow in 1868. On April 10, F. B. Johnson reported that, through Tucksing, he would be able to get the "complete support of the guild in the way of freight."[30] Besides freight, Jardine's would also benefit from the banking and insurance business that would result from the establishment of the new line.[31] Johnson was confident by October that, through the influence of Tucksing, Jardine's could obtain the support of virtually all the Chinese shippers:

The estimates confirm the information I have previously received from Chinese about the quantity of cargo now conveyed in the wretched boats on the line & the room for development of the traffic, & I have as much confidence as before that we could obtain the support of all or nearly all the Native shippers through the influence of Tuck Sing if we lay ourselves properly out to secure it. The necessity of regular communication between this port & Foochow is every day becoming more apparent. Already a large exchange business has been done.[32]

To encourage Tucksing's interest in the line, Jardine's permitted him to "take shares to a certain extent."[33] The steamer line was finally launched and soon became a lucrative business.[34]

---

29. "My principal object, however, is to keep best informed about our Hong, as he is the best informed Native, I know, on all matter connected with local business" (Johnson to Keswick, Sept. 28, 1867, JMA).

30. Ibid., Apr. 10, 1868.

31. "Tucksing says a capacity of 400 or 500 tons will be all that is requisite for the trade & that if we undertake the line we may depend upon its bringing banking & insurance business to us in the way of advances upon shipments to Foochow" (ibid., Apr. 11, 1868).

32. Ibid., Oct. 26, 1868.

33. Ibid., Apr. 11, 1868.

34. For later developments, see Kwang-Ching Liu, *Anglo-American Steamship Rivalry in China, 1862–1874* (Cambridge, Mass., 1962), p. 135.

Ekee (Kin Cheequi, Kin Tzu Kwei), an active Cantonese merchant on the coast, also actively cooperated with Jardine's in the sixties and seventies. Starting in 1864 he frequently shipped cotton from Shanghai to Hong Kong, where the firm served as his agent.[35] Two years later he was the firm's teaman in securing green teas from Woochow.[36] Meanwhile, he bought British goods from the firm, often receiving sizable advances. After 1865 he also bought opium from Jardine's.[37] Ekee not only traded with Jardine's Shanghai office, but also, with the help of the firm, directly exported tea and silk to England and France. In 1865 complications developed out of his sale of silk to Lyons, and he requested legal and financial assistance from the firm. William Keswick's desire for Ekee's friendship prompted him to write to Jardine's head office at Hong Kong: "You would oblige Ekee by sending to Lyons for presentation, the enclosed Dft. [Draft] No. 717, Shanghai, 30th October 1865, for fcs [francs] 12500. It may not be accepted, and probably it may not be paid. In any case, request your correspondents to take such legal steps as may be necessary for the interest of this native friend."[38]

They also cooperated in operating traditional, Chinese-style businesses, such as native banks. Ekee proposed to Keswick at Shanghai in 1864 that a native bank, capitalized by Jardine's, Tong King-sing, Ekee himself, and other Chinese merchants, be set up in that port as soon as possible. Keswick, regarding it as a promising undertaking, reported favorably to James Whittall on February 18, 1865:

The Native Bank I spoke to you about I am endeavouring to bring into shape and in a few days hope to report progress. My intention is to limit the capital to 3 lacs [$300,000], of which we supply one & 2 natives the remaining 2 lacs. The more I think over & study the project, the more impressed I became with the advantages such an establishment well conducted will afford us. I have secured

35. "Ekee is anxious to have his late shipments of Cotton to your address sold without delay, of which please take note" (Keswick [Shanghai] to Jardine, Matheson & Co. [Hong Kong], Apr. 20, 1864, JMA).

36. "I hope you will not object to an arrangement being made to buy Woochow Greens which are doing very well indeed. You will recollect having bought them through Ekee in 1866 & the result was very satisfactory" (F. B. Johnson [Shanghai] to W. Keswick [Hong Kong], Feb. 12, 1868, JMA).

37. Concerning advances, see Keswick (Shanghai) to Jardine, Matheson & Co. (Hong Kong), July 29, 1864, JMA. One year later, Keswick wrote: "Ekee on behalf of some Chinamen has given me an order for 100 chests Patna to be purchased on your market on the best terms at which it is procurable, so long as you do not pay more than $560 per chest. $5,000 bargain money will be deposited with me, and for the cost you will please value upon me in the event of your thinking it right to execute this order" ([Shanghai] to James Whittall [Hong Kong], Nov. 27, 1865, JMA).

38. Keswick (Shanghai) to Jardine's, Oct. 24, 1865, JMA.

the services of a very experienced Native and in April the Bank will probably be opened.[39]

This native bank, named "Ewo Bank," was established in June 1865. Eight months later, Keswick reported that this bank earned a handsome profit of about 2.5 percent per month, adding, "There is every reason to believe the establishment will continue to be a great success."[40] The bank continued to be profitable and all concerned were satisfied with its performance.

Jardine, Matheson & Co. profited through the bank in several ways. It could receive interest for its deposits and also get loans in time of need. William Keswick wrote of this factor on June 29, 1865:

Instead of keeping all our cash with the comprador, I have transferred to the Ewo China Bank the custody of most of our money on the understanding that we receive interest at the rate of 8 per mil [0.8 percent] per 30 days on all sycee in the Bank's possession and pay the same rate on all sycee for which we overdraw our account. I consider this a very good arrangement and one by which we shall reap the advantage & profit hitherto derived by the Comprador alone when the Treasury was well filled.[41]

The firm reduced the possibility of the comprador's malpractice, especially by overspeculation, by leaving "as little cash under his care as possible."[42] Jardine's also quietly engaged in silver dollar speculation through the Ewo Bank. Because large amounts of Mexican dollars were shipped from Shanghai to India, Keswick, in anticipation of a strong market, purchased the silver dollars through the bank.[43]

Finally, and most importantly, Ewo Bank greatly enhanced Jardine's tea and silk purchases by providing short-term loans to Chinese traders to buy native produce upcountry. The bank was staffed from manager to clerks by Chinese alone, and its average monthly business was Tls. 550,000. Besides engaging in the banking business, Ekee was a silk merchant who maintained silk firms and warehouses in Shanghai as well as

39. To Whittall (Hong Kong), JMA. Also see Liu Kuang-ching, "T'ang T'ing-shu," p. 146.
40. "The year will run on until 30th June so as to make it accord with our Commercial Year" (to Whittall [Hong Kong], Feb. 12, 1866, JMA).
41. Ibid. See also Liu Kuang-ching, "T'ang T'ing-shu," p. 146.
42. Keswick to Whittall, June 29, 1865, JMA.
43. Keswick wrote to Whittall: "The purchase I alluded to in my letter of the 30th ultimo is bearing interest and will I doubt not continue to do so. This was arranged through the Ewo Bank, and as the sums are distributed in small amounts, and only to good people, I conceive there is no danger" (ibid., Dec. 2, 1865). See also Accounts, Ewo Bank, JMA.

in the silk districts of Chekiang. From June 1865 to April 1867, the bank furnished the large sum of about 10 million taels to Chinese merchants for the purpose of buying tea, silk, and cotton from the interior.[44] Most of the native produce then purchased was sold to Jardine's in Shanghai. Jardine's was by no means the only Western house involved in the joint venture of a native bank. The foreign commissioner of the Maritime Customs at Shanghai reported that there were 116 native banks in that port in 1866, and "some of the principal foreign mercantile houses are largely interested in native banks."[45]

Jardine's also cooperated with other Chinese merchants. On the advice of the company, Matheson & Co. of London advanced £2,000 to two native silk traders, Esing and Chun Yun-chang, in 1859. These merchants used the money to buy forty bales of silk and shipped them from Shanghai to Lyons in 1860. Both made money by engaging in this export business, and Jardine's similarly profited by shipping and insuring the silk. Jardine's also made advances to Yakee to expand his cotton trade on the coast in the sixties, with the understanding that the cotton would be shipped by Jardine's steamer *Queensbury* and that "the insurance and freight" would be "paid by himself at time of shipment."[46] This arrangement was successfully carried out. At one time when Yakee was short of cash at the time of shipment, he sold to Jardine's some of his shares in the Canton Insurance Office, a subsidiary of Jardine's to which he had subscribed.[47] In like manner, Augustine Heard & Co. worked closely with the Chinese merchants. Through the arrangement of the house, See Yong made a shipment of tea from Canton to the United States via the steamer *Alabama* in the early sixties. His tea incurred some damage on the route, and Heard's gave him legal help regarding the so-called "Alabama claims."[48]

This cooperation in overseas shipments was later extended to China's domestic trade. In the sixties, Heard's helped Tong Loong-maw to

44. Wang Ching-yü, "Shih-chiu shih-chi wai-kuo ch'in-Hua shih-yeh chung ti Hua-shang fu-ku huo-tung," *Li-shih yen-chiu* 4:52 (1965). Wang states that Ewo bank started in 1864, but the Jardine archives show that it was planned in 1864 but did not open until June 1865 (W. Keswick [Shanghai] to J. Whittall [Hong Kong], June 29, 1865, JMA). When Ekee went bankrupt, it was temporarily closed at the end of 1866 and the beginning of 1867 (ibid., Jan. 3, 1867). It was "dissolved by mutual consent" on Apr. 23, 1867 (*NCH*, May 6, 1867, p. 51).

45. BPP, *Report on Trade by the Foreign Commissioners at the Ports in China Open by Treaty to Foreign Trade for Year 1866*, vol. 69, p. 20.

46. James Whittall (Shanghai) to Jardine, Matheson & Co. (Hong Kong), Apr. 6, 1861. For Esing and Chun Yun-chang, see ibid., May 5, 1860.

47. Ibid., Apr. 6, 1861.

48. EA-2, HC.

establish his tea-purchasing facilities in the Yangtze Valley, especially in the tea districts of Hunan and Hupei. In return for this favor, Tong sold the bulk of his tea to Heard's at Shanghai and provided market intelligence to the firm regarding other commodities, such as tea, sugar, pepper, and opium. In a letter to G. B. Dixwell of Heard's at Shanghai on February 23, 1863, Tong urged the firm to ship sugar from Shanghai to Hankow to make money.[49] In another letter of May 19, he reported on a variety of things: "The sugar market at present is lower.... As to tea, the spring rains have been excessive. During the third month there were more than twenty rainy days and this is the month for gathering leaves . . . and I do not therefore see any chance of a good business in early tea. . . . Opium has gone down."[50] Equipped with such accurate and detailed market intelligence, Heard's business became increasingly profitable in the sixties.

In collaboration with the Chinese, Heard's even tried to explore the possibility of mining. The firm reached an agreement on February 6, 1873, with Atai, who was to go to Hainan Island for this purpose. The house was to give $600 to Atai for his travel expenses. He would then proceed to the island to "obtain the consent of the authorities and the inhabitants near and in Cheong-fa-hien to his working sundry copper and other mines in that vicinity." If Atai succeeded, "he then is to offer to Mr. A. F. Heard the privilege of working these mines with him either as owning half share therein or with such other parties as they select to own the privilege with them."[51] Even though we do not know whether or not this project worked out, it nevertheless shows the symbiosis of both parties in the pursuit of mutual profit.

"Symbiosis" by definition means a close two-way relationship. If one party fails to perform his function, the other party will quickly desert him. Takee's silk business with Jardine's in 1852 was a good example. Takee, an important silk merchant at Shanghai, received an advance from Jardine's for the purchase of silk from the interior of Chekiang and Kiangsu. Under contract, he was to sell a certain amount of silk to Jardine's at Shanghai. The initial stage of his upcountry silk purchase was so successful that he asked the firm to sponsor with him a shipment of silk to Europe on joint-account. He suggested a share of one-quarter to one-third for the firm (one to three thousand bales).[52] Despite

49. Tong Loong-maw (Hankow) to Dixwell, HM-30, HC.
50. Ibid., May 19, 1863.
51. Agreements, Case 9, HC II.
52. A. G. Dallas wrote to the head office at Hong Kong in 1852, asking authority to

the initial approval from David Jardine, A. G. Dallas finally rejected Takee's request on the ground that Takee had been slow in fulfilling other obligations: "I note what you say in regard to Takee's silk, but as he is very slow in fulfilling his Contracts, I do not think he will be entitled to any share."[53] It is thus clear that only efforts that proved mutually beneficial could ensure business cooperation.

Friends and relatives of Chinese merchants also benefited from this Sino-Western symbiotic relationship. One example was Yowloong, a Chinese tea merchant who had close connections with Jardine's. His brother often borrowed money from James Whittall of Jardine's at Shanghai in the early sixties, to be repaid to Jardine's by Yowloong in Canton.[54] Yowloong usually settled his debt in two months when he sold tea to Jardine's. In fact, it was the tea trade that led Whittall to grant the loan in the first place. A Chinese merchant might often help a friend to get a job from foreign houses. Chun Fai-ting (Ch'en Hui-t'ing) of China Merchants' S. N. Co. was a case in point. He wrote to James Keswick of Jardine's in 1885, inquiring whether one of his friends could apply for a clerical position in the firm's shipping office.[55] Chun's request was apparently cleared through Keswick, for his friend, Chaikokhing, later sent in the application.[56] We are not sure whether or not Chaikokhing

grant Takee's request: "Takee also has applied to me for an interest say 1/3d or 1/4th in our Silk purchases. This I think he would hardly do did he expect to see a very large crop. He says we may expect to see 20,000 Bs. [bales] brought forward, but not much more unless high prices are paid. I quite agree in what he says, & leave it to you to appropriate to his account one, two, or three thousand bales of all our purchases as you may be disposed. Please let me know when you decide, & what rate of exchange you draw against the shipments. He acknowledges that all my purchases from him are bona fide, & that he has no claim to any share. He would I dare say be quite satisfied with 500 bales, & I think it would be better if you leave the appropriation of it to me, letting me know, say on arrival of next mail, the quantity you would wish disposed of in this manner, & leaving it to me to settle the rate of exchange with him" (Dallas [Shanghai] to David Jardine, July 21, 1852, JMA).
      53. Dallas continued: "Should he fail in completing them, I think I shall be able to replace them otherwise" (ibid., Aug. 31, 1852).
      54. "Yowloong's brother applied to me to pay passages of himself & two Chinamen to Hankow, amounting to Tls. 190, stating that his brother would repay the sum in Canton, and you would oblige me by applying to him for & recovering the same" (Whittall to Jardine, Matheson & Co. [Hong Kong], July 30, 1861, JMA).
      55. "I hear that a Chinese clerk who can read and write English is required in your shipping office. If so, a young friend of mine who has been in our office for the last five years and writes a good hand wishes to apply for it. I wrote to Mr. Allum about it some time ago and he told me that perhaps you would get some one from Hong Kong. Will you kindly inform me if my friend can send in his application or not" (Chun Fai-ting [Shanghai] to Keswick [Shanghai], Mar. 20, 1885, JMA).
      56. "Being informed that you are in want of a respectful person to fill the situation of clerkship in your Company, I beg to offer you my services. I have been in school for six

got the job, but the fact that Chun could explore the possibility is noteworthy.

The advances that Western houses made to Chinese merchants gained influence or leverage for them as creditors and were useful in facilitating the purchase of native produce as well as the sale of imported goods, especially cotton drills.[57] Commenting on making advances to Chinese teamen, A. F. Heard wrote in 1858: "Some houses have very large connections of this description and it is the best commission business we can have."[58] Less wealthy houses needed Chinese capital to start modern enterprises; for instance, there were considerable amounts of Chinese shares in the first three foreign steamship companies in China (1862–1868)—Shanghai S. N. Co., Union S. N. Co., and North-China Steamer Co.[59] This was also true of manufacturing companies. The Hou-i Cotton Spinning and Weaving Co., the first modern factory of its kind ever operated in China, was established in Canton in 1871 by an American merchant, Vrooman. Its initial capital was only $20,000, but Vrooman was unable to convince foreign merchants to subscribe to it. Instead, he successfully persuaded his Chinese friends to invest in the enterprise.[60]

With the help of Chinese shareholders, Western firms could expand their businesses. Some British merchants tried to establish a sugar refinery near Canton in the late sixties, but they failed, partly because they had no Chinese shareholders and consequently had to pay high prices for the local raw sugar. But other foreign-owned sugar-refining companies around Canton, with Chinese capital, had successful businesses, partly because of the ease with which they could obtain cheap raw sugar. The suppliers of the raw sugar were none other than the Chinese merchants who had invested in the refineries.[61]

Even though in most cases it was the Chinese merchants who invested in Western-owned enterprises, occasionally companies with foreign capital were registered under the name of their Chinese friends. This was particularly true in the eighties when Chinese officials strongly resisted

---

years, after out of which I left this port for Foochow, and where was to be a clerk in the firm of Messrs. Bathgate & Co. The said vacancy, which I beg for, I believe that I can fulfill perfectly" (Chaikokhing [Shanghai] to Keswick [Shanghai], July 14, 1885, JMA).

57. For cotton drills (cotton fabrics in twill weave), see Lockwood, p. 48.
58. (Shanghai) to John Heard III, Feb. 28, 1858, HL-13, HC.
59. Yen-p'ing Hao, *Comprador*, pp. 123–24.
60. Wang Ching-yü, "Fu-ku," pp. 56, 70.
61. Ibid., p. 71.

the establishment of foreign-owned factories in the treaty ports. Jardine's started to organize a cotton-spinning mill in Shanghai in 1889. To honor official policy, Jardine's allowed some of their Chinese friends to own the mill in name, although its capital was to be furnished by a Bombay yarn merchant. Meanwhile, Jardine's would act "as managers for a small percentage on gross, say 2%."[62] Jardine's plan was aborted, but it reflects the wide scope of the economic symbiosis between Chinese and foreign merchants along China's coast.

WESTERNERS' CULTIVATION OF CHINESE FRIENDSHIP

No other business attested more vividly to the Westerners' efforts to improve their Chinese connections than the shipping trade. The American firm of Russell & Co. provides a good example. Edward Cunningham (1823–1889), its managing partner at Shanghai, was particularly good at cultivating Chinese friendship by virtue of his being able to speak pidgin English. He proposed in early 1861 to concentrate the firm's resources in a steamship enterprise in Chinese waters for the shipping trade, but other senior partners at home showed little interest. He then successfully raised capital in China and maintained a profitable operation. To achieve this, he relied to a high degree on his ability and willingness to cultivate the goodwill of the Chinese in the treaty ports. Around August 1861, when the freight rates on the Yangtze were high and the profit from the steamship business soared, he arranged to have his Chinese friends share the ownership of a steamer, the *Willamette*, which was immediately profitable. Earlier, however, after this vessel had a shipwreck, Cunningham alone took the risk of repairing it and making it shipworthy again. He later recalled: "Though I took the risk myself, I took none of the profits, dividing her up, as soon as she was safely running, among our Shanghai Chinese, in order to induce them to enter the grander scheme of the SSN [Shanghai Steam Navigation] Company."[63]

Cunningham's effort was not in vain: he raised more than one-third of the total capital of 1 million taels for the Shanghai Steam Navigation Company from the local business community in 1862. This was of special significance because in the same period three other commercial houses were contemplating a similar project but could not obtain the

62. Jardine's to J. Macgregor (Hong Kong), July 22, 1889, Private Letter Book, JMA. See also LeFevour, p. 46.
63. To P. S. Forbes, Nov. 10, 1865, FC. See also Kwang-Ching Liu, *Steamship Rivalry*, pp. 27–28.

much-needed capital from the Chinese.[64] When he purchased waterfront sites for the company, Cunningham chose properties situated near the Chinese business sections. The Kin-lee-yuen (Chin li yuan) wharfage site in Shanghai, for example, was selected because it was next to the Chinese city; it proved to be one of the company's great attractions for the Chinese shippers and contributed to its profitable operations.[65] A shipping office was also located at Kin-lee-yuen in 1870 in order to better accommodate the Chinese. Chinese capital in the company doubled by 1874, to the amount of 600,000 taels.[66]

In sharp contrast to the success of their fellow Americans of Russell & Co., Augustine Heard & Co. could not achieve a satisfactory Chinese connection despite their willingness to do so. A. F. Heard wrote apologetically in 1858: "I am anxious to get up a shipping business among the Chinese but never have been able to do it."[67] The British firm of Jardine's fared better. At the end of 1859, James Whittall used 10,000 taels to acquire a piece of land in Shanghai next to the Chinese business district from Takee in order to attract Chinese merchants. The firm also built an office-godown complex on the lot, which cost an additional 30,000 taels.[68] Jardine's Chinese business was greatly enhanced by the employment of an able comprador, Tong King-sing, in 1863. Another British firm, Butterfield & Swire, refused to fall behind Jardine's. Their cordial relationship with the Chinese was mainly attributable to the ability of William Lang, their "Eastern Partner" managing the Shanghai office, to find a competent Western shipping clerk to be in charge of public relations with the local business community. This clerk was Henry B. Endicott, a Chinese-speaking American, who was employed in 1872 for the purpose of drumming up Chinese business. Their Hankow office was equally satisfactory, because, as John H. Scott, another "Eastern Partner," reported to John Samuel Swire in 1885: "The work of this branch has never been so efficiently cared for as at present. All friction with Natives disappeared."[69]

Western firms often competed among themselves to obtain Chinese business in shipping freight. For this purpose, after 1860 Jardine's made

64. Kwang-Ching Liu, *Steamship Rivalry*, p. 25.

65. Ibid., p. 26; and Robert B. Forbes, *Personal Reminiscences* (Boston, 1882), pp. 364–66.

66. F. B. Forbes to Edward Cunningham, Apr. 10, 1870, FBF. See also Kwang-Ching Liu, *Steamship Rivalry*, p. 90; *Shen pao*, Apr. 10, 1874, p. 3; and Hsu Jun, *Nien-p'u*, p. 24.

67. (Shanghai) to John Heard III, Feb. 28, 1858, HL-13, HC.

68. Whittall (Shanghai) to Joseph Jardine (Hong Kong), Dec. 20, 1859, JMA.

69. (Shanghai) to Swire (London), Mar. 11, 1885, SP. For Endicott, see Yen-p'ing Hao, *Comprador*, pp. 31–34.

advances to Chinese merchants of tea, silk, and opium. Meanwhile, William Keswick reported from Shanghai in 1865 that "Heard & Co. are doing the utmost to encourage business of this nature on Native a/c [account]. Their object is of course to secure freight for their steamer, and business for their [opium] receiving vessels."[70] Another example was Tucksing, an influential businessman on the coast who had close connections with the principal shippers. He was an old friend of Jardine's but Heard's endeavored to lure him away in 1866. William Keswick wrote angrily to James Whittall on February 4, 1866: "Heard tried very hard to get Tucksing to promise to become connected with the Coast Steamer scheme."[71]

Chongfat was a prominent freight broker in Canton in the mid-nineteenth century, and Russell's did their utmost to solicit his support of their Shanghai Steam Navigation Company.[72] Russell's effort was successful, and Chongfat frequently made shipments on the coast via Russell's steamers after 1868. Meanwhile, Jardine's also discovered that Chongfat "was the most influential shipper" in that port.[73] Consequently, the house wanted his business very much. The competition between Russell's and Jardine's for Chongfat's freight ended up amicably; Chongfat subsequently did business with both houses.

But more often than not, this competition for Chinese friendship resulted in unpleasant friction among Western merchants. Achea, another freight broker at Canton, was of particular help to the Shanghai Steam Navigation Company of Russell's in the sixties. He was, however, tempted by Olyphant & Co.'s promise to give him a better deal in 1868. Enraged by Olyphant's obviously empty promises, John M. Forbes of Russell's wrote from Canton on May 27:

Olyphant's have been trying to get hold of one of our freight brokers (Achea) and I sent him there to find out what they wanted. They told him, as a great secret!, that they had bought four steamers and had a large capital subscribed, that they would give him a much better chance than we could, etc., etc. I told Achea that he must decide which company should have his freight for himself, but that my advice to him was to wait a short time until the four steamers came, before deciding anything.[74]

70. To James Whittall (Hong Kong), Dec. 18, 1865, JMA.
71. Ibid.
72. John M. Forbes of Russell's wrote from Canton: "At present I am trying to get Chongfat to give the S. [Shanghai] S. N. Co. the support of his patronage" (to Edward Cunningham [Shanghai], May 27, 1868, Case 26, RA).
73. F. B. Johnson wrote from Shanghai in 1870: "Captain Russell tells me that when he ran the *Corea*, a broker named Chongfat at Canton was the most influential shipper" (to William Keswick [Hong Kong], Apr. 11, 1870, JMA).
74. Forbes to Edward Cunningham (Shanghai), Case 26, RA.

Achea's final decision concerning his freight is not known, but it is never-theless clear that competition among Western houses to improve their Chinese connections was keen.

Drumming up freight business took time, money, and imagination on the part of the Western firms, because they had to please Chinese freight brokers on a competitive basis. No sooner had Jardine's and Russell's started the practice of "entertaining Chinese brokers every [Chinese] New Year at dinner" in 1869[75] than Butterfield & Swire followed suit. Butterfield's took the matter most seriously, for the firm gave a big din-ner at which the foreign clerks assisted. Another way to woo the Chinese shippers was to make liberal rebates, or "returns," to them for their freight. Russell's, Jardine's, and Butterfield & Swire competed in earnest with one another in offering this extra attraction. Frank B. Forbes wrote in July 1873 that on the Shanghai-Tientsin line Russell & Co. had "for some time past been obliged to make returns" to every shipper.[76] But-terfield & Swire had a more flexible program, as Cheng Kuan-ying, the firm's comprador (1873–1881), later recalled: "We either gave them an extra commission of 5 percent, or gave them allowance for expenses such as [office] rent, or permitted them to recommend men to serve as steam-er compradors—the best posts going to men recommended by those who brought the largest amount of freight."[77] The Shanghai Steam Naviga-tion Company further wooed Chinese shippers by allowing them free storage in the company's warehouses for fifteen days in late 1873, and the Butterfield's China Navigation Company matched the offer immediately.[78]

Commercial competition among the Western merchants was by no means limited to the shipping trade. In view of the "great development of trade in the East," Jardine's began in 1870 to give more attention to an art long-practiced by its Amercian rivals—the cultivation of Chinese friendship. To improve the Chinese business in general, Jardine's allotted some of their shares to the Chinese who most likely could achieve that goal, such as Tong King-sing and Tucksing. F. B. Johnson reported to William Keswick in 1870: "I have alloted to Tucksing the half-share you apportioned to Tong King-sing with the concurrence of the latter & I

75. *NCH*, Oct. 7, 1875, p. 358.
76. Forbes (Shanghai) to W. S. Fitz (Hankow), July 8, 1873, FBF. Earlier Forbes wrote: "Butterfield's have given a big *chin-chin* [goodwill] dinner to all the freight brokers, at which the foreign clerks assisted" (ibid., Apr. 10, 1873).
77. Cheng Kuan-ying, *Sheng-shih wei-yen* (1893) 5:34 (Kwang-Ching Liu's transla-tion). See also Kwang-Ching Liu, *Steamship Rivalry*, p. 131.
78. *Shen pao*, TC 12/10/1, p. 7, and TC 12/10/2, p. 5.

hope the allotment will lead to an increase of Native business."[79] Again in announcing the issue of 100 new shares of its Canton Insurance Office, the firm decided to reserve two-thirds of the profits, instead of one-third, for distribution among contributing shareholders. This arrangement immediately attracted the investments of seven "reputable Chinese" in Shanghai in March 1874.[80] The major Western commercial houses in China, such as Jardine's, Butterfield's, Russell's, Heard's, and Olyphant's, all competed vigorously in the improvement of their Chinese connections in general and the recruitment of efficient brokers and compradors in particular, throughout the late Ch'ing period.[81]

JOINT-ACCOUNT TRADE

It was common practice for the Western houses in China to engage in trade with either their constituents at home or Chinese friends in the treaty ports on a joint-account basis during the nineteenth century. When Robert B. Forbes was in Canton in the 1830s, he had joint commercial ventures with friends in New England, such as Dan Bacon, T. H. Perkins, Samuel Cabot, and T. J. Cary.[82] This method of trading became more popular after the sixties. Until the early sixties, the bulk of the business of most foreign agency houses in China was the commission business of the merchandise trade—the sale of Western-manufactured goods and the export of tea and silk from China. Acting mainly as agents on orders from constituents and supplying services at the risk of capital located in London or New York, the agency houses handled large quantities of imports and exports. This type of business involved minimum risk, but it also produced meager profits.

This traditional way of doing business underwent revolutionary changes in the sixties because of the opening of the Suez Canal and the introduction of steamship and telegraphic lines to China. The growth of business in a new direction saw the concomitant decline of the traditional commission agency business. Edward Cunningham of Russell & Co. wrote in 1861: "I think we are sliding into a great change.... I see all our business gone and I look around to find who has it. Not Heard's or any house on commission. It is being done by parties on their own account.... The business has become too complicated to be done by agents."[83]

79. Johnson (Shanghai) to Keswick (Hong Kong), Mar. 12, 1870, JMA.
80. Ibid., Apr. 1, 1874.
81. Yen-p'ing Hao, *Comprador*, pp. 32–36.
82. Cases 1 and 2, RA.
83. To P. S. Forbes, June 4, 1861, FC.

Marketeering and investment activities gradually took the place of pure commission business for the agency houses.

Even though direct investment was the new way of doing business, it was financially impossible for many middle-sized houses to do so entirely on their own. They could risk only enough capital for two or three cargoes a year. Gradually, they found that a compromise arrangement with the merchants at home to share the investment and risk opened possibilities for greater profit. Besides reducing risk, joint-account shipping employed temporarily idle capital, financed larger operations than the house could afford by itself, and attracted new constituents in China and at home. Its main purpose, however, was to minimize commercial risk. Those who did business "on their account" necessarily had to take risks and felt the need to reduce the risk of heavy investment and at the same time to control it. For this purpose, foreign merchants in China made various arrangements for risk sharing in trade, and an important one was joint-account shipping. Under this arrangement, capital was contributed by two or more parties, and the profit or loss was determined by the ratio of investment; this kind of arrangement was widely used in foreign and domestic trade, especially after the sixties.

FOREIGN TRADE

Augustine Heard & Co. witnessed the change in business patterns after the fifties and tried to increase profits by experimenting with two variables. The first was the marketing of its ancillary services to the trade as a whole, and the second was the adoption of joint-account shipping. Joint-account shipping did not become a major concern for Heard's until the late 1850s when the newly organized smaller agency houses started to use it to attract constituents. One example was the newly reconstructed firm of Olyphant & Co. whose meteoric rise, due to the increase in joint-account shipping, alarmed Heard's. Albert Heard observed: "We stand to be #3 this year if Olyphant and Co. go on cutting their big swash. Our orders are for low limits and it will be a hard scratch to pick up a lac [$100,000]."[84] Heard's balance sheet of 1859 shows that it had sixty-seven running accounts with European, American, and Chinese constituents.[85] By 1861, Albert Heard was even more convinced that house investment would be more important than

84. To John Heard III, July 10, 1858, EM-7, HC.
85. EA-1, HC.

commission business: "I am becoming more and more convinced that
we must change somewhat our style of business. . . . Comm. [Commis-
sion] pur. [purchases] . . . are a myth. How have Olyphant & Co. and
others wheedled away the floating constituency which we had?"[86] The
joint-account system was regularly used by the firm after the sixties.[87] In
the early sixties, Heard's made a proposal to an official on Taiwan for
joint-account monopolies of exporting camphor from the island.[88]

Augustine Heard & Co., however, was by no means the leading company to adopt the joint-account trade. In fact, this system was more
widespread among the British houses. Edward Cunningham of Russell's
remarked in 1861: "I think we are sliding into a great change. The
American business is following or had followed the English and like that
can no longer be done on commission."[89] Jardine's adopted this practice
as early as July 1849. Around 1850, it exported tea from China to Europe
regularly on joint-account with "a reputable Shanghai Hong," the Manfoong Hong. This Chinese firm, as we have seen in chapter 3, was operated by Takee and some of his friends in the opium trade.[90] This
arrangement was made by A. G. Dallas of Jardine's through Ahee, the
firm's chief teaman at Shanghai.[91] Dallas left Shanghai in 1852, but the
joint-account shipping of tea with Chinese continued. James Whittall
and Edward Whittall cooperated closely with a group of Chinese merchants led by Ekee in the fifties and sixties.[92] Besides tea, silk was also
frequently exported on joint-account: Jardine's and Takee cooperated in
shipping silk to Europe on a large scale in the summer of 1852.[93] Furthermore, the firm vigorously sought joint-investment opportunities
with the Chinese merchant community in the sixties and seventies.[94]

These joint-account ventures in trade were also carried out between
China and Japan, especially between the ports of Shanghai, Nagasaki,

86. To Augustine Heard, Jr., Oct. 22, 1861, HL-36, HC.
87. For detailed joint-account records of Augustine Heard & Co., see EA-1, EA-2,
EJ-1, and EJ-2, HC.
88. EA-1, HC.
89. To P. S. Forbes, June 4, 1861, FC.
90. For Jardine's joint-account trade with the Manfoong Hong, see LeFevour, p. 148.
However, this practice did not start in 1851; it can be traced back as early as July 1849
(A. G. Dallas [Shanghai] to Donald Matheson [Hong Kong], July 5, 1849, JMA).
91. From 1855 on Ahee was Jardine's teaman at Foochow, purchasing tea from the
Bohea districts (George V. W. Fisher [Foochow] to Joseph Jardine [Hong Kong], Nov. 5,
1855, JMA).
92. Edward Whittall (Shanghai) to William Keswick (Hong Kong), Oct. 6, 1865,
JMA.
93. A. G. Dallas (Shanghai) to Jardine, Matheson & Co. (Hong Kong), July 21,
1852, JMA.
94. LeFevour, p. 57.

Yokohama, and Kanagawa. Jardine, Matheson & Co. was engaged in this trade frequently after the late fifties. James Whittall, for example, reported in May 1859 that 300 packages of Chinese merchandise, valued at Tls. 9,884, were shipped to Nagasaki via its steamer *Troas* on joint-account with Yakee.[95] The volume of this trade increased in the summer of 1860, and many shipments were made. Takee and Yakee were among the Chinese who actively participated in these adventures.[96] This type of joint-account trade became so numerous and intricate by October 1863 that William Keswick, on the request of the head office in Hong Kong, was unable to produce the accounts readily.[97] In like manner, Augustine Heard & Co. had joint accounts with Chinese and American merchants in the trade between Shanghai, Nagasaki, and Yokohama in the sixties and seventies.[98] Impressed by the profitable prospects of exporting tea from Japan, Heard's sent an envoy to the daimyo of Satsuma in Japan in the early sixties to seek joint-account shipment of tea with him from his domain.[99]

DOMESTIC TRADE

Overseas joint-account commercial ventures were sometimes extended to upcountry purchases of tea and silk. Jardine's, for example, purchased and exported silk jointly with Takee in 1852.[100] In the same vein, the tea that Jardine's and Ekee shipped to Europe on joint-account in 1865 was bought from the interior.[101] In 1859 when the overseas joint-account trade of Augustine Heard & Co. was prosperous, the house had about sixty instances of joint interest in local shipments, mainly with Cantonese merchants.[102]

95. "In compliance with the request contained in your letter of 22nd ultimo, I beg to hand you enclosed the following Invoice: No. 1. 300 pkgs [packages] Chinese merchandize, shipped per 'Troas' to Nagasaki, on joint account with Yakee costing Tls. 9884, the half of which Tls. 4942 I have paid him and place to your debit" (Whittall [Shanghai] to Jardine, Matheson & Co. [Hong Kong], May 11, 1859, JMA).
96. Ibid., July 30, 1860.
97. Under the heading of "Yeakee [Yakee] & Takee's Nagasaki accounts," Keswick wrote: "I have been examining into this matter very carefully but find the account so intricate & in such confusion that I cannot prepare a Statement of it for this opportunity, but will let you have it at an early date" ([Shanghai] to Jardine, Matheson & Co. [Hong Kong], Oct. 24, 1863, JMA).
98. EJ-2, HC.
99. EJ-1, HC.
100. A. G. Dallas (Shanghai) to Jardine, Matheson & Co. (Hong Kong), July 21, 1852, JMA.
101. Edward Whittall (Shanghai) to William Keswick (Hong Kong), Oct. 6, 1865, JMA.
102. FG-1, HC.

The upcountry joint-account system was also involved in commodity speculations between Chinese and foreign merchants. They bought tea and silk from the interior and sold them in the treaty ports for profit.[103] A. G. Dallas of Jardine's at Shanghai arranged with the Manfoong Hong to purchase tea and silk from the interior on joint-account in the late 1840s. When these commodities were shipped to Shanghai, they were insured with Jardine's.[104] This method of purchasing tea was extended to a grand scale in the sixties. Aleet, a tea merchant, strongly suggested in 1867 that a packhouse be built "without delay" in the tea district on joint-account with Jardine's in order to expedite purchasing.[105] Aleet's suggestion was subsequently approved.

At the same time, Jardine's cooperated with another Chinese merchant, Yowloong, in the upcountry purchase of tea. With the consent of Jardine's, Yowloong set up four tea hongs in the tea districts in 1868 and bought large amounts of tea on joint-account. Jardine's, however, did not think that the tea trade would be profitable the next year and wanted to reduce its share in this venture. As Yowloong was deeply committed to the upcountry purchasing scheme in terms of personnel and physical plants, F. B. Johnson felt strongly that Jardine's should not suddenly leave him without financial support. The firm therefore committed the respectable sum of Tls. 100,000 and a loan of Tls. 60,000 to Yowloong (at an annual interest of 12 percent).[106]

With the introduction of steamships to China's waters after the mid-century, the joint-account trade for overseas ventures was extended to coastal shipping. Under the initiative of Edward Cunningham, who was both willing and able to cultivate Chinese friendship, Russell & Co. engaged in this trade from as early as 1861.[107] In the summer of that year,

103. BPP, *Commercial Reports of Her Majesty's Consuls in China*, China, No. 1 (1875), Chinkiang, p. 205.
104. Dallas to Donald Matheson (Hong Kong), July 5, 1849, JMA.
105. "Aleet has represented that it would be necessary to engage a packhouse in the Tan Kai district without delay should we require to make one or two chops during the ensuing season. I have authorized him to engage a building on our joint account, & as he proposes to proceed to the South shortly you will be able to talk with him on the subject" (F. B. Johnson [Shanghai] to William Keswick [Hong Kong], Dec. 27, 1867, JMA).
106. Johnson reported to Keswick: "Yowloong arrived by the [steamer] 'El King' & informed me that you had arranged to let him have a lakk [100,000] of taels on our own account but acting upon the basis settled with you when here, that we should do as little as possible in the Country. I have allowed him Tls. 60,000 on House a/c, & agreed to advance Tls. 60,000 on his own at 12% interest. He assures me that on the strength of an implied understanding he last year engaged four hongs in the Tea districts, & as I believe this is really the case I think we cannot suddenly leave him without support" (ibid., Mar. 29, 1869).
107. Cunningham (Shanghai) to F. G. Dexter, June 1, 1861, DP.

Cunningham invested Tls. 5,000 for F. G. Dexter of Boston in the pea trade between Newchwang and Foochow on a joint account with a Chinese merchant.[108] But Jardine, Matheson & Co. adopted the joint-account trade more frequently and on a grander scale. One such shipment with some Chinese in 1861 involved the large sum of 100,000 taels.[109] Among the coastal Chinese, Jardine's cooperated frequently with Tucksing, an aggressive merchant from Swatow. After the sixties, they shipped "north produce of peas, beancake, and oil" from Newchwang to the central and southern ports, especially Foochow and Canton. At the same time, they shipped "southern goods," such as sugar and nankeen, to the northern ports of Newchwang and Tientsin.[110] The trade thrived throughout the sixties and seventies, with profit ranging from 15 to 20 percent each shipment.[111]

Under the supervision of F. B. Johnson, Jardine's Shanghai office arranged to ship rice from Chinkiang to Canton "on joint account with the Chinese friends of Tong King-sing" in August 1871. Because of the current tight market, William Keswick at first doubted "somewhat the prudence of the arrangement." However, he finally approved: "We shall see. I hope you have secured sailing vessels."[112] A large shipment was again made several months later. In this shipment, only 4,000 piculs were on the house account; 10,000 piculs were on joint-account with "native friends."[113] This proved to be a successful venture.

The joint-account ventures also included "purely native institutions, such as pawnshops and theatres."[114] Jardine's and some Chinese merchants planned to establish jointly a pawnshop at Shanghai in 1866. Realizing that there were few well-established pawnshops in that port and that a pawnshop business would yield an annual profit of 40 percent, Tong King-sing proposed to William Keswick that they would

108. Cunningham wrote to Dexter: "One of our Chinamen is shipping a cargo of peas [from Newchwang] to Foochow and for a little I thought of investing 5,000 taels for you" (ibid.). Dexter consented to this suggestion.
109. Part of the cargo was stolen by either the Ch'ing or the Taiping soldiers (ibid., June 1, 1861).
110. William Keswick (Shanghai) to James Whittall (Hong Kong), Jan. 6, 1866, JMA.
111. F. B. Johnson wrote of this trade from Shanghai in 1867: "I have arranged to take an interest with Tucksing in a venture with Nankeen to Newchwang to the extent of Tls. 20,000. He says he does command the market which shows 15% or 20% profit" (to James Whittall [Hong Kong], May 6, 1867, JMA).
112. (Hong Kong) to Johnson (Shanghai), Aug. 29, 1871, JMA.
113. Johnson (Shanghai) to Jardine, Matheson & Co. (Hong Kong), Oct. 4, 1871, JMA.
114. BPP, *Commercial Reports of Her Majesty's Consuls in China*, China, No. 1 (1875), Chinkiang, p. 205.

jointly operate one with Jardine's, Accum, and Tong himself as partners. Although Jardine's finally declined to join, Accum and Tong were
still able to get a loan for Tls. 100,000 from the firm for this purpose.
These two Chinese merchants established the Ken Yue pawnshop in 1866
and repaid the loan by the spring of 1870.[115]

DIVERSIFIED INVESTMENTS

Besides joint-account trading, another way to enhance the chances of
profit making was through diversified investments. In the words of John
H. Scott, a "Eastern Partner" of Butterfield & Swire, "It is not desirable
to have all our eggs in one basket."[116] Coastal merchants, Chinese and
Western alike, were as a rule engaged in a great variety of enterprises,
usually at the same time.

CHINESE MERCHANTS

Tong King-sing, a noted coastal merchant, invested in various enterprises in the later half of the nineteenth century. Among the traditional
modes of investment, he was at first interested in the pawnshop. During
the late fifties, he was the owner of two pawnshops in Hong Kong for
four years, with an annual profit of 25 to 40 percent. As we have just
seen, in 1866 Tong and his friends borrowed Tls. 100,000 from Jardine's
to operate a pawnshop in Shanghai, believed to be capable of yielding an
annual profit of 40 percent. This pawnshop was later moved from Shanghai to Yangchow. After the early sixties he was a merchant in Shanghai
selling export commodities of tea, silk, and cotton.[117] Among these, tea
seems to have been the most important. In the late sixties Tong was a
partner in a large tea firm operated by Acum and Aleet, which sold tea
to Jardine's as well as to other Western firms in Shanghai.[118] In 1869
Tong borrowed Tls. 20,000 from Jardine's and became a Chinese
government-licensed salt merchant, shipping salt from Yangchow to
Hankow in pursuit of 60 percent annual returns. He engaged in this
business for at least three years.[119] Meanwhile, Tong, together with
Accum and Aleet, invested in three native banks in the late sixties and

---

115. Liu Kuang-ching, "T'ang T'ing-shu," pp. 156–58.
116. (Shanghai) to John Samuel Swire (London), Nov. 18, 1884, SP.
117. Liu Kuang-ching, "T'ang T'ing-shu," pp. 156–58; and Hsu Jun, *Nien-p'u*, p. 12.
118. Liu Kuang-ching, "T'ang T'ing-shu," p. 147.
119. Ibid., pp. 160–61.

early seventies, financing the purchase of tea from inland to Shanghai.[120] With time, however, Tong became more interested in modern enterprises. In 1868 Tong and his friends purchased a piece of land near Chinkiang with the notion of working its graphite deposits, but operation was not permitted by the Ch'ing government. From about this time, a great part of Tong's energies were devoted increasingly to steamship investments. He was a shareholder and a member of the board of directors in two British steamship companies, the Union and the North-China. In 1870 he invested in a ship that Jardine's managed, and in the next two or three years he also invested in a tramp steamer that plied the Yangtze, and another ship managed by Augustine Heard & Co. When Jardine's consolidated its shipping interests into the China Coast Steam Navigation Co. in 1872, Tong was elected a director.[121] To a lesser extent, Tong also invested in mining and newspaper enterprises.[122]

In like manner, Tucksing maintained highly diversified commercial operations. First of all, he was a prominent opium merchant. Having engaged in this trade in his home province of Kwangtung, he expanded it to Shanghai when he went there in the fifties. As noted in chapter 3, it was common practice in that time for Chinese merchants in Shanghai to buy opium from the foreign receiving vessels anchored in Woosung, the outer port of Shanghai, and bring it to Soochow for sale. They then used the proceeds to purchase local silk and sold it in Shanghai. This was called the "Soochow system" in which Tucksing, like Takee, participated actively during the late fifties.[123] During the next decade, Tucksing purchased opium from Jardine's on a large scale. In one case, on April 12, 1869, he bought 100 chests of Malwa opium from the firm.[124] Given the market price of about Tls. 580 per chest at the time,[125] the transaction involved a large sum of money—about Tls. 58,000.

With time, Tucksing became a shrewd opium merchant, buying from various foreign traders and easily determining the quality of the commodity.[126] While maintaining contacts with Jardine's, Tucksing be-

120. Ibid., pp. 148–51.

121. Ibid., pp. 162–69; and Kwang-Ching Liu, Steamship Rivalry, pp. 141–43.

122. Ellsworth C. Carlson, The Kaiping Mines, chap. 2; and Ko Kung-chen, Chung-kuo pao-hsueh shih (Shanghai, 1927), chap. 4.

123. James Whittall, e.g., wrote: "Tucksing informed me there will be more [opium] doing in Foochow" ([Shanghai] to Jardine, Matheson & Co. [Hong Kong], Sept. 3, 1859, JMA).

124. F. B. Johnson (Shanghai) to William Keswick (Hong Kong), Apr. 13, 1869, JMA.

125. Ibid., Mar. 29, 1869.

126. "Tucksing's man was with me today for 30 chests [of opium] but after examining 12 chests . . . would select none except at a reduction" (James Whittall [Shanghai] to Jardine, Matheson & Co. [Hong Kong], Sept. 3, 1861, JMA).

came more closely connected with Sassoon & Co. at Shanghai, a leading British opium firm in China. Through Tucksing, Jardine's and Sassoon's tried to manipulate the opium market by fixing the price at Tls. 540 per chest.[127] With the extension of foreign merchants' activities toward the northern ports after the treaties of Tientsin in 1858, Tucksing's opium trade was also expanded northward along the coast. Starting from the summer of 1861, he began to purchase opium from Jardine's Tientsin office. On June 10, he bought ten chests at Tls. 595 per picul, and another six chests at Tls. 575 per picul.[128] He thus was active on the market in northern China until his retirement two decades later. Tucksing was so deeply immersed in the opium trade in the north that he became the principal customer of Jardine's Tientsin office.[129] On a smaller scale and less frequently, Tucksing also bought opium from other foreign houses, including the American firm of Augustine Heard & Co.[130]

Tucksing moved one step northward by selling opium on the coast of Manchuria. After the port of Newchwang was actually opened to foreign trade in 1864, Tucksing proceeded to that port to assess the local situation. Convinced that opium would have a receptive market, he immediately purchased opium from Shanghai and shipped it to Newchwang. From that time on, he bought most of his opium from Jardine's Shanghai office, where F. B. Johnson was pleased with the ample supply of opium from Hong Kong. Johnson wrote Keswick on January 31, 1868: "Tucksing anticipated a considerable report from Newchwang. I will realize our various invoices as advantageous opportunities offer after the goods come to hand, & I am well pleased to notice the liberal supplies we are to receive on consignment."[131]

Tucksing traded in other commodities along the coast as well. He was

127. F. B. Johnson reported from Shanghai: "Through Tuck Sing I have come to an understanding today with both the firms of Sassoon not to sell at present under Tls. 540 [per chest], & I have reason to believe that any reaction here will be followed by considerable business at the [Whangpu] River stations [at Woosung] & also at the North" (to William Keswick [Hong Kong], Apr. 3, 1869, JMA). We do not know how successful this effort was.

128. Dan Patridge (Tientsin) to James Whittall (Swatow), June 10, 1861, JMA.

129. Jardine's agent at Tientsin reported in 1865: "Malwa [opium] is very firm now. I have waited for an opportunity to place 10 chests at Tls. 540 per picul. I am now asking higher [price] with hopes of obtaining an advance, should no steamer arrive with surplus for the natives especially Tucksing who is out of stock and is in the market for purchase. The above sale was made to him and is the only one at that price" (Dan Patridge to Jardine, Matheson & Co. [Swatow], July 8, 1865, JMA).

130. G. B. Dixwell (Shanghai) to A. F. Heard (Hong Kong), Nov. 29, 1865, HM-30, HC.

131. To Keswick (Hong Kong), JMA.

intimately involved in the important, time-honored trade of bean and bean products between Manchuria and the southeast coast. In the spring of 1861 he went to Newchwang, and in June and July he made several shipments of bean and bean products through native junks from that port to Shanghai and Canton, pocketing handsome profits.[132] In July 1862 he made another two shipments of bean and barley, valued at Tls. 5,811, from Chefoo to Shanghai where he sold it to a local merchant. In early August he again proceeded to Newchwang where he bought more than Tls. 5,000 of bean products to be shipped directly to Canton.[133] Meanwhile, he was engaged in the coastal trade of nankeen, investing in September 1868 at least Tls. 15,000 in this trade.[134] To sum up, Tucksing, in order to enhance the chances of making profit, traded diversely, engaging in opium business at Canton, Hong Kong, Swatow, Shanghai, Tientsin, and Manchuria and also trading in other commodities, such as bean, bean products, barley, and nankeen.

Cheng Kuan-ying, a noted merchant in Shanghai and Canton, went to Shanghai to trade in 1859 when he was seventeen years old. In the next decade or so he acted as a retail merchant of tea, foreign piece goods, and other miscellaneous goods in Shanghai and ended up as a wholesale merchant in Shanghai, Newchwang, and Swatow. Because of his nine-year experience as a freight broker for the British firm of Dent, Beale & Co. in Shanghai, he was knowledgeable about the steamship business. He consequently set up his own freight brokerage firms in Shanghai, Foochow, and Hankow and a transshipping company in Shanghai.[135] Meanwhile, he was a shareholder of the Union Navigation Co., which was organized by the British firm of Glover & Co. in 1867.[136]

Cheng Kuan-ying made other investments in the seventies, such as newspapers, bookstores, paper-manufacturing plants, maritime and fire insurance companies, seafood-gathering firms, salt businesses at Yangchow, and various mining enterprises in Kaiping, Shantung, and Anhwei. In the meantime, he strengthened his investments in shipping by purchasing shares in the China Merchant's S. N. Co. In the eighties he put some of his capital in dairy farming, land reclamation, telegraph companies, and precious metal mines in Jehol, but his major investment

132. James Whittall (Shanghai) to Jardine, Matheson & Co. (Hong Kong), July 30, 1861, JMA.
133. Ibid., Aug. 2, 1862.
134. F. B. Johnson (Shanghai) to Jardine, Matheson & Co., Sept. 11, 1868, JMA.
135. Cheng Kuan-ying, *Sheng-shih wei-yen hou-pien* (Shanghai, 1920), 8:31–32, 42–43.
136. *NCH*, Dec. 22, 1868, pp. 623, 625–26. See also Wang Ching-yü, "Fu-ku," pp. 42–43.

seems to have been the Shanghai Cotton Cloth Mill. After 1879 he was the head of the business affairs department of the enterprise and was able to solicit Tls. 352,800 of the initial paid-up capital of Tls. 500,000. From the nineties on, he established a freight brokerage firm in Canton and became increasingly interested in the new investments he made in the railroads.[137] In 1906, after the Canton-Hankow Railroad had become a private joint-stock enterprise, Cheng was one of its biggest shareholders.[138]

The investment pattern of these coastal merchants was thus unmistakably diverse, but a complete record of their investments is not available. Thanks to the autobiography of Hsu Jun, we know more about his investments. In the late nineteenth and early twentieth centuries, Hsu invested in many diverse enterprises in the interior and in the treaty ports. He was at first engaged in the import-export business in the fifties and sixties, dealing in tea, silk, cotton, cereal, and piece goods at Shanghai and in the tea and silk districts. At the same time, he became a partner in such time-honored enterprises as pawnshops and native banks. With time, however, he was increasingly attracted by modern undertakings, investing large amounts of money in steamship, insurance firms, and wharf companies in the seventies, and in modern-style coal and silver mining companies during the eighties. In the last decades of the century, he also purchased shares in numerous manufacturing enterprises, such as cotton textile plants, sugar refineries, and glass and paper companies. Meanwhile, he continued to make investments in traditional enterprises, particularly in land reclamation in Chihli and real estate in Shanghai and Tientsin. In the forty-eight years from 1859 to 1907, Hsu invested in at least fifty-five business undertakings—traditional and modern, commercial and industrial.[139] This testifies eloquently to the extent to which Hsu diversified his investments.

The tendency of the Chinese merchants to diversify their investments is also demonstrated by the fact that foreign shares of small denomination were more attractive to them than more expensive stocks. The Shanghai Steam Navigation Co. decided in February 1868 to change the denomination of the company's stock from Tls. 1,000 to Tls. 100 in order to solicit more Chinese interest in its shares. Its directors explained:

137. Cheng Kuan-ying, Hou-pien, 8:42–43; 9:1; 10:118–119; 11:16–17, 25b. For the Shanghai Cotton Cloth Mill, see Yen Chung-p'ing, Chung-kuo mien-fang-chih shih-kao (Peking, 1955), p. 103.
138. Hua-tzu jih-pao, May 6, 1906.
139. Hsu Jun, Nien-p'u, passim.

"Many parties interested in the traffic on the [Yangtze] river, particularly Chinese, are unwilling . . . to invest so large a sum as Tls. 1,000 in a
share. . . . This [new arrangement] will place the stock within reach of all
parties and in the opinion of the Directors will bring to the Company a
great increase of contributing shareholders."[140] This policy proved to be
successful. Admittedly, many Chinese investors were not rich and thus
preferred to buy stock in smaller denominations, but their preference for
diversified investments also figured prominently in the situation.

WESTERN TRADERS

Perkins & Co., an important American mercantile house in China
during the early nineteenth century, not only handled its own trade and
many other ventures in which it had shares, but it also received consignments from others on commission. This firm mostly traded ships and the
use of ships, dealt in insurance and storage, and performed the functions
of a bank, trading in specie, credit, and bills of exchange. John P.
Cushing, Perkins's partner in residence at Canton, followed this tradition of commercial diversification after his return to Boston in 1828, for
example, his joint ventures with Perkins and Bryant, Sturgis & Co. in
the China trade.[141] (In 1829 they sent three ships to Canton, in which he
took a quarter-share.)

In fact, the China traders of New England almost never risked all
their wealth in one bottom, nor did they risk owning all the goods in one
ship. Instead, they minimized their risk by taking shares in many ventures. Cushing's record of investment in the China trade on January 1,
1832, is a case in point. On that day, he had a one-third share in the
voyage of one ship; a one-fourth share in five other ships; and interests of
various degrees in another six vessels with tea, silk, and tortoiseshell on
board.[142] Even though Cushing shifted a considerable part of his capital
from China trade to the American domestic market after the mid-
thirties, he continued to invest diversely. From 1835 to 1851, for instance,
he invested simultaneously in personal loans, real estate, government
and railroad bonds, and stocks in insurance, bank, manufacturing, and
railroad companies, totaling from U.S. $785,158 in 1835 to $1,574,930 in

140. Shanghai S. N. Co., "Report," Feb. 21, 1868, cited in Kwang-Ching Liu,
Steamship Rivalry, p. 91.
141. Henrietta M. Larson, "A China Trader Turns Investor," *Harvard Business Review*
12:348–51 (1933–1934).
142. Ibid.

1851.[143] Furthermore, within each of these fields "there was considerable distribution" among firms.[144]

The American China trade witnessed a considerable change by the end of the nineteenth century. Young firms gradually replaced the one-time famous houses, such as Russell & Co., but none of them was large. Because most of the houses that appeared after the American Civil War were not well-supplied with capital, they preferred to do business in China in an even more diverse way than their giant predecessors.[145] The uncertainty of the political and economic scene in China after the fifties further encouraged foreign houses to diversify. Because no one source of income in the trade was reliable enough to risk specialization, foreign firms were not only concerned with the normal commission business of buying and selling, but also acted as banks, handled exchange operations, served as agents of shipping and insurance ventures, acted in legal matters, and directly engaged in a number of investments.

The establishment of auxiliary commercial facilities on an independent basis exemplifies the trend toward diversification. Two cases in point are the modern banks and steamship firms that stemmed from what had originally been sidelines or parts of a complete agency business. In 1864 many Western merchants invested in the Hongkong and Shanghai Banking Corp., which was the leading financial institution on China's coast for more than half a century. Although a single commercial house might gradually lose control of a rapidly developed bank, it was still able to retain loose control of a steamship enterprise, for example. After having promoted the Shanghai Steam Navigation Co., a joint-stock firm in 1862, Russell & Co. acted as the new firm's "permanent agents and treasurers." Russell's also furnished all the managerial personnel and the offices for the steamship company. By the same token, Butterfield & Swire established the China Navigation Co. in 1872, and Jardine's founded the China Coast Steam Navigation Co. the next year.[146]

The foreign merchants were active in investing in almost all fields related to trade. To carry on their main business, the external trade, they were eager to see that related fields were also being developed. This was particularly true of the well-established British trading firms, such as Jardine, Matheson & Co. (table 12). In addition to importing and

143. Ibid., p. 356, table 2.
144. Case Book, pp. 130–31, CP.
145. Dennett, *Americans*, pp. 579–80.
146. Kwang-Ching Liu, *Steamship Rivalry*, chaps. 2 and 4.

TABLE 12.   ACCOUNT OF JARDINE, MATHESON & CO., SHOWING
DIVERSE OPERATIONS, SHANGHAI, APRIL 30, 1875
(TAELS)

Debit Balances	Amount	Remarks
Cash	54,806	Balance of account
Hongkong & Shanghai Banking Corp.	79,103	Balance of account
Shares in C. [China] C. [Coast] S. N. Co.	258,766	As per memo
Woosung Road [Railroad] Co. a/c IV–1	1,386	Original incorporators a/c
Woosung Road [Railroad] Co. a/c IV–2	25,850	Includes Tls. 11,000 cost of land on Souchow Creek
Chinese Loan	186,013	Closed in May
Shanghai & Hongkew Wharf	9,600	Shares
Chow Wan Kee	2,220	Advance on 37 shares in C.C.S.N. Co.
Tong King Sing	25,000	Tls. 10,000 repayable Aug. 25, 1875
Him Shum Oan [Bank]	40,000	Advance guaranteed by Aleet
Aleet	20,000	Advance
Takee	602	Expenses of transfer of property
Hung Ching Kung	3,000	Advance on nankeens in Ewo godown
Cutcheong	47,564	Advance on opium
Kessowjee & Co.	106,154	Advance on opium
Wharves: Hunts, Heards, Pootung	94,201	Current advances
Silk advances	1,438	Current advances
D. Burjorjee	3,000	Advance on gray shirtings
A. J. Howe	9,958	50 shares in C.C.S.N. Co.
E. A. Fabris	3,906	Mortgage on "Alpha Farm" Property

Source: Shanghai Trial Balance Sheet, Memoranda, JMA.

exporting, this firm established the Canton Insurance Office in 1836 and the Hongkong Fire Insurance Co. in 1868. It also invested in such financing institutions as the Hongkong and Shanghai Banking Corporation in 1864 and the British and Chinese Corporation in 1898. External trade still dominated the firm's investment picture in the mid-seventies, but shipping trade investments received increasing attention. In fact, the firm reorganized the various steamers under its management into the China Steam Navigation Co. in 1873 and established the Indochina Steam Navigation Co. in 1882. Meanwhile, it established shipyards, wharves, and warehouse companies as auxiliary businesses to shipping. The firm increased its investment in industrial enterprises after the eighties, especially in such fields as silk reeling, packing, breweries, utilities, cold storage, engineering, sugar refineries, cotton textiles, and railroads. Taken together, these large-scale enterprises dwarfed the firm's real estate investments as well as its loans to the Chinese government.[147] Jardine's was not alone in diversifying its investments; this was also the case with Augustine Heard & Co., which after the sixties invested in steam navigation, insurance, and such industrial undertakings as an ice company, a rice cleaning mill, barges, pile drivers, and a floating dock.[148]

147. Jardine, Matheson & Co., *An Outline of the History of a China House for a Hundred Years, 1832–1932* (Hong Kong, 1934), pp. 1–87. For a detailed list of Jardine's major investments, see Yen-p'ing Hao, *Comprador*, p. 22.

148. For a full account of Heard's diverse investments, see Case 9, HC II.

CHAPTER NINE

Toward Maximum Profit

Lucrative as the legitimate means of trading were, the coastal merchants also tried hard to maximize profits through illegal maneuvers. Some foreign-owned factories were occasionally registered under the name of their Chinese friends, but it was usually the Chinese merchants who sought the haven of Western protection. The presence of foreign traders in China gave some Chinese merchants more opportunity to take advantage of them or to elude the Ch'ing officials' pressure. Consequently, the Chinese merchants not only bought capital shares in Western enterprises, but also illegally traded under foreign auspices. Most of these legal and illegal practices produced handsome profits in a short period of time.

FU-KU: CHINESE INVESTMENT IN FOREIGN ENTERPRISES

The activities of Chinese merchants in buying capital shares in foreign enterprises, called *fu-ku* in Chinese, were common in the treaty ports starting from the 1860s. The Chinese invested significant amounts in Western enterprises, especially in steamship lines, banks, insurance companies, and goods warehouses. To a lesser extent, this was also the case in silk filatures, electric light and power companies, and, after 1895, in the newly established cotton textile mills.

Fu-ku activities, began after the Treaty of Nanking in 1842, increased after the sixties when modern steamers were introduced to China's waters, and intensified with time. According to the China Association, composed mainly of British merchants, "shares in British joint stock companies" in China were "largely held by Chinese" at the end of the nineteenth century.[1] More British industrial companies were set up after the Treaty of Shimonoseki of 1895. The extent to which *fu-ku* activities existed in these enterprises can be seen in a memorandum of the London head office of the China Association on March 14, 1899:

> Every year our commercial relations with China became more important, and the interests of British and Chinese capitalists more involved. The Industrial Companies that have been founded recently at Shanghai under foreign management contain numerous Chinese shareholders. Chinese are also shareholders in the local fire and marine insurance companies, and in most of the local banks.[2]

The Chinese who subscribed to the shares in foreign enterprises included officials as well as merchants. The memorandum went on: "Chinese, both merchants and officials, have for years been shareholders in foreign companies, and have enjoyed all the advantages which such a position gave."[3]

THE SHIPPING TRADE

Thanks to the company records of Heard's and Jardine's, we know more about *fu-ku* activities in the shipping enterprises than in any other field. The American firm of Augustine Heard & Co. took advantage of Chinese capital in this way. In 1859 the firm raised $100,000 to acquire its first steamship, the *Fire Dart*, for the Shanghai-Hankow line. Two Chinese are known to have subscribed to the investment from the beginning: Apoon, the firm's comprador at Shanghai during the late fifties and early sixties, invested $5,000, and Kong Yoc Tong, who frequently traded with Heard's, purchased $10,000. Three years later, Chun Yuechong (Choping) joined the scheme by putting up another $5,000.[4] Chun was later the comprador to Russell & Co. in Shanghai from 1865 to 1874.[5]

By 1863 Chun Yuechong had also invested $69,000 in Heard's ship,

---

1. Shanghai Branch of the China Association to Sir C. MacDonald (Peking), Nov. 3, 1898, FO 405/84, p. 274.
2. Memorandum on the Need of a Code of Chinese Mercantile Law, China Association, London, FO 405/84, p. 273.
3. Ibid.
4. Augustine Heard & Co. (Hong Kong) to ibid. (Shanghai), Aug. 1, 1862, EQ-5, HC. Chun Yuechong was referred to as "Choping" after 1866 in Russell & Co. correspondence, RA.
5. Yen-p'ing Hao, *Comprador*, pp. 28–29.

the *Shantung*, which was 85 percent of its purchasing price. Yen Chong and Wyune Chong invested $10,000 each in the steamer *Kiang Loong*.[6] Twelve Chinese shareholders contributed Tls. 73,500 toward the purchase of the *Hai Loong*, and another eight Chinese invested $50,000 in the *Tom Hunt*. In 1863–1864, Heard's purchased two steamers from the United States, the *Kin Shan* and *Suwonada*, for the Canton–Hong Kong line. Seven Chinese invested in the *Kin Shan*, and ten in the *Suwonada*. The purchasing price for *Kin Shan* was $170,000, and Chinese capital constituted $45,000.[7] They likewise invested an unknown amount of money in the *Washington*.[8] Another Chinese merchant, Tai Hong Cheong, also invested an unknown amount of money in Heard's steamship projects.[9] Augustine Heard & Co. and Douglas Lapraik established the Hongkong, Canton and Macao Steamboat Co. in 1865, capitalized at $750,000. Its Chinese shareholders, led by Quok Acheong (Kuo Kanchang), Lee Sing, and Sin Tak Fan, played an important role through the nineteenth century.[10]

Chinese capital figured prominently when Russell & Co. in 1862 organized the Shanghai Steam Navigation Co., the first steamship company ever established in China and by far the largest one during the sixties and early seventies. It was organized by Edward Cunningham, the managing partner at Shanghai. Because the firm's own capital resources were never large and Warren Delano, Jr., the managing partner at Hong Kong who had control of the firm's funds, was conservative,[11] Cunningham had to organize subscriptions from individuals in Shanghai. (In the middle of March 1861, he succeeded in getting some "Chinese friends and constituents" to join him in the purchasing of the steamer *Surprise*, costing some $45,000.[12]) From August 1861 to March 1862 Cunningham raised the capital to 1,000,000 taels. Chinese were the largest owners of the concern, purchasing more than half of these shares.[13]

Encouraged by this initial success, Cunningham soon set up a $320,000 subscription plan. Finally, $17,000 was subscribed in Shanghai, about $75,000 in Hong Kong, and about $75,000 was reserved for

6. Augustine Heard & Co. (Hong Kong) to ibid. (Shanghai), Mar. 21, 1863, EL-1, HC.

7. *American Neptune*, Jan. 1957, pp. 45–50.

8. Memorandum, HL-19, p. 486, HC.

9. Jardine, Matheson & Co. (Shanghai) to ibid. (Hong Kong), July 13, 1880, JMA.

10. Wang Ching-yü, "Fu-ku," p. 42.

11. Delano was the grandfather of President Franklin Delano Roosevelt.

12. Kwang-Ching Liu, *Steamship Rivalry*, p. 18.

13. Ibid., pp. 29–30; and Wang Ching-yü, "Fu-ku," p. 40.

subscription by partners not in China. Much of the allocation for Shanghai was filled by the firm's "old Chinese friends" from the coastal region, including Ahkai, Ahyou, Ahyune (Hsu Jun), Chongfat, Chun Yuechong (Chan Yue-chang), Hupkee, Koofunsing, Lyongchong, and Wong-yong-yee.[14] Among them, Chun Yuechong, a businessman from Chekiang, was probably the wealthiest. He invested Tls. 130,000 in Russell's steamship scheme.[15] As we have just seen, he also invested in steamships operated by Augustine Heard & Co. His total investment in these houses reached Tls. 215,000 in 1863, an amazingly large amount of money in those days.[16] Koofunsing,[17] Russell's onetime comprador at Shanghai, came from Swatow.[18] He invested Tls. 150,000 in Russell's steamship company by 1862,[19] and his silk firm was one of the largest in Shanghai.[20] Hsu Jun later became the deputy manager of the China Merchants' S. N. Co.

As mentioned in chapter 7, in February 1868 the directors of the Shanghai S. N. Co. decided to change the denomination of the company's stock from Tls. 1,000 to Tls. 100 for the sake of promotion. They were right, for the company's capital increased to Tls. 1,875,000 that year, then to Tls. 2,250,000 in 1872.[21] Chinese capital investments further increased to Tls. 600,000 in 1874, and those of Koofunsing and Chun Yuechong constituted one-third of the amount. Hsu Jun remained a shareholder in 1876.[22]

The North-China Steamer Co. was organized in 1866 by the British firm of Trautmann & Co., operating between Shanghai and Tientsin. The paid-up capital was Tls. 194,000, of which one-third was subscribed to by Chinese merchants who were connected with the northern trade.[23] The Union Steam Navigation Co. was organized in Shanghai by the British firm of Glover & Co. the following year with a view to competing

---

14. Otto Asverus (Swatow) to Jardine, Matheson & Co. (Hong Kong), Nov. 3, 1874, JMA. See also Kwang-Ching Liu, *Steamship Rivalry*, p. 26.

15. A. F. Heard (Shanghai) to Augustine Heard, Jr., Apr. 18, 1862, HL-36, HC.

16. Yen-p'ing Hao, *Comprador*, p. 121.

17. Also known as Kiukee, Ku Feng-sheng, and Ku Ch'un-ch'ih.

18. Hsu Jun, *Nien-p'u*, p. 24.

19. A. F. Heard (Shanghai) to Augustine Heard, Jr., Apr. 18, 1862, HS-36, HC.

20. Ibid. The silk quotations of the "chop" of Koofunsing appeared frequently in *NCH* and the Chinese newspaper *Shen pao* (e.g., TC 11/7/9, p. 1, and TC 11/7/16, p. 7).

21. Wang Ching-yü, "Fu-ku," p. 45.

22. Hsu Jun was also known as Yu Kee or Yuchee. Others included Foo Chong, Koo Fung Kee, and Lee Ki (ibid., pp. 45–46). In his chronological autobiography, however, Hsu Jun did not specifically mention this investment.

23. Ibid., p. 43.

with Russell's steamship company. Among its Chinese shareholders, many were prominent coastal merchants, such as Quok Acheong, Tong King-sing, Li Sung-yun (Soong-yin), Sinchong, Akeong, and Cheng Kuan-ying.[24] In addition to Quok Acheong, Tong King-sing, the chief comprador to Jardine's at Shanghai, was an influential merchant. Li Sung-yin was the company's own comprador, and Sinchong was the comprador to Hongkong and Shanghai Banking Corp. at Hankow.[25] Akeong was a merchant at Hankow and Kiukiang who frequently did business with Heard's in the sixties.[26] Cheng Kuan-ying was then a clerk in Dent, Beale & Co., dealing in the silk and freight business.[27]

In 1868 Jardine's planned to open the Shanghai-Foochow steamer line. Two steamers were to be built, costing £11,500, and the firm sought to raise a capital of Tls. 50,000 in shares of Tls. 500 each. In April 1868 F. B. Johnson found that the *Dragon* was "a most successful boat" and thus desired to purchase her for the line.[28] Her price was about Tls. 60,000, and Johnson was confident that he could enlist Chinese investors to buy it: "I believe there will be no difficulty in getting shares taken by some of the best hongs."[29] Meanwhile, Johnson admitted that Jardine's would "take shares to a certain extent."[30]

Even though Jardine's was engaged in steamship enterprises in the sixties, it was not until 1873 that the firm established the China Coast Steam Navigation Co. Among the 4,600 shares (at Tls. 65 each), the ship *Nanzing*, owned by Tong King-sing and others, represented 400 shares. Through Tong, another 300 were subscribed for. In a similar manner, 235 shares were sold through Awei, the firm's comprador at Foochow. In total, the Chinese had 935 shares or Tls. 60,775, representing 20.5 percent of the total initial paid-up capital.[31] In the seventies, Tong King-sing and his brother Tong Mow-chee were elected as directors, and Tong King-sing even once served as the company's assistant manager.[32]

24. Ibid., pp. 42–43; and Kwang-Ching Liu, *Steamship Rivalry*, p. 189.
25. *NCH*, May 9, 1868, p. 215.
26. EL-1, HC.
27. Cheng Kuan-ying, *Hou-pien*, 8:42–43.
28. "I have discussed the conditions of a suitable boat & I think the 'Dragon' carrying 500 tons will suit us. She consumes only 7½ tons of coal per day to produce a speed of 9 knots & I hear on all hands that she is a most successful boat" ([Shanghai] to William Keswick [Hong Kong], Apr. 10, 1868, JMA).
29. Ibid.
30. Ibid., Apr. 11, 1868.
31. Kwang-Ching Liu, *Steamship Rivalry*, pp. 140–41; and Yen-p'ing Hao, *Comprador*, p. 122.
32. Wang Ching-yü, "Fu-ku," p. 44.

Meanwhile, the steamers *Tungting* and *Hanyang* of Morris, Lewis & Co. were also owned in large part by the Chinese, led by Tong King-sing.[33]

In addition to these conspicuous cases, there also are, before the mid-seventies, other foreign shipping companies in which there existed limited Chinese participation. Two coastal merchants, Li Chen-yü of Chekiang and Kow-Ku-San of Kwangtung, joined the American merchant M. G. Holmes and established the firm of Holmes & Co. at Shanghai in 1860. They purchased the steamer *Dragon* at Tls. 63,750 and plied on the Shanghai-Chefoo-Tientsin line.[34] In the early 1860s attempts were made to introduce steamships on the Yangtze by such large foreign houses as Jardine, Matheson & Co., Dent, Beale & Co., Fletcher & Co., and David Sassoon, Sons & Co. Some smaller firms also participated. Many of these steamships were partially purchased with Chinese capital.[35] In 1872 the China Trans-Pacific Steamship Co. was organized in London, planning to operate ships between Hong Kong and California. In addition to two Russell's partners, some Chinese merchants in Hong Kong also invested.[36]

The prospects for the carrying trade on China's water brightened increasingly after the mid-seventies for two reasons. First, it became easy to transfer the ownership of vessels. Prior to 1875 merchants at Shanghai had to register their purchases and sales of British-registered ships in Hong Kong, which was the only British ship-registration port on China's coast. But vessels plying under the British colors could be easily bought and registered in Shanghai after 1875 when that port became one of the British ship-registration ports. Because the great majority of the steamers on China's coast, whether actually owned by Chinese or foreigners, were under the British flag, the ease of transferring the ownership of these ships increased the liquidity of capital. Consequently, numerous investors were attracted to steamers. Second, the British commercial laws, especially those concerning limited liability, were generally accepted by the British steamship companies in China after the late seventies. Thus, greater convenience and more security combined to attract even more Chinese capital in the foreign-owned enterprises, particularly in the steamship and insurance fields.[37]

No one used these opportunities better than Jardine's. Besides estab-

---

33. Ibid.
34. *NCH*, Mar. 1, 1882, p. 238, and Mar. 15, 1882, p. 294.
35. Wang Ching-yü, "Fu-ku," pp. 39–40.
36. These two Russell's partners were Edward Cunningham and P. S. Forbes (Kwang-Ching Liu, *Steamship Rivalry*, pp. 127, 205).
37. Wang Ching-yü, "Fu-ku," p. 46.

lishing the China Coast S. N. Co., the house also organized the Yangtze Steamer Co. in 1879, primarily with Chinese capital. Thanks to the efforts of William Keswick, the firm's Head in East (1874–1886), the Indo-China S. N. Co. was set up in 1881. It took over the ships of the China Coast S. N. Co. and those of the Yangtze Steamer Co. The original Chinese investors of these two companies thus became shareholders of the new firm. Of the initial paid-up capital of £449,800 (Tls. 1,370,000), £150,000 was raised in China and Hong Kong.[38] One "zealous Chinese investor" was Ho Tung (1862–1956) who had been the chief comprador to Jardine's (1883–1900) in Hong Kong and was the richest and most prominent Chinese merchant in that port at the end of the nineteenth century.[39]

In 1882 the China Shippers' Mutual Steam Navigation Co. was established in London for transocean operations. One month after its establishment, many Chinese invested "with zeal." By April 1883 Chinese subscribed to more shares than the original amount assigned to China.[40] In the same year, the Co-operative Cargo Boat Co. of Shanghai was established with an initial capital of Tls. 100,000, a considerable proportion of it being held by Chinese investors. After the eighties, some of the steamship companies in China were officially owned jointly by Chinese and foreign merchants, such as the Hua-an Steam Navigation Co. at Shanghai in 1886, the Taku Tug and Lighter Co. at Tientsin in 1889, and the Hung-an Steam Navigation Co. (Greaves & Co.) at Shanghai in 1890.[41] As joint concerns, these companies had an even greater proportion of Chinese capital. The last company, for example, was jointly owned by Chinese and British merchants with a capital of probably over Tls. 200,000, and at least 70 percent of its capital was supplied by Chinese.[42]

Chinese merchants also invested in fields closely related to shipping, such as goods warehouses, wharves, and ship docks. Half of the shares of Kin-lee-yuen, the warehouse of Russell's Shanghai S. N. Co., for instance, were owned by Chinese, led by Koofunsing, in the late sixties.[43] Chinese also invested in the Shanghai and Hongkew Wharf Co. after it was established in 1872, particularly when its capital was increased from

38. Kwang-Ching Liu, "Steamship Enterprise," p. 439.
39. Yen-p'ing Hao, *Comprador*, p. 100; and Wang Ching-yü, "Fu-ku," p. 46.
40. Wang Ching-yü, "Fu-ku," p. 48.
41. Ibid.
42. Tōa Dōbunkai, *Shina keizai zensho* (Osaka, 1907), II, 495.
43. John M. Forbes (Canton) to Edward Cunningham (Shanghai), May 27, 1868, Case 26, RA.

Tls. 130,000 to Tls. 200,000 in 1895. One big investor was Ho Kin Chow who was a representative of the Chinese shareholders.[44] Another foreign wharf company, the Birt's Wharf Co., which was founded in 1882, eagerly solicited Chinese capital.[45] The building and repair of ships was the first industrial enterprise in China operated by foreigners, and many foreign houses, including Farnham, Boyd & Co. in Shanghai and Brandt & Co. in Hong Kong, were partially financed by Chinese investors.[46]

INSURANCE AND BANKING

As soon as the British firm of Dent, Beale & Co. established the Union Insurance Society in Macao in 1835, many Chinese merchants subscribed to its shares. Jardine's followed suit by founding the Canton Insurance Office in Canton in 1836. Some Chinese capital was probably involved from the beginning. At any rate, many Chinese definitely became shareholders after the sixties.[47]

In June 1862 Edward Cunningham of Russell's founded the Yangtze Insurance Association with an eye on the Yangtze shipping. It was a joint-stock company and absorbed Chinese capital from the beginning. With Russell & Co. serving as its agent, this association obtained most of its business by underwriting cargoes shipped in the Shanghai S. N. Co's steamers. After 1878 when its capital expanded from Tls. 157,000 to Tls. 420,000, Chinese investors became more numerous.[48] In 1863 North-China Insurance Co. was established in Shanghai by David Sassoon & Co., Travers & Clark, Scott Harding & Co., and other foreign houses. It soon became a tough competitor of the Yangtze Insurance Association. It welcomed Chinese investors, large or small. Its capital of Tls. 125,000 was increased to Tls. 250,000 in 1867, and to Tls. 1,000,000 in 1883. It was so profitable and Chinese investors were so zealous to invest that the firm had to make investment conditional in the seventies, for example, the shares would be distributed proportionately according to the amount of business that could be brought to the firm.[49]

Five Western insurance companies were organized in Hong Kong and Shanghai between 1864 and 1871: The China Fire Insurance Co. in

44. Wang Ching-yü, "Fu-ku," p. 55.
45. Ibid.
46. Ibid., p. 62.
47. Yowloong's Account, Memorandum, Hong Kong, Feb. 1875, JMA.
48. Kwang-Ching Liu, *Steamship Rivalry*, p. 35; and Wang Ching-yü, "Fu-ku," pp. 45, 49.
49. Wang Ching-yü, "Fu-ku," pp. 49–50.

1864, the China Traders Insurance Society in 1865, the Hong Kong Fire Insurance Co. in 1868, the China and Japan Marine Insurance Co. in 1870, and the Chinese Insurance Co. in 1871. Except for the first one, all are known to have had Chinese investors at one time or another. Although the exact amount of Chinese investment in these companies is unknown, we do know that more than half of the Chinese Insurance Co.'s capital was provided by the Chinese.[50]

No other Western insurance companies have a more detailed record of *fu-ku* activities than the China Traders Insurance Society. Heard's papers show that quite a few Chinese subscribed to its shares. It was organized by Augustine Heard & Co. in Hong Kong in 1865, with a projected capital of $1,000,000 in 200 shares of $5,000 each. Due to the lack of capital, Heard's did not invest much, allocating only 10 shares "for [our]selves and [American] constituents."[51] Meanwhile, other British and American firms in Hong Kong had interests in the new company, including Olyphant & Co., John Burd & Co., Oxford & Co., and Adam Scott & Co. But the bulk of the shares was purchased by local Chinese merchants.[52] Chinese businessmen continued to invest in this company in the sixties and seventies, and Chung Hing Kee and Yee On were two prominent shareholders in the late seventies.[53]

The Hongkong and Shanghai Banking Corp. emphasized the recruitment of Chinese capital from its establishment. After its stocks were issued in July 1864, almost every firm and individual doing business in Hong Kong, Shanghai, and Japan were interested in it. Its initial paid-up capital of Tls. 5,000,000 was entirely subscribed to in less than six months. In the eighties some Chinese were representatives in the shareholders' meetings, for example, Chow Ming Kee, Lo Shou-sung, Hsu Tzu-ching, and T'ang K'uei-sheng.[54] Lo Shou-sung was the bank's comprador.[55]

Efforts to organize the Bank of China were begun at Shanghai in 1872 by some foreign merchants, including A. A. Hayes, Jr., of Olyphant & Co., and O. C. Behu of Pustau & Co. Chinese capital was solicited and obtained in Shanghai and Hong Kong. Due to problems of registration, however, the plan to establish this bank did not materialize.[56] The Trust

50. Ibid., pp. 50–51.
51. Memorandum of China Traders Insurance Society, HQ-1, HC.
52. Ibid.
53. Wang Ching-yü, "Fu-ku," p. 50.
54. Ibid., p. 53.
55. *NCH*, Mar. 1, 1881, p. 207, June 6, 1890, p. 709, and Apr. 8, 1892, p. 469.
56. Wang Ching-yü, "Fu-ku," pp. 52–53.

and Loan Co. of China, Japan and the Straits, Ltd., was established in 1890, with the support of Chinese capital. In 1893 when the bank increased its capital, eighteen Chinese who represented the interests of Chinese shareholders announced that Chinese capital constituted more than half of the total amount.[57] These Chinese investors were headed by Li Kuan-chih, a prominent merchant at Shanghai who traded opium in Chinkiang in the late seventies.[58] In 1898 conspicuous Chinese shareholders included Wai Poo Kee, comprador to Jardine's, and Woo Chee Dong, comprador to Schultz & Co. Woo had purchased 1,000 shares of the bank stock.[59]

Another foreign bank, the National Bank of China, was established in 1891. Its Chinese capital must have been substantial, for among the seven directors in the head office at Hong Kong, three were Chinese. Futhermore, all the members of the advisory committee of its Shanghai office were also Chinese.[60] The Chinese who subscribed to the shares of foreign banks were probably rich businessmen. At the same time, however, there were many small investors. For instance, when the Oriental Bank was liquidated in 1892, numerous Chinese were found to be small shareholders.[61]

EXPORT PROCESSING AND OTHER COMPANIES

To a lesser degree, Chinese also invested in the export-processing enterprises owned by foreigners. The Chefoo Silk Filature Company was established by the German firm of Crasemann and Hagen at Chefoo in 1877. Its capital was increased from Tls. 40,000 to Tls. 100,000 in 1881, and the majority of the new shares were bought by Chinese.[62] The Ewo Silk Filature was established at Shanghai by Jardine's in 1881. By March 1883 it had "a staff of 10 men as shroffs, engineers, etc.," and also employed some 170 women. The company had Chinese capital from the beginning. In response to the inquiry of the British consul, Jardine's wrote on March 7, 1883: "For your private and special information, we may add that several Chinese, who are desirous to see its development,

57. Ibid., p. 53.
58. *Shen pao*, Sept. 3, 1879, p. 3.
59. Wang Ching-yü, "Fu-ku," p. 54.
60. Ibid., p. 53.
61. Ibid.
62. Ibid., pp. 58–59; and Hsu Jun, *Nien-p'u*, p. 73b.

are interested in the enterprise, although the control is solely in our hands."[63] Chinese capital probably constituted 60 percent in the eighties. Among its six directors, three were Chinese. In addition to Ewo, there were seven other foreign silk filature companies. Even though we do not know exactly how these firms were financed, all of them involved Chinese capital.[64]

As sugar was produced mainly in southern China, almost all of the foreign sugar-refining companies were set up in the southern ports of Canton and Hong Kong. As early as 1869, some British and Chinese tried to establish a sugar refinery in Whampoa near Canton but failed due to the strong opposition of the local handicraft sugar producers. This abortive scheme did not dampen the hope of Western merchants to continue the effort, and another sugar refining company was successfully established in the same year. This company, renamed the "China Sugar Refining Co." after 1877 and operated by Jardine's, attracted many Chinese investors.[65] Butterfield & Swire established the Taikoo Sugar Refinery in Hong Kong in 1881, and its stock shares were valued at $200 each in 1882. The Swire papers indicate that at least six Chinese from different hongs were shareholders in 1882: one with 200 shares, three with 300 shares each, and two with 400 shares each. The total Chinese investment was thus more than $380,000, a sizable amount.[66]

Two modern soybean oil companies were established in Newchwang by British businessmen in 1868 and 1888, respectively, and one of them was closely connected with a Chinese merchant who operated an oil workshop in that port. The China Tannery Co. was organized in Shanghai in 1882, with the German firm of Siemssen & Co. as its general agent, and two of its Chinese shareholders were prominent businessmen in that city. By March 1883 the shareholders of the China Tannery Co. "were chiefly Chinese."[67] J. C. Bois, the "Eastern Manager" of Butterfield & Swire at Shanghai, reported to John Samuel Swire in 1895 that some Chinese investors were interested in jointly establishing a rice mill with the firm: "C. T. Wong, co-owner of the Amoy property . . . is

63. Jardine, Matheson & Co. (Shanghai) to British Consul Hughes (Shanghai), FO 405/27, p. 82.

64. Wang Ching-yü, "Fu-ku," p. 59.

65. *NCH*, May 13, 1887, p. 515; and Wang Ching-yü, "Fu-ku," p. 60.

66. Box 1175, SP.

67. Jardine, Matheson & Co. (Shanghai) to British Consul Hughes (Shanghai), Mar. 7, 1883, FO 405/27, p. 52. For the soybean oil companies and the China Tannery, see Wang Ching-yü, "Fu-ku," pp. 60–61.

very anxious to go in with us & he and his friends are prepared to put up
⅔rd of the capital for a [rice] mill with a capacity of 100 tons per day....
This mill is to be controlled by a Board of Directors [instead of solely by
Butterfield & Swire]."[68]

Various public utility companies were established in the treaty ports,
such as Shanghai Gas Co. (1864), Compagnie de Gaz (1865), Shanghai
Waterworks Co. (1881), Shanghai Electric Co. (1882), and Tientsin Gas
Co. (1888). All of them had Chinese capital. Among the prominent
Chinese investors were Tong King-sing, Li Sung-yun, and Tong Mow-
chee.[69] Chinese capital was also behind other companies operated by
foreigners. Although its amount was not known in many enterprises,
such as Hua Hsing Glass Co. (est. 1882), Tientsin Chinese Match Factory (1886), Major Brothers & Co. (1889), Shanghai Chromo and
Photo-Lithographic Co. (1890), Shanghai Ice Co. (1890s), and China
Flour Mill Co. (late 1890s),[70] the picture was clearer in other instances.
The shareholders of China Paper Mill Co. (1881), for example, were
virtually all Chinese,[71] and the Cantonese invested heavily in the
Chinese Glass Works Co. (1882) at Shanghai, representing about 80
percent of the initial paid-up capital of Tls. 100,000.[72]

After 1895 foreigners were permitted to set up manufacturing factories in China's treaty ports. Four cotton-manufacturing companies were
organized by foreign merchants in Shanghai in 1895: Loau Kung Mow
Cotton Spinning and Weaving Co., Ewo Cotton Spinning and Weaving
Co., International Cotton Manufacturing Co., and Soy Chee Cotton
Spinning Co. Except for the first company whose capital was Tls.
800,000, the rest all had Tls. 1,000,000 each in capital.[73] Judging from
the number of shares allocated for Chinese subscription and the number
of Chinese on the boards of directors, it is likely that Chinese capital
constituted from 40 to 50 percent of the initial paid-up capital of the four
companies.

68. To Swire (London), July 19, 1895, SP. Unfortunately, the Swire papers do not
yield more details of the mill.
69. Wang Ching-yü, "Fu-ku," pp. 62–64. Wang doubts that the French firm Compagnie de Gaz had any Chinese capital, but one of Jardine's letters in 1883 indicates that
its shareholders came from all nationalities, including the Chinese (Jardine, Matheson &
Co. [Shanghai] to British Consul Hughes [Shanghai], Mar. 3, 1883, FO 405/27, p. 82).
70. Wang Ching-yü, "Fu-ku," pp. 65–66. Wang does not mention the Shanghai Ice
Co. which was a British firm and had Chinese capital. See Jardine, Matheson & Co.
(Shanghai) to British Consul Hughes (Shanghai), Mar. 3, 1883, FO 405/27, p. 82.
71. Jardine, Matheson & Co. (Shanghai) to British Consul Hughes (Shanghai), Mar.
3, 1883, FO 405/27, p. 82.
72. Wright, *Impressions*, p. 548; and *Shang-hai ch'ien-chuang*, p. 37.
73. Wang Ching-yü, "Fu-ku," p. 56.

AMOUNT AND SIGNIFICANCE

Among these *fu-ku* enterprises, many had 40 percent Chinese capital, and some of them, such as Shanghai S. N. Co., China Coast S. N. Co., and Shanghai Water Works Co., had more than 50 percent. Chinese capital constituted at least 60 percent in Chefoo Silk Filature, Ewo Silk Filature, and Hua Hsing Glass Works Co., and was as high as 80 percent in the Chinese Glass Works Co. and the Trust and Loan Co. of China, Japan and the Straits. The total capital of these *fu-ku* enterprises was more than Tls. 40,000,000,[74] and the Chinese capital in them, probably constituting an average of 40 percent,[75] was at least Tls. 16,000,000.

The Treaty of Shimonoseki of 1895 provided the legal basis for foreign merchants to establish manufacturing factories in the treaty ports, and consequently many cotton mills were founded. Seventy-eight Chinese individuals and firms invested in seventeen such factories in 1896 to 1910, eight of them being cotton and flour mills in Shanghai.[76] More than one hundred prominent Chinese investors were either representatives of Chinese shareholders or on the foreign firms' boards of directors during the second half of the nineteenth century. Eighteen of them invested in the sixties, and their *fu-ku* activities involved five foreign houses. The numbers of the conspicuous Chinese investors and foreign firms increased after the sixties, as shown by the following figures:[77]

Period	Number of Chinese investors	Number of foreign firms
1860s	18	5
1870s	27	6
1880s	21	14
1890s	64	19

Actually, these figures would have been higher if adequate foreign shares had been available to Chinese investors, but the limited availability of foreign shares could not meet the local demand after the eighties. Consequently, many Chinese were denied the opportunity to buy shares in

74. Ibid., pp. 68–69.
75. There were many foreign enterprises in Shanghai in 1882–1891 that had at least 40 percent of Chinese capital (IMC, *Decennial Report, 1882–1891*, Shanghai, p. 340). This was also the case in 1893 (Murphey, *Shanghai*, p. 6).
76. Among these enterprises, six were cotton mills and two were flour mills; most were in Shanghai (Wang Ching-yü, *Kung-yeh shih*, II, 1065).
77. Wang Ching-yü, "Fu-ku," p. 69.

such foreign companies as Shanghai Water Works Co. in 1881, China
Shippers' Mutual Steam Navigation Co. in 1882, Shanghai Electric Co.
in 1882, Hua Hsing Glass Works Co. in 1882, and Major Brothers & Co.
in 1889.[78]

The economic implications of *fu-ku* activities were many. First, nothing testifies better to the existence of large amounts of readily available
Chinese funds for modern enterprises than these activities. Second,
Chinese investors responded promptly to the prospect for profits. They
were quick to select foreign firms in which to invest but were not indiscrim-
inate in their choices. Some contemporary foreign enterprises failed as
a result of lack of funds, and the Chinese sometimes switched their investments to Chinese enterprises if the latter were equally profitable with
foreign firms. After the *kuan-tu shang-pan* (merchant undertaking under
government supervision) projects were established, some of those who
had invested in foreign firms, such as Tong King-sing and Hsu Jun, also
invested in these ventures.

Fu-ku activities closely tied together the interests of Chinese and Western merchants in the treaty ports as they pursued their respective profits.
F. B. Johnson of Jardine's believed that the wisest course for the firm in
the eighties was to continue organizing joint-stock enterprises with
Chinese investors, especially in the fields of cotton manufacturing and
silk reeling. In order not to alienate Chinese investors, he felt that it was
of paramount importance to secure their participation, especially those
who did not like to risk their capital in the *kuan-tu shang-pan* enterprises.[79]
Fu-ku activities also unmistakably showed that Chinese businessmen
were afraid of the exaction of officials of their government. They tried
their best to prevent their wealth from being exposed to the attention of
the officials. Whereas China Merchants' Company, a *kuan-tu shang-pan*
enterprise, had a hard time in raising capital in the early seventies, the
shares of Russell & Co.'s Shanghai S. N. Co. were in heavy demand by
Chinese investors. The major problem in China's economic development
was not the lack of capital, but the lack of trust on the part of the investors toward bureaucrats.

CHINESE BUSINESSES UNDER
WESTERN NAMES

Under the treaty system, a Western trader enjoyed privileges that
were denied to the Chinese merchants. A principal aim of the treaty

---

78. Ibid.
79. (Hong Kong) to William Paterson (Shanghai), Jan. 25, 1883, JMA.

system had been to facilitate foreign commerce; accordingly, the treaty tariff was set at fixed monetary rates, which in many cases represented 5 percent ad valorem in 1858, but generally were lowered as prices rose in subsequent decades. Foreign imports and Chinese goods for export, as they passed in either direction between treaty ports and the interior, were to pay an additional 2.5 percent (half the tariff duty) as transit dues and were subsequently free from all the likin and other taxes that goods in China's purely domestic commerce had to pay. Similarly, an additional 2.5 percent could be paid as "coast trade" duty to avoid all further taxes on Chinese goods carried in foreign ships from one Chinese port to another. Because the Chinese merchants could not better their position through legislative channels, they eventually found their way out by putting themselves under foreign protection.

COASTAL SHIPPING

In order to pay lower tariffs, many Chinese shipped their cargoes in Western vessels. This practice was prevalent after 1845 because of the confusion between foreign and native trade. British merchants enjoyed the privilege of reexport, that is, Western imports that had entered one treaty port and paid duty there could be reexported and taken into another treaty port without paying any further import duty. When Englishmen dealt in Chinese produce, and Chinese merchants shipped their cargoes in British vessels, the former clear-cut distinction between foreign and native trade began to break down. This in turn confused the application of the tariff, because there were two tariffs now in force—the old Chinese tariff and the new foreign treaty tariff. Under the Chinese tariff, native produce, upon leaving a port, paid export duty; on entering a second port, it paid import duty, and if it left the second port it again paid export duty. The foreign treaty tariff operated on a different principle. Although its rates were usually higher than those of the native tariff, it was applied to suit the convenience of the foreign merchant, who could move his Western imports from port to port indefinitely without paying more than a single import duty.[80]

The stage was thus set for disputes over borderline cases. By which tariff were goods to be taxed when in the hands of a Chinese merchant shipping on a British vessel? These disputes wee complicated and confusing. In general, practice varied from port to port and from time to time at the same port. The object of the merchants in most cases was to

80. Fairbank, *Trade and Diplomacy*, I, 317.

enjoy both the privileges of the foreign tariff and the lower rates of the native tariff. In the spring of 1847, the Amoy authorities warned Chinese merchants not to ship their goods on British ships, but this warning was abandoned after the governor of Hong Kong protested. The British claimed that Chinese could ship Chinese goods on British ships and pay duties according to the Chinese tariff, rather the treaty tariff. This amounted to full British participation in the coastal carrying trade. Whether Ch'i-ying had actually granted the use of the native tariff was uncertain, but the consuls assumed that he had.[81]

Many Chinese went one step further by running their vessels on the coast under foreign flags. This practice was profitable for several reasons.. First, the exaction of the Chinese officials was minimized. A memorial of China's minister to France dated 1907 described in detail how the officials had illegal "squeeze" on Chinese-owned ships in the late Ch'ing period.[82] A contemporary document points out that "once a Chinese ship has a foreign flag on it, clerks of the customs house dare not to exact duties. Otherwise, foreign merchants will come to protect them."[83] Moreover, pirates would think twice before they took action against foreign ships, and, in time of domestic disorder, such as the Taiping uprising (1850–1864), vessels with foreign flags were best able to command the respect of insurgents and most likely to have their claims paid in case of loss by capture. Finally, the Chinese owners of the vessels wanted to pay lower duties for their cargoes.[84]

The use of Western flags in coastal shipping immediately after the Opium War raised eyebrows among Chinese officials. British vessels in Chinese waters were required to carry sailing letters after 1843 entitling them to the use of the British flag. This gave them a recognized status in British law, but their status under the treaties was less clear. The Supplementary Treaty of 1843 freed from tonnage dues all small British vessels that carried only passengers and letters, while vessels carrying dutiable goods and not weighing over 150 tons were to pay at the rate of

81. Ch'i-ying's supposed concession of 1847—that native goods owned by Chinese shippers should pay duty at the native rate—was inoperative in Shanghai in 1848, the high authorities of Kiangnan having decided that the new treaty tariff should apply (ibid., I, 318–19).
82. Enclosure of Circular 1497, Apr. 28, 1908, IMC, *Circulars*, X, 367.
83. *Kuang-hsu ch'ao tung-hua hsu-lu*, comp. Chu Shou-p'eng, 198:16.
84. Jardine's wrote on the different duties: "Referring to a conversation with Mr. Johnson a few days ago, we have the honour to lay before you a scale of the differential duties levied on Chinese produce shipped hence to Foochow by vessels under foreign flag as compared with Chinese owned vessels" ([Shanghai] to Thomas Dick [Shanghai], Apr. 27, 1869, JMA).

one mace (one-tenth of a tael) per ton; and vessels over 150 tons would be charged the regular rate of five mace per ton. Every British vessel required a sailing letter, to be obtained at Hong Kong and deposited with the British consul while in the port of Canton.[85]

By treaty, this arrangement was applicable only to Canton, but a few years later this type of British craft (with a sailing letter from Hong Kong) was active along the entire southeast coast. The use of sailing letters was abused by British merchants: once a vessel had received a sailing letter, its owner could renew it from a distance without presenting either himself or the vessel for further formalities. The general result of this practice was that each of the opium ship captains on the coast was listed as the owner of several vessels, and sometimes as the master of two at once. It is clear that some Chinese merchants were using these vessels for trade.[86]

The practice of registering Chinese vessels with foreign authorities became more popular after the fifties, thanks to the improvement of steam navigation. The number of small steamers in China increased because many Chinese lorcha owners obtained the right to fly a foreign flag over their vessels. This was accomplished by an ingenious transaction in which the technical ownership of the lorcha was transferred to the foreigner who in turn gave back to the Chinese a mortgage for the full value of the vessel, which carried with it the right to operate the craft. The foreign flag was then hoisted as evidence of foreign ownership, but the foreigner named in the vessel's papers never appeared except in case of trouble. The lorcha *Arrow*, which caused disputes at Canton in 1856 and finally led to the Anglo-French War with China from 1858 to 1860, had been flying the British flag under such an arrangement.[87] By the late fifties it was common for Chinese vessels to ply in coastal waters under foreign, especially British, flags.[88] This practice existed not only in the southern ports of Hong Kong and Canton, but also in the Yangtze ports of Shanghai. In fact, this practice was so widespread on the coast that some foreign merchants "specialized in this class of business" during the sixties and seventies.[89]

85. Fairbank, *Trade and Diplomacy*, I, 127, 322.
86. Ibid., I, 324, 332. See also A. G. Dallas (Shanghai) to David Jardine (Hong Kong), Sept. 19, 1848; and Alexander Perceval (Shanghai) to Joseph Jardine (Hong Kong), Apr. 7, 1856, JMA.
87. Dennett, *Americans*, pp. 583–84. For the disputes over the *Arrow*, see Eitel, p. 307.
88. Letter of W. Davidson, enclosure of the commercial report of Consul D. B. Robertson, Canton, 1858, FO 405/2, p. 353.
89. Dennett, *Americans*, pp. 583–84.

By the late sixties even ordinary Chinese junks were under Western colors. In 1868, 38 junks, under Western flags and totaling 3,314 tons, arrived at Chinkiang from Hankow.[90] Similar cases existed in Tientsin. In order to transport tribute rice from Tientsin to Tungchow, the impressment of cargo boats by the Chinese authorities at Tientsin became a routine practice. Although there were 1,436 government lighters available for use in 1869, no less than 560 private boats were impressed in the first four and a half months of 1869. Because those cargo boats owned or employed by foreigners had the privilege of exemption from the impressment, the Chinese officials took pains in identifying these boats. They asked these boats to supply a boat pass under the seal and signature of a foreign consul, to be countersealed by the taotai. Nevertheless, many Chinese junk owners purchased these passes when they traded in Tientsin and resold them when their junks departed from the port. To keep the misuse of these passes to a minimum, the Chinese authorities asked that these passes be kept pasted on the masts of the boats. These official efforts notwithstanding, the abuse of boat passes continued. The British consul openly admitted that it would be difficult to guard against the abuse of these passes.[91]

Whereas some Chinese merchants operated their vessels under Western colors, others bought steamships and put them under Western management. In February 1869 "a Chinese hong of some standing in Chefoo and Tientsin" bought the steamer *Dragon* for $85,000, but the "nominal owner" was Holmes & Co. One year later the owners of the ship transferred the management of the ship to Jardine's, which was to receive for the service "5% commission on gross earnings and any wharfage charges."[92] The Shanghai Steam Navigation Co. was founded by the American firm of Russell & Co. in 1862, and some Chinese subscribed to its shares, as we have just seen. When this shipping company was sold to the Chinese-owned China Merchants' S. N. Co. in 1877, some Swatow shareholders refused to transfer their shares and instead bought some steamers and formed the Ningpo S. N. Co., which sailed under the American flag.[93]

The practice of running Chinese vessels under Western flags con-

90. Report of C. F. Allen, Assistant in Charge, Chinkiang, May 20, 1869, FO 17/531, p. 2.
91. Report of Consul J. Morgan, Tientsin, Apr. 16, 1869, FO 17/535, p. 3.
92. When the *Dragon* was put under Jardine management, F. B. Johnson arranged to make a short-term loan of Tls. 40,000 to the ship's owners ([Shanghai] to William Keswick [Hong Kong], Feb. 2, 1869, and Feb. 16, 1870, JMA).
93. Wang Ching-yü, "Fu-ku," p. 73.

tinued into the eighties, and Chinese officials, particularly those on the Yangtze, frequently complained about it.[94] However, this practice substantially declined in the nineties. In the first place, Chinese authorities decided to treat Chinese and foreign vessels as equal for tax purposes, thus eliminating the special privileges enjoyed by foreign-owned vessels.[95] Also, Chinese officials, particularly the governor-general of Liang Kwang, began to vigorously enforce the rule that only foreign nationals were allowed to hoist foreign flags.[96]

TRANSIT PASSES AND "PSEUDOFOREIGN HOUSES"

In order to avoid likin and other restrictions, some Chinese merchants tried to disguise their business as Western. They frequently traded between inland and the treaty ports by illegally using transit passes that were reserved for foreign traders. In the sixties quite a few merchants from Tientsin transported hides from Mongolia to that port by using transit passes that they bought from British firms, including Collins & Co. and David Sassoon & Co.[97] The abuse of these transit passes was in vogue during the 1860s and 1870s, and the Sugar Taxation Bureau of Shanghai complained in 1874 that its tax revenue was steadily deteriorating. This situation did not improve even though the Bureau reduced the sugar tax by half in August 1874, in an effort to induce the Chinese merchants to trade in their own right.[98]

Robert Hart, the inspector-general of the Chinese Maritime Customs, admitted in 1876 that "there has been quite sufficient reason for supposing that the transit privilege was being abused."[99] Hart's opinion was attested to not only by the discovery of this malpractice by the customs itself,[100] but also by the report of the British consul from Chinkiang. The consul pointed out in 1882 that the Chinese trader took full advantage "of the provisions of the British treaty . . . by employing a foreign merchant as his agent to bring down the goods [from upper Yangtze] and pay the duties [instead of likin] on them."[101] Protests from the Chinese

94. IMC, *Circulars*, I, 669; III, 272.
95. Circular no. 846, Sept. 5, 1898, IMC, *Origin*, II, 138.
96. *Chiao-t'ung shih* (Nanking, 1930—), XII, 155.
97. *NCH*, Nov. 19, 1884, p. 579.
98. *Shen pao*, Aug. 20, 1874, p. 5.
99. "Proposals for the Better Regulation of Commercial Relations," Jan. 23, 1876, IMC, *Origin* VI, 367.
100. IMC, *Circulars*, III, 68.
101. BPP, *Consular Report, Chinkiang, 1881–1882*, p. 3.

officials notwithstanding, the abuse of transit passes continued until the
end of the Ch'ing dynasty.[102]

The opium trade figured prominently in this business pattern. In a
letter dated October 16, 1862, Dan Patridge of Jardine's at Shanghai
reported that, in order to avoid the taotai's "squeeze of 10 Taels per
chest," many Chinese merchants dealing in opium "are clearing their
drug through foreigners who take it into their houses at [a commission
of] Tls. 5 c [to] 10 pr. chest, whereby the Taoutae [taotai] loses his old
squeeze of 25 Tls. as the drug is redelivered during the night."[103] Under
Western names, the Chinese merchants not only traded in foreign opium
but also in Chinese-produced opium as well.[104]

A perusal of the local Chinese and English newspapers reveals that
whereas some Chinese merchants occasionally traded by using a Westerner's transit pass, other Chinese regularly did business under the names
of foreign firms. These "pseudoforeign houses," which were completely
financed and managed by the Chinese, could avoid paying likin and
other taxes by trading under foreign names, and in turn they passed half
of their "savings" to the foreigner who "lent his name" to them.[105] It
was in this way that W. F. Walker, a British merchant at Chinkiang who
had three Chinese hong names under which the Chinese could trade,
cooperated with the Chinese merchants from Canton and Swatow in
that port. This was by no means an isolated case: at that time, nearly
every foreign firm in Chinkiang had three or four Chinese names to trade
under. One Chinese observed in 1879 that it "was the general practice"
that many "foreigners lent their names to the Chinese."[106] This practice
was particularly popular in Shanghai, Chinkiang, and Hankow after the
seventies.[107]

As soon as Chungking was opened as a treaty port in 1890, some
Chinese merchants immediately began to trade under foreign names.[108]
In his private correspondence, an employee of the maritime customs
wrote from Ningpo in 1892 that on the coast and on the Yangtze there
were many such "lie hongs . . . who prostitute their names to make a
living" throughout the late Ch'ing era.[109] Because of its profitability, this

102. H. F. Merrill (Ningpo) to Robert Hart (Peking), Jan. 4, 1891, IMC, *Origin*, V, 10.
103. Patridge to Jardine, Matheson & Co. (Hong Kong), JMA.
104. Cheng Kuan-ying, *Tseng-ting*, 3:1.
105. *NCH*, Sept. 16, 1865, p. 146.
106. *NCH*, Oct. 17, 1879, p. 388.
107. *Shen pao*, May 1, 1878, p. 3, and Oct. 14, 1879, p. 3.
108. Consular report, Chungking, 1903, FO 405/152, p. 40.
109. H. F. Merrill (Ningpo) to Robert Hart (Peking), Mar. 12, 1892, IMC, *Origin*, V, 20.

practice was introduced from commerce to industry in the eighties. A group of Fukienese merchants tried to set up factories under British and German names in order to produce iron pans at Amoy in 1883. The local officials, however, were successful in stopping these enterprises, because the treaty did not grant foreigners the privilege of manufacturing in China.[110] When the foreigners obtained such privileges in 1895, some Chinese did start to manufacture under foreign names.[111]

A small number of Chinese merchants benefited from trading under Western names, but this practice inhibited the flow of Chinese commerce in certain ways. Some merchants would not invest their capital until they found a foreign trader who would lend his name to them. In his celebrated book on reform, *Warnings to the Prosperous Age*, Cheng Kuan-ying fiercely attacked this practice for its disturbing effects on the Chinese economy. The most important way for the Ch'ing government to deal with this situation, Cheng argued, was to abolish the likin altogether.[112] Some high officials, on the other hand, emphasized the importance of improving Chinese commercial law. Chang Chih-tung and Liu K'un-i jointly memorialized at the turn of the century, calling for positive government policy to create a desirable atmosphere for Chinese merchants.[113]

In the foreign concessions of the treaty ports, the treaties forbade, "under forfeiture, the sale, letting, or transfer of ground or premises to any native."[114] However, because some Chinese wanted to reside or to do business in the concessions, they often bought or rented real estate under foreign names, especially after the sixties.[115] A group of Chinese merchants at Chinkiang purchased land from Gibb, Livingston & Co. in 1882 under the name of George Cowie, a British subject who was "well known as an agent for the Chinese,"[116] and there were several similar cases at that port. This practice continued to exist at the treaty ports through the late eighties and early nineties.[117]

110. Circular no. 215, Apr. 3, 1883, IMC, *Circulars*, III, 42.
111. A case in point was the opium-processing factory at Swatow, which operated under the British colors in 1897 (P'eng Tse-i, comp., *Chung-kuo chin-tai shou-kung-yeh shih tzu-liao* [Peking, 1957], II, 401–2).
112. *Tseng-ting*, 3:1–1b. For a standard account of the likin system, see Lo Yü-tung, *Chung-kuo li-chin shih* (Shanghai, 1936). For a new study of the system, especially its detrimental effects on commerce, see Ho Lieh, *Li-chin chih-tu hsin-t'an* (Taipei, 1972).
113. Hatano Yoshihiro, *Chūgoku kindai kōgyōshi no kenkyū* (Kyoto, 1961), p. 268.
114. British Office of Works (London) to Foreign Office (London), Feb. 20, 1882, FO 405/55, p. 11.
115. For Hsu Jun, see Wright, *Impressions*, p. 566.
116. British Office of Works (London) to Foreign Office (London), Feb. 20, 1882, FO 405/55, p. 11.
117. Cheng Kuan-ying, *Tseng-ting*, 3:1.

The Chinese merchants who associated themselves with Western traders also received legal protection from the foreigners, for example, in 1845 Rutherford Alcock at Foochow vigorously intervened between the Chinese authorities and some Cantonese.[118] This kind of legal protection motivated some Chinese companies to invite foreign merchants to serve on their boards of directors. When the Pao-an Insurance Co., a Chinese enterprise, was established in 1871, it invited the partners of the American house of Olyphant & Co. to be its directors. The chairman of the board of directors was also a Westerner.[119] Even Sheng Hsuan-huai, an official-entrepreneur, registered his cotton mill under a foreign power in Hong Kong.[120] Chinese merchants even changed their citizenship through naturalization; Ho Fu (Ho Fook) became a British subject, and Hsi Li-kung became a Portuguese citizen.[121]

The Western trader under whose name the Chinese were operating businesses accepted the obligation to protect them.[122] Occasionally, he backed them up by using force. In the fifties when the main tea-producing areas were disturbed by the Taipings, Chinese often transported their own tea from upcountry to Shanghai under the protection of Dent & Co. and Jardine, Matheson & Co.[123] This was also the case with Augustine Heard & Co. in the early sixties.[124] German troops even landed at Swatow in 1883 in order to support a German firm's claim to a piece of disputed land (that probably in fact belonged to a Chinese).[125]

Because of the practice of trading under false names by both Chinese and foreign merchants, the well-established Western mercantile houses paid special attention to assure that their names would not be abused in this way. Jardine's specified that its special agents were not permitted to use the name of the firm.[126] David Sassoon & Co. was equally strict, and

118. Fairbank, *Trade and Diplomacy*, I, 220–21.
119. Wang Ching-yü, "Fu-ku," p. 51.
120. Marion J. Levy and Kuo-heng Shih, *The Rise of the Modern Chinese Business Class* (New York, 1949), p. 52.
121. Wright, *Impressions*, p. 178.
122. Report of C. F. Allen, Assistant in Charge, Chinkiang, May 20, 1869, FO 17/531.
123. A. G. Dallas (Shanghai) to Jardine, Matheson & Co. (Hong Kong), Dec. 18, 1851, JMA; and James Whittall (Shanghai) to Joseph Jardine (Hong Kong), Dec. 21, 1859, JMA.
124. A. F. Heard to John Heard, Aug. 16, 1860, HL-16; and G. F. Weller to A. F. Heard, May 15, 1862, HM-49, HC.
125. *NCH*, Mar. 11, 1883, p. 525.
126. E.g., F. B. Johnson gave instructions in 1883: "Please note that we only recognize Mr. Craig as our special agent at Swatow. He is not authorized to use the name of our firm. I have instructed him to this effect. He will sign letters on the firm's general agency

it particularly instructed its comprador that in no way could he use its name except when he received payments for the firm.[127] During the late nineteenth and early twentieth centuries, some Chinese companies added the term *yang-hang* to their names. Although this term meant "brokerage firms dealing with foreign goods" in the time of the hong merchants,[128] it changed meaning during the last decades of the Ch'ing period, meaning literally "foreign firms" and referring to the foreign mercantile houses in China.[129] Consequently, the foreign traders contended that it was misleading for the Chinese hongs to use this term.[130]

LARGE AND QUICK PROFITS

The handsome profit returns from modern commerce can be understood against the traditional pattern of investment. Although based on incomplete data, it seems conclusive that by the 1870s, profits from trade had become considerably greater than those from landholding, especially as land prices rose in response to the continued population increase.[131] The rate of return on landed investments, which seems to have been constantly decreasing in the nineteenth century, was already rather low. In the late eighteenth century, the rate of return before taxes was about 10 percent. In the 1870s the rate of return was reduced to about 4 percent. In the 1880s rent per *mou* (0.15 acre) at certain places in Shangtung was less than Tls. 3, but the price of land had soared to Tls. 150. The rate of return in this case was less than 2 percent, the same as that given by J. L. Buck in his field study on the Republican period. Not only was the rate of return on land investments low, but with time full rents became more difficult to collect. In short, in the nineteenth century, especially the

---

business in his own name as 'Agency for JM & Co.' All policies of Insurance & letters & documents for the Indo-China S. N. Co. he will sign 'R. Craig, Agent,' simply" ([Hong Kong] to William Paterson [Shanghai], Apr. 5, 1883, JMA).

127. *NCH*, Nov. 19, 1884, p. 577.

128. Liang chia-pin, *Shih-san hang*, pp. 278–79.

129. See the entry under *Yang-hang* in *Tz'u-yuan* (Taipei, 1955).

130. In a letter to the Chinese General Chamber of Commerce at Shanghai, dated December 12, 1923, the foreign Shanghai General Chamber of Commerce wrote: "We are directed by our committee to draw your attention to the use of the title 'foreign firm' (*yang-hang*) by certain Chinese firms and enclose herewith several chop tickets which have been brought to the notice of our committee. We are to request you to kindly bring the matter to the attention of your committee with the suggestion that suitable action be taken with a view to preventing the practice" (Uchida Naosaku, "Yōkō seido no kenkyū," *Shina kenkyū* 50:189–90 [Mar. 1939]). It is not clear whether or not this letter was effective in restraining the Chinese firms from using the term *yang-hang*.

131. Chung-li Chang, *The Income of the Chinese Gentry* (Seattle, 1962), pp. 138–39.

second half, the profits obtainable from landholding were declining.[132] At the same time, profit returns from traditional government monopolies, such as salt, were at best static, or even declining.[133] Perceiving and acting on the changed circumstances, Chinese investors found modern commercial and industrial enterprises attractive outlets.

LARGE PROFITS

Although the overall rate of profit of the opium trade is not known, the evidence indicates that it was very profitable. A mid-nineteenth century estimate shows that, during the first decades of the century, the semi-annual net profit rate of India-China opium traffic was more than 15 percent of capital invested. Foreign opium merchants, "in consequence of realizing such sure gains, in so short a time and with so little trouble in the trade . . . [were] unwilling to embark in any other branch of commerce or business."[134] Andrew Jardine of Jardine's is said to have divided with his partners in the 1840s the immense sum of £3,000,000 (almost $15,000,000) of profits, much of which had been accumulated from the opium trade during the previous decade. In 1848 one British ship carried 1,800 chests of opium from Bombay to Hong Kong and sold it for $750 per chest, receiving a total of $1,350,000. With an average of 15 percent profit, this single cargo would net the owner $202,500. In November 1852 the steamship *Ganges* shipped 2,500 chests of opium from Bombay to Hong Kong. With the same price and profit rate, this cargo would bring the owner a handsome profit of $281,250.[135]

The tea trade was also highly lucrative.[136] For example, the net profit from the *Empress of China* in 1784–1785 was estimated at $30,727 (U.S.), 25 percent of the original investment.[137] The net proceeds of the *Betsey* in 1797–1798 exceeded $120,000 (U.S.), and the profits came to $53,118 (U.S.).[138] During the era of the tea clippers, the rate of return was even

132. Ibid., pp. 139–42.
133. For the changing profitability of alternate uses of investment capital, see P'eng Tse-i, "Shih-chiu shih-chi hou-ch'i Chung-kuo ch'eng-shih shou-kung-yeh shang-yeh hang-hui ti ch'ung-chien ho tso-yung," *Li-shih yen-chiu* 1:81–90 (1965).
134. Allen, *Opium Trade*, p. 62.
135. Ibid., pp. 62–63. Calculations of profit figures are mine.
136. For a discussion of the profitability of the Sino-American tea trade and its economic, social, and cultural ramifications, see Yen-p'ing Hao, "The Early Chinese-American Tea Trade," in John K. Fairbank, ed., *American–East Asian Economic Relations*, Harvard University Press, forthcoming.
137. Samuel Shaw, *The Journals of Major Samuel Shaw*, ed. Josiah Quincy (Boston, 1847), p. 135.
138. Dennett, *Americans*, p. 11.

higher due to the speed of these ships. The *Oriental* made a profit of $48,000 (U.S.) in a single voyage in 1850; this sum equaled two-thirds the cost of the ship. Another clipper ship, the *Rainbow*, paid for her cost two times over in just one trip.[139]

If the profit of tea trade was handsome, it also involved much risk, and the opening of Foochow as a tea port in 1854 eminently illustrates this. Although Foochow was close to tea-producing districts, tea was seldom shipped abroad from Foochow before 1854. In 1853 the walled Chinese city of Shanghai was occupied by the rebellious Small Sword Society, a Triad offshoot, and the approaches to that city were in the hands of the Taipings. Canton was also besieged by the rebels. Thus, the two tea-exporting centers were closed to trade. Wu Chien-chang, the taotai of Shanghai, was a former hong merchant who was acquainted with the American merchants of Russell & Co. After they saved his life during the Small Sword rebellion, he suggested to them "that it was a good opportunity to try a shipment [of tea] from Foochow."[140]

Augustine Heard, Jr., later recollected that "the hint was immediately taken." Early the next year, four foreign firms, Dent's, Jardine's, Heard's, and Russell's, "commenced vigorous action. Men and money in large quantities were sent into the interior." This way of purchasing tea involved three kinds of risk. First, it was new and experimental; Heard pointed out: "We were doing something that had never been attempted on a large scale before." Second, the foreign merchants were not protected by treaty in this respect: "At first money went into the country to some extent in January, and more largely in February and March, and did not come back in the shape of tea till May. It was a great risk to run. We had no right by treaty to buy produce in the interior, and could make no reclamation in case of loss."[141] Therefore, they had to take the risk of depending entirely on the fidelity of their Chinese employees.

Another factor that made this tea purchase risky was the social disturbance in the interior. Heard continued: "We did not know how far we could trust our men [Chinese employees], and as the country was in a most disorganized condition [due to the Taiping uprising], they had only to come back and say they were very sorry, but they had been robbed and lost everything in their possession." To show that this was by no means rumor, Heard mentioned his own experience: "Before going up [to the interior] myself, I sent up a staff of Chinamen overland

---

139. Carl C. Cutler, *Greyhound of the Sea* (New York, 1930), p. 169.
140. Augustine Heard, Jr., "Old China and New," p. 30, GQ-2, HC.
141. Ibid., pp. 30–31.

from Amoy to hire premises, and have everything in order for my arrival. When I did arrive, I found they had never reached their destination. They had been attacked, robbed and turned back." In short, the entire operation involved great risk, as Heard aptly remarked: "The question was whether the probable profits and prestige were worth the risk." Thanks to the integrity of their Chinese employees, the outcome was a happy one: "The profit was large."[142]

The Chinese merchants dealing in tea also benefited from the opening of Foochow. After 1854 the upcountry purchase of tea in the Bohea districts proceeded smoothly, and many tea merchants, teamen, and compradors became prosperous as a result. They included Ahone of Russell's who went from Shanghai to Foochow to take advantage of the newly developed trade of tea; Akit, Sickqua, and Tong Loong-maw who worked closely with Heard's; and Ahee, Alum, Taising, Tonghing, and Yuntai who usually made contracts to provide Jardine's with tea at Foochow. Even the operators of tea warehouses in the interior profited.[143] They took commissions for purchasing and examining teas in the upland, and received additional fees for preparing and shipping off teas to Foochow. All these profits, in the words of George V. W. Fisher, Jardine's agent at Foochow, "should pay the keeper of the Hong handsomely."[144]

Acum, a comprador-merchant, shipped a cargo of silk to Lyons, France, via Jardine's ship in 1868 and made "¼ profit on the shipment."[145] In many cases the profits were much larger. In 1861, for instance, a Chinese could buy a picul (a bale) of silk at the Shanghai market for $360. The freight and insurance to ship it to Marseilles totaled about $30. As the silk price in Marseilles was $575 a picul, he made $185, and his profit rate was 47 percent for a period of six to nine months.[146] This profitability was unchanged in the seventies.[147] Actual-

---

142. Ibid., p. 31.

143. Ibid., pp. 30–31.

144. One of the operators was Awy whose tea hongs made handsome profits: "I see no reason why things should not go on perfectly smooth at the Hong, for I have told Awy that half the commission of all teas bought, where there is any, for sometimes when the Teamen are very firm it is settled without commission, is to go towards the expenses of the Hong, which with the difference between the Canton weight, paid into the Hong for the payment of Teas, & the Foochow weight, paid to the Teamen as is custom here, amounting to fully $20 per box of $5,000 besides the $5 per 100 packages paid for examining & shipping off, & the profit on the marking papers should pay the keeper of the Hong handsomely" (Fisher [Foochow] to Joseph Jardine [Hong Kong], May 4, 1856, JMA).

145. Memoranda, May 1868, JMA. See also F. B. Johnson (Shanghai) to William Keswick (Hong Kong), May 10, 1868, JMA.

146. James Whittall (Shanghai) to Jardine, Matheson & Co. (Hong Kong), Jan. 24, 1861, JMA.

147. Kai Cheong-loong (Hong Kong) to Jardine Matheson, May 29, 1874, JMA.

ly, his profits could be larger, because he could (and many Chinese merchants did) buy silk directly from the silk districts of Chekiang and
Kiangsu where the price was lower (around $250) than in Shanghai and
ship the silk to London where the price was higher (about $600) than in
southern France. Therefore, he could realize an annual profit of 65 percent of capital invested.

The Ch'ing government seriously considered contracting with American merchants to supply rice to Peking during the last months of 1860,
when the traditional grain-tributary routes were disrupted by the Taiping Rebellion, the Sino-British War, and the shift of the Yellow River
channels. Thanks to neutrality, fast speed, and modern armament,
American shipping was by and large safe from the British, rebels, and
pirates. In response to the proposal of the Ch'ing government, A. F.
Heard of Augustine Heard & Co. and Edward Cunningham of Russell
& Co. worked out a joint plan in December. It specified that each house,
by placing cash advances of $600,000 to $700,000, would purchase one
million piculs of rice from the major ports of Southeast Asia and ship it
to Tientsin, to be picked up by Chinese junks. Through careful calculations on rice prices, freight charges, insurance costs, exchange rates, and
expenses of Chinese staff, it turned out that each firm would need a little
more than $1,000,000 of capital, with 60 to 70 percent of it being placed
as cash advances in order to secure rice. The joint profits would be about
$1,200,000;[148] the operation would thus yield a handsome profit of about
50 percent. That the rice trade was profitable in the mid-nineteenth century was further attested to by some high Ch'ing officials, for example,
Shen Pao-chen, governor of Fukien, pointed out in a memorial of 1862
that Chinese and foreign merchants made a handsome profit by trading
rice between Southeast Asia and the provinces of Kwangtung and
Fukien.[149]

QUICK PROFITS

That large and quick profits resulted from the coastal trade was borne
out by the fact that a great number of merchants on the coast rose "from
rags to riches" and accumulated a considerable amount of wealth in a
short period of time. Actually, many of them, by their own account, had
made and lost several fortunes in this lucrative and unstable coastal

148. A. F. Heard (Shanghai) to John Heard (Hong Kong), Jan. 21, 1861, EA-1, HC.
The managing partners of Heard's and Russell's in Hong Kong later vetoed the plan
because it involved too much risk. See also Lockwood, pp. 81–84.
149. *Shen Wen-su-kung cheng-shu*, 1:24.

trade. Indeed, they became rich so fast that they were frequently referred to as the "quick-fortune-makers" (*k'uai-fa-ts'ai*).[150]

This was true not only for the newly rising merchants under the treaty system, but also for some of the rich hong merchants. Although a few, like Houqua, inherited family wealth to a certain extent, most assembled their fortunes in their own lifetime. One case in point was Kingqua (Liang Ching-kuo, 1761–1837) of Canton. His father, a village teacher, died in 1767 when Kingqua was six years old, and the destitute family of four could hardly make a living. At such a tender age, he peddled in the daytime and helped his mother in weaving at night. When he grew up he went out to earn a living as a hired laborer and for more than ten years worked as a clerk and then as manager of a hong merchant. He was loyal, honest, and hardworking. Finally he himself became a hong merchant in 1808, and the amount of tea he sold increased more than threefold in the sixteen years from 1811 to 1827. He thus accumulated a sizable fortune. After becoming rich, he made successive monetary contributions to the state and eventually purchased the title of intendant, the highest rank money could buy. He served as a hong merchant for nineteen years and retired in 1827.[151]

Thanks to Hsu Jun's autobiography, we know in considerable detail the rapid rise of this noted Cantonese merchant. Going to Shanghai in 1852 at the age of fourteen, he worked for sixteen years in the British house of Dent, Beale & Co., first as an apprentice and then as a comprador. As we discussed in chapter 8, by 1859 Hsu had begun investing, and he operated many enterprises, including native banks, real estate, and various shops dealing in tea, silk, cloth, and other kinds of produce. By November 1883 he was one of the richest businessmen in Shanghai (table 13). The *North-China Herald* reported in August 1883 that the average income of a peasant was about 15 dollars per annum;[152] thus Hsu's assets were equivalent to the annual income of about 316,000 peasants, and his net worth, that of 82,150 peasants.

Hsu's counterpart on the southern coast was Ho Tung who, though a native of Canton, lived and did business in Hong Kong for most of his life. His father died when he was young, and the family was so impover-

---

150. *Shang-hai ch'ien-chuang*, p. 29.
151. Liang Chia-pin, *Shih-san hang*, pp. 261–66; and Ping-ti Ho, *The Ladder of Success in Imperial China* (New York, 1962), pp. 299–301. Kingqua sold 7,000 chests of tea in 1811, 12,000 chests in 1816, 16,500 chests in 1821, and 22,834 chests in 1827 (Morse, *Chronicles*, III, 159, 191, 207, 244, 313, 350, 371; IV, 9, 72, 147).
152. *NCH*, Aug. 3, 1883.

TABLE 13.   HSU JUN'S FINANCES, NOVEMBER 1883
(TAELS)

Assets	
Real estate	2,236,940
Stocks	426,912
Pawnshops	348,571
Accounts receivable secured by stocks	397,000
Total	3,409,423
Liabilities	
Native bank loans	1,052,500
Loans secured by stocks	419,920
Loans secured by real estate	720,118
Individual loans	329,709
Total	2,522,247
Net Worth	887,176

Source: Hsu Jun, *Nien-p'u*, pp. 2b, 5b, 34–35b.

ished that it could not afford to send him to school. He nevertheless managed to learn some pidgin English on his own. From 1879 he worked as a clerk in the Chinese Maritime Customs at Canton, and in 1883 he became the comprador to Jardine's at Hong Kong, a post that he held for seven years. At the age of thirty, he was already a millionaire. His businesses included shipping, insurance, real estate, and foreign trade. In the early twentieth century, he was the director of eighteen of the leading companies in Hong Kong and Shanghai, and chairman and largest shareholder of a number of them.[153]

The Chekiang merchants also benefited from coastal trade quickly, as exemplified by four colorful merchants. In the mid-forties Takee went from Ningpo to Shanghai where he started as a poor laborer but gradually engaged in business in his own right, especially in the silk trade. His shrewdness and the ample opportunities for profit making on the coast made him almost a millionaire in less than two decades. He was particularly noted in Shanghai for the quickness with which he acquired

153. Wu Hsing-lien, *Hsiang-kang Hua-jen ming-jen shih-lueh* (Hong Kong, 1937), I, 2–3; and Wright, *Impressions*, p. 176.

his fortune.[154] Another Chekiang merchant who made extremely large profits from the silk trade was Chun Yuechong (Choping, Ch'en Chup'ing). Coming to Shanghai destitute in the early fifties,[155] he accumulated wealth so fast that he became a man of means by 1862. A. F. Heard wrote of him from Shanghai on April 18: "The sale of [steamer] *Shantung* was a great hit, as it has opened a connection with Chun Yue Chong (alias Choping) who is one of the largest [richest] men here. . . . He is a new man [of wealth] and has grown up within my recollection, in silk."[156] Another rich businessman from Chekiang was Hu Kuang-yung. Partly because of his experience in a Hangchow money shop and partly because of his close connections with high officials, he came to play a leading role in the Chinese financial world. In addition to trading in rice and silk, he set up native banks and customs banks at Shanghai, Ningpo, Hangchow, Wenchow, Foochow, Amoy, Hankow, and Peking, and became a millionaire by 1883.[157]

The family of Yeh Ch'eng-chung (1840–1899) had for generations been poor peasants of Chen-hai, Ningpo. In 1845 his father died, leaving him an orphan at the age of five in an impoverished family of six. Their only property was rice land of eight *mou* (totaling 1.2 acres). Yeh had to work on the farm and in a vegetable-oil workshop in order to make a living. When he was fourteen years old, a certain Ni, an old family friend, took him to Shanghai where he was apprenticed to the trades. Through his patron's influence, he obtained a position in a grocery shop in the French concession. In 1862 he opened business on his own account, rowing a sampan on the Whangpu River to sell groceries to foreign vessels. His diligence, honesty, and, more importantly, pidgin English, all made him a successful trader. His business expanded, and he opened several branch stores. With an eye to doing more business with foreigners, he hired an English teacher to teach his employees English at night. At the end of the nineteenth century, he had six stores in Shanghai, two in Hankow, and one each in Kiukiang, Wu-hu, Chinkiang, Chefoo, Tientsin, Ying-k'ou, Ningpo, and Wen-chou, engaging in foreign trade and machine business. Meanwhile, he also operated several native banks. In the nineties he moved on from commerce to industry by establishing silk filatures and a match factory in Shanghai and Hankow.

154. Toyama Gunji, "Shanhai no shinsho Yō Bō," *Tōyōshi kenkyū*, 1.4:17–34 (Nov. 1945).
155. *Shang-hai hsien hsu-chih* (Shanghai, 1918), 21:13.
156. To Augustine Heard, Jr., Apr. 18, 1862, HL-36, HC.
157. For Hu's career, see John C. Stanley, *Late Ch'ing Finance* (Cambridge, Mass., 1961).

By the time of his death, he was reported to have accumulated a fortune of Tls. 8 million, a surprisingly large amount of money.[158]

There were also wealthy merchants in the small cities and towns. A case in point is the town of Nan-hsun in northern Chekiang, a center of silk production and trade. The rich silk merchants there were dubbed according to their wealth: an "elephant" had Tls. 1 million or more; an "ox," from Tls. 0.5 million to Tls. 1 million; and a "dog," from Tls. 300,000 to Tls. 500,000. Thus, sometime after the 1860s, the town had four elephants, eight oxen, and seventy-two dogs. With the growth of their fortunes, later on there were also two "lions," each reportedly having Tls. 10 million or more.[159]

Western businessmen refused to fall behind in the pursuit of large and quick profits along the coast. A cardinal feature of the foreign communities in the treaty ports was that they consisted mainly of merchant-adventurers whose sole aim was to amass great wealth within the shortest possible time.[160] John P. Cushing, for example, returned from Canton to Boston in 1828 at the age of forty-one, bringing home over $600,000. He then retired from business and entrusted William Sturgis to manage his funds.[161] Indeed, many of them were hard-pressed by financial difficulties at home and had to come to China in pursuit of quick profits. For example, Robert B. Forbes, after having made money by engaging in the China trade, returned to Boston in the early 1830s. His financial losses in the panic of 1837 with the failure of some enterprises (U.S. $20,000) forced him to come to Canton again in 1838.[162] He was admitted to Russell & Co. on January 1, 1839, and became the chief of that house.[163] A similar situation was true for Augustine Heard in the late 1830s. John Heard III, one of his nephews, wrote in his diary: "The cause that led my uncle to return to China was the loss of some of the money that he had brought home a few years before, through speculation, recommended by his friend R. [Robert] B. Forbes and, perhaps, others."[164]

To the Western merchants, life in China was not necessarily pleas-

158. *Shang-hai ch'ien-chuang*, p. 743; *Shang-hai hsien hsu-chih*, 21:14b; Wang Ching-yü, *Kung-yeh shih*, II, 955; and Wright, *Impressions*, p. 560. See also Ping-ti Ho, *Ladder*, pp. 308–310.

159. Liu Ta-chün, ed., *Wu-hsing nung-ts'un ching-chi*, cited in Liu Shih-chi, "Ch'ing-tai Chiang-nan shang-p'in ching-chi ti fa-chan yü shih-chen ti hsing-ch'i" (M.A. thesis, National Taiwan University, 1975), pp. 54–55. Certainly these amounts were exaggerated.

160. Rutherford Alcock, *The Capital of the Tycoon* (London, 1863), I, 37–38.

161. Larson, p. 350.

162. *Personal Reminiscences*, pp. 139–40.

163. Hunter, *Fan Kwae*, pp. 156–57.

164. Diary, p. 21, FP-4, HC.

ant; the hot, humid climate and special diseases constituted the major hardships. The profit returns on their China trade had to be attractive enough to sustain the hardships. Once their fortunes were made, they usually went home. A case in point is John Murray Forbes who was in Canton as a supercargo in 1835. Under the encouragement of Houqua, he accepted the offer to become a partner in Russell & Co. in Canton. In two years he made a handsome profit of $150,000. He then returned to Boston where he established himself as a China trader and Russell's agent, and finally became a noted entrepreneur in railroad enterprise. Other partners of Russell's were also successful; they included Samuel Russell, Philip Ammidon, John C. Green, and Joseph Coolidge in the period from 1834 to 1836.[165] They shared the firm's net profit of around $100,000 in 1834, and the profits on the entire term of partnership of 1834–1836 exceeded $400,000. The average annual profit was around $133,000, and prospects for the future were bright.[166] Russell's probably lived up to expectations, because it regularly distributed dividends in the seventies.[167]

We do not know the exact rate of return of Augustine Heard & Co., but it must have been impressive. John Heard III indicated that as a partner he was highly satisfied with what he got from the house. His diary reveals that he received an average annual profit of $50,000 in the period from 1847 to 1852,[168] and the profits drastically increased during the next five years. He wrote in his diary in 1857: "On the whole, I was very profitable, running from $180,000 to $200,000 a year."[169]

The exact rate of profit return for the coastal commerce is not known, but it is clear that the international trade was more profitable than the domestic. My estimate is that the annual profits probably constituted about 20 percent of capital invested for the interregional trade within China and 40 percent for the international trade. The average annual rate of profit for the coastal merchants was therefore around 30 percent, considerably higher than that of rural land investments—a mere 4 percent in the 1870s. Although the coastal merchants, by using legal and illegal practices, usually accumulated huge commercial profits in a relatively short period of time, they had to face political uncertainties and commercial risks of various kinds at the same time.

165. Hunter, *Fan Kwae*, p. 156.
166. Samuel Russell to Augustine Heard, Mar. 31, 1837, BM-9, HC.
167. *Shen pao*, July 3, 1875, p. 1.
168. Diary, p. 71, FP-4, HC.
169. Ibid., p. 123.

Market Risks and Uncertainties

A salient feature of commercial capitalism is the immense business risks and uncertainties that are contingent to the lush opportunities for making profit. John Samuel Swire's remarks on a British China trader in Hankow illustrate the situation: "R. Anderson informs me that he is retiring from the China trade. He has either made enough, or lost enough, to satisfy him."[1] Indeed, unlike the traditional masters of the workshop who produced only on order, or at least for customers whose tastes and demands were known in advance, the modern merchant sold goods in faraway places, to persons unknown. He had to deal with many variables, such as what products distant customers wanted, where they would sell, in what quantities, and at what price people would buy. In this kind of business, a new type of man developed—the merchant-entrepreneur—a man who had to face many political and economic uncertainties.

POLITICAL DISTURBANCES

A proper business climate is vitally important to economic development. Because Sino-Western commercial capitalism depended heavily on foreign markets as well as on upcountry purchases, political disturbances naturally affected its development, no matter whether these disturbances occurred in foreign lands, along the Chinese coast, or in the interior of China.

1. (London) to William Lang, John H. Scott, and Edwin Mackintosh (China), Sept. 1, 1882, SP.

Large-scale wars on foreign land clearly affected China's coastal economy. China's trade with Europe, for example, declined substantially
during the period of the Napoleonic wars. The American Civil War also
had a negative effect on the trade along China's coast. The business of
the gigantic British firm of Dent, Beale & Co. declined in 1864, and
worsened in 1865 and 1866. Hsu Jun, its comprador, made this observation in 1867: "After 1866 it was difficult for Dent's to make profit. Its
business in China's ports recessed partly due to the American Civil
War."[2]

China's coastal trade was also subject to the disturbances of wars with
foreign countries during the nineteenth century. From the Houqua correspondence (only recently available to scholars), it is clear that the
Opium War (1839–1842) had a detrimental effect on the coastal trade.
For one thing, it created a money shortage, as Houqua noted when he
wrote in 1841: "The operations of the British on the coast have alarmed
all trading people, and those that have money do not let it out as usual to
the shroff shops so that there is very little disposition or means for speculation in foreign goods."[3] The hong merchants were particularly hard
hit by the Opium War. In May 1841 after the season's teas had been
shipped, Captain Charles Elliott started to attack Canton, but the British force withdrew from outside of the city walls after Elliott secured a
"ransom" of $6,000,000 from the hong merchants. Houqua wrote to
John M. Forbes and Robert B. Forbes on May 11, 1842 that a sum of
$2,000,000 was "then raised by the Hong merchants and $4,000,000 provided by the Imperial Treasurer—the Poochingsze [Pu-cheng-shih],"
which the hong merchants were asked "to replace in the Treasury by
instalments." In addition, he continued:

The Hong merchants have been called upon to subscribe heavily during the
past ten months for the purpose of erecting fortifications, building war junks,
casting cannons and organizing troops, which, added to the large amount required to be paid from annual dividends on the estates of Hongtai, Monqua,
Kingqua, and Siuqua, made an aggregate of a very heavy burthen of which not a
small share falls upon my poor old shoulder.[4]

Complaining about the additional sufferings of the hong merchants

2. *Nien-p'u*, p. 14.
3. (Canton) to Forbes (Boston), Nov. 22, 1841, HLB.
4. (Canton) to J. M. and R. B. Forbes (Boston), HLB.

because of the war, Houqua again wrote the Forbes brothers on April 5, 1843:

The Hong merchants are to be done away with in July and in the meantime the Authorities are forcing us to pay up the old debts of Hingtai and Kingqua (which were agreed to be paid off in annual instalments). One million has been paid within three months and two millions remain to be paid by the first of July. Besides, the mandarins claim the Canton ransom money and about five millions more. So you see we have plenty of trouble and no cheering prospect ahead.[5]

Among hong merchants, Houqua probably suffered the most. The decline of the princely merchant Houqua during the Opium War clearly illustrates how military operations could damage the business of the merchants. Houqua wrote in 1840 to his American friends in Boston and New York, worrying about the long-range effect of the war on the Canton trade: "I very much fear that it will be a long time before the dispute is settled and trade allowed to go on regularly." He was correct, for he wrote to John M. Forbes the next year, expressing his unhappiness with the war: "The English business [Opium War] makes me very unhappy; it has caused me the loss of a great deal of money, and as every day it is becoming complicated and extended, I do not know when it will be settled."[6]

Houqua's private trade with the outside world virtually stopped during the Opium War. Although American merchants could continue their business, Houqua was so deeply troubled by officials that he refrained from doing business through his American friends altogether. In writing to John C. Green, who handled Houqua's silk in New York, Houqua gave this direction in the summer of 1840: "When proceeds are realized, please remit the same to Russell & Co. in such a way as I may deem best, avoiding merchandise."[7] Meanwhile, he wrote to John M. Forbes to take good care of his investments abroad:

I have now a large amount of funds in America and Europe of which you must take the best care you can. Place them in safety and where they will be productive of interest. After this British business [Opium War] is settled, send all my funds back to China to my friends, Russell and Company, in Hard Dollars or bills on Bengal, whichever you think may be best for me. If any accident should occur to me by which I may be prevented from giving instructions regard-

5. Ibid.
6. (Canton) to J. M. Forbes (Boston), June 28, 1840 and Oct. 4, 1841, HLB. See also Houqua's letters to John C. Green (New York), May 31, 1840, and J. P. Cushing (Boston), June 1, 1840, HLB.
7. (Canton) to Green, July 5, 1840, HLB.

ing the management and disposition of my property in Europe and America, my agents, Russell and Company, will have my full authority to act as they may think best for and in behalf of myself or my heirs.[8]

Houqua was afraid that he might be imprisoned or even executed by the Ch'ing officials during the war. Indeed, he was so frustrated by the war that he contemplated withdrawing completely from international trade after the war.

When the war came to an end, Houqua understandably expressed his delight, even though he had lost over $2,000,000 because of the conflict. He wrote to W. H. C. Plowden of London: "In the attack on Canton of May 1841, I had a pack house destroyed with eight laks [$800,000] of property, and I paid eight laks of the Canton ransom money, and my losses altogether by the war are over two millions of dollars. . . . I have reason to feel glad that the war is ended."[9] According to the Treaty of Nanking, signed on August 29, 1842, Cohong was to be abolished. Houqua wrote to the Forbes brothers on April 5, 1843, directing them to pursue a "more extensive sale of teas, especially of those remaining of shipments in 1841 of which I wish to see the final account. The sale of my tea generally I must leave to your direction. My own idea is that when a fair profit can be had, it will be best to sell."[10] Now, perhaps for the first time in his entire life, he wanted to limit his business, rather than expand.

The Opium War not only brought physical damage to some of Houqua's property but also resulted in extra expenses. As the Ch'ing government was in need of immense sums of money, Houqua came to bear the brunt of mandarin exactions because the delicate balance of the Cohong system was upset. In 1841, for example, he paid to the officials a total of about $2,000,000 (Spanish), some $1,100,000 of this sum being his personal contribution to the "ransom" of Canton. Before his death in August 1843, Ch'ing officials also succeeded in extorting from Houqua and the other hong merchants at Canton another $1,000,000.[11] The second Sino-British War inflicted further damages on Houqua's family, whose extensive buildings and shops in the Canton factory site were utterly destroyed by fire in December 1856 as a result of the war.[12]

8. (Canton) to J. M. Forbes (Boston), June 28, 1840, HLB.
9. (Canton) to Plowden (East India House, London), Apr. 2, 1843, HLB. He mentioned his losses earlier to J. P. Cushing on Nov. 21, 1841.
10. (Canton) to J. M. and R. B. Forbes (Boston), Apr. 5, 1843, HLB.
11. Kwang-Ching Liu, "Houqua: The Sources and Disposition of His Wealth," pp. 9–10.
12. Ibid., p. 12.

In 1883 the Sino-French conflict over Annam touched off a financial crisis at Shanghai in which many prominent merchants went bankrupt, as we will see in detail in chapter 11. During the first Sino-Japanese War of 1894–1895, the money market was tight at Shanghai, with only 13 million taels in circulation.[13] Furthermore, the foreign community in that city believed that, in view of a possible rebellion in China, a great disturbance of the tea trade might take place.[14]

Even though China's treaty ports were relatively free from the direct influence of internal political disturbances, they were indirectly affected. Coastal commerce relied heavily on the interior for both the sale of imported goods and the supply of produce for export, and political disturbances and social unrest in the interior inhibited the development of commercial capitalism on the coast in general. The internal disturbance that most severely affected China's commerce was the Taiping uprising from 1850 to 1864. According to Rev. I. J. Roberts, the religious teacher of Hung Hsiu-ch'uan, the Taiping leader was against commerce. Commenting on Hung, Roberts wrote from Nanking in 1862: "He is opposed to commerce, having had more than a dozen of his own people murdered since I have been here, for no other reason than trading in the city, and has promptly repelled every foreign effort to establish lawful commerce here among them, whether inside the city or outside."[15]

The general destruction of the Taiping Rebellion can vividly be seen from the eyewitness account of the American merchant John Heard III. Starting from Shanghai on April 11, 1861, he took a business trip up the Yangtze and found that the cities along the river were either destroyed, like Chinkiang, or deserted, like Nanking. He first visited Chinkiang: "This was the first of the new ports and we were anxious to see what it amounted to. Alas! What a failure! It was one of the saddest I have ever seen. The place was destroyed and redestroyed by the Rebels, and the whole population at this time consisted of a few hundred vagabonds of the lowest and most filthy description."[16] This miserable situation was only slightly improved by 1862, as a British report stated: "The present condition of this port is melancholy indeed. . . . One very inferior street and a most squalid suburb still constitute Chinkiang."[17] In fact, the port

13. Hsu Jun, *Nien-p'u*, p. 82.
14. FO 405/65.
15. FO 17/377, p. 101. After staying with the Taipings in Nanking for fifteen months, Rev. Roberts began to disagree with them.
16. FP-2, HC.
17. Report by A. Adkins in 1862, cited in report of C. F. Allen, Assistant in Charge, Chinkiang, May 20, 1869, FO 17/531, p. 2.

did not substantially recover from the Taiping disturbance until 1869.[18]
The ports on the upper Yangtze were no exception. Heard described
the scene of Kiukiang during his trip up the Yangtze:

The chief impression remaining in my mind from the trip is the desolation
caused by the Great Rebellion. The cities on the banks of the river were only
masses of ruin. Kiukiang I recollect distinctly. Only one or two houses stood on
the main street which ran through the town. All the rest were gone, and the
people, too, had disappeared. Here and there an old man crawled about, and
tried to find the site of the house where he had lived.[19]

He complained about the difficulty of doing business, as the people had
not come back for fear of the rebels, and the remaining residents took
goods in barter only. This was no surprise because, as Heard put it, "the
wretches won't buy."[20]

Water transportation was likewise affected. Commercial vessels were
seized by both the government and the Taipings for military purposes.
A. G. Dallas of Jardine's wrote on September 15, 1852, concerning government activities: "There is a stoppage [of business] at Hangchow from
want of boats. The Government now requires them to send to Hunan
(not Honan) with troops, where it is said, & I believe with truth, that the
Rebels are making great progress."[21] This was also the case with the
Taipings. Joseph Jardine wrote from Canton on January 7, 1855: "The
rebels have taken a large number of Imperialist junks (30 to 40) near to
[sic] Whampoa.... The Chinamen are very anxious that foreigners
should interfere. Tungmow the shroff had, I understand, some 3 or 4
junks among them, which he used to send formerly to Namoa."[22] Tributary rice transportation through the Grand Canal was disrupted when
the Taipings occupied Chekiang and Kiangsu in the mid-1850s. For a
time the tributary rice was transported by sea, but even this arrangement was interrupted in 1853–1854 when Shanghai was occupied by the
members of the Small Sword Society. Sea transportation was again suspended in 1861–1863 during the last days of the Taiping uprising, and
the food supply to Peking had to be temporarily transported by foreign
vessels.[23]

By 1853 the Taiping Rebellion had completely demoralized the trade

18. Ibid.
19. FP-3, p. 11, HC.
20. Ibid.
21. (Shanghai) to David Jardine (Hong Kong), JMA.
22. To David Jardine (Hong Kong), JMA.
23. Chang Che-lang, *Ch'ing-tai ti ts'ao-yun* (Taipei, 1969), pp. 68, 70.

of Shanghai. On March 3 Rutherford Alcock reported that "at the bare supposition of Nanking being taken, trade is at a stop."[24] George Bonham found eight days later "a kind of panic amongst the Chinese merchants and traders, . . . [and] there is at present little or no business carried on and money is very scarce."[25] On the scarcity of silver due to the Taipings, Alexander Perceval wrote from Shanghai in 1856 that the price of silver in terms of copper coins would be sharply higher.[26] The rebellion also affected industry. Coal mining in Kwangtung was at a standstill during the Taiping disturbance, because of the departure of most businessmen.[27]

The indirect effects of the Taiping uprising were equally detrimental to China's commerce. To meet the financial crisis, a small tax on merchants and traders was instituted in 1853, which became known as likin. It hampered commerce because it was collected on trade of articles of consumption, being levied either as a transit tax on goods as they passed a likin barrier or as a sales tax on the shops where the goods were sold. As for the Taipings, A. F. Heard wrote in 1861: "The Rebels are establishing fixed taxes & in addition the imperialists are enforcing theirs so that produce is well sweated before it can reach Shanghai."[28] We are not sure whether or not the Taipings levied likin in the same manner as did the Ch'ing government, but they nevertheless imposed taxes on commerce in certain ways.

One consequence of the new taxes on commerce was an increase in the cost of living in China in general and in the treaty ports in particular. James Whittall was forced to raise the salary of Jardine's clerks at Shanghai in October 1862. He reported this change to the head office at Hong Kong: "In the account current you will notice that you are debited with T. 100 for the Remedios salary instead of T. 80 as formerly. I raised the above on account of the great expense of living here, which has much increased of late."[29]

Another indirect effect of the Taiping Rebellion on business conditions in the treaty ports was a wide range of fluctuation in real estate values. To escape from the Taipings, a great number of well-to-do Chinese swarmed to Shanghai in the 1850s and early 1860s. This sudden increase in population prompted many Chinese merchants to invest in

24. FO 17/200.
25. Ibid.
26. To Joseph Jardine (Hong Kong), June 10, 1856, JMA.
27. *Kuang-tung ts'ai-cheng shuo-ming-shu*, 5:22b.
28. (Shanghai) to Charles Fearon, June 3, 1861, HL-35, HC.
29. To Jardine, Matheson & Co., Oct. 4, 1862, JMA.

real estate, and they profited from it soon afterward. But the suppression of the uprising in 1865 caused them tremendous losses on their speculation. Charles A. Winchester, British consul at Shanghai, reported on March 16, 1866: "Probably no year ever opened on the trade of this port with gloomier prospects than 1865. The vast exodus of Chinese after the defeat of the rebels had left stranded in serious difficulties many traders, whom the enormous return yielded by Chinese houses had induced to embark their own, and such funds as they could raise, in real estate."[30]

Besides the Taipings, China's coastal commerce was influenced in various ways by other internal disturbances, such as the Triads, the Nien Rebellion, and the Boxers. In 1853, on the eve of the insurgency of the Small Sword Society, the Shanghai market was notably affected. Hoarding of the Carolus (Spanish) dollar and the lack of demand for foreign manufactured goods caused severe monetary stringency. Even the opium market was upset and soon was reduced to a barter basis. Five of the leading British houses at Shanghai complained that the illiquid market retarded the sale of imports, resulting in the detention of several seabound ships.[31] In his report to the Foreign Office on April 12, 1860, Charles A. Winchester, British consul at Canton, mentioned that because of the disturbance of the Triads, "trade has again almost stopped."[32] In his next report eleven days later, he stressed "the peculiar sensibility of commerce in this country [China] to disturbing political causes."[33]

As regards the Nien Rebellion, W. H. Medhurst, British consul at Hankow, reported in 1866: "Another important source of hindrance in the way of the commercial progress of this port may be traced to the periodical visits to which it is subjected by rebellious and disaffected bodies of men." They induced timidity and distrust in the minds of the people and discouraged the influx into the market of the native capital. He concluded that "a convincing proof of this effect is given in the diminished sales of grey shirtings for the three months which have elapsed since the Nienfei commenced to annoy us."[34] The Boxer uprising of 1900 also brought about a general business depression in China. At that time, Hsu Shu-p'ing (Chu Sok Pin), son of the noted merchant Hsu Jun, was a comprador to a German firm at Shanghai that engaged in shipping,

30. BPP, *Commercial Reports from Her Majesty's Consuls in China, Japan, and Siam, 1865*, vol. 71, p. 54.
31. Quoted in R. Alcock to British Community, Mar. 10, 1853, FO 17/204.
32. FO 17/340.
33. Ibid., Apr. 23, 1860.
34. Mar. 3, 1866, FO 17/456.

import, and export business. This depression caused the firm "heavy losses," and Hsu personally "suffered to the extent of $500,000."[35]

THE INFLUENCE OF WARS ON FOREIGN TRADE

If it was true that military operations were detrimental to commercial development in general, their negative influence on foreign trade was even more marked. The compradors—the bridge between foreign merchants and Chinese commerce—were usually prohibited by the Manchu government to serve in the firms of the particular country with which China was having a war.[36] In the same vein, the internal disturbances might put the compradors and their staffs in such a panic that many would desert their foreign employers. A. F. Heard wrote on September 4, 1860, when the Taipings were threatening Shanghai: "The only way I could keep the tea boy [in the firm] was by telling him that I would shoot him if I saw him out."[37] This was also the case with the Chinese cooks, coolies, and shroffs.

It was not always easy for the Chinese merchants to sell imported goods, especially during times of war. Houqua mentioned this problem in November 1841 when the Opium War was in progress: "I have about 8 lacks [$800,000] of cargo (England goods) on hand, which I fear I shall not be able to realize for a long time to come."[38] The import trade was generally disorganized during the period of the Taiping Rebellion,[39] which reduced the Chinese demand for all imports. The junkmen who shipped foreign goods inland on the Yangtze were discouraged from placing orders for imported cottons for fear of Taiping piracy and foreign blockades. Many American firms, including Heard's and Russell's, were overstocked with unsalable cotton goods.[40] A resolution passed at the meeting of the Shanghai British Chamber of Commerce on February 24, 1862, stated that the ongoing stagnation of the import trade at Shanghai was "directly attributable to the presence of the Taepings in this province."[41] The remark of A. F. Heard about the Taipings in 1860 summed up the feelings of the foreign merchants: "I think it would be

---

35. Wright, *Impressions*, p. 566.
36. Yen-p'ing Hao, *Comprador*, pp. 194–195.
37. To John Heard III (Hong Kong), HL-16, HC.
38. (Canton) to R. B. Forbes (Boston), Nov. 22, 1841, HLB.
39. For 1853–1859, see Morse, *Conflict*, pp. 464–66.
40. A. F. Heard (Shanghai) to John Heard III (Hong Kong), May 10, 1862, HL-16, HC.
41. FO 405/8, p. 44.

better for the benefit of China and humanity, to say nothing of cotton goods, to exterminate the whole party."[42] Jardine papers indicate that the Tientsin massacre of 1870 was detrimental to the piece goods market not only in Tientsin, but also in the Yangtze ports, especially Hankow.[43]

As to native goods for export, its amount and value slightly increased during the years of the Taiping disturbance,[44] but the increase would probably have been greater if there had been no war. One visible effect of the war on China's export trade was that the prices and supplies of tea and silk were uncertain and irregular. On two accounts, the Taiping uprising changed the way in which tea was transported from the interior to the treaty ports for export. First, during the early years of the uprising, instead of taking the dangerous way by the Yangtze, tea was transported by road over the mountains from Anhwei, Kiangsi, Fukien, and Chekiang, until it finally reached Shanghai. Second, as mentioned in chapter 6, Foochow became a significant port for the export of tea after 1854. The export of tea from Shanghai in the season of 1852 was about 60 million pounds and increased to 69 million pounds in the next season. However, it declined to 50 million pounds in 1854 and 39 million pounds in 1859.[45] On the other hand, the export of tea from Foochow rose from 15.7 million pounds in 1855 to 40 million pounds in 1860 (table 14).

The Taiping Rebellion caused a tightening of credit in the cities and a destruction of crops in the interior—two conditions that were detrimental to the export trade. When Taiping expansion reached the Yangtze delta in the late fifties and the early sixties, the tea trade was conspicuously disrupted. A. F. Heard wrote from Shanghai in 1860 that numerous teamen "withdrew from the trade" as the native banks tightened credit. The "usual facilities were unavailable," and the practice of "native exchanges between Soochow, Hangchow and Kiating [Chiating]" was disrupted, with about half of the tea hongs being occupied.[46] He again wrote about this region in 1861: "The internal business of these provinces is so disorganized, workmen have gone away, whole districts are devastated, money is buried. Dealers will not launch out as usual."[47]

The network of trade routes for purchasing native produce was similarly damaged. Ahee was purchasing tea for Jardine's in the Bohea tea districts in the 1850s. In April 1856, in his letters to George V. W.

42. (Shanghai) to John Heard (Ipswich, Mass.), Sept. 13, 1860, HL-34, HC.
43. Henry Beveridge (Hankow) to F. B. Johnson (Shanghai), July 2, 1870, JMA.
44. Morse, *Conflict*, pp. 464–66.
45. Ibid., p. 466.
46. To John Heard III (Hong Kong), July 16, 1860, HL-16, HC.
47. To Charles Fearon, Mar. 5, 1861, HL-35, HC.

TABLE 14.   TEA EXPORTS FROM SHANGHAI AND FOOCHOW,
1855–1860
(MILLION POUNDS)

	Shanghai		Foochow		Total
	Amount	*Percent*	*Amount*	*Percent*	
1855	80.2	84	15.7	16	95.9
1856	59.3	59	41	41	100.3
1857	41	56	32	44	73
1858	51	65	28	35	79
1859	39	46	46.5	54	85.5
1860	53.5	57	40	43	93.5
Total	324	61	203.2	39	527.2

Source: Morse, *Conflict*, p. 466. Calculations are mine.

Fisher, Jardine's agent at Foochow, he expressed his concerns for the disturbances in the surrounding provinces.[48] The situation deteriorated in mid-May, as Fisher reported to Joseph Jardine, the firm's head at Hong Kong, on May 17, 1856: "Just now Ahee says Ningchow, Moning, Oonam & Oopack are overrun with rebels and any man [dealing in tea] is afraid to go there."[49] In the early 1860s Ahee was replaced by Taising. On August 29, 1861, Taising reported from the interior of Fukien to M. A. Macleod, Jardine's new agent at Foochow: "At Hohow there is still nothing to be done, as the rebels continue there in force."[50]

In reply to the inquiry of the British consul at Shanghai, Edward Webb (partner in Dent's and chairman of Shanghai Chamber of Commerce) in March 1862 dwelt on the effect of the Taipings on the export of silk and tea from Shanghai. As regards silk, Webb stated that, even though the short distance between the silk country and Shanghai favored the transport of the product, nevertheless "many [silk] boats have been robbed" by the rebels, and "in other cases large sums have been paid as ransom." Meanwhile, "the imperial authorities, professing to need money to meet their military expenditure, levy heavy inland taxes upon the silk." Both added significantly to the cost of silk, and "the

48. Fisher (Foochow) to Joseph Jardine (Hong Kong), May 1, 1856, JMA.
49. Ibid., May 17, 1856.
50. (Sueykut) to Macleod, Aug. 29, 1861, JMA.

export has thus fallen off some 14,000 bales as compared with the same period the preceding season." But the prospect of the next season was even gloomier, as the Taipings occupied such important silk centers as Nantsin [Nan-hsin], Chen-tse, and Ling-hu. Webb continued: "Nantsin, the center of the silk trade, has been burnt and was occupied several times by the Rebels and no doubt a considerable quantity of seed has been lost." Furthermore, the coming crop might be affected in two ways: "either by the Rebels cutting down the mulberry trees to use as fuel or by their marauding parties plundering and destroying the villages at the time of hatching the seed."[51] Unfortunately, Webb's prediction proved to be true. Silk production was in fact reduced during the next few years, because many mulberry trees were felled during the Taiping uprising.[52]

With reference to tea, Webb noted that, as none was grown near Shanghai, the Taipings "prevented it altogether from arriving by any of the inland routes.... No tea has been brought to this port since the early part of 1860 when the rebels captured Soochow and Karhing [Chiahsing] excepting what was sent here from Ningpo and what since last April has come down the Yangtze." As Ningpo was soon lost, the green teas of the P'ing-hu districts could not be brought in. The black teas from Ningchow and Ho-k'ou could only come by way of the Yangtze. Thus, Shanghai depended completely on the Yangtze for the supply of tea. Webb concluded: "If the rebels should carry out their expressed intention of taking the river ports of Hankow and Kiukiang, not a chest of tea of any kind can come into Shanghai." As to the next season, he was also pessimistic: "The Hokou country and large portion of the Ningchow have been devastated by the rebels and the destructions of the tea hongs and scattering of the peasantry will of course lessen the production."[53] The prospect was indeed dismal.

During 1865, the first year after the suppression of the Taiping Rebellion, business was not necessarily profitable either. Charles A. Winchester, British consul at Shanghai, reported that the reopening of the Yangtze tea districts, coupled with the sluggish market in the United States due to the Civil War, resulted in an unusually large amount of tea ex-

51. To W. H. Medhurst, Shanghai, Mar. 18, 1862, FO 17/377, pp. 145–46.
52. The *Hong Kong Daily Press* reported on Feb. 10, 1856: "Trade was seldom or ever so bad in China as it is at the present moment . . . and there appears to be a fatality attending commerce at present. Raw silk, to begin with. The supply of China has fallen off materially, and there does not appear to be much chance of it recovering itself. The reason undoubtedly is that during the Taiping occupation of the provinces of Kiangsu and Chekiang, fuel became very scarce, and the mulberry trees were felled for culinary purposes."
53. To W. H. Medhurst, Shanghai, Mar. 18, 1862, FO 17/377, p. 146.

ported to England that year, and "a rapid fall in home prices was the consequence."[54] This situation had a striking effect on Chinese and Western merchants in Shanghai, as Winchester continued:

Mercantile houses of world-wide reputation were reported to have sustained enormous losses, . . . [and] the fortunes made by former generations of merchant princes were to be called out. The expression of men's faces was sombre and depressed. Exchange fell because sellers could see no way to the profitable employment of their funds. Freights went down so low as 30 s. [shillings] a ton for tea. . . . The port was rapidly deserted by its mercantile fleet; and the crowd of storekeepers and artisans, foreign and Chinese, supported by its presence, soon became straitened in their business operation.[55]

It was indeed ironic that the coastal businessmen should have incurred huge losses at the same time that China's commerce began to recover from political disturbances.

MARKET FLUCTUATION

The price of commodities, especially that of tea, silk, and opium, in coastal regions rose and fell considerably over short periods of time. This was due, in large part, to the effect on coastal commerce of foreign factors.

PRICES OF COMMODITIES

Tea and silk, China's two most important export commodities, were no exceptions to price fluctuations. Their prices responded quickly to changes in demand and supply. In September 1852, for instance, in anticipation of a bad crop, A. G. Dallas of Jardine's stepped up the purchase of tea at Shanghai: "I am daily more confirmed in the opinion that the Crop of Tea will fall short in this quarter by 2 to 3 chops, & I am therefore extending my purchases, which I trust will be satisfactory to you. I will now require to use all the sycee on *Iona*, as well as that sent up from *Lookong*."[56] Sometimes the situation worsened, because the commodity was not purchasable at all. James Whittall of Jardine's wrote on the export of green tea from Shanghai in 1859: "Extract of a letter from Messrs. Redfern & Alexander suggests our including in the next Teas

54. Mar. 14, 1866, BPP, *Commercial Reports from Her Majesty's Consuls in China, Japan, and Siam, 1865*, vol. 71, p. 54.
55. Ibid.
56. To David Jardine (Hong Kong), Sept. 27, 1852, JMA.

shipped on their account 500 to 1000 chests of Hyson, but at present there are no Greens procurable, neither is there a prospect of obtaining any until the new season's produce comes to market."[57]

The price of green tea fell sharply at Shanghai in January 1852. As a result, many Chinese tea merchants suffered losses. The loss of Hsu Jung-ts'un, a Cantonese merchant who also was the comprador to the gigantic British firm of Dent, Beal & Co., was especially heavy. Reporting to his firm's head office at Hong Kong, Jardine's A. G. Dallas wrote on January 13, 1852: "Dent, Beale & Co.'s comprador is deeply in with teas & has a large lot of Greens in the market, upon which he must lose heavily."[58] Tea prices in the United States fell in 1857, and many American China traders lost money. Augustine Heard & Co. suffered heavily. The firm survived the crisis, as John Heard III explained: "Teas were generally losing money that year, but the business of the house was so good that it could stand much heavier losses."[59] In 1874 there was a similar case in which the low price of tea at Shanghai caused a loss of money to coastal merchants.[60]

Silk was China's second most important export commodity. The fluctuation of its price in Shanghai during the late 1840s forced Takee, a silk merchant from Ningpo, temporarily out of business in 1849. He then cooperated closely with Jardine's in securing silk from upcountry. A. G. Dallas wrote in 1849: "In my silk and other operations at this season I have been a good deal put out by the loss of Takee, the managing partner of the Man-foong Hong. . . . He is now winding up their business with the view of going himself into the silk country for a time, & to prosecute that branch almost exclusively in conjunction with us."[61] Their cooperation lasted about three years.

Prices tend to fluctuate quickly in a limited market, and the mid-century silk market along the coast is an example. When the demand did not live up to expectations, the price immediately fell. A. G. Dallas of Jardine's had this to report from Shanghai in 1852: "From various circumstances I come to the conclusion that the total export this season will not much exceed 22,000 Bs. [bales] & it may not be so much. The price is falling here, because there are few buyers at present, & holders are anxious to square their accounts."[62] There was a similar case in 1874,

57. To Jardine, Matheson & Co. (Hong Kong), June 14, 1859, JMA.
58. To David Jardine, JMA.
59. Diary, p. 132, FP-3, HC.
60. *Shen pao*, Nov. 23, 1874, p. 2.
61. To Jardine Matheson (Hong Kong), Oct. 23, 1849, JMA.
62. To David Jardine (Hong Kong), Aug. 31, 1852, JMA.

when the sudden low price of silk resulted in the loss of money to Chinese and foreign merchants alike.[63] Three years later, the British consul at Shanghai observed that the silk price in the West fell considerably due to the "overstocked European markets." Many foreign merchants lost money, but quite a few Chinese silk merchants went bankrupt. He continued: "The effects of these Chinese failures on foreign houses were severe."[64]

Some Chinese merchants at Shanghai, including the prominent silk dealer, Aleet, contracted with Jardine's to buy silk in the interior for the firm in 1869, but the price went up unexpectedly, causing a loss to the merchants. F. B. Johnson made note of this when he reported from Shanghai to the head office at Hong Kong in the summer of that year: "Aleet is buying [silk] for us in the country & reports a sudden advance from Tls. 350 to 530 [per bale]. He had only secured up to latest account, a few bales."[65] Nearly three months later, Johnson had this observation to make: "Aleet has brought down 10 bales of dear silk which he says represent the balance of our funds. I accept them but I feel they will lose heavily."[66]

Probably no market fluctuation at Shanghai in the nineteenth century was as dramatic as cotton prices in 1863. In that year British manufacturers, being unable to obtain adequate cotton from the United States due to the American Civil War, started to buy cotton from India and China. The price of cotton at Shanghai rose from its ordinary rate of Tls. 9.8 per picul to Tls. 13 in less than forty-eight hours, and to Tls. 18 within ten days. It further soared to Tls. 26 in half a month.[67] However, for reasons unknown to C. B. Robertson, British consul at Canton, the price of cotton fell considerably at that port in 1868. The consul expressed his puzzlement in a report of April 1869: "Native cotton, chiefly from the north, has fallen off considerably. It is almost impossible to account for these fluctuations, nor do we know sufficiently the economy which regulates supply and demand in China to be able to attribute them to any certain cause."[68]

With the assistance of Tong King-sing, Jardine's entered a contract in the early 1880s with a Chinese merchant at Shanghai named Lin Yew

63. *Shen pao*, July 6, 1874, p. 1.
64. BPP, *Commercial Reports of Her Majesty's Consuls in China* (1879), No. 1, Shanghai, p. 5.
65. To W. Keswick, June 10, 1869, JMA.
66. Ibid., Sept. 2, 1869.
67. Hsu Jun, *Nien-p'u*, pp. 11b–12.
68. Commercial report, Apr. 16, 1869, FO 17/533, p. 2.

Mae to purchase copper from him at a fixed price. The copper cost more in the interior, and its price fell at Shanghai; consequently, both parties suffered losses. As Lin's loss was heavier than Jardine's, he asked the firm to share his loss with him. On behalf of Lin, Tong King-sing wrote on May 13, 1884, to William Patterson, Jardine's manager at Shanghai: "He [Lin] admits that you have lost money, but says his loss is greater. . . . His loss would come to nearly Tls. 1,200. However, he is willing to accept half the difference as a compromise."[69] As it took a long time for foreign merchants to reach a settlement with an absconding Chinese debtor, Jardine's accepted the compromise.[70]

The wide range of market fluctuation was also evidenced by opium prices, especially in the early nineteenth century. The price of a chest of Patna opium varied from $550 to $1,375. The price of Malwa opium was about a third as much. These price fluctuations were due to at least five factors: the amount of Patna and Benares sold at Calcutta; the quantity and quality of Malwa exported from Bombay and Damaun; the stock of both in India and China; the activities of market speculators; and the attitude of the mandarins toward native dealers.[71]

SOME IMPORTANT REASONS

The inelastic demand for these commodities and the wide fluctuation in the supply partly accounted for the price fluctuations. Other important reasons include the complex and unstable monetary system. Chinese currency before the end of the nineteenth century was by and large a dual currency of silver and copper, but the Ch'ing government could not exert effective control over the supply of these two kinds of metal. The bimetallic monetary system thus lacked the flexibility of adjusting money supply to market demand for circulating media. Also, the traditional bimetallism lacked uniformity. In the silver sector, the silver tael was the basic money account, but taels varied in value from place to place and trade to trade.[72] H. B. Morse described the situation at Chungking:

Here the standard weight of the tael for silver transactions is 555.6 grains, and this is the standard for all transactions in which the scale is not specified. Fre-

69. JMA.
70. W. Paterson (Shanghai) to Jardine, Matheson & Co. (Hong Kong), May 18, 1884, JMA.
71. Fairbank, Trade and Diplomacy, I, 133–34.
72. For a comprehensive list of taels, see H. B. Morse, Currency, Weights, and Measures in China (Shanghai, 1906).

quently, however, a modification of the scale is provided for, depending in some cases upon the place from which the merchant comes or with which he trades, and in others upon the goods in which he deals.[73]

Meanwhile, as noted in chapter 3, silver dollars gradually found a place in the system—first by the importation of Spanish, Mexican, American, and other dollars, and then by coinage in China.[74] An examination of the quality of silver dollars in Shanghai in 1856 shows that there were several descriptions: the unexceptionables; those which would pass in ordinary transactions at Shanghai but would not be received by silkmen; those at 10, 20, and 30 percent discount; and finally the "black dollars."[75] Parallel with the silver sector was the copper or "cash" sector, which most of the people used in daily transactions. The value of copper coins varied not only with the number, but also with the quality of mix.

These silver and copper sectors were part of a bimetallic system, and their relative values were determined by market forces. Although theoretically one tael equaled one thousand copper cash coins, the price of silver in terms of cash was actually subject to both long-term and short-term influences. In the long run, the state of national security, the general factors affecting the price of copper at the mints, and the fluctuations in silver and copper prices on the world market all affected the supply and demand of silver and coins in China. In the short run, seasonal variations in the relative demand for silver vis-à-vis cash influenced the exchange rate as well. A case in point was the high price of coins in relation to silver at the end of the Chinese year. Because it was customary for the Chinese to settle all debts before the Chinese New Year Day, the rate of exchange at that time moved heavily against silver because people wanted cash coins in order to settle their accounts.[76] On some occasions, however, the price of silver against copper cash would rise, for example, during a war, when silver, being easy to store and carry, was in heavy demand. Alexander Perceval wrote from Shanghai in 1856 when the Taiping uprising reached its height: "Rebels are gaining ground. Silver in any shape will be very valuable."[77]

A major factor, which influenced the stability of China's market, was

73. Cited in John K. Fairbank, Alexander Eckstein, and Lien-sheng Yang, "Economic Change in Early Modern China," *Economic Development and Cultural Change* 9:10 (Oct. 1960).

74. King, *Money*, pp. 169–81.

75. *NCH*, Nov. 29, 1856, p. 70.

76. King, *Money*, p. 58.

77. To Joseph Jardine (Hong Kong), June 10, 1856, JMA.

the price of silver on the world market. Up to November 1935, China was the only commercially important country in the world that was on a silver standard, and world silver prices witnessed wide fluctuations after the 1870s (by which time most large nations had adopted the gold standard). The rise and fall of world silver prices, reflected unmistakably in China's foreign exchange, subjected China's foreign trade to constant vicissitudes. Sir Rutherford Alcock reported from Peking in 1868: "Now the rate of exchange of the dollars or silver in reference to Europe may be very low, while its value in cash in the interior and at the ports may be very high, owing to various causes wholly independent of foreign trade."[78] This situation caused China's commerce to be quite vulnerable to price fluctuations.

Indeed, foreign factors had a considerable effect on Chinese economy in general and coastal commerce in particular. The fluctuation of the world price of silver called the tune of the Chinese economy up to the early twentieth century. The Chinese economy was aggravated or stimulated according to the movement of silver, the fluctuation in foreign investment and commodity trade, and real estate and financial speculations. Foreign traders, bankers, and entrepreneurs in China, because of their powerful commercial, industrial, and financial interests, were responsible, in part, for the major economic actions taken under the protection of treaty privileges, without the knowledge of and free from the control of Chinese authorities.[79] A case in point was the bank notes issued by foreign banks in China during the late nineteenth century, as discussed in chapter 3.

Another reason for the unstable market was that the native banks, in terms of their own paid-up capital, usually received large deposits and made large loans. The British consul reported from Chinkiang in 1868 that there were twenty-seven native banks in that port. Their capital varied from Tls. 5,000 to Tls. 20,000, but many of the larger banks held deposits from Tls. 60,000 to Tls. 100,000.[80] The ratio of paid-up capital and deposit was even smaller in the case of the Fu-k'ang money shop at Shanghai. From 1896 to 1907, the partners of this native bank maintained an investment of only Tls. 20,000, but the deposits were large, ranging from Tls. 103,152 in 1896 to Tls. 825,123 in 1906. At the same time, the bank made equally large loans. On the average, the paid-up

78. To Foreign Office (London), May 29, 1868, FO 405/13, p. 127.
79. See Yu-kuei Cheng, *Foreign Trade and Industrial Development of China* (Washington, D.C., 1956).
80. Commercial report of C. F. Allen, Chinkiang, May 20, 1869, FO 17/531.

capital constituted a meager 5.9 percent of the deposits and 5.1 percent of the loans. (See table 15.) At the same time, one must keep in mind that the amount of paid-up capital on the books was probably less than the actual amount invested. The native banks were thus particularly vulnerable to financial crises.

As mentioned in chapter 4, native banks also received "chop loans" from foreign mercantile houses. The normal annual rate of interest of those loans was 14 percent but, under the manipulations of a comprador in a tight market, it sometimes reached as high as 28 percent.[81] China's money market was thus also affected by the availability of the chop loan. Finally, as we have seen in chapter 7, the market fluctuations on China's coast, in contrast to those in the interior, were further affected by the keen competition among the coastal merchants.[82]

SPECULATIVE TRADING

Even though many groups were active in speculative trading, the merchants along the coast were especially prone to speculation, because they were constantly exposed to a commercial milieu full of temptations. Coastal merchants, Chinese and Western alike, were often engaged in speculation, sometimes in a reckless manner. Many of them were convinced that it was more profitable to speculate than to trade in the ordinary way. Even the businessmen in industry tended to speculate.[83]

CHINESE AND WESTERN SPECULATORS

Many Chinese merchants on the coast speculated. In the early nineteenth century a comprador working under the hong merchant Houqua speculated with his foreign factory's money to the extent of $50,000 and incurred losses. After learning of this malpractice, Houqua, who was responsible for the conduct of the compradors who worked for him, immediately made up the money to the foreigners.[84] Speculative trading in commodities on China's coast became more marked after the abolish-

81. F. B. Johnson (Shanghai) to William Keswick (Hong Kong), May 20, 1868, JMA. See also *Shang-hai ch'ien-chuang*, p. 29.
82. "The suspension of business that now exists will I hope continue, but there are such sanguine people always ready to enter the market that I dare not look for a prudent course being pursued" (William Keswick [Shanghai] to James Whittall [Hong Kong], Oct. 7, 1864, JMA).
83. For Shanghai, see D. K. Lieu, *The Growth and Industrialization of Shanghai* (Shanghai, 1936), passim.
84. Connolly, *Canton*, p. 229.

TABLE 15. DEPOSITS AND LOANS OF THE FU-K'ANG MONEY SHOP, SHANGHAI, 1896–1907

(TAELS)

	Deposits	Loans			Paid-up capital		
		Unsecured	Secured	Total	Amount	As percent of deposits	As percent of loans
1896	103,152	134,766	0	134,766	20,000	19.4	14.8
1898	177,547	182,820	0	182,820	20,000	11.3	10.9
1899	318,988	371,621	0	371,621	20,000	6.3	5.4
1900	398,244	215,736	168,718	384,454	20,000	5.0	5.2
1901	432,563	395,014	0	395,014	20,000	4.6	5.1
1902	506,292	407,176	107,260	514,436	20,000	3.9	3.9
1903	547,748	340,944	485,550	826,494	20,000	3.6	2.4
1904	488,951	356,024	561,800	917,824	20,000	4.1	2.2
1905	768,041	443,578	426,734	870,312	20,000	2.6	2.3
1906	825,123	613,995	317,500	931,495	20,000	2.4	2.1
1907	817,069	539,424	501,443	1,040,867	20,000	2.4	1.9
Average	489,429	363,736	233,546	597,282	20,000	5.9	5.1

Source: Shang-hai ch'ien-chuang, pp. 774–75, 778, 780–81. Calculations are mine.
Note: The Fu-k'ang money shop was established in 1894, with a capital of Tls. 20,000. Figures for 1894, 1895, and 1897 are not available.

ment of the Cohong system in 1842. For example, the *North-China Herald*, a Shanghai newspaper, reported in May 1857 that Takee was engaging in speculative trade, "probably finding such more lucrative." Speculative trading reached its high point in the 1860s. This local newspaper commented on July 19, 1867: "Speculations for a rise or fall in the market have been carried to an extreme of rash trading, and frequent failures have been the result."[85]

Ekee, a tea merchant at Shanghai in the 1860s, did business with Jardine's. In 1867 he experienced financial difficulties that, according to Tong King-sing, were attributable to "reckless trading and speculation."[86] Ekee finally went broke at the end of that year.[87] Yowloong, Jardine's comprador at Hankow in the 1860s, privately used the firm's funds for his own speculations. In September 1867, S. I. Gower, Jardine's agent at Hankow, discovered that Yowloong had privately used the firm's capital to the extent of Tls. 74,000, which had been entrusted to his care. Gower, after having inspected the godown, "found that 3 cases white shirtings, 478 bags copper cash, 10 chests Malwa, 1 chest Patna and 1 chest Benares had been delivered without my orders, & had been taken" by Yowloong. Gower then decided to put the money in a foreign bank: "I therefore drew a cheque for Tls. 70,000 in favor of the Mercantile Bank, & this at once brought out the truth of the case, for, after great difficulty, he [Yowloong] managed, after about 3 or 4 days, to produce about Tls. 3000 in sycee & the balance of cash in [native] bankers' orders, due in 3 or 4 days up to over a month—Tls. 12,500 of which were eventually not paid at all." As a result, Yowloong went bankrupt, and some of his friends failed shortly afterward.[88]

The coastal merchants speculated not only in China, but also in Japan. In late April 1860, Augustine Heard & Co. employed a Chinese named Akow (Ch'en Yü-ch'ih) as its new comprador to serve at Yokohama, Japan.[89] John Heard was highly satisfied with Akow's ability and family background, but he worried about the possibility of his doing speculative trade. He wrote from Hong Kong on May 2, 1860: "He seems to me an active, intelligent man. . . . I don't think there is the slightest risk of dishonesty, as his family are respectable and perfectly well-known in Macao. The only danger with him is that he may lose

85. *NCH*, May 16, 1857, p. 166; and July 19, 1867, p. 153.
86. F. B. Johnson (Shanghai) to James Whittall (Hong Kong), Jan. 16, 1867, JMA.
87. Johnson to Jardine, Matheson & Co. (Hong Kong), Sept. 11, 1868, JMA.
88. "When this [fund] was suddenly withdrawn, of course they had to stop" (Gower to F. B. Johnson [Shanghai], Sept. 3, 1867, JMA).
89. For the detailed arrangements, see Yen-p'ing Hao, *Comprador*, pp. 161–62.

money by over-speculating, and this should be carefully watched over by our Agent."[90] Whereas we are not sure whether or not Akow actually conducted speculative trading in Japan, John Heard's concern was not without reason. A dispatch from Nagasaki in 1876 stated: "It is here that the Chinese are met by their weak point. Trade without speculation is as little tasteful to them as fish without sauce."[91]

The speculative disposition of the coastal Chinese was such that most foreign merchants disliked clever compradors. Asam, the comprador of Jardine's at Shanghai, had to leave the firm in 1846 because of illness.[92] Atow, a Cantonese, was sent from Canton to Shanghai to take his place. Dallas wrote: "Atow's being not too clever is in his favor. Ayoke or any other Chinaman may get on very well if he confines himself solely to brokerage business."[93] Thus, the fact that Atow was not particularly smart was, from the point of view of the foreign manager, a merit instead of a drawback.

Many Western traders on the coast also rashly speculated. For them, the China trade was generally more speculative than trade with other parts of the world. They thus assumed greater risks over longer periods of time in exchange for higher returns. William Cole of Boston aptly observed in 1860: "China offers some chances for speculation to a man with capital and knowledge."[94] Augustine Heard, after his return to Boston from Canton, still speculated in Chinese goods. He lost and went again to Canton.[95]

CONVENTIONAL AND RECKLESS SPECULATION

The simple and popular way to speculate was to buy an article inexpensively and then sell it, after having stored it for a short period of time or transported it quickly to another place, at a considerably higher price. This practice applied to both Chinese produce and foreign goods. Speculation in opium was a common practice for the coastal merchants. One of them was Ah-fun, who bought opium at Shanghai during the 1860s when the price was low and sold it when its supply decreased.[96]

90. To A. F. Heard (Shanghai), HM-5, HC.
91. *NCH*, Feb. 13, 1876, p. 90.
92. A. G. Dallas (Shanghai) to Donald Matheson (Hong Kong), Mar. 21, 1846, JMA.
93. Ibid., May 9, 1846.
94. To F. G. Dexter, June 10, 1860, DP.
95. "The cause that led my uncle [Augustine Heard] to return to China were [*sic*] the loss of some of the money that he had brought home a few years before, through speculation recommended by his friend R. B. Forbes" (John Heard III, Diary, p. 21, FP-4, HC).
96. *NCH*, Jan. 8, 1867, p. 348, and July 19, 1867, p. 153.

Some of Ah-fun's fellow townsmen, however, bought opium from foreign vessels anchoring at Woosung and immediately reshipped it to the northern and Yangtze ports for sale before the article could be transported there by the foreign merchants themselves. James Whittall of Jardine's commented on the firm's opium business at Shanghai in 1863: "Hitherto a considerable business has been done by the Chinese speculators on the spot for resshipment to Tientsin, Hankow &c [etc.] which interfered with our trade at these ports, especially the Yangtze ones."[97]

Speculation in Chinese products was even more common. For one thing, the readily available goods on the market tempted the trader to speculate. The *North-China Herald* recorded in 1865: "The enormous quality of native produce has poured from every province into the great central market of Hankow . . . renders speculation rife, and presents an irresistible temptation to the enterprising Chinese mind."[98] Many Chinese merchants speculated in cotton, especially during the 1860s. As mentioned before, English manufacturers, unable to obtain adequate cotton from the United States during the Civil War, stepped up their purchase of cotton from other parts of the world, including China. In addition to exporting cotton from China on their own account, Jardine's also served as the agent for some Chinese merchants in Shanghai who similarly shipped cotton to the Liverpool market. This cooperation helped to bring Jardine's into close contact with a group of Chinese merchants willing to speculate in foreign trade. They were regular customers of the Ewo native bank, which, as we have seen in chapter 7, was established by Jardine's, Ekee, and other Chinese merchants in 1865. In 1864 one Chinese merchant at Shanghai, "being of a speculative disposition, dealt largely in cotton. . . . He, on one occasion, bought a large quantity from Liu Chow-fan, which he resold" to foreign merchants.[99]

Speculation in tea and silk by Chinese and Western merchants on China's coast after the 1860s was caused mainly by the tremendous demand on the foreign markets during the early season of each year.[100] Regarding this factor, W. H. Medhurst, British consul at Shanghai, reported in 1869: "The exceptional prices paid in the home markets for the early cargoes of each season's tea and silk has had its natural effect in inducing a spirit of reckless speculation out here when the first arrivals of produce are placed on the market . . . bringing about an enhancement of

97. To Alexander Perceval (Hong Kong), Mar. 30, 1863, JMA.
98. *NCH*, Sept. 16, 1865, p. 146.
99. *NCH*, Apr. 16, 1864, p. 62. This was observed by an eyewitness, a Prussian merchant in Shanghai.
100. *NCH*, May 6, 1867, p. 51.

value." Meanwhile, "enormous supplies" were "hurried forward" to the British markets, which became "in a few months so overstocked that they never recover for the remainder of the year." The consequence obviously was "positive loss for the mass of speculators."[101]

The speculation in silk was usually conducted by rich Chinese, as Alexander Perceval of Jardine's wrote from Shanghai in 1856: "The Chinese talk of 70,000 bales for export and I see no reason why it should not be more unless the scarcity of dollars forces prices down below what the rich Chinese consider safe to purchase on speculation."[102] Similarly, A. F. Heard wrote about Choping from Shanghai in 1862: "He has grown up in *silk* and all the wealthy men here are *silk* men."[103] The biggest speculator in silk was probably Hu Kuang-yung, as we will see in chapter 11.

Cantonese merchants were the largest group of provincial merchants in China to trade and speculate in tea. One of them was Coekeye who traded with the British firm of Dent, Beale & Co. In the season 1851–1852, the firm was reported to have purchased an unusually large amount of tea, to the extent of 1,200 tons.[104] A. G. Dallas of Jardine's wrote in late 1851: "The large shipments making by Dent Beals & Co. are on account of Coekeye, their compradore, who was a large speculator this year."[105] As the tea price fell, Dallas maintained that Coekeye "could not now sell excepting at a loss of 2 to 3 taels [per picul]."[106] This situation continued until early 1852, as Dallas again wrote : "Dent Beale & Co.'s compradore is deeply in with teas & has a large lot of Greens in the market, upon which he must lose heavily."[107] Speculation in tea was sometimes profitable. After Foochow was opened for tea export in 1854, the volume of tea exported from that port increased steadily. With the rise in the price of tea, speculative trading in tea was pursued by many Chinese merchants. In August 1856, for example, a coastal merchant bought 1,000 chests of tea at Foochow, and then quickly resold at the profit of one-half to one tael per picul.[108] But speculation in tea could be

101. Apr. 20, 1869, FO 17/531, p. 9.
102. To Joseph Jardine (Hong Kong), July 9, 1856, JMA.
103. To Augustine Heard, Jr., Apr. 18, 1862, HL-36, HC.
104. "It is said that D. [Dent] B. [Beale] & Co. have altogether 1,200 tons [of tea] waiting shipment, & I dare say this is not far from the truth" (A. G. Dallas [Shanghai] to David Jardine [Hong Kong], Jan. 13, 1852, JMA).
105. Ibid., Dec. 18, 1851.
106. Ibid.
107. Ibid., Jan. 13, 1852, JMA.
108. Jardine's agent at Foochow wrote: "Of the 6,000 chests above notices as being settled during the week are 1,000 chests bought some time ago by a Cantonese on specula-

as risky as in silk. A British consular report indicated that 1868 "was the worst year of speculation in tea" at Foochow. Encouraged by the London market, foreign merchants purchased tea at high prices that year, but they lost money, except for those who were able to load the tea on board the first few ships bound for England.[109]

In addition to commodities, fluctuations on the local and international exchange market provided opportunities for lush profits, though the risks were high. The difference between the intrinsic value and market value of various kinds of silver dollars tempted Western and Chinese merchants to speculate in currency. Aheen, a Cantonese merchant at Shanghai, sometimes engaged in buying and selling dollars. His speculative trading in silver dollars was closely connected with his business function as a comprador. When he lost money and defaulted, his sureties pointed out in the court: "If he had not been employed by the bank in purchasing and disposing of dollars, he would not have fallen into temptation to make time bargains."[110] Yu Tze-hiang, another merchant at Shanghai, speculated in copper in the 1860s, incurred losses, and absconded in September 1870.[111]

There were fluctuations in the exchange rate, as A. G. Dallas wrote from Shanghai in 1851: "Exchange on Canton is fluctuating from 1% to 1½% premium on Shanghai dollars for 10 day drafts, and may probably go higher as some of our neighbours are hard pressed for funds."[112] The shipment of sycee from one port to another was therefore profitable. Dan Patridge, the Jardine agent at Tientsin, wrote in June 1865 that for this purpose some Shansi merchants shipped Tls. 100,000 from that port to Shanghai via the steamer *Yuntzefei*, and consigned them to Choping, a prominent merchant who was the comprador to the American firm of Russell & Co.[113]

Speculations in stock shares in Hong Kong culminated in 1878. Shares were steadily rising in the 1870s, but a change took place in 1878: "Wild speculation took possession of the share market, with the usual result in inflation followed by subsequent depreciation." Several local

---

tion and resold at Ts. 0.5 c [to] 1 per pecul profit" (Thomas Larken to Joseph Jardine [Hong Kong], Aug. 29, 1856, JMA).

109. Report of Charles Sinclair, FO 17/534.

110. *NCH*, June 4, 1864, p. 91.

111. *NCH*, Sept. 22, 1870, p. 228.

112. To David Jardine (Hong Kong), Oct. 4, 1851, JMA.

113. The sycee was shipped "through a comprador of a foreign firm unknown to his employer" (To William Keswick [Shanghai], June 19, 1865, JMA).

firms of old standing failed. A general depression followed, which prevailed not only in Hong Kong, but also in other Chinese treaty ports and
Japan.[114] Again, as F. B. Johnson of Jardine's wrote from Hong Kong in
early 1884, "there is great trouble amongst bank share speculators" in
that port, because there was "a fraud in Yokohama involving loss of
$150,000."[115] In Shanghai, speculative activity was likewise manifest in
the history of shares on the city's stock market, over which the government exerted little control.

As expected, the most reckless activities occurred with new issues. As
we will see in the next chapter, the speculators' overenthusiasm for the
shares of the newly established mining companies in 1882 prompted a
business recession the following year. Two decades later, for the purpose
of exploiting the "rubber rush," several Western adventurers in Shanghai formed a shaky joint-stock rubber company in 1908 and started to
sell shares. Expecting huge profits, individual and institutional speculators (especially the native banks) quickly drove the shares' price sky-high.
But this firm proved to be a "bubble" company; its foreign partners left
China in 1910 and never came back. The speculators incurred heavy
losses, and several prominent native banks went bankrupt, which led to a
serious financial crisis.[116]

Other reckless speculations occurred along China's coast in the second half of the nineteenth century. There were numerous brokers whose
major business was rash speculation, not unlike that in Amsterdam
during the seventeenth century: "One sees . . . that without possessing actions or even a desire to acquire any, one can carry on a big business in them. . . . The seller, so to speak, sells nothing but wind and the
buyer receives only wind."[117] A. F. Heard described in his diary how a
Chinese broker was doing speculative trade in opium at Shanghai. He
wrote on August 22, 1855:

Had a row with an opium broker yesterday and today. He bought 20¢ [chests] on
the 14th, selected 20¢ on the 14th but sent no money. I sent the comprador after the
money three times, each time in vain, the fellow giving now one and now another
excuse; price $362. And as the comprador has since found out he was speculating
in Malwa on the 20th, I told him if the money wasn't paid by nightfall, bargin
should be off. It was not paid and I tore up the order.[118]

114. Eitel, p. 550.
115. To W. Paterson (Shanghai), Jan. 26, 1884, JMA.
116. King, *Money*, p. 236; *Shang-hai ch'ien-chuang*, pp. 74–76; and Yang Yin-p'u, p. 26.
117. Violet Barbour, *Capitalism in Amsterdam in the 17th Century* (Baltimore, 1950),
pp. 78–79.
118. Diary, HP-1, HC.

A Prussian businessman at Shanghai in 1864 described the speculative trading in commodities of a Chinese merchant in that city: "His transactions were, to a great extent, fabulous. That is to say, he sold where he had not bought, and bought without money to pay, according to his anticipations of a rise or fall in the market."[119] The Chinese magistrate, sharing the Prussian's resentment, declared in the Shanghai Mixed Court in December 1867 "his determination to punish speculators . . . who bought without capital and repudiated their engagement if the market were unfavorable."[120] This shows that there must have been many such speculators at Shanghai. They usually obtained credit from the native banks, and the overextension of credit by these banks resulted in financial crises. One example was the instance in 1894, when half of the native banks at Shanghai went out of business.[121] After their failures, however, some speculators used the government as the scapegoat, blaming the economic slumps entirely on official exaction.[122]

OPTIONAL AND CONDITIONAL TRADING

A more risky way to speculate on a large scale with a limited amount of money was through the optional contract, by which a person purchased the right to call for or make delivery within a specified time of particular stocks and commodities at a predetermined rate. Thus, the optional trade was virtually always conditional in nature. Sometimes a sum of money was agreed upon to be paid by the party who "repented himself of the bargain."[123] Trade in option, being proper for the stocks and commodities whose price rose and fell quickly, was attractive to some adventurous merchants, for it offered the advantage of leverage—a potentially large profit from a relatively small investment. Such transactions were common on China's coast during the nineteenth century. In most cases, the optional contract involved trading commodity futures. Tea and silk, for instance, were traded before they were actually produced. And many foreign traders made advance payments to Chinese merchants for "the right of first refusal" to buy the latter's commodities.

Nothing illustrates better the nature of optional trading as it existed on China's coast than Jardine's silk trade with Takee at Shanghai in the

119. *NCH*, Apr. 16, 1864, p. 62.
120. *NCH*, Dec. 24, 1867, p. 426.
121. Yang Yin-p'u, pp. 25–26.
122. *NCH*, Mar. 28, 1883, p. 352.
123. Barbour, p. 74.

early 1850s. A. G. Dallas, the firm's agent, had a substantial silk contract with Takee. Having previously agreed on the amount and price, the firm was to make an advance to Takee to help his purchase. For Takee's part, he was to sell to the firm, under certain conditions, amounts of silk in installments. The amounts must have been large, because Takee asked an advance of $100,000. Takee in turn made contracts with the small merchants for silk. But for several reasons Takee later failed to fulfill his part of the contract. He was ill and "incapable of exercising a proper personal superintending over his extensive business," and he was "deceived by the silkmen to whom he made an advance of $50 a bale."[124] Finally, "the great & hurried demand for silk early in the season, by buyers with hard dollars, seriously interfered with Takee."[125] Takee was thus unable to hand over the silk to Dallas on schedule in accordance with the contract.

Dallas then reported to the Hong Kong office on September 15: "On this account I declined making him further advances to enable him to carry out his operations and preferred cancelling the silk contract. . . . I have now determined to receive no more silk from him except at market rates." For fear of disapproval from the head office, Dallas further explained: "Those are contingencies to which any one carrying on large speculative operations here must be at all times liable, & my anxieties are sometimes greater than I can express. In this instance the failure of the contract is no loss, as we have already a good stake in the article, & I can now buy on better terms in open market."[126] However, David Jardine, head of the firm, was uneasy about the contracts. In response, Dallas pointed out the uncertainties contingent on transactions in options: "We must always be liable to many contingencies in such large operations & dependent not alone on the good faith & ability of one man, but on those qualities in his instruments. . . . Had the price of silk ultimately advanced I should have pressed for & obtained some indemnity from Takee had he ultimately failed in his engagements."[127]

Many Chinese merchants engaged in cotton speculation at Shanghai, including Hsu Jun and Tong King-sing.[128] Cotton prices suddenly rose in 1863, and many cotton contractors pulled out. William Keswick of

124. Dallas to David Jardine (Hong Kong), Sept. 15, 1852, JMA.
125. Ibid., Sept. 27, 1852.
126. Ibid., Sept. 15, 1852.
127. Ibid., Sept. 27, 1852.
128. Hsu Jun, Nien-p'u, pp. 11b–12.

Jardine's at Shanghai reported to Alexander Perceval, the firm's head at Hong Kong, on November 24:

> I thank you for cautioning me about advances on account of rumours having reached you to the effect that many of the contractors have run away. This is no doubt the case, and I am certain many more will also take to flight, as they have really not the means with which to complete their engagements. I am assured however that all or nearly all of the men with whom I have contracted will fully carry out their engagements, & judging from the way they have lately been delivering cotton I am disposed to believe they will do so. Many people however who contracted to deliver cotton cannot possibly do so for the simple reason that they have not capital to represent their losses.[129]

Optional contracts for tea were most often carried out at Foochow. For example, tea prices at Foochow rose substantially in 1867 over those of the previous year because of speculation. Charles Sinclair, British consul at that city, reported on March 9: "Speculation was active during the first month of the year in the interior for the purchase of the leaf, and higher prices were paid for the article by the native teamen and Chinese agents for foreigners than were ever before known. Some foreign merchants paid 20 to 25 percent over the previous year's prices—a range of price never before known at Foochow."[130] Given these political and economic uncertainties, it is no wonder that grave commercial consequences followed, including many bankruptcies.

129. JMA.
130. FO 17/483.

Commercial Losses and Bankruptcies

Chinese and Western merchants on the coast not only were haunted by political and economic uncertainties, but they also frequently suffered from heavy business losses. In many cases these losses were so heavy that quite a few businessmen, among them some prominent ones, went broke. These risks and losses, taken together, precipitated several economic crises along the coast.

BUSINESS LOSSES

In addition to political disturbances and official exactions, coastal merchants had to deal with routine and unexpected losses. Indeed, risks and uncertainties haunted the China traders. In the mid-1850s, for instance, John Heard of Augustine Heard & Co., while on a worldwide tour, wrote a letter to his uncle saying that he took no pleasure in traveling while he was worried about business risks in China.[1]

THE HONG MERCHANTS

Risks and uncertainties were constantly with the hong merchants. In addition to their own luxurious life-styles and the squeezes exacted by officials, they often had to cope with other business losses.[2] First, competing with one another for business, they sometimes paid unrealistically high prices to foreign merchants and lost money in the process. Sec-

1. (London) to Augustine Heard, Feb. 10, 1855, EM-6, HC.
2. Liang Chia-pin, *Shih-san hang*, p. 113.

ond, many hong merchants borrowed money from foreign traders. As the latter could get higher interest rates in Canton than in the West, they were willing to make loans and extend the loan periods. Sometimes, however, the accumulated loan became too large a sum for the hong merchants to repay.

In addition, because officials demanded that the hongs be collectively responsible for the debts of bankrupt hongs, the risk of losing money on the part of all the hong merchants was increased. This principle of joint liability for debts can be traced back as early as 1780.[3] By 1794 it was firmly established, as evidenced by the bankruptcy of Shy Kinqua; the whole burden of his debt was assumed by the hong merchants collectively.[4] Another example was Conseequa who died in 1823 and owed duties and foreign loans amounting to more than Tls. 300,000; other hong merchants were forced by the officials to take responsibility for his debts.[5] Finally, the hong merchants might suffer unexpected losses. In a petition to Li Hu, the governor of Kwangtung, eight hong merchants reported in 1777 that they suffered unanticipated losses in transporting tea from Hui-chou and Bohea districts to Canton. According to them, the porters and coolies secretly substituted inferior tea for the good tea, and hong merchants had to make up the losses.[6]

Many hong merchants owed money to Western traders. In 1759 Khiqua (Li Kuang-hua) owed more than Tls. 50,000 to the British East India Company.[7] His debt prompted the promulgation of an edict by Governor-General Li Ch'ih-yao in the same year, to the effect that no hong merchants could legally borrow money from foreign merchants.[8] But this law was mostly ignored; in 1779 eight hong merchants owed debts to British merchants totaling $3,808,076.[9] According to a memorial of Governor-General Chiang Yu-hsien in 1815, the hong merchants in that year had a foreign debt of Tls. 1,061,914 (table 16). Actually, the hong merchants' foreign indebtedness was such a common phenomenon that in 1829 the number of entirely solvent firms was reduced to three—

3. In 1780 the hongs attempted the practice of price-fixing, and the resultant profits were to go toward an annual sum, jointly raised to meet debts and buy gifts for officials. Yet it was not an established practice for the Hoppo to demand from the hongs, as a group, the duties owed by a bankrupt hong. Hence, in the same year, "Coqua . . . had been bankrupt for two years; his estate was in the hands of the officials, who put in a preferred claim for the duties owing to the Emperor" (Morse, *Chronicles*, II, 56–57).
    4. Ibid., II, 255–64.
    5. Ibid., IV, 73.
    6. Liang Chia-pin, *Shih-san hang*, pp. 109–11.
    7. Ibid., pp. 71–72.
    8. Ibid., p. 76.
    9. Most of the debt was owed by four hong merchants: Coqua, Seunqua, Yngshaw, and Kewshaw (Morse, *Chronicles*, II, 44–45).

TABLE 16.   HONG MERCHANTS' DEBTS TO WESTERN
MERCHANTS, 1815
(TAELS)

Name of firm	Hong merchants		Amount of debts
	Western name	Chinese name	
Fu-lung	Manhop	Kuan Ch'eng-fa	338,929
Hsi-ch'eng	Pakqua	Li Kuang-yuan	295,194
Li-ch'üan	Conseequa	P'an Ch'ang-yao	228,905
Tung-yü	Goqua	Hsieh Ch'ing-t'ai	91,981
T'ung-t'ai	Poonequa	Mai Chin-t'ing	88,903
Wen-yuan	Fatqua	Li Hsieh-fa	11,040
T'ien-pao	Kingqua	Liang Ching-kuo	6,962
Total			1,061,914

Source: Liang Chia-pin, Shih-san hang, pp. 131–32, 246, 251, 255, 261, 267, 268.

Howqua, Puankhequa, and Goqua.[10] In addition to foreign debts, the hong merchants also owed duties to the Ch'ing government. The total amount of unpaid duties in 1833 was Tls. 1,306,600.[11]

Mouqua, a prominent hong merchant, was in financial trouble in 1832. Augustine Heard of Russell & Co. reported from Canton to Samuel Russell on May 15, 1832: "Yesterday Houqua sent for me to say that Mouqua was *shaking*, and must stop payment. I immediately called upon Mouqua and was told by him that he had been in the habit of borrowing from foreign houses, particularly Dent & Co., Magniac & Co., and ourselves."[12] Heard papers indicate that in May 1832 Mouqua's debts totaled Tls. 186,000, as follows (in taels):[13]

Creditor	Amount
Dent & Co.	50,000
Magniac & Co.	25,000
Blitterman & Co.	26,000
Russell & Co.	15,000
Parsees	30,000
The Hoppo	40,000

10. Ibid., IV, 209.
11. Liang Chia-pin, Shih-san hang, p. 150.
12. BL-1, HC.
13. Ibid.

The merchant prince Houqua often incurred losses in his overseas operations in the early nineteenth century. In early 1837, for example, a shipment of his silk, consigned to Baring Brothers & Co., arrived in London. The price was low at the moment, so John M. Forbes, Houqua's manager in Boston, instructed the London firm to hold Houqua's silk "for a rise in the market." Instead, Baring Brothers & Co. hastily sold the silk. Houqua wrote from Canton to Forbes on December 30, 1837: "My silk . . . I am sorry to say, was sacrificed at very miserable prices. Owing to this hasty step on the part of B. [Baring] B. [Brothers] and Co., I am a very heavy loser."[14] In fact, Houqua was so indignant with the firm that he changed his agents in London from Baring Brothers & Co. to Forbes, Forbes & Co.

To minimize business losses, Houqua indicated in the same letter that he would order British dry goods, including manufactures, directly from Canton:

> Of your instructions to Baring Brothers and Co. to remit my funds from London in manufactures at certain limits, I approve, but in [the] future I wish you not to give any similar orders, for I find that shippers of Dry Goods in England form the most erroneous opinions of the quantity exported, and are liable, if left to their own discretion, to ship when this market [Canton] is overstocked, and entail on their friends serious losses. For this reason I prefer that my orders for dry goods should always go direct from hence, and that as little as possible should be left at the option of my agents in England.[15]

However, Houqua continued to give John M. Forbes considerable authority over his business operations, as he explained: "I allow you a wider range of authority because I consider that you have the advantage of long training under my personal care, and must therefore necessarily be better acquainted with my wishes, and be able to determine what course I would myself pursue under particular circumstances, and willing to adopt it."[16]

John M. Forbes exercised this prerogative in the next year, to the dissatisfaction of Houqua. With the advice and consent of John P. Cushing, Forbes deviated from Houqua's instructions by remitting £25,000 from London to Canton in cotton goods. This form of investment was probably the best (for example, Russell & Co.'s agent in Lon-

14. Robert B. Forbes, *Reminiscences*, p. 247. Houqua continued: "I feel so chafed in my temper that I have diverted, and shall divert very considerable consignments from them to Forbes, Forbes & Co., who I trust will exercise more care to judgment in promoting my interest" (ibid.).

15. Ibid., pp. 247–48.

16. Ibid.

don also shipped £72,000 of cottons). But, when the shipment arrived in Canton, it found an overstocked market, and Houqua again suffered heavy losses. Consequently, Houqua immediately withdrew Forbes' authority over shipments to Europe and revoked Forbes' prerogative to decide the best way to remit from the United States to Canton.[17] Robert B. Forbes, brother of John M. Forbes, also handled a part of Houqua's business. In late 1837 he remitted to Houqua by sending a shipment of cotton goods to Canton. In 1838 it too unfortunately came to "a bad market." Because he did not give Forbes specific instructions in advance, Houqua did not complain, despite his loss.[18]

THE RISKS OF THE COMPRADORS

The compradors were Chinese managers of foreign firms in China, serving as middlemen in the companies' dealings with the Chinese. The comprador system was based on the Chinese institution of "complete responsibility" (*pao*); thus the comprador was fully responsible for the conduct of his staff, for the credit of the company's Chinese constituents, and for the dependability of the native bank orders that he received and kept for the company.[19] Consequently, the comprador always faced the risk of loss.

One common risk that a comprador had to face was the probability that not everyone on his staff was trustworthy. In 1874 the comprador office of Augustine Heard & Co. at Shanghai lost treasure boxes containing Spanish dollars, for which the comprador had to make good.[20] The comprador often sued his clerks for having made forged seals of the comprador office for their own illegal gains.[21] Many corrupt comprador employees absconded before the discovery of their wrongdoings.[22] Because one of the important functions of the comprador was to guarantee the

17. Forbes, however, still had authority over Houqua's shipments to America. Forbes and Cushing wrote to Houqua, explaining why they had deviated from his previous instructions. Houqua was satisfied and soon restored all privileges to Forbes (Russell & Co. [Canton] to J. M. Forbes [Boston], Aug. 7, Sept. 15 and 17, 1838, File 12, FC). See also Cushing (Boston) to Houqua (Canton), June 25, 1838, vol. 12, BSP; and Forbes (Boston) to Joseph Coolidge, Mar. 6, 1839, F-8, FC.

18. "The cotton goods you have sent me have unfortunately come to a bad market, but I don't complain of the remittance" (Houqua [Canton] to R. B. Forbes [Canton], Mar. 8, 1838, HLB).

19. Yen-p'ing Hao, *Comprador*, p. 160.

20. *Shen pao*, Sept. 6, 1874, p. 6, Sept. 9, 1874, p. 2, and Sept. 11, 1874, p. 2.

21. *Shen pao*, Sept. 30, 1874, p. 2, and Jan. 17, 1882, p. 3.

22. The treasurer of the comprador office of Russo-Chinese Bank, e.g., absconded in 1907 (*Hua-tzu jih-pao*, Nov. 18, 1907).

solvency of the Chinese constituents, he was likely to lose money on their account. H. G. Bridges, agent of Augustine Heard & Co. at Hankow, wrote in June 1866 that Soyseng, the firm's Hankow comprador, "acknowledged his liability for all sales made by him."[23] This practice was universally accepted by all compradors, as Bridges continued: "Three years ago [1863] there was a general crash among the [native]Bankers. Russell & Co.'s comprador lost Tls. 20,000 by holding against cargo sold orders of Banks that were failed. . . . Goldsmith, who is the oldest resident in Hankow, says their (Dow & Co.'s) comprador has made repeated losses and always paid them up."[24] The comprador also might lose in the process of exchange. On December 24, 1863, Jardine's agent at Amoy reported: "The comprador says that the banker would not accept the sycee at its proper value, and therefore he would lose by it."[25] In a similar manner, Sung Ts'ai, comprador to Sassoon & Co. at Chinkiang, lost 0.2 percent on opium proceeds in the 1870s.[26]

It was uncommon for the compradors of large firms to go bankrupt. The *North-China Herald* commented from Shanghai in 1883: "The Compradores who have come before the [Mixed] Court criminally have generally been those of young firms. The Compradors of large and old-fashioned firms . . . are generally well connected, and able, when the depredations to which they have been driven by ill-success of speculations are discovered, to secure the assistance of their friends and arrange the matter with their masters."[27] Nevertheless, many prominent compradors failed. The business risk of the compradors of smaller firms was even greater. Y. C. Tong, a Chinese merchant, wrote in the early twentieth century: "Within the last decade or two, foreign adventurers have appeared on the scene, mushroom companies have sprung up, trading on Chinese credit and money and leaving their Chinese compradors in the lurch."[28] The results were losses and frequent defaults on the part of the smaller compradors.

The extent to which compradors were affected by the failure of Western firms was illustrated by Young Ateong. Starting in the early 1850s he was engaged in the tea trade at Foochow. In the late fifties he became the comprador to King & Co. in that port. In 1862, however, he "lost much

23. To A. F. Heard (Shanghai), June 28, 1866, HM-23, HC.
24. Ibid.
25. Henry Beveridge to Jardine, Matheson & Co. (Hong Kong), JMA.
26. *Shen pao*, May 5, 1876, p. 3.
27. *NCH*, Mar. 28, 1883, p. 352.
28. Julean Arnold, *Commercial Handbook of China* (Washington, D.C., 1919, 1920), II, 254.

money by the failure of that firm."[29] He then went to Kiukiang to engage in the tea business. His ability impressed H. G. Bridges, Heard's agent at Kiukiang, who tried to hire him as comprador.[30] But his old debts at Foochow prevented him from serving Heard's, because G. F. Weller gave an unfavorable report on him to A. F. Heard in October: "I believe he is in debt, so that it would not be for our interest to have him, and [our] old comprador will know that very well."[31] Heard's finally decided not to employ him.

The failure of a comprador naturally caused losses for many other Chinese merchants. The Shanghai taotai commented in 1867: "Many hundred innocent native merchants have been brought to ruin in property and person by the defalcation of the compradors of foreign firms."[32] When their losses were extremely heavy, some of the compradors even committed suicide. The *North-China Herald* observed in 1883: "Occasionally they [compradors] become too deeply involved for extrication; but in such cases suicide generally [*sic*] withdraws them from the action of the law."[33] As all the compradors were at once independent merchants in their own right, the risks and uncertainties that were concomitant with their compradorship were naturally detrimental to their business.

RISKY COMMODITIES

It was especially risky to trade in certain commodities, such as opium and tea. Opium was easily stolen because of its light weight and divisibility. Foreign merchants kept an eye on compradors and other Chinese in the firm, but the risk of loss still existed, because, evidently, not all Western employees were honest either.[34] Another risky feature of trading

29. "The mandarin Atong [Ateong] has lately spoken twice to me about his nephew, Young Atong, as an eligible man to be comprador for the house at this port." (H. G. Bridges [Kiukiang] to A. F. Heard [Shanghai], July 28, 1862, HM-23, HC).

30. "I had a half hour conversation with him, and was very favorably impressed. He seemed to have a good store of general information on trade everywhere, knew everything that was being sold, and at what prices, and what business everyone was doing. . . . He looks intelligent, speaks English very well, and says everything to the point" (ibid., Aug. 27, 1862).

31. (Kiukiang) to Heard (Shanghai), Oct. 2, 1862, HM-49, HC.

32. *NCH*, Feb. 8, 1867, p. 367.

33. *NCH*, Mar. 28, 1883, p. 352.

34. One of Jardine's clerks at Shanghai reported to the Hong Kong office in October 1862: "On this occasion I beg to hand you a memo. of the outturn of 3 of the 5 chests of Malwa weighed in the presence of Mr. [James] Whittall of the 3rd and reweighed to a broker on the 13th current, shewing [showing] an average loss of 10 taels p. [per] chest in 8 days. Every care was taken, no Chinese were allowed near the scales, neither were they

in opium was that it was illegal until 1858. As such, it was not protected by foreign governments. In the United States, both the government and public opinion condemned the trade. Even the official British policy prohibited the British from engaging in the opium business. In his proclamation of February 24, 1843, Sir Henry Pottinger declared that any British subject dealing in opium would do so at his own risk and would not receive British official protection.[35] In a dispatch to Lord Aberdeen on April 17, 1843, Pottinger reiterated this policy.[36]

In contrast to opium, tea was a safer commodity to trade. Being bulky, it was difficult to steal, and the tea trade was legal. But for the merchants, the tea business was by no means free from risk. For one thing, tea leaves were likely to be damaged by bad weather, such as draught, heavy rain, or cold temperatures. Through the comprador-merchant Aleet, Jardine's was actively engaged in the upcountry tea purchase in the Hankow area in the late 1860s and early 1870s, but unexpected heavy rains and unseasonable cold temperatures there in the spring of 1871 damaged the tea leaves. Consequently, F. B. Johnson reported from Shanghai that he was not sure whether the firm's efforts in the upcountry tea business would yield a profit.[37] (The cold weather was also "prejudicial to the silk worms" and severely hampered Jardine's upcountry silk purchase.[38])

Foreign merchants were subject to even more risks. In order to acquire the best tea cheaply, quickly, and surely, they often purchased tea from Chinese teamen, entering into contracts with local tea merchants and advancing money or opium to them. This kind of advance, without the guarantee of the comprador, was sometimes hazardous. M. A. Macleod, the Jardine agent at Foochow, reported to Alexander Perceval in

---

allowed to handle the opium" (Dan Patridge to Jardine, Matheson & Co., Oct. 16, 1862, JMA).

35. "To point out to all whom it may concern, that opium being an article, the traffic in which is well known to be declared illegal and contraband by the laws and imperial edicts of China, any person who may take such a step will do so at his own risk, and will, if a British subject, meet with no support or protection from Her Majesty's consuls or other officers" (*Chinese Repository*, 12:446 [1843], cited in IMC, *Origin*, VI, 6).

36. Pottinger to Aberdeen, dispatch no. 34, FO 17/67.

37. "The Accounts from the Tea districts are less favorable in respect to the quality of the first Congou pickings, heavy rain accompanied by a fall in temperature having interfered with the caring of the leaf. There is little probability of our being interested in any but the investment in the early purchases & I fear if Aleet's statement as to the cost in the Country be correct of our contracts yielding a profit" (to William Keswick [Hong Kong], May 17, 1871, JMA).

38. "It is impossible as yet to form any opinion as to the coming silk crop" (ibid.).

Hong Kong on May 11, 1861, concerning an advance of $12,000 to a teaman, Yantai, who became critically ill, a fact that caused Macleod "a good deal of anxiety."[39] Jardine's experienced another bad debt in 1862 when teaman Chunsing, to whom the firm had made an advance of Tls. 996, disappeared from Shanghai.[40] This kind of risk was faced by other foreign merchants as well.

The Chinese teamen might likewise lose money. In 1856 Jardine's Foochow office advanced $10,000 worth of opium to a Chinese teaman named Awy. Awy in turn advanced a part of the opium to some of the smaller tea merchants. Awy lost heavily in the Moning tea districts because some of these local merchants "ran off without paying him."[41] A similar incident followed two weeks later. Ahee, another teaman, was active in the Bohea tea districts in the fifties. According to George V. W. Fisher, the Jardine agent at Foochow, "the man Ahee sent to these districts to buy the tea cheated him. He gave him an inferior Tea & charged him first class price."[42] As a result, Ahee lost about $9,000.

Like their counterparts in the tea business, the Chinese merchants dealing in cotton, especially those who entered into contracts with foreign merchants, sometimes suffered heavy losses. As mentioned in chapter 10, the cotton price at Shanghai in 1863 was Tls 9.6 per picul. When it suddenly rose to Tls. 13 in two days, several cotton hongs contracted with the foreign firms, promising to deliver more than 100,000 piculs at this price in that year. Meanwhile, the world market for cotton continued to go up because of the American Civil War, and its price in Shanghai increased to Tls. 18 eight days later. Such a high price attracted Chinese cotton merchants as far away as Ch'ung-ming Island, and they similarly entered into contracts with foreign merchants. The price, however, soared to an all-time high of Tls. 26 five days later, increasing two and a half times in fifteen days. It was estimated that at least 1,000,000 bales of contracted cotton were transacted under these circumstances, 300,000 to 400,000 bales of which were contracted by merchants from nearby Sung-chiang and T'ai-ts'ang districts. As the

39. "Yantai, one of our teamen, is causing me a good deal of anxiety just now, as he is said to be in great danger, & hardly expected to live any time. You will no doubt remember that he is one of our Contract people, and has had an advance from me of $12,000 for operation in the Paklum district. In the event of his death I will endeavour to do the best I can for the protection of our interests" (JMA).

40. "I am afraid that this is a bad debt, for the man has some time since left Shanghai and is not in a position to refund the amount" (James Whittall [Shanghai] to Jardine, Matheson & Co. [Hong Kong], Oct. 4, 1862, JMA).

41. George Fisher to Joseph Jardine (Hong Kong), May 4, 1856, JMA.

42. Ibid., May 17, 1856.

lowest price at the village cotton shops (*hsiang-chuang*) in the cotton districts was Tls. 23 to 24, virtually all of the Chinese contractors lost money. To minimize their losses, many of them tried to fulfill their contract obligations by adding water to the cotton in order to increase its weight. The foreign merchants receiving this damaged cotton also incurred heavy losses.[43]

Cotton could also be stolen—sometimes mysteriously. In a shipment of cotton from Hong Kong to Shanghai in March 1861, for example, James Whittall of Jardine's Shanghai office discovered short weight but was puzzled as to how it could have happened.[44] Another risky commodity to trade in was silk. Its price fell sharply in 1877 "due to the overstocked European markets." Consequently, many Chinese silk merchants suffered losses, and some foreign houses were also severely affected.[45]

NATURAL CALAMITIES AND ACCIDENTS

In the nineteenth century, it was common for China to suffer from natural calamities, such as drought, flood, and famine. They led to business depressions, and both Chinese and Western merchants suffered losses. The drought in eastern China during the first half of 1852 resulted in the partial suspense of tea trading at Shanghai in the summer. Chinese merchants, in A. G. Dallas' words, were "quite knocked up." He wrote: "The new Teas are coming in very slowly, & little or no progress has been made since I last wrote to you. Owing to the excessive heat & drought, all business is partially suspended & the Chinese themselves are quite knocked up."[46] Western traders were similarly affected.

In 1875–1876 North China was devastated by drought. Henry Beveridge, the Jardine agent at Tientsin, reported in August 1876 that this calamity "has caused the greatest depression to trade in the north of

43. Hsu Jun, *Nien-p'u*, pp. 11b–12.

44. "With regard to the short weight in the shipment of *Cotton* to Mr. [William] Keswick, I beg to assure you that I am as little satisfied as yourselves with the reasons given, for, the cotton going direct from our own godowns, in our own boats & with our own men, I know that no robbery could have taken place here, as it would have been impossible to open and re-close the bales again in a proper manner, in the short distance from our Jetty to the vessel. Besides, shipments have been made of the same article to Amoy & Foochow, whence no complants [complaints] whatever have reached me" (to Jardine, Matheson & Co. [Hong Kong], Mar. 21, 1861, JMA).

45. BPP, *Commercial Reports of Her Majesty's Consuls in China* (1879), No. 1, Shanghai, p. 5.

46. (Shanghai) to David Jardine (Hong Kong), July 21, 1852, JMA.

China."[47] One month later, he explained to Jardine's Shanghai office why he could not sell sugar: "There has been an utter absence of demand all during the spring & summer. The instructions I received from Hongkong on the 6th [of] June relative to this sugar would certainly have been carried out had it been in my power to have done so. . . . The stocks of all grades of sugar in this port is very large, & some importers have [had] sugar in their godowns for a year."[48]

Accidents, such as fire and death, could also cost the merchants dearly. Fire was a constant hazard to the hong merchants and Western traders in Canton during the old Cohong times. The fire of 1822 caused heavy damages to the foreign "factories." They, together with the establishments of the former hong merchants, were virtually demolished in the big fire of 1856.[49] After the Treaty of Nanking, fires occasionally broke out in foreign firms. The head office of Russell & Co. at Hong Kong, for example, suffered from fire in June 1875.[50]

Unexpected death in China was a risk that foreign merchants had to face. After its establishment at Canton in 1823, Russell & Co. handled Houqua's personal trade with the West. On the eve of his return to Boston in 1828, John P. Cushing, head of Russell's, recommended that Thomas T. Forbes of the firm take care of Houqua's business. In the fall of 1829, however, Thomas Forbes was drowned in the sea off Macao. As soon as he received the news at London, Cushing rushed back to Canton where he stayed from August 1830 to March 1831 to settle the problems arising out of Thomas's untimely death. John M. Forbes was then sent to Canton. There was another accidental death in the firm a few years later. Handsayd Cabot, the son of Samuel Cabot who was a partner of Perkins & Co., worked at Russell & Co. in Canton in 1834. At the age of twenty-one, he suddenly died there from smallpox the next year.[51]

The defalcation of a merchant might result in losses for both Chinese and Western entrepreneurs. David Welsh was such a merchant. Residing at Pakhoi in 1875, he "had goods in his hands consigned to him by Jardine, Matheson & Co. for sale." Meanwhile, "he entered into an understanding with a Chinese hong to purchase Cassia from them. On a visit he paid to Hongkong immediately after, he found the price agreed

47. To Jardine, Matheson & Co. (Shanghai), Aug. 2, 1876, JMA.
48. Ibid., Sept. 9, 1876.
49. Liang Chia-pin, *Shih-san hang*, p. 176.
50. *Shen pao*, June 25, 1875, p. 1.
51. J. M. Forbes (Canton) to Samuel Cabot (Boston), Apr. 27, 1835, Samuel Cabot Papers.

to would cause a loss for him. He therefore decided not to return and went to Australia."[52] As a result, both the Chinese hong and Jardine's lost money.

BANKRUPTCIES

Frequent business losses often led to bankruptcy. A great deal of wealth passed through coastal merchants' hands, but many of them did not remain wealthy for long due to their propensity for disastrous speculative enterprises. In fact, business conditions were occasionally so unpredictable that a coastal merchant faced bankruptcy all the time. G. W. Cooke, the noted *London Times* correspondent, was correct when he wrote of the China trader that "an extremely farsighted commercial man must always run the risks of bankruptcy, for the most absolutely certain sequences are often the most uncertain in point of time."[53]

WESTERN TRADERS

With the exception of Jardine, Matheson & Co. and Butterfield & Swire, many prominent Western houses in China ended in failure, including Dent, Beale & Co. in 1867, Augustine Heard & Co. in 1875, Olyphant & Co. in 1879, and Russell & Co. in 1891. C. A. Winchester, British consul at Shanghai, wrote that quite a few "old and respectable foreign firms" went broke in the mid-sixties, and that "the losses of English merchants have been very great."[54] Several additional firms collapsed in 1867, including Maitland, Bush & Co. and Mackellar & Co.[55] Dent & Co. was an old and gigantic British house. In 1861 when the noted merchant, Hsu Jun, became its comprador, it did a considerable business, amounting to at least Tls. 10,000,000 a year at Shanghai alone. In terms of capital and business volume, according to Hsu Jun, "it was probably the number-one foreign firm in China."[56] However, its business declined after 1864 partly because of the American Civil War. The firm also faced intense competition, because "numerous foreign firms were established on the northern coast and the Yangtze River, as well as

52. W. G. Stronach, British consul (Pakhoi), to Jardine, Matheson & Co. (Hong Kong), July 26, 1879, JMA.
53. *China* (London, 1858), p. 25.
54. *NCH*, Feb. 8, 1867, p. 368.
55. *NCH*, June 1, 1867, p. 85, Aug. 5, 1867, p. 191, Sept. 28, 1867, p. 277, and Oct. 9, 1867, p. 286.
56. *Nien-p'u*, p. 9

in such ports as Shanghai, Hong Kong, an Foochow."[57] Dent's finally wound up its business in 1867.[58]

Augustine Heard & Co., a leading American firm in China, was established in 1839. After thirty-six years in business, the firm went bankrupt on April 19, 1875. John Heard III wrote to Augustine Heard that their "troubles began" in 1873. His letters to Augustine Heard showed that the decline of their business actually started in the early seventies.[59] The immediate cause of Heard's failure was that Everett & Co., their agents in the United States, misappropriated funds and that Augustine Heard, Jr., the ablest of the brothers, was not in China after 1871. But more fundamental factors lay in the nature of trade in China during the seventies. The possibilities for easy profits were disappearing, and competition with fellow merchants became keener with time.

On April 28, 1875, nine days after its bankruptcy, Heard's issued a circular at Hong Kong, announcing that their "entire property in all parts of the world" was entrusted "to two trustees for the benefit of their creditors."[60] Meanwhile, John Heard and Albert F. Heard announced bankruptcy in the United States and sold their land in Boston.[61] On learning of Heard's bankruptcy in 1875, *Shen pao*, the leading Chinese newspaper at Shanghai, commented: "This firm was one of the oldest foreign houses at Shanghai, and was highly regarded by both Chinese and foreign merchants. Its failure shows that the Western merchants have been in bad shape in recent years."[62] It was difficult to resume business once it failed. Both Augustine Heard, Jr., and John Heard III wrote that they doubted the wisdom of trying to resume business. John Heard III, at the urgent appeals of his brothers, later wrote to John M. Forbes, William Endicott, F. W. Channery, and others, asking them to subscribe funds for the reestablishment of Augustine Heard & Co. under the name of "Heard & Co." The sum of $30,000 was raised,[63] and the

57. Ibid., pp. 13–14.
58. *NCH*, Aug. 5, 1867, p. 192.
59. FL-18, HC.
60. The two trustees were William Keswick and T. G. Linstead. Heard's circular reads: "We beg leave to inform you that the late firm of Augustine Heard & Co., hitherto engaged in business in Hongkong, China, and Japan, as Merchants and Commission Agents, having through unavoidable necessity been compelled to go into liquidation, have executed a deed of assignment, pursuant to the bankrupt laws of this Colony, of their entire property, in all parts of the world, to two trustees for the benefit of their creditors" (Circular, Hong Kong, Apr. 28, 1875, EQ-7, HC).
61. They "presented a petition to sell land on Commonwealth Ave., Boston, containing 6,972 square feet, to E. Rollins Morse, for $26,145 cash" (bankruptcy announcement in the newspaper, EQ-7, HC).
62. *Shen pao*, Apr. 19, 1875, p. 1.
63. Folder description, p. 19, HC. See also the diary of Augustine Heard, Jr., GQ-2, HC.

new firm was finally established on April 28, 1875.[64] Its business, however, did not prosper, and it ceased operations on February 1, 1877.[65] As was the case with Robert B. Forbes, the family of Augustine Heard experienced bankruptcy twice.

In 1879 several Western firms failed, including the noted German firm of Renter, Brockelmann & Co. (Lu-lin yang-hang) and the American firm of Olyphant & Co. (T'ung-fu yang-hang).[66] The failure of foreign firms at Shanghai was so frequent in the seventies that even Li Hung-chang lost faith in them. In his reply on a proposed cotton-cloth factory in Shanghai, Li charged in 1879 that "the foreign hongs in Shanghai excel in the powers of cheating."[67] The first months of 1892 saw the bankruptcy of Russell & Co., a prominent American firm in China, and the failure of the New Oriental Bank. In a letter to G. L. Montgomery, Jardine's New York agent, William Keswick lamented "how disastrous Eastern trade has been for some time." Jardine's then circulated a confidential statement among their agents to allay suspicion of the firm's insolvency.[68]

CHINESE MERCHANTS

Numerous Chinese merchants on the coast went bankrupt during the last decades of the eighteenth century. In the days of the Canton system, many hong merchants accumulated debts, and, when these debts became too large for them to repay, bankruptcy naturally followed. Wayqua (Ni Wen-hung) owed British merchants more than Tls. 11,000 and was banished to Ili in 1777. He was followed by Yngshaw (Yen Shih-ying) and Kewshaw (Chang T'ien-ch'iu) three years later.[69] For their indebtedness, Eequa (Wu Chao-p'ing) and Shy Kinqua (Shih Chung-ho) were banished to Ili in 1791 and 1795, respectively.[70]

Hong merchants went broke even more frequently in the nineteenth century, including Lyqua (Mu Shih-fang) in 1809 and Gnewqua (Cheng Ch'ung-ch'ien) in 1810.[71] Both of them were banished to Ili for punishment, but Inqua (Teng Chao-hsiang) managed to abscond in 1810 with-

64. See the printed circulars announcing the establishment of Heard & Co., EQ-7, HC.

65. Folder describing Augustine Heard & Co.'s archives, p. 13, HC.

66. *Shen pao*, Jan. 9, 1879, p. 2.

67. *NCH*, Jan. 10, 1879, p. 35.

68. LeFevour, pp. 122–23.

69. Liang Chia-pin, p. 108.

70. Ibid., p. 113.

71. Ibid., p. 125.

out being officially punished.[72] Exchin (Pakqua, Li Kuang-yuan) was banished to Ili in 1822, leaving a debt of more than Tls. 667,000. He was followed by Poonequa (Mai Chin-t'ing) in 1827, Manhop (Kuan Ch'eng-fa) in 1828, and Chunqua (Liu Ch'eng-shu) in 1829.[73] Sinqua held the office of purser, or foreman, for Pantinqua, a tea merchant. Osmond Tiffany, Jr., an American who visited Canton, commented about Sinqua in 1844: "Since my return from China the revulsion of trade has overtaken him, and always inflated, he has finally 'busted.'"[74] The enormous risks that hong merchants took are clear when one looks at the great speed with which some of them went broke. Eequa was made a hong merchant in 1786 and went bankrupt five years later.[75] Munqua (Ts'ai Shih-wen), during his eight years (1788–1796) of tenure as the head hong merchant, accumulated foreign and domestic debts to the extent of more than Tls. 500,000. He committed suicide in 1796.[76]

After the abolition of the hong merchants in 1842, numerous Chinese businessmen along the coast continued to go broke. Some of them were independent traders, such as Ekee and Hu Kuang-yung, and some of them were comprador-merchants, such as Sung Ts'ai and Yang Kuei-hsuan. Virtually all of them were connected directly or indirectly with foreign trade. As we have seen in chapter 8, Ekee was an active trader along the coast who cooperated closely with Jardine's. During the heyday of his business career, however, Ekee started to encounter financial difficulties. He lost money due to the decline in the silk market; the Ewo Bank, established jointly with Jardine's, was not as profitable as expected; and, most importantly, his business operations were overextended in general. He was forced to declare bankruptcy at the end of 1866, owing to Jardine's alone some Tls. 67,000.[77] Jardine's later tried vigorously to collect the debt (F. B. Johnson asked Chinese officials' assistance in this regard in 1868).[78]

72. Ibid., p. 126.

73. Ibid., p. 136.

74. *The Canton Chinese* (Boston, 1849), p. 114.

75. Liang Chia-pin, p. 237.

76. Ibid., p. 118; and Morse, *Chronicles*, II, 284.

77. Edward Whittall reported from Shanghai in January 1867 on the debt of Ekee: "The only dependencies at credit are the Tea & Silk shipped to England on his account, to which has been added the difference between the contract price of the Green Tea & what it sold for, also our profit said to have been made & our interest in the Ewo Bank" (to James Whittall [Hong Kong], Jan. 3, 1867, JMA).

78. "I have annexed to the statement of Ekee's Estate a copy of the original memo of assets & a statement of their realization so far. I have discovered the owner of some property in Tychow valued at Tls. 3,000 c [to] 4,000 mortgaged to Ekee & transferred to us & I

Another leading independent merchant who ended up in bankruptcy was Hu Kuang-yung. Hu, a native of Chekiang, was probably the most prominent silk merchant at Shanghai in the early 1880s. He accumulated wealth by serving under Tso Tsung-t'ang. From 1867 Tso had him take charge of the forwarding office at Shanghai, where he was mainly responsible for the procurement of supplies for Tso's army. Hu also operated native banks, and his own Fu-k'ang bank was one of the most respectable and dependable native banks in China. The exact point in Hu's career when he began to branch out into commodity speculation is not known, but it is probable that speculative activities accounted for part of his wealth. From 1881 he speculated extensively in silk, and by 1882 he was reported to have held a large amount. But he miscalculated the market and went broke in 1883.[79]

Many coastal businessmen were comprador-merchants. The risks and uncertainties that were inherent in compradorship always haunted them. Because a comprador, according to Chinese practice, usually carried unlimited responsibility, any accumulated losses inevitably led to the deterioration and even the complete collapse of his own business as an independent merchant. Ahee, comprador to James Bowmann & Co., absconded in October 1859.[80] The failure and absconding of compradors became more common from the sixties on, especially at Shanghai. The outstanding failures of the Chinese comprador-merchants in the sixties included Fung Heen, a native of Whampoa, Canton, who was the comprador to the Oriental Bank at Shanghai from July 1861 to January 1864. Due to speculation and overextended business, he failed on January 4, 1864.[81] Ahien provided a similar case. A Cantonese who went to Shanghai in the fifties, he established himself as a tea merchant in the next decade. He became comprador to Gibb, Livingston & Co. in the early sixties and went broke in 1869.[82]

In the seventies there were two conspicuous bankruptcies. Ch'en Li-t'ang, comprador to Kelly, Wash & Co. at Shanghai, failed in 1874.[83] Sung Ts'ai, comprador to Sassoon & Co. at Chinkiang, owed the firm

---

have moved the Chinese Authorities to order the value to be paid to us" ([Shanghai] to Jardine, Matheson & Co. [Hong Kong], Sept. 11, 1868, JMA).

79. For an account of Hu Kuang-yung's career as a merchant-banker, see Stanley, *Late Ch'ing Finance*.

80. *NCH*, Oct. 15, 1859, p. 42.

81. *NCH*, June 4, 1864, p. 91.

82. F. B. Johnson (Shanghai) to William Keswick (Hong Kong), Apr. 24, 1869, JMA.

83. *Shen pao*, TC 13/1/18, Mar. 6, 1874, p. 1.

"tens of thousands of taels" and decamped in 1876.[84] At the same time, there were numerous compradors with relatively small debts who absconded.[85] One of them was Achow, Jardine's comprador at Swatow, who failed in 1874.[86] More compradors took to flight in the eighties, especially those of the smaller foreign houses. The *North-China Herald* commented on March 28, 1883:

> The compradors of the smaller houses, lightly chosen on the recommendation and security of some man as shaky as themselves, debarred from the systematic squeezing on which compradores exist, not infrequently resort to open robbery, flying when discovery is imminent. In several cases compradors have been brought up for running away, leaving a balance against them of several thousand taels.[87]

Yang Kuei-hsuan, comprador to Butterfield & Swire at Shanghai, accumulated a large debt of Tls. 100,000 to the firm over a three-year period from 1881 to 1884. This debt represented his losses as a comprador as well as a speculator.[88] In 1892 the bankruptcy of the comprador to the Hongkong and Shanghai Banking Corporation at Shanghai, a man of immense influence in the treaty port communities, considerably disturbed the financial market.[89]

In the twentieth century, many Chinese compradors in Hong Kong went bankrupt. On May 1, 1905, for example, Jung Cho-sheng and Wei Lin-shih legally declared bankruptcy.[90] Most of them were compradors to small foreign firms, and the *Hua-tzu jih-pao*, a leading Chinese newspaper at Hong Kong, suggested that a more careful process of recruiting compradors should immediately be adopted.[91] Other ports besides Shanghai and Hong Kong had problems with absconding compradors, and these cases occasionally involved the compradors of large foreign houses. Han Teng-t'ang, comprador to Caslowitz & Co. at Hankow, and Han Mei-ch'ing, comprador to Arnhold Karberg & Co. at the same port, absconded in 1902, leaving a considerable amount of debt behind them.[92]

84. *Shen pao*, Feb. 22, 1876, p. 3.
85. *Shen pao*, June 5, 1879, p. 3, and June 17, 1879, p. 3.
86. Otto Asverus (Swatow) to A. Curtis (Hong Kong), Nov. 16, 1874, JMA.
87. *NCH*, Mar. 28, 1883, p. 352.
88. Cheng Kuan-ying, *Hou-pien*, 10:119. For a "Mixed Court" hearing of the case, see *NCH*, Oct. 29, 1884, p. 473.
89. LeFevour, p. 122. Unfortunately, the name of the comprador is not known.
90. *Hua-tzu jih-pao*, May 1, 1905.
91. Ibid., June 3, 1905.
92. P'eng Yü-hsin, p. 28.

Wang Shao-yun, merchant at Shanghai, was the manager of the Ching-lun textile factory, founded by his fellow townsman Hsu Jun. In 1904 he also became the comprador of an Austrian firm. Because of the failures of some Chinese businessmen whose solvency he had guaranteed for the firm, he lost Tls. 50,000 during the first three months of his compradorship, which ended in his absconding.[93] Wei Lang-shan, vice-comprador to the gigantic Hongkong and Shanghai Banking Corporation, declared bankruptcy at Hong Kong in 1908.[94] Liu Hsin-sheng, a native of Hankow, was one of the wealthiest and best-known Chinese businessmen in that port at the turn of the century. Besides being a comprador to Racine, Ackerman & Co. and the Banque de l'Indochine, he was an entrepreneur in his own right. He operated an iron factory, a lumber factory, and a beancake oil mill, and was the vice president of the Chinese Chamber of Commerce at Hankow. However, he overextended his operations and went bankrupt in 1911, reportedly owing Chinese and Western merchants some Tls. 5,000,000.[95] Similar cases occurred in other cities, where many Chinese merchants and native banks suffered heavy losses.[96]

The careers of two prominent Chinese merchant-entrepreneurs in Shanghai, Tong King-sing and Hsu Jun, give eloquent testimony to the business risks and uncertainties along China's coast in the nineteenth century, because they personally experienced political and military disturbances, market fluctuations, speculation, business losses, and, finally, bankruptcy. The financial collapse of Tong and Hsu in late 1883 was partly caused by the unfortunate situation created through the Sino-French disputes over Indo-China.[97]

THE FINANCIAL CRISIS OF 1883

Sino-Western trade in the nineteenth century witnessed many crises that were attributable to all the risks that were contingent to burgeoning commercial capitalism. In the West, the depression of 1837 affected a few China traders, and the crisis of 1857, in which the American stock market almost crashed, led to the failure of two leading American com-

93. Hsu Jun, *Nien-p'u*, p. 103b.
94. *Hua-tzu jih-pao*, Nov. 21, 1908.
95. Wang Ching-yü, *Kung-yeh*, II, 961–63.
96. Teng Chün-hsiang, comprador to Hongkong and Shanghai Banking Corp. at Peking, absconded in 1927, reportedly leaving a debt of around Tls. 4,000,000 (*Hua-tzu jih-pao*, May 4, 6, 7, 9, and 11, 1927).
97. Hsu Jun, *Nien-p'u*, pp. 35a–b, 81b–82b.

mission houses in China, Wetmore & Co. and King & Co.[98] The financial crisis of 1873 in Europe was partly responsible for monetary stringencies on the Shanghai market in that year, and the financial crisis of 1890, in which the Baring Brothers of London failed, resulted in the bankruptcy in 1891 of Russell & Co., the most prestigious American firm in China.[99] At the China end, "the year 1866," a British consul observed, "closed on a state of depression never before witnessed in the China trade," which led to the closing of some Chinese businesses in Shanghai the following year.[100] In addition, native banks in Shanghai experienced various degrees of liquidity problems and failures in 1871, 1873, 1878, 1879, and 1910,[101] but the most serious economic crisis occurred at Shanghai in 1883.

BACKGROUND OF THE CRISIS

This crisis can be traced back to the severe natural disasters in the interior of China in 1876–1877, which reduced the treaty ports' trade with the interior. In this period, there were hordes of flying locusts in North China, storms in Kiangnan, droughts in Hunan and Kwangsi, and floods in Fukien and Kwangtung. The drought in North China was especially protracted and widespread, causing millions of deaths. These disasters led to economic decline and reduced purchasing power on the market, as we have just discussed.[102] In 1883 the Yellow River floods once again affected wide areas, which caused purchasing power in the interior to decline even further and thereby weakened the foundations of the Shanghai market.[103] On the international front, China experienced an unfavorable balance of trade (caused partly by the fall of silver prices on the world market) from 1877 on, reaching an unprecedented annual total of more than Tls. 20,000,000 in 1881 (table 17). This trend led to tight money along China's coast, particularly on the Shanghai market.[104]

98. George William Edwards, *Finance Capitalism*, pp. 149–50; and Lockwood, p. 26.

99. The immediate cause of the suspension in 1890 of Baring Brothers, closely associated with the London capital market since the eighteenth century, was the default of the Argentine government (Edwards, *Finance Capitalism*, pp. 36–37).

100. Report of Consul Charles Winchester, Shanghai, May 6, 1868, PO 17/503, p. 51; and Hsu Jun, *Nien-p'u*, p. 14.

101. For the financial crisis of 1910, see Marie-Claire Bergère, *Une crise financière à Shanghai à la fin de l'ancien régime* (Paris, 1964), esp. pp. 1–11.

102. See footnote 48 of this chapter.

103. Han-sheng Ch'üan, "The Economic Crisis of 1883 as Seen in the Failure of Hsu Jun's Real Estate Business in Shanghai," in Chi-ming Hou and Tzong-shian Yu, eds., *Modern Chinese Economic History* (Taipei, 1979), p. 496.

104. Liang-lin Hsiao, *Statistics*, p. 22; and Liu Kuang-ching, "I-pa-pa-san nien Shanghai chin-yung feng-ch'ao," *Fu-tan hsueh-pao*, 1983. 3 (May 1983), p. 95.

TABLE 17.   CHINA'S FOREIGN TRADE: IMPORTS AND
EXPORTS, 1876–1884
(IN 1,000 HAIKUAN TAELS)

	Net imports	Exports	Export balance (+) Import balance (−)
1876	70,270	80,851	+ 10,581
1877	73,234	67,445	− 5,789
1878	70,804	67,172	− 3,632
1879	82,227	72,281	− 9,946
1880	79,293	77,884	− 1,410
1881	91,911	71,453	− 20,458
1882	77,715	67,337	− 10,378
1883	73,568	70,198	− 3,370
1884	72,761	67,148	− 5,613

Source: Liang-lin Hsiao, *China's Foreign Trade Statistics, 1864–1949*, p. 22.

But the basic reason—and also the immediate cause—for the financial crisis was market speculation. Encouraged by the success of China Merchants' Steam Navigation Co. and the Kaiping Mines, many provinces in the early 1880s tried to establish joint-stock mining companies by issuing stocks and selling them on the Shanghai market. By 1882 there were at least fourteen such new firms. Many individual businessmen as well as native banks speculated in these capital shares, driving prices sky-high by September 1882:[105]

Company	Face value (taels)	Market value on Sept. 26, 1882 (taels)
China Merchants S. N. Co.	100	253
Shanghai Cotton Textile Co.	100	110
Kaiping Mines	100	216.5
Ch'ang-lo Copper Mine, Hupei	100	168
P'ing-ch'uan Copper Mine, Jehol	105	256
Ho-feng Copper Mine, Hupei	100	155

Many such new enterprises were unsuccessful, and the price of their

105. Chang Kuo-hui, *Yang-wu yun-tung yü Chung-kuo chin-tai ch'i-yeh* (Peking, 1979), pp. 300–301, cited in Liu Kuang-ching, "Feng-ch'ao," p. 97.

stocks nose-dived in 1883; various native banks suffered heavy losses. Commenting on the bankruptcies of so many native banks in August and September of 1883, a local newspaper wrote in October that it was not so much the withdrawal of funds by individual depositors that caused the failures: "We have inquired of insiders for the real cause of the collapses, and all have informed us that since last year, the various stocks rose and fell quite irregularly and many have suffered great losses thereby."[106] Other local newspapers held similar views.[107] William Patterson, the Jardine partner at Shanghai, wrote on October 10: "There has been several failures among Native Banks and there are likely to be more. This has mostly been brought about by share speculation in Chinese Coys [companies]."[108]

The tension of war between China and France over Annam exacerbated the crisis. There is a scholarly debate on the degree to which the Sino-French War affected the Shanghai crisis of 1883. Hsu Jun maintains that there is a direct, causal relationship between the war and the crisis because French naval forces had reached the Woosung estuary before the crisis occurred. C. John Stanley and Kwang-Ching Liu, on the other hand, argue that Hsu Jun has erroneously ascribed events that occurred in 1884 to the preceding year, because there is little evidence to substantiate Hsu's memory that in 1883 French naval forces had arrived at the Woosung estuary and that the French had threatened to attack the Kiangnan Arsenal in Shanghai.[109] Stanley and Liu may be correct in pointing out the time of actual military conflict around Shanghai, but a financial market always anticipates events and reacts sensitively to the probabilities of military conflict.

The fact of the matter is that in May 1883 the stock price of Kaiping Mines was high at Tls. 210, but by August it had plummeted to Tls. 120. What happened in the summer is that, though China and France had not declared war formally, in June the Chinese local forces (the Black Flag army) began engaging the French troops in Haiphong, and the Ch'ing court dispatched regular troops into Tongking. In July French naval forces reached northern Annam, and in August the French blockaded all Annamese ports. In other words, the war was threatening

106. *Tzu-lin Hu-pao*, Oct. 18, 1883, cited in Kwang-Ching Liu, "Credit Facilities in China's Early Industrialization," in Chi-ming Hou and Tzong-shian Yu, eds., *Modern Chinese Economic History*, p. 508.

107. *Shen pao*, Oct. 19 and 20, 1883; and *NCH*, Oct. 24, 1883.

108. To J. B. Irving, Oct. 10, 1883, JMA, cited in Kwang-Ching Liu, "Credit," p. 503.

109. Hsu Jun, *Nien-p'u*, p. 35; Stanley, *Late Ch'ing Finance*, p. 76; and Kwang-Ching Liu, "Credit," p. 507.

China's coastal areas. It was this ominous sense of war hovering over Shanghai that aggravated the ongoing financial crisis. *Shen pao* reported that, during summer and fall 1883, many depositors, for fear of war, withdrew their funds from the native banks.[110] A British consul reported from Chinkiang concerning the last quarter of 1883: "A general belief in the imminence of war induced the rich bankers of Shansi to withdraw their silver from native banks at Shanghae [Shanghai]."[111]

THE CRISIS

In 1883 Shanghai witnessed a severe financial crisis unprecedented in the history of Sino-Western trade. Banks closed, businesses failed, money was scarce, prices fell, the stock market plummeted, and prominent merchants went broke. The crisis started on January 12 when the Chin-chia-chi silk firm collapsed, losing Tls. 560,000 and in debt to forty native banks. Because this happened at the end of Chinese New Year, a time when the monetary market was always tight, this failure touched off a chain reaction, leading to the bankruptcy of some fifty firms (engaging in tea, silk, sugar, clothing, cotton, iron, groceries, and coastal junk trade) by February 7, involving more than Tls. 1,500,000. In default, forty-one of the ninety-nine native banks went out of business by February 11. Between October and December, of the fifty-eight banks that survived, as many as forty-eight went bankrupt, and quite a few other prominent firms collapsed with them.

This severe depression sent prices into collapse. General commodities lost 30 to 50 percent of their values, and real estate was altogether unsalable.[112] The share price of common stocks similarly plunged, Tong King-sing's personal support notwithstanding. William Paterson of Jardine's reported from Shanghai on August 1, 1883:

I believe he [Tong] holds some 3,000 Kaiping mine shares upon which he has received large advances from the Natives. Six or eight months [ago] he went to the market & bought shares and Chinese at once followed him & the result was for a time a firm and higher market. He wired out the other day [from England, where Tong was on a visit] to buy shares to steady the market & some 500 were bought for him up to Tls. 120 per share, but instead of the Chinese following, they were prepared at the finish to sell freely at Tls. 115 or less.[113]

110. *Shen pao*, Jan. 12 and 23, 1884.
111. BPP, *Consular Report, Chinkiang, 1884*, p. 197.
112. Hsu Jun, *Nien-p'u*, p. 82.
113. To F. B. Johnson (Hong Kong), JMA, cited in Kwang-Ching Liu, "Credit," pp. 502–3.

With time, the crisis intensified, as Paterson reported again two months later: "Kaiping mine shares which at one time touched Tls. 260 are now offered at Tls. 70 without finding purchasers, and China Merchants' shares which were also very high are offered freely at Tls. 90."[114] As the crisis protracted into 1884, their stocks sank to the bottom; Kaiping Mine shares fell to Tls. 29, and China Merchants' shares to Tls. 34.[115] Compared with their prices in September 1882, these two stocks experienced an average of an 87 percent drop in price.

Many native banks had made advances secured by these shares. In his trade report for the year 1883, the British consul in Shanghai wrote:

Advances were freely made [by the native banks] on shares in native mining and other companies, the majority of which never got beyond the initial stage, and the bankers were burthened with depreciated securities. The want of confidence resulting from the collapse of these projects was one cause of the tightness of the money market which prevailed in the latter half of the year.[116]

A reporter of the *North-China Herald* held a similar view: "[In early 1883] nearly all the native bankers had made advances on Chinese stocks and shares, most of which markets have become either of diminished value, or, in very many cases, positively worthless."[117] A perusal of other local newspapers in both Chinese and English indicates that this view was widely held.[118] It was not without reason that the native banks were willing to take these dubious capital shares as collateral for loans. After the early 1860s, these banks had two, new, large financial resources— the Shansi remittance banks and "chop loans"—that made their loan business more competitive, and, as a consequence, the requirement for loans became less strict.

After 1860 the rapid rise of Shanghai as China's leading commercial center attracted many Shansi banks, and their number had increased to twenty-four by 1864. Shansi banks received large deposits from high officials, with whom the banks had close ties and in turn lent the funds to the money-shop native banks. This type of loan was called *ch'ang-ch'i* (long-term) but actually was recallable at any time. In a good market,

114. To J. B. Irving, Oct. 10, 1883, JMA, cited in Kwang-Ching Liu, "Credit," p. 503.
115. *NCH*, Oct. 24, 1883; and Hsu Jun, *Nien-p'u*, p. 81b.
116. Stanley, *Late Ch'ing Finance*, p. 77.
117. *NCH*, Oct. 24, 1883.
118. These include the *Tzu-lin Hu-pao*, which was owned by the British but edited by Chinese and frequently criticized foreigners. For an article in its Oct. 18, 1883, issue, see *Shang-hai ch'ien-chuang*, pp. 49–50. An editorial in *Shen-pao* also ascribed the recent failures of Chinese banks chiefly to speculation in joint-stock shares (Oct. 19 and 21, 1883). All cited in Kwang-Ching Liu, "Credit," pp. 504–8.

the amount of such loans could reach Tls. 2,000,000 to 3,000,000. As the financial crisis of 1883 deteriorated in the fall of that year, the Shansi banks on October 30 recalled all their *ch'ang-ch'i* loans, amounting to more than Tls. 1,000,000.[119]

After the mid-1860s, it was common practice for the Western banks and mercantile houses to grant large, short-term chop loans to native banks—their second new resource. On October 29, 1883, F. B. Johnson, the Jardine manager at Hong Kong, wrote to his partner at Shanghai that foreign banks had withdrawn the substantial amount of more than Tls. 2,000,000 from the native banks at these two ports:

The Chinese say that the fear of war with France causes the existing stagnation but in my opinion the principal reason why trade is so dull is to be found in the withdrawal of all foreign capital from the Native Banks here & in Shanghai. The average advances during recent years have not been less than 2 million of taels & the withdrawal of this sum following on the losses incurred by Native speculators in land here and in mining & other schemes in your part of the world is quite sufficient to account for the collapse of enterprise.[120]

In his trade report for the year 1883, the British consul in Shanghai gave a similar assessment: "The native local banks were also hampered by the inability to borrow money from foreign banks, which prudently declined to make the short loans which they were in the habit of making."[121]

In October as the war situation became increasingly tense, more businessmen liquidated their assets, and money became scarce. Meanwhile, individual depositors quickly withdrew their funds from the native banks. More business failures prompted the recall of *ch'ang-ch'i* loans and chop loans. This worsened the liquidity problem. As the year 1883 drew to a close, panic swept Shanghai, causing a flight of capital. The silver stock in Shanghai was reduced 90 percent to a meager Tls. 380,000.[122] It was under these circumstances that two of the richest businessmen in Shanghai, Hsu Jun and Hu Kuang-yung, went bankrupt.

Hsu Jun made handsome money as the comprador to the leading British agency house of Dent & Co. from 1861 to 1867. As an independent merchant, he speculated on the currency market, founded the noted

119. *Shen pao*, Oct. 24, 1883, and Jan. 12, 1884, cited in Liu Kuang-ching, "Feng-ch'ao," pp. 98, 96; and *Tzu-lin Hu-pao*, Feb. 9, 1884, cited in *Shang-hai ch'ien-chuang*, pp. 51–52.
120. To William Paterson, JMA; cited in Kwang-Ching Liu, "Credit," p. 504.
121. Stanley, *Late Ch'ing Finance*, p. 77.
122. Hsu Jun, *Nien-p'u*, p. 82b.

Pao-yuan-hsiang tea firm, and after the seventies invested in and managed various commercial, industrial, and insurance enterprises. He put his principal resources in real estate in the foreign settlement of Shanghai, by early 1883 amassing 2,900 *mou* of land in addition to 320 *mou* on which buildings had been constructed. It was in real estate that Hsu overextended himself, and he collapsed financially in mid-November 1833. Under the pressure of native bankers who were themselves in difficulty, Hsu surrendered all his real estate holdings (which originally had cost Tls. 2,200,000) as well as all his stocks in modern enterprises and pawnshops (the total current value of these having been determined at Tls. 982,530), in order to meet his obligations totaling Tls. 2,500,000.[123]

The noted banker Hu Kuang-yung, as we have seen, was a man of means. He made money by speculating in rice in the early sixties and was deeply involved in silk speculation by the early eighties. He purchased a large quantity of 3,000 bales of silk in June 1881. His stock rose to 8,000 bales in May 1882, and to 14,000 bales by October, which naturally drove up the price of silk in Shanghai. By the end of September 1882, the silk price at Shanghai had risen to a high of 17s. 4d. for one grade then worth only 16s. 3d. in London. Meanwhile, in 1883 the Italian silk production had recovered and begun to rise. The Western merchants sensed that Hu would have to sell sooner or later, so they ceased buying at current prices. From August to October 1883, Hu remained firm in his asking prices, and buyers were equally persistent in their attitudes. The majority of Shanghai silk merchants stopped their operations. As the depression proceeded, all commodities fell in price, and Hu reluctantly began to sell his silk in November, and was said to have lost more than Tls. 1,000,000.[124] His finances finally collapsed on December 5; with him the reputable Fu-k'ang Bank went down.

By the end of 1883, the financial crisis at Shanghai had already afflicted damages to the coastal commerce from Kwangtung to Kiangsu. As a number of the native banks in Shanghai, especially Hu Kuang-yung's Fu-K'ang Bank, had close ties with commerce in Chekiang, Kiangsu, and other neighboring provinces, Hsu's bankruptcy had considerable adverse effects on China's coastal commerce in general. More importantly, because these native banks played a significant role in financing the purchase of tea and silk from inland, their collapse retarded commerce and agriculture in the interior as well.

123. Ibid., pp. 34–36, 82b; and Kwang-Ching Liu, "Credit," pp. 504–5.
124. Li Wen-chih, *Chung-kuo chin-tai nung-yeh shih tzu-liao*, p. 536; Stanley, *Late Ch'ing Finance*, pp. 73–78; and *Shang-hai ch'ien-chuang*, pp. 47–49.

IMPLICATIONS

The economic crisis of 1883 reflected the strengths and weaknesses of Sino-Western commercial capitalism. For more than two decades after 1860, commerce on China's coast, thanks to free trade and monetary and credit expansion, witnessed unprecedented development. But fast economic expansion bred economic contraction, and the ensuing depression shows that the coastal financial institutions were fragile, credit resources limited, and the stock market volatile. Business uncertainties abounded, as evidenced by speculative maneuvers, price fluctuations, bank runs, war panics, business losses, and bankruptcies.

The financial disasters that befell the Chinese business community at Shanghai had detrimental effects on China's industrialization. They not only afflicted many traders and bankers who had no interest beyond commerce and finance, but also dealt a near-fatal blow to a number of businessmen who were interested in modern enterprises.[125] These businessmen included those who were engaged in traditional-style businesses but had just started to show interest in modern enterprises. The native banker Hu Kuang-yung, for example, wrote in early 1882 to Governor-General Tso Tsung-t'ang, indicating his willingness to undertake single-handedly the construction of telegraphic lines along the Yangtze River. After his bankruptcy, China could no longer tap his reportedly large fortune of about Tls. 10,000,000 for industrial purposes.

More importantly, these businessmen also included a group of energetic, modern-minded entrepreneurs, such as Tong King-sing, Hsu Jun, and Cheng Kuan-ying, who were the pioneers of modern enterprise in China, actively involved in the steamship-borne industry, in modern-type mining, and in industrial manufacturing enterprises. Hsu Jun, for example, in addition to his interests in real estate and pawnshops, invested in various modern undertakings.[126] (See table 18.) The financial disasters suffered by Tong King-sing and Hsu Jun resulted in their leaving the China Merchants' Steam Navigation Co., and Cheng Kuan-ying's losses led to the long interruption of the establishment of the Shanghai Cotton Textile Co., which was on the verge of production by 1883. Their financial failures therefore had the effect of nipping in the bud, as it were, the nascent Chinese industrial capitalism that, up until 1883, had a chance of uninterrupted growth. After that date, other

125. Kwang-Ching Liu, "Credit," p. 499.
126. Hsu Jun, *Nien-p'u*, pp. 34–35b, 81b–82b.

TABLE 18.   HSU JUN'S INVESTMENTS IN THE EARLY 1880s
(TAELS)

Enterprise	Amount
China Merchants' Steam Navigation Co.	480,000
Five mines (excl. Kaiping Mines)	280,000
The Kaiping Mines	150,000
Two insurance companies	150,000
Shanghai Cotton Cloth Mill	50,000
China Glass Co., Shanghai	30,000
Sugar refinery, Hong Kong	30,000
Dairy company, Hong Kong	30,000
Land reclamation company near Taku	30,000
Silk filature in Shanghai	25,000
Paper mill in Shanghai	20,000
Investments in Western companies	100,000[a]
Real estate in Shanghai	2,237,000
Eight pawnshops	349,000
Native banks	50,000[a]
Total	4,101,000

Source: Hsu Jun, *Hsu Yü-chai tzu-hsu nien-p'u*, pp. 34–35b, 81b–82b.
[a]My estimate.

modern-minded Chinese had to start all over again. Precious time was lost in China's early industrialization.[127]

Furthermore, the economic crisis of 1883 was a turning point for the rise of bureaucratic capitalism. As Hu Kuang-yung was no longer in a position to pursue his interest in the construction of a telegraphic line along the Yangtze River, the project was later undertaken by the newly established Imperial Telegraph Administration, a *kuan-tu shang-pan* (merchant undertaking under government supervision) enterprise headed by Sheng Hsuan-huai, an official who hardly considered himself a businessman.[128] Other *kuan-tu shang-pan* enterprises, after the exodus of such professional and entrepreneurial businessmen as Hsu Jun, Tong

127. Kwang-Ching Liu, "Credit," p. 500; and Liu Kuang-ching, "Feng-ch'ao," p. 100.
128. Liu Kuang-ching, "Feng-ch'ao," p. 100; and Albert Feuerwerker, *China's Early Industrialization* (Cambridge, Mass., 1958), pp. 190–207.

King-sing, and Cheng Kuan-ying, saw a reorientation in management policy. For instance, Governor-General Li Hung-chang in 1884 appointed Sheng Hsuan-huai to replace Tong and Hsu in managing the China Merchants' Company. Under Sheng's administration, the Chinese company had little progress, and the fleets of the Western rivals grew by leaps and bounds. Within a decade, its predominate position in the steamship trade in Chinese waters was fast disappearing because it was outdistanced by Jardine's and by Butterfield & Swire in the number and net tonnage of steamships.[129] In other words, after 1883 bureaucrats, headed by Sheng Hsuan-huai, unfortunately got a firm grip of the *kuan-tu shang-pan* enterprises (which had earlier spearheaded China's industrialization), and bureaucratism began to play a much more important role than entrepreneurship in China's industrial development.

Finally, the financial crisis of 1883 made it more difficult to raise capital for industrial undertakings in later years. The financial resources of the Ch'ing government in supporting modern enterprises was extremely limited, because the total tax revenue constituted only 2.4 percent of China's net national income by the end of the Ch'ing period.[130] Consequently, a business structure based on large-scale, joint-stock companies was indispensable to China's early industrialization, but the crisis of 1883 discredited these joint-stock enterprises in the eyes of both Chinese promoters (who at one time were eager to lead) and Chinese investors (who did have capital to invest). From the late 1870s on and as late as the end of 1882, the general economic expansion, together with the early successes of the China Merchants' Company and the Kaiping Mines, led to a public enthusiasm toward modern Chinese companies.[131] But by the end of 1883 stock prices nose-dived, and many newly formed joint-stock companies, including some bubble schemes, proved to be disastrous. It was reported that "bogus companies have depleted the Shanghai natives by nearly three millions of taels."[132]

In 1885 one could still find along the banks of the Whangpu River in Shanghai "the empty, useless, and deserted structures, monuments of abortive enterprises which are dotted here and there. . . . They are the

129. In 1894, whereas the Chinese company still had a fleet of twenty-six ships (23,284 net tons), the Indo-China S. N. Company's fleet had grown to twenty-two ships (23,953 net tons) and the China Navigation Company's fleet had expanded to twenty-nine ships (34,543 net tons) (Kwang-Ching Liu, "British-Chinese," pp. 71–75).

130. This is Yeh-chien Wang's estimate for the year 1908 (*Land Taxation in Imperial China, 1750–1911* [Cambridge, Mass., 1973], p. 133).

131. Chang Kuo-hui, *Yang-wu yun-tung*, pp. 300–1, cited in Liu Kuang-ching, "Feng-ch'ao," p. 97.

132. *NCH*, Oct. 24, 1883, cited in Kwang-Ching Liu, "Credit," p. 508.

silent ghosts of factories—the graves of enterprises which were strangled
at their birth."[133] A Chinese entrepreneur familiar with modern-style
mining commented in 1887 on the business trend: "In Shanghai alone,
several scores of *kung-ssu* (modern firms) had been set up but few were
successful, especially with respect to those of mining. The promoters,
after having lost all they have, still owe creditors money. Consequently,
for a long time people have been fed up with the word *kung-ssu*."[134] Indeed, the financial structure of the treaty port economy proved too volatile for a stable market in industrial securities to exist, and after 1883 it
became much more difficult to raise industrial capital through joint-
stock companies.

133. *NCH*, Dec. 16, 1885, pp. 674–75.
134. Li Chin-yung's remarks. See Sun Yü-t'ang, *Chung-kuo chin-tai kung-yeh shih tzu-liao*,
I. 719, cited in Liu Kuang-ching, "Feng-ch'ao," p. 99.

CHAPTER TWELVE

Conclusion

The net result of the vigorous trade along the coast in modern China was the emergence of a commercial revolution in the form of Sino-Western mercantile capitalism. Something new and important had developed in the commercial sector of the Chinese economy during the nineteenth century, especially from the 1820s to the 1880s. Sino-Western commercial capitalism was a significant form of development, and, viewed from the perspective of worldwide economic history, so many substantial changes in commerce are seldom seen on so large a scale in so short a time.[1] It therefore seems appropriate to call this process a *commercial revolution.*

New economic forces fermented in China during the late eighteenth century, but, in modern Chinese economic history, the 1820s saw what Fernand Braudel calls a "conjuncture"—a multitude of factors that occurred simultaneously.[2] A fundamental commercial change was in the making, which came into full bloom by the 1860s and maintained strong

1. An economic revolution is not as sharply defined as a political one. The American Revolution broke out in 1776 and attained its goal by 1783, but it is virtually impossible to single out an initial and a terminal date for the Industrial Revolution or for a commercial revolution. In China the "commercial revolution" that occurred after the eighth century (when the transition from classic to early modern China was in progress) lasted for more than 400 years. For a general survey of commercial history of China, see Ch'en Ts'an, *Chung-kuo shang-yeh shih* (Taipei, 1965), esp. I, 54–71. The West also experienced protracted commercial revolutions. See Samuel B. Clough and Charles W. Cole, *Economic History of Europe* (Boston, 1952); Robert S. Lopez, *The Commercial Revolution of the Middle Ages, 950–1350* (Cambridge, England, 1976); and Laurence B. Packard, *The Commercial Revolution, 1400–1776* (New York, 1927).

2. For the idea of conjunctures in history, see Braudel, *The Mediterranean and the Mediterranean World in the Age of Phillip II,* tr. Sian Reynolds (New York, 1975), II, 892–900.

momentum into the 1880s. This development is all the more impressive given the fact that the Ch'ing government, unlike its counterparts in the West, did not play an active role in promoting it.

This commercial revolution had many salient features. All that has proved most typical of the modern sector of Chinese economy during the late Ch'ing times appeared, at least in embryo, by the turn of the nineteenth century. Contrary to the conventional view, China's coastal commerce was, in large measure, "free" in the days of the old Canton system (1757–1842), as evidenced by the activities of the "shopmen," the opium-smuggling trade, the independence of the "country" trade, and the ingenuity of the "free merchants." This situation had existed for decades, but in the 1820s, with the rise of British and American agency houses, the tempo of change accelerated.[3] In the ensuing decades, the treaty system ushered in an era of bona fide free trade. The Treaty of Nanking was therefore not as epoch-making as is generally believed; it was only one factor in facilitating a commercial capitalism that had already been set in motion.

The expansion of money, as evidenced by the Mexican silver dollars and Chinese paper notes (ssu-p'iao), was another fresh economic force in the 1820s. In time monetary stock became unprecedentedly large, increasing a hefty nine times during the Ch'ing period and outpacing the population growth. Thanks to the bills of exchange on London and the Chinese draft (hui-p'iao), trade on credit became an established practice by the 1820s, breaking an old business practice. Meanwhile, the opium trade typified the widening of the market. In the 1820s coastal merchants introduced such innovative practices as the "outer anchorages" and the "coastal system." Later on the "Soochow system" was developed. Average annual amount imports of opium increased from some 4,000 chests in the first decades of the nineteenth century to a peak of some 83,000 chests in 1879.

China's commercial revolution gained further momentum in 1860 with the conclusion of the prolonged war with Britain and France and the defeat of the Taiping uprising. The economies of the interior, especially those of silk-producing Kiangnan, the Bohea tea districts of Fukien and Kiangsi, and the Yangtze tea-growing region of Hunan and Hupei, were revitalized by the innovative practice of upcountry purchases. The

---

3. Magniac & Co. was founded in 1824. It was the forerunner of Jardine, Matheson & Co., the largest British house in China, which was established in 1832. Russell & Co., the largest American commission house in China, was also established in 1824.

expansion of the tea trade typified the commercialization of agriculture, and new commercial centers, such as Ch'ung-an, Chien-ning, and Foochow, rose to prominence. Tea exports reached a peak of 250,000,000 pounds in the 1880s; tea represented 60 percent of China's total exports and 88 percent of the world's exported tea. Silk exports increased similarly. Tea and opium led the market expansion, but the irony is that the Chinese were no more traditional opium smokers than the British were traditional tea drinkers. To a large degree, these habits were a product of two salient features of nineteenth-century capitalism—efficient production and ingenious marketing.

There is virtually no capitalism without competition, and keen commercial rivalry emerged after 1860 in all areas of trade—upcountry purchases, exports, imports, and the shipping trade along the coastal areas. Although the Western traders believed in laissez-faire, including the spirit of competition, their Chinese counterparts were often motivated by economic nationalism—a strong desire to compete with foreign merchants. In the pursuit of profit, the coastal merchants usually benefited from Sino-Western cooperation: the Chinese merchants received advances, low-interest loans, modern expertise and facilities, and political protection; the Western businessmen obtained market intelligence, quality produce, and shipping and insurance business. Diversified investments and the joint-account system of trade proved profitable for all. Meanwhile, market uncertainties and commercial risks loomed large. In contrast to their counterparts in the interior, coastal merchants at once had golden opportunities and deadly risks.

Thus, although new economic forces fermented along China's coast in the late eighteenth century, the commercial revolution did not gather momentum until the 1820s when a cluster of fundamental changes took place in the organization of enterprises and in the techniques of exchange: the "country" trade grew by leaps and bounds; the old commercial framework (the Canton system and the British East India Co.) was disintegrating; the agency houses rose to prominence; money stock substantially increased; credit in commerce entered a new era; and the opium trade assumed worldwide importance. Taken together, the aggregate change in trade was so great that it may be considered as the beginning of a commercial revolution. After 1842 the "treaty system," which facilitated free trade, gave new impetus to the process. When peace was restored domestically and internationally after 1860, this commercial revolution, revitalized by a revolution in worldwide communication, quickened its tempo: commercial rivalry stepped up; commercialization of agriculture intensified; and the widening of the market accelerated (as evidenced by the upcountry purchase system). Meanwhile, lush opportunities were accompanied by precarious market conditions.

Changes in the commercial world during the 1820s were mainly functional, but those of the 1860s, being faster in tempo and larger in scope, were structural as well as functional changes. The commercial revolution, on balance, reached its zenith in the seventies, as measured by the size of the money supply, the expansion of credit, the volume of opium trade, the vitality of upcountry purchases, the dominant position of Chinese tea and silk in the world market, and the stiff competition in both foreign trade and the coastal trade. The revolution symbolically came to an end with the market panic of 1883. The financial crises, however, were not unmitigated misfortunes. They were in a sense the growing pains of the Chinese economy, of Sino-Western commercial capitalism groping for solutions to new and baffling financial problems. In fact, the Chinese economy continued to expand throughout the nineteenth century.

All in all, one finds modern China's commercial revolution in the rise of Sino-Western commercial capitalism along the coast from the 1820s to 1883. These commercial changes were closely intertwined and reinforced one another. Pecuniary security and financial flows, for instance, created and sustained low interest rates. These low rates in turn attracted further flows and led to commercial and industrial investments that were sources of financial profit. And the pecuniary gains thus obtained were relatively safe in the treaty ports. This chain reaction, like so many others, was spiral in form, each act contributing to making the next more possible, until a peak was eventually reached.

The rise of Sino-Western commercial capitalism was a complicated process. On the one hand, one finds flourishing activities in the "country" trade, agency houses, exports and imports, and money and credit. On the other hand, silver outflow caused economic contraction during the second quarter of the nineteenth century, and the scarcity of money during times of political unrest prompted the frequent use of opium as a medium of exchange. In addition to foreign wars, there were financial crises with devastating consequences. And the Taiping uprising all but aborted the commercial revolution. Indeed, there is no single conjuncture in history: we must visualize a series of overlapping histories, developing simultaneously.[4]

4. Braudel, *The Mediterranean*, II, 892.

How did this commercial capitalism compare with commercial developments in traditional China and in the West? In China a kind of "commercial revolution" lasted from the mid-T'ang period (eighth century) to the Southern Sung period (thirteenth century). But the commercial revolution during the nineteenth century not only was quicker in tempo, but led to an economic form that was in many ways considerably different from that of traditional China.

It was, first of all, based on Sino-Western trade, a hybrid system imposed on China by the Western powers. Second, viewed in a larger perspective, Chinese merchants along the coast in the nineteenth century were under much less government control than their counterparts of the previous centuries. In traditional China, the merchant class was generally under close control of the state;[5] a case in point is the thriving commercial development in eighteenth-century Yangchow that was spearheaded by government-licensed salt merchants.[6] Sino-Western commercial capitalism, however, took a different path: it emerged from this time-honored pattern, but it triumphed as a system based on genuine private undertakings. In the nineteenth century, Chinese merchants along the coast accumulated sizable fortunes mainly by engaging in various economic activities on their own initiative rather than resorting to official patronage. Thus, they were the first independent, modern-minded, commercial capitalists in Chinese history. It is not surprising, then, that full-fledged capitalism occurred not in the interior, but along the coast where the Ch'ing state had only loose control, and that it did not thrive in the eighteenth century of Pax Sinica, but bloomed instead in the nineteenth century when the Ch'ing state was declining.[7]

Third, Sino-Western commercial capitalism was large in scope and quick in tempo. The opium trade, for instance, is highly significant because of its sheer volume. It was no petty smuggling trade, but probably the world's largest commerce of the time in any single commodity. The trade in tea and silk gained a preeminent position unprecedented in

5. Commerce was always subject to the supervision and taxation of the officials. Government monopolies of staple articles, such as salt and iron in ancient times or tea, silk, tobacco, and salt later on, were expressions of the overriding economic prerogatives of the state.

6. See Ping-ti Ho, "The Salt Merchants of Yang-chou," *Harvard Journal of Asiatic Studies*, 17:130–68 (June 1954).

7. This does not mean that the Ch'ing government of the nineteenth century was entirely without control over treaty-port merchants. Indeed, it could tax their merchandise, at least outside of the treaty ports. The transit pass was not foolproof, and likin taxes were still a hurdle. See, e.g., the rich material on the Swatow Opium Guild case in the *NCH* in 1878.

Chinese history. China's monetary stock reached an all-time high, and credit activities were never livelier. As profit opportunities and business risks abounded, it took little time for one to rise from rags to riches or to lose a fortune.

Fourth, whereas wealthy merchants in traditional China tended to spend a great deal of their fortune in conspicuous consumption, the modern Chinese merchants along the coast invested a considerable part of their wealth in commercial and industrial enterprises. Another difference is that Sino-Western commercial capitalism was extremely unstable. This system, however innovative and vigorous it may have been, suddenly collapsed in the financial crisis of 1883. The panic destroyed more than 85 percent of the native banks in Shanghai. Throughout the late Ch'ing period, all of the American firms among the old China houses failed, and all but two of the British companies went bankrupt. Why was the system so extremely precarious?

Part of the explanation is related to the speculative, risk-taking mentality of Chinese and Western entrepreneurs, as we have stressed. Another reason is that the mutually beneficial Sino-Western symbiosis was at times mutually parasitical. A heavy reliance on Chinese connections, for instance, inhibited many Western merchants from being more innovative and diversified, contributing to their eventual demise. And the Chinese businessmen's activities under the foreign merchants' protection were not always in their best interests either. Some of them waited too long before investing their capital. Furthermore, although an awareness of profit opportunity was important to economic development, exaggerated expectations of profit, which were the case on the coast because of illegal Sino-Western dealings, were a drawback.[8] As a result, many investors kept their funds in liquid form or engaged in speculative operations by investing in foreign exchange, inventories, and real estate. In a larger sense, except for a few businessmen like Cheng Kuan-ying, their contentment with foreign protection reinforced their inertia and thus inhibited them from aggressively seeking sociopolitical reforms through Chinese channels.

Nor was the intense commercial competition always a sign of health and vitality. It forced businesses, Chinese and Western alike, into high-risk situations in which, through advances, upcountry trade, and freight-

---

8. An excessive alertness to new opportunities often led to the postponement or abandonment of useful ongoing ventures in favor of the new get-rich-quick activities. For further discussion, see Albert O. Hirschman, *The Strategy of Economic Development* (New Haven, Conn., 1958), pp. 20, 23.

rate wars, their credit was easily overextended, and their businesses were thus nearly always in jeopardy. This situation, with its attendant proliferation of brokerages and guilds, each taking a portion of profits, rendered Chinese tea and silk unprofitable vis-à-vis Japanese and Indian products and contrasted vividly with the more sober state of affairs in other countries at this time. Behind this unstable business milieu lay the basic fact that China was a semi-colonial country: unlike India, China maintained her political independence; but unlike Japan, China was far from being fully independent. As neither a foreign power nor a native government was in firm control of the situation, fierce competition ensued.

Finally, the nineteenth-century commercial revolution, in contrast to commercial developments in traditional China, brought a cluster of new business organizations and practices to China. Insurance and modern-style banking thrived, joint-stock companies represented the trend of the future, and the stock market became an instrument of raising capital. Sino-Western symbiosis prospered, legally or otherwise. Silver dollars were in wide circulation. Credit transactions became easy, inexpensive, and impersonal. Credit instruments were by and large standardized, and credit was extended not as a recognition of social status, but as a means of expanding business. Many business loans were secured by such non-traditional means as stock shares, promissory notes, cargoes carried through steamships, and produce stored in warehouses. New commercial practices came into being: the coastal system of selling opium; the Soochow system of buying silk; the upcountry purchase system of procuring tea and silk from the interior; trade on margin; option trading, including the right of first refusal to buy; and trade in futures under the contract system.

New commercial centers, such as Shanghai and Hong Kong, rose to national and international prominence. They were great population centers, which, unlike earlier Chinese cities as centers of political administration, were primarily great emporiums of trade.[9] It was in these economic centers that those who traded could usually count on a quick sale, prompt payment, and a broad choice of opportunities to invest the proceeds. It was here, too, that one found expert knowledge of market conditions the world over, skill in appraisal and classification of mer-

9. Shanghai was what Braudel calls a *place marchande* (*Afterthoughts*, p. 26). It was a trade and change center, like Amsterdam or London in the seventeenth and eighteenth centuries, which had currency quotations, money changers, and usually a bourse. Hong Kong was the other such center along China's coast in the nineteenth century.

chandise, informed brokerage services, and sophisticated facilities handling credit, exchange, insurance, and distribution.

The commercial revolution in nineteenth-century China and its counterparts in the West share some similar patterns: all originated and thrived along the coastal areas, and commercialization did not spread evenly in both Europe and China. In many ways, too, China's nineteenth-century commercial capitalism brings to mind the classic model of Western commercial capitalism that bloomed in Holland in the seventeenth century. In both cases, trade moved freely with little government control; political safety attracted large deposits from different places; credit business for distant centers was lively; pecuniary security and financial flows resulted in low rates of interest; and speculative trading in commodities and company shares flourished.[10] China's speculative boom in the early 1880s reminds one of similar situations in early eighteenth-century France (the "Mississippi Bubble") and England (the "South Sea Bubble"). And China was not alone in experiencing unstable market conditions: before 1850 the West witnessed frequent financial crises in which dozens of local banks failed.

One outstanding difference between the commercial developments in China and in the West is that in the West commercial capitalism was primarily a natural, spontaneous development,[11] whereas in modern China commercial capitalism was largely imposed from the West. A natural consequence of this situation is that the commercial revolution in nineteenth-century China had a quicker pace: in a few decades the West introduced to China the commercial institutions that had already slowly evolved in the West. A difference between Chinese capitalism and its Dutch counterpart is that whereas Amsterdam's reign, like those of Venice and Antwerp before her, was the reign of a city, Sino-Western commercial capitalism blossomed on the periphery of the economy of a very old empire. More importantly, a large portion of the mercantile capital in Amsterdam was channeled to financial operations, but a con-

10. In Europe, the commercial revolution of the Middle Ages developed along the coastal areas of the northern Mediterranean Sea, and the modern commercial revolution thrived on the Atlantic coast. See Lopez, *The Commercial Revolution of the Middle Ages*, chap. 3; and Packard, *The Commercial Revolution*, chaps. 1 and 2. The commercial revolution in nineteenth-century China centered on the coastal areas of the South China Sea and the East China Sea. The uneven diffusion of commercialization occurred in all the three commercial revolutions: in the inner recesses of Europe and China, business tended to be carried out in a lower key. For commercial development in Holland, see Barbour, *Capitalism in Amsterdam*.

11. When misfortune overwhelmed Antwerp in the late sixteenth century, the scepter passed to Amsterdam without political pressure.

siderable part of the new commercial wealth along China's coast found its way into industry.

The commercial capitalism in nineteenth-century China cannot be compared with its contemporary counterparts of the Western nations in terms of scope and sophistication: the stock market was limited and without government regulation; modern commercial law did not develop; most monetary stock was in metallic form; financial institutions were weak; Chinese private notes had a debilitating effect upon the economy; and for such high-value commodities as tea, silk, opium, and sugar there was no genuine national market that was an integral part of a modern economy.[12] In other words, China did not have a true "national economy"—a political space transformed into a coherent, unified economic space whose combined activities tend in the same direction.[13] Viewed in a larger perspective, Sino-Western commercial capitalism was only a peripheral aspect of the worldwide capitalistic system dominated by Great Britain.

Braudel divides all economic activities into three categories. The bottom level concerns everyday material life, involving basic necessities, habits, inertia, and daily routines. The second level is that of a market economy that links production with consumption, involving simple and direct exchanges. The highest level of the triptych is that of a capitalist mechanism that is highly sophisticated, complicated, unpredictable, and dominant, involving huge capital and high profits.[14] Sino-Western commercial capitalism, however, did not fit neatly into any one of these three categories. It obviously did not fall into the level of daily material life, because all commercial activities involve conscious decision and calculation. It reached out to the other two levels. On the one hand, as evidenced in chapters 2, 4, 9, 10, and 11, it showed, in some degree, the complexity, unpredictability, internationalism, and large profits of a capitalist mechanism. On the other hand, it was not extremely sophisticated, nor was it overwhelmingly dominant. As attested to in chapters 3, 5, 6, 7, and 8, it touched on the lower level of a market economy: simple, daily market exchanges; direct transactions that were almost, in

12. China had national marketplaces, such as Shanghai and Hankow, into which goods flowed from all over the country. While a *national marketplace* is simply a central place into which goods are channeled for exchange, in a *national market*, on the other hand, the prices of goods are determined by the interaction of supply and demand on a nationwide scale. For a fuller discussion, see Moulder, pp. 32–33. See also Feuerwerker, *The Chinese Economy*, p. 47.

13. Braudel, *Afterthoughts*, pp. 99–100, discusses the rise of the first national economy, that of England, in the mid-eighteenth century.

14. Braudel, *Capitalism*, p. xiii, and *Afterthoughts*, pp. 6, 50.

Braudel's word, "transparent"; and numerous participants including coolies, stevedores, peddlers, boatmen, money handlers, shopkeepers, operators of upcountry hongs, brokers, and money lenders. Sino-Western commercial capitalism therefore occupied a position in both the domain of the market economy and of high-flying capitalism, but belonged to neither. Instead, it was a mixture of the two.

The commercial revolution affected modern China's economic development in many ways, including some that were crucial. The role of silver dollars and bank notes in expanding China's commerce was very important because China's traditional monetary system was inadequate to meet the challenge of modern times. My estimate is that China's monetary stock was around $2.5 billion in 1910. For the sake of comparison, the average annual value of China's exports was $107,000,000 (Tls. 77,000,000) in the 1880s and $185,000,000 (Tls. 133,000,000) in the 1890s, and the annual revenue of the central government was about $124,000,000 (Tls. 89,000,000) in the early 1890s.[15] The amount of money used in late Ch'ing China was exceedingly large, and new forms of money constituted about 71 percent of the total amount.

The new money instruments played several important roles. Financially, they afforded a degree of flexibility to the money supply, increased the cash flow of financial institutions, expanded the credit market, and eased the problem of fiscal fluidity. Because these new forms of money were circulated on the coast as well as in the interior, they facilitated China's external trade and played an important role in her domestic commerce. Moreover, they enhanced business productivity. The traditional currency and exchange system was unusually complex; thus, every time goods or funds passed through the commercial network, a percentage was levied for the costs of exchange operations. This situation led to an inefficient proliferation of services, in which the distributive process involved more layers and more manpower than really necessary. This inevitably impeded the flow of commodities, causing numerous delays. And the distributive margin between buying and selling prices was increased because of the excessive number of persons who derived support from it. Consequently, the use of new forms of money not only increased efficiency but also reduced costs.

An economy that is characterized by sophisticated commercialization

15. For China's exports, see Feuerwerker, *The Chinese Economy*, pp. 48–49; calculations are mine. For the revenue of Chinese central government, see ibid., p. 66.

depends on a mechanism for the transfer of unused purchasing power accumulated in some parts of the economy to other parts where the surplus may be more useful. Yet this important credit system was not fully developed in China before the late Ch'ing period. After the mid-nineteenth century, however, credit became indispensable in trade along the coast. I have discussed its features, but, in terms of economic development, none is more important than that of low interest rates. My estimate is that the annual rate was about 12 percent. This rate was somewhat higher than that in contemporary Europe (6 to 8 percent), but was substantially lower than the prevailing rate in both traditional China (usually 40 percent or more) and the interior in modern times (35 to 50 percent or more). The low rates of interest resulted partly from the competition among Western firms in making loans, the ease with which security was handled, and the Ch'ing government's role as a light borrower on the financial market. But a more important reason was that the treaty ports offered an environment where capital was relatively secure from political disturbance.[16]

The upcountry purchase of tea and silk had several economic implications. It linked the upper two layers in the Braudelian three-tiered economy: the sophisticated "capitalistic mechanism" of the big cities on the one hand, and the "market economy" of the villages and towns on the other. It also increased productivity because, as a well-institutionalized practice conducted on a large scale, operation costs were reduced while the quality of the commodities improved. More importantly, the upcountry purchase system, reinforced by the penetration of silver dollar coins to the interior, at once related the hinterland commerce to the littoral trade and bridged China's agriculture with the world market.

One of the salient features of Sino-Western commercial capitalism was the competitive market—"the first computer available to men."[17] Commercial competition along the coast under the treaty system was virtually pure competition: no single merchant or group could dominate the market; there was little government intervention in the marketing process; and the entry into, and exit from, the market was relatively free and easy.[18] The Chinese merchants by and large outcompeted Western

16. It is interesting to note that in 1864 Jardine, Matheson & Co. had more confidence in the private Chinese coastal merchants than in the local authorities of Nagasaki, Japan (William Keswick [Shanghai] to James Whittall [Hong Kong], Oct. 7, 1864, JMA).
17. Oskar Lange, quoted in Braudel, *Afterthoughts*, p. 44.
18. Strictly speaking, the situation did not even resemble that of an oligopoly, because

traders because of their familiarity with local conditions, their ability to dispense with additional middlemen, and their satisfaction with a relatively small profit margin. The modern facilities and cheap credit offered by the Western traders were readily available to the Chinese, who quickly learned the modern way of doing business. But the most important reason was that the Chinese indigenous socioeconomic institutions remained effective. Organizations based on trade, kinship, and geographical considerations helped Chinese merchants to capitalize and market their goods. Particularism and functional diffusiveness were strong assets in the Chinese merchants' successful competition with foreign traders.[19]

The coastal merchants were highly motivated by the large profits to be made in trade. My estimate is that the average annual rate of profit was around 30 percent. In contrast, the rate of return on investment in farmland before taxes seems to have constantly decreased in the late Ch'ing, ranging from about 10 percent in the eighteenth century to around 4 percent in the 1870s, and less than 2 percent by the end of the dynasty.[20] Returns from traditional government monopolies, such as salt, were becoming at best static and were often declining. Given the economic climate of the late Ch'ing, the modern commercial enterprises along the coast were an attractive outlet for investment. It is important to remember that an awareness of profit opportunity is essential to call forth the initiatives that lead to economic development.

There are several economic implications of these profit-oriented activities. For one thing, contrary to the generally held view, an important reason for China's relatively slow economic development in the nineteenth century was not the scarcity of capital, because large amounts of Chinese fund were readily available. Besides, Chinese businessmen were wary of government exactions. Because they could not improve their position through legislative channels, they looked to Westerners for help. Third, Chinese investors responded, promptly yet

---

there were far too many relatively large firms. The competitors were well-informed and acted independently of one another.

19. For a recent study of the strengths of the Chinese merchants vis-à-vis their foreign rivals, see Murphey, *Outsiders*, chap. 10.

20. In the 1880s, profit from trade had become even greater than that from landholding, especially as land prices rose in response to continued population increase. The claim that land was a valuable investment was generally applicable only to the large, powerful landowners who, backed by their privileged position, could count on their landed estates as secure investments.

selectively, to the prospect for profit. Finally, in contrast to traditional China, a large portion of the fortunes accumulated on the coast during the late Ch'ing period became investment capital, which vigorously regenerated capital through commercial and industrial activities.[21]

The market risks and business losses that led to financial crises were due partly to the fact that China's coastal commerce was closely influenced by the world market. The Chinese economy was considerably aggravated and also stimulated as a result of the fluctuation of the world price of silver, changes in foreign investment or in the commodity trade, and real estate and financial speculations. Domestically, the Ch'ing government failed to play an active role in promoting commerce. A case in point is the financial crisis of 1883 in which the Chinese businessmen, without government support, were denied loan privileges by private Chinese and Western banks precisely because, ironically, these businessmen needed such financial assistance most urgently. Also there were many unhealthy financial institutions and practices in the Chinese economy.

It was common for the coastal merchants, Chinese and foreign alike, to engage in speculative trading, sometimes in a reckless manner. Speculation necessarily involved risk taking. It is important, however, to distinguish between the "gambling" instincts of speculators and the normal risk taking of the entrepreneur. It is also important to make a distinction between risk taking in long-term investments and speculation for immediate profit. In any event, the speculative activities of coastal merchants must be considered against the broader economic, social, and political background of the time. Sharply fluctuating prices provided strong temptations for speculation to those who possessed even small amounts of money. Speculation in this form permitted quick and not easily detected movement of capital from one venture to another, and mitigated the danger of attracting unwelcome attention to the accumulation of wealth. Most industrial or long-term commercial enterprises could not match the speculative ventures for security, anonymity, and rate of return. Widespread speculation also reflected the lack of adequate professional training in the modern sense, as well as the passive role of the government in the economy. Although the Ch'ing government did not directly hinder China's economic development in a fundamental

21. The accumulation of private fortunes did occur in traditional China, but such wealth did not necessarily constitute capital, because it was generally not devoted to the production of more wealth. Nor did it have a significant economic role until the nineteenth century, when private fortunes became useful capital.

way, it nevertheless failed to perform several functions important to the context of economic activity, such as the maintenance of peace and of commercial law and the standardization of weights and measures.

Speculation was detrimental to China's economic development in two significant ways. Individually, although a great deal of wealth passed through the hands of coastal merchants, many of them did not remain wealthy for long due to their propensity for speculative enterprises. If they had been financially successful for long periods of time, their positive influence on the Chinese economy and society as a whole would have been greater. In addition, the speculative market placed new industry in an unfavorable situation for the absorption of capital. It is true that business crises often occur in many societies, but, given the particular international and domestic conditions in China, coupled with the permeating mentality of speculation, the panic of 1883 in Shanghai was devastating.

The financial crisis of 1883 was detrimental to the development of agriculture, commerce, and industry at once, but its negative effect on China's industrialization was especially grave, because it occurred at a crucial time of transition from commercial capitalism to industrial capitalism. The early eighties saw a vital juncture in China's commercial development—a time when there was the possibility that it might grow into full-fledged industrialization. The disasters that befell the Chinese mercantile community at Shanghai afflicted many aggressive Chinese investors-entrepreneurs. Their financial failures had the effect of nipping in the bud, as it were, the nascent Chinese industrial capitalism, which had had a chance of uninterrupted growth until 1883. After that date, other modern-minded Chinese had to start all over again. China's early industrialization was thus slowed down.[22] This financial crisis did not deal a fatal blow to China's industrial development, because after a temporary setback the movement showed some progress, but the crisis of 1883 demonstrated that industrialization without a strong economic foundation could never thrive. Indeed, industrial capitalism was borne up by the strength and vitality of the market economy, and of the underlying economy as well.

Commercial activities on the coast served as a springboard for China's industrial development for two significant reasons. In the first place, one of the outstanding sources of economic development for a

22. For recent assessments, see Kwang-Ching Liu, "Credit," pp. 499–500; and Liu Kuang-ching, "Feng-ch'ao," pp. 98–101.

less-developed economy is the technology imported from more advanced economies. As the Western traders' expertise lay in commerce, they first invested in those industries that served the trade. They established more than 100 industrial enterprises in China from 1842 to 1895, and the great majority of these, including shipyards, docks, silk filatures, bean mills, sugar refineries, and other export-import processing industries, were closely related to Sino-Western trade. Consequently, commerce served as a medium in the transfer of technology from the West to China.[23]

More importantly, industrialization required a constant flow of fresh capital, and here the old commercial community supported the young industrial sector. Like the tobacco merchants of Glasgow and the tea merchants in London and Bristol who were instrumental in financing Britain's early industrial projects, many of the Chinese merchants on the coast who made fortunes in trade (Hsu Jun and Tong King-sing in tea, Takee and Chun Yuechong in silk, Tucksing and Tong Mow-chee in opium, and Yeh Ch'eng-chung and Cheng Kuan-ying in yarn and cloth) later invested substantial commercial capital in the pioneering enterprises of China's industrialization. These enterprises included China's first steamship undertaking (the China Merchants' Steam Navigation Company, 1872), first modern mining (the Kaiping Mines, 1878), first large-scale machinery production (the Yuan-ch'ang Machinery Company, 1883), first textile manufacturing (the Shanghai Cotton Cloth Mill, 1890), and such early major railroads as the Nanking-Shanghai Railroad and the Canton-Hankow Railroad (at the end of the nineteenth century). The capitalization of China's early industrialization, therefore, relied heavily on commerce, not agriculture. In the same vein, virtually all of China's prominent industrial managers started as merchants, acquiring modern management skills through commercial enterprises.[24] The thriving commercial development on the coast thus provided the much-needed capital, managerial skills, and entrepreneurship for China's early industrialization.[25] However unimpressive this industrial development might be when compared with that of Japan, it could not have started if there had not been a commercial revolution.

23. For the importance of cultural elements in the transfer of technology from the West to China, see Shannon R. Brown, "The Transfer of Technology to China in the Nineteenth Century," *Journal of Economic History* 39:181–97 (March, 1979).
24. The scholar-entrepreneur Chang Chien was a notable exception (Samuel C. Chu, *Reformer in Modern China* [New York, 1965]).
25. Commerce was important to industrial development in still another way. The expansion of trade carried with it the seeds of drastic change in the character of the modern sector of economy, because it put increasing pressure on the supply of manufactured goods and eventually ushered in the era of industrialization.

All told, the commercial revolution along the coast enhanced China's economic development in general. It not only fundamentally changed coastal trade, but had a concrete impact on the economy of the interior. It considerably accelerated the flow of goods, provided better services, and promoted innovation. In particular, it reduced cost, increased efficiency, facilitated market flexibility, and actively employed financial resources. Although commercialization is highly desirable in its own right as part of the process of economic development, the burgeoning Sino-Western commercial capitalism along the coast also helped China, in a fundamental way, come to grips with the crucial problem of long-term industrial development. Viewed from a Keynesian perspective, it is important to note that the immense supply of money, the rapid expansion of credit, and the remarkably low rate of interest all encouraged business investment and augmented the economic development of modern China. This was especially true in view of the fact that much of the Chinese economy's resources were not employed in the late Ch'ing period.[26]

In examining Sino-Western commercial capitalism in detail, this study also sheds light on three controversial issues in Chinese socioeconomic history: incipiency of capitalism, which is related to a worldwide debate on the question of transition from feudalism to capitalism; economic imperialism, which concerns not only China but the world at large; and the role played by the treaty ports in affecting modern China, which is an academic controversy with political overtones.

The first topic is that of indigenous sprouts of capitalism. I have noted the new aspects of Sino-Western commercial capitalism, contrasting them with China's traditional economic patterns. But to a considerable extent the new wine was sedulously poured into old bottles, which were durable and readily available. In fact, the commercial revolution of the nineteenth century was in many ways an indigenous movement, and China's traditional economic organization was sufficiently sophisticated to provide a framework that enabled Sino-Western commercial capitalism to thrive. It is no wonder, then, that there were no similar commercial revolutions in modern Africa and Latin America.

Viewed in a larger perspective, the major tradition of China's agrarian-bureaucratic empire from early times was accompanied by the

26. The classic work of John Maynard Keynes, *General Theory of Employment, Interest, and Money* (New York, 1936), has a detailed and technical discussion of the issue.

minor tradition of maritime China. In this minor tradition, sea trade and naval power flourished between the twelfth and fifteenth centuries.[27] On the seacoast south of Shanghai, there were merchants and their hangers-on who developed a lucrative trade with Southeast Asia. Maritime China grew up under less government control in the trade of large-scale commercial junks, which sailed throughout Asian waters, and in the coastal mercantile communities, which lived by coastal and foreign trade. Meanwhile, a vast water-borne domestic commerce evolved on the rivers and lakes of central and southern China, which fed into the maritime trade.[28] Thus, by the nineteenth century there were two Chinas: a maritime China, lively, flexible, enterprising, caught up in the economic growth of the modern times and looking beyond her frontiers; and a continental China, agrarian, bureaucratic, conservative, accustomed to her local horizons, and unaware of the economic advantages of international capitalism. It was this second China that consistently controlled political power.

It was the trading world of maritime China, into which the Westerners intruded, that provided a ready-made milieu for the blossoming of Sino-Western commercial capitalism. After all, treaty ports were situated in maritime China where commerce had considerably developed after the sixteenth century, as attested to by the vigorous trade in silk in the Kiangnan area, in rice and cotton along the Yangtze River, and in bean, rice, and sugar along the coast. All these were indigenous developments, and in this sense Sino-Western commercial capitalism represents a continuation of the secular trend in Chinese history.

Indeed, many of the main features of Sino-Western commercial capitalism were deeply ingrained in China's economic traditions. The old native banks were revitalized and expanded. They not only were crucial in financing Sino-Western trade, but also played a much more important role than the modern-style banks in financing China's early industrialization. Chinese paper notes, which transformed the Ch'ing monetary system from an awkward bimetallism to a troika by the turn of the nineteenth century, had its origins in the "flying money" (*fei-ch'ien*) of the T'ang period (618–907). Some of the loans were still guaranteed by such traditional means as title deeds of property. The old smuggling

27. The world's first large-scale maritime expedition between 1405 and 1433 took Chinese ships to India, the Persian Gulf, and the East African coast almost a century before the Portuguese reached those places by sea around Africa.

28. John King Fairbank, "Ewo in History," in Maggie Keswick, ed., *The Thistle*, pp. 245–47.

networks became more sophisticated with the help of international col-
laborators. Commercial centers, such as Soochow and Hankow, had
been well-known for centuries prior to the modern commercial revolution. The amassment of profits through cooperation, diversification, and
the cultivation of customers' friendship had been time-honored practices
for Chinese merchants. And China's close economic relations with the
world market relied heavily on her old, domestic, commercial networks
and institutions, such as the guild.

Furthermore, it was the Chinese merchants who demonstrated vitality and ingenuity in bringing about the commercial revolution. It was on
Chinese initiative that a number of new institutions and practices started
and developed, including the "chop loan" (*ch'e-p'iao*), the native bank
drafts (*hui-p'iao*) and orders (*chuang-p'iao*), the paper notes (*ssu-p'iao*)
issued by various private institutions, the activities of Chinese investors
in buying capital shares in foreign enterprises (*fu-ku*), the upcountry
purchase system, the new way of buying tea and silk under the contract
system, and the freight war in the steamship trade. It was mainly
through the day-to-day activities of Chinese merchants that these immense, pacesetting commercial changes evolved.

The presence of Western traders on the Chinese scene, however, sped
up the ongoing process of commercialization, because some of the new
features of this commercial capitalism, including the silver dollars, London bills of exchange, modern banks, insurance business, and steamship
trade, came from the West. Without this catalytic force—however su-
perficial it might be in view of China's huge economy—it would have
been difficult for China to experience a commercial revolution from the
1820s to the 1880s. The fact of the matter is that the commercial revolution affected a large sector of the Chinese economy and developed new
mechanisms for trade and finance that were grafted onto indigenous
business institutions. Therefore, though it is very likely that China would
have evolved in a capitalistic fashion in the absence of the Western impact, it would probably have taken a long period of time to wage a commercial revolution of her own that was comparable to this one both in
scope and in intensity.

Any discussion of the presence of foreign traders in China raises the
issue of economic imperialism. In certain categories, the picture is not
entirely clear. We do not know for certain, for example, the Western
traders' reinvestment ratio.[29] In other categories, their role in imperialis-

29. One definition of imperialist exploitation is that it is a process whereby foreigners

tic exploitation is minimal, at least until the last years of the nineteenth century. The Westerners seem not to have paid Chinese employees (for service) or peasants (for raw materials) less than was paid by their local competitors.[30] Nor did they distort the development of China's agrarian economy by introducing extractive industries (plantations, mines, oil wells) and exporting raw materials for processing in Western factories.[31] Finally, in commerce, Western traders not only failed to bar Chinese merchants from entering the business, but also were generally outcompeted by the natives.[32]

It is in the category of government-business relations that economic imperialism was most conspicuous in the Sino-Western commercial capitalism. Under the "treaty system," which was backed by the military forces of his home government, a foreign trader enjoyed certain privileges that were denied to Chinese merchants. For instance, he received special tax treatment and political protection from the Ch'ing government. Further, the Western businessman was partly responsible for the major economic actions taken under the protection of treaty privileges, often without the knowledge of—and free from the control of—Chinese authorities. Many Chinese sought his protection in order to pay lower rates of tariff or to avoid paying the local trade tax (likin) altogether. Chinese businessmen sailed under foreign colors, transported goods on land using Westerners' transit passes, and otherwise generally did business under Westerners' names. Chinese merchants also invested in foreign-owned enterprises: my estimate is that by the last decade of the Ch'ing period the Chinese capital in foreign firms totaled more than Tls. 16,000,000.

From the beginnings of Sino-Western trade in the sixteenth century down to the end of the eighteenth century, China was not an integral part of what Wallerstein calls the "modern world-economy."[33] After the

---

drain wealth from the economies of poor countries for use in the imperialists' home countries (Chi-ming Hou, *Foreign Investment*, pp. 93–94, 131, 254).

30. David S. Landes, "Some Thoughts on the Nature of Economic Imperialism," *Journal of Economic History* 21.4:499–500 (1961), discusses the relations between imperialist management and local labor.

31. China's economy did not become a monoculture, which abandoned various food crops in favor of the one cash crop demanded by the imperialists. For a detailed discussion on this issue, see Ernest Mandel, *Marxist Economic Theory*, tr. Brian Pearce (New York, 1968), II, 459–65.

32. Some foreign industrial companies in China, however, did commit this kind of economic imperialism in the early twentieth century.

33. The reasons for this are that exchanges between China and the West were largely bilateral, the balance of trade was persistently unfavorable to Europe for a long period of

turn of the nineteenth century, however, China was gradually "incorporated" into the modern capitalist world economy.[34] After "incorporation," China manifested many features that were typical of a periphery status.[35] Did the "incorporation" and "peripheralization" of China, then, result in Western economic exploitation? The dependency theory asserts that the degree of underdevelopment of satellite countries is proportional to their contact with the metropolitan West. In China, however, the southeastern littoral and the lower Yangtze Valley, where the Western appearance was most apparent, remained as more developed regions than the interior. In view of the fact that by the late nineteenth century China's coastal region manufactured goods in exchange for raw materials from the interior and then exported them to the West, we may even argue that coastal China had shifted from what Wallerstein calls the status of periphery to that of semiperiphery in the modern world-economy, standing between the core states of the West on the one hand and the peripheral zone of North China, the upper Yangtze Valley, and southwestern China on the other.

The central theme of the dependency theory is that capitalism creates underdevelopment. To what extent is the concept of "capitalistic underdevelopment" applicable to China? Admittedly, China experienced certain negative consequences of the opening of the country to trade with the industrial nations.[36] And viewed in a larger perspective, the treaty system in general and the opium trade in particular were in many ways detrimental to China economically, socially, politically, and psychologically. But this situation does not mean that Sino-Western commercial capitalism created underdevelopment in China. For one thing, despite

---

time, and the commodities involved were luxuries. For a discussion of the distinction between trade within the capitalist world-economy and trade between any particular world-system and its external arena, see Wallerstein, *Modern World-System II*, pp. 108–9.

34. Using Wallerstein's criteria, one may say that "incorporation" was complete because in Sino-Western trade currency was required, and exchanges were basically multilateral and notably facilitated by the use of paper, including bills of exchange and paper notes. Not only trade substantially increased in volume, but its nature changed from exchanges of preciosities to those of staples, because by then tea and opium were vital to the functioning of the economies of the core nations in the West.

35. The absence of the strong state, a sign of weakness in the peripheral zone, was obvious—which made Western economic intrusion possible in the first place. Moreover, China remained a raw-material-producing country whose coastal economy tended to produce some primary products for export to the core states.

36. These negative consequences included an unfavorable balance of trade (virtually for the first time in Chinese history), fixed tariffs and extraterritoriality, price instability in exports, and the secular trend of the commodity terms of trade moving against China.

the deterioration of the commodity terms of trade, both the total gain from trade and the capacity to import were measurably improved during the late Ch'ing period.[37] Moreover, there was by and large a persistent coexistence between Chinese and Western enterprises in the modern sector, and many Chinese businessmen and their foreign counterparts had symbiotic relationships. If imperialism promotes commercial capitalism rather than industrial capitalism, as Andre Frank contends, then it was the Chinese entrepreneurs who successfully converted much of their commercial profits to industrial capital. Finally, some aspects of the Western-induced benefits were not tangible, such as the rise of economic nationalism, the emergence of modern entrepreneurship, the changes in attitude toward economic affairs, and the advancement in the level of technology and inventiveness. Indeed, the balance sheet of China's economic contact with the West is not entirely clear as to which party benefited the most.

Actually, in sharp contrast to the contention of some proponents of the world-economy thesis and the dependency theory, nineteenth-century China was not altogether "tightly integrated as a satellite."[38] The fact of the matter is that unlike most of the "underdeveloped" countries and despite a considerable degree of economic imperialism, China was never colonized. Foreign economic intrusion was thus mainly limited to the coastal areas, as evidenced by the upcountry system of purchase and the way in which Western traders pursued their profits. In doing so, they often encountered vigorous competition from Chinese businessmen regarding exports, imports, and the shipping trade. As a consequence, foreign trade and investments could not enjoy unrestricted development, and in fact, China was singularly successful in checking foreign economic penetration of her interior. In contrast to South America, the lack of foreign mining and latifundia in modern China is striking. Therefore, for the most part the dependency theory is not applicable to China (though it may still be valid in other developing countries, especially those of South Asia and Latin America).[39]

37. Chi-ming Hou, *Foreign Investment*, p. 220.
38. Moulder, p. 145. In fact, despite the title of her book, *Japan, China and the Modern World Economy*, and frequent use of the term "world economy" throughout the book, Moulder actually refers to the dependency theory, especially Frank's thesis of "development of underdevelopment," instead of Wallerstein's world-economy perspective.
39. The Taiwan model of development since 1945 refutes many of the assumptions of the dependency theory, because the Nationalist government has been able to encourage foreign trade and investment without losing political independence to various multinational corporations. See A. James Gregor, with Maria Hsia Chang and Andrew B. Zimmerman, *Ideology and Development* (Berkeley, Calif., 1982), chap. 5.

Another controversial issue concerns the role of the treaty ports in affecting modern China. I have attempted to identify how and why these new centers had an impact on the Chinese economy and society, with special reference to the rise of a new "merchant-business class" in China. It is clear that in these maritime centers a different kind of market economy—in the form of commercial capitalism—had been created over a number of decades through business expansions and failures and through the competition and cooperation of Chinese and Western businessmen. These entrepreneurs played an active role in China's modernization. Chinese investors, operating in symbiosis with Western merchants, quickly responded to opportunities for joint investment with foreigners, preferring their enterprises to Chinese officials' economic projects. Consequently, most of what China did end up having as a result of commercial and industrial development was the result of their entrepreneurship.

The political implication of the coastal ports is evidenced by the fact that trade in the ports usually overshadowed the political framework under which it operated. China's foreign trade had traditionally been an important element for the implementation of foreign policy, but in time expanding trade undermined the tributary system. British private merchants and Chinese "shopmen" finally supplanted the British East India Company and eclipsed the Canton system altogether by 1842. After that, the economic motivation of the Western merchants played a crucial role in shaping the treaty system. At the Chinese end, nationalism emerged in the treaty ports, and commercial fortunes accumulated under the treaty system constituted a wealth that was, in marked contrast to the usual practice, largely free from government supervision and exaction. Socially, the nouveaux riches Chinese merchants along the coast made up a new type of elite who performed many traditional gentry functions in the treaty ports. They typified the rise of merchants and symbolized modern China's reorientation to the West.

Ironically, at a time when scholars in the West have begun to deemphasize the role of the treaty ports in affecting modern China, the People's Republic launched its awesome "Great Leap Outward" programs in the late 1970s. The coastal ports, such as Shanghai, Canton, and Amoy, figure prominently in China's ambitious Four Modernizations project.[40] Sino-Western economic relations today are, of course, on a

40. To attract foreign capital and technology, e.g., China in 1979 established four "special economic zones" (*ching-chi t'e-ch'ü*) in Amoy, Swatow, Chu-hai, and Shen-tsun along the Fukien-Kwangtung coast. In April 1984 China opened an additional fourteen

very different political basis from that of the unequal treaty system, but it is improbable that China can ignore the modern history of Sino-Western commercial contact. By the twenty-first century, it is likely that China's three decades of isolation from the West in the mid-twentieth century will be viewed as an aberration. China was not remade in the image of the treaty ports, but they did play, and will probably continue to play, an important role in her quest for modernity.

---

coastal port cities to foreign trade and investment: Shanghai, Canton, Tientsin, Dairen, Chinwangtao, Yentai (Chefoo), Tsingtao, Lien-yun-kang, Nan-t'ung, Ningpo, Wenchow, Foochow, Chan-chiang, and Pakhoi (Pei-hai) (*Jen-min jih-pao*, Apr. 8, 1984). The majority of these port cities were treaty ports in the nineteenth century (e.g., the first five treaty ports opened by the Treaty of Nanking in 1842).

Glossary

Akit, T'ang Ying-chai 唐英齋
Akow, Ch'en Yü-ch'ih 陳玉池
Amoy, Hsia-meng 廈門
Ao-meng. *See* Macao.

Bohea, Wu-i 武夷

Canton, Kuang-chou 廣州
ch'a-chan 茶棧
Chan-chiang 湛江
Chan Yue-chang. *See* Chun Yuechong.
Chang Chih-tung 張之洞
Chang T'ien-ch'iu 張天球
ch'ang-ch'i 長期
Ch'ang-lo 長樂
Chao-hsing 肇興
Chefoo (Yentai) 芝罘(煙臺)
ch'e-fang 拆放
ch'e-k'uan 拆款

Chen-tse 震澤
Ch'en Hui-t'ing. *See* Chun Fai-ting.
Ch'en Yü-chang. *See* Chun Yuechong.
Ch'en Yü-ch'ih. *See* Akow.
Cheng Ch'ung-ch'ien 鄭崇謙
Cheng-ho. *See* Chunghow
Ch'i-ying 耆英
Chia-hsing 嘉興
Chia-ting. *See* Kiating.
Chiang-nan. *See* Kiangnan.
Chiang Yu-hsien 蔣攸銛
Chien-ning. *See* Kienning.
Chien-yang. *See* Kingyong.
ch'ien-chuang 錢莊
ch'ien-p'iao 錢票
Chin-chia-chi 金嘉記
Chin li yuan. *See* Kin-lee-yuen.

Chinchew, Ch'üan-chou 泉州

ching-chi t'e-ch'ü 經濟特區

Ching-lun 景綸

Chinkiang 鎮江

Chinwangtao 秦皇島

Chiu-chiang. *See* Kiukiang.

Choping. *See* Chun Yuechong.

Chu Ch'i-ang 朱其昂

Chu-hai 珠海

Chu Sok Pin. *See* Hsu Shu-p'ing.

chuang-p'iao 莊票

Chusan, Chou-shan 舟山

ch'u-tzu fu-ku 出資附股

Chun Fai-ting, Ch'en Hui-t'ing
陳輝庭

Chun Yuechong, Ch'en Yü-
ch'ang, Choping 陳裕昌

Chunghow, Cheng-ho 政和

Chungking 重慶

Ch'ung-an. *See* Shung-oan.

Ch'ung-ming 崇明

Ch'üan-chou. *See* Chinchew.

Dairen 大連

Foochow, Fu-chou 福州

Fu-k'ang 阜康

fu-ku 附股

Fu-lung 福隆

Han-k'ou. *See* Hankow.

Han Mei-ch'ing 韓梅卿

Han Teng-t'ang 韓登堂

hang. See hong.

Hang-chou. *See* Hongchow.

Hankow, Han-k'ou 漢口

Hao-kuan. *See* Houqua.

Heng-feng 恒豐

Ho Amei, Ho Hsien-ch'ih 何獻墀

Ho-feng 鶴峰

Ho Fu, Ho Fook 何福

Ho Hsien-ch'ih. *See* Ho Amei.

Ho-k'ou. *See* Hohow.

Ho Tung 何東

Hohow, Ho-k'ou 河口

hong, hang 行

Hong Kong, Hsiang-kang 香港

Hongchow, Hang-chou 杭州

Hou-i 厚益

Houqua (Hao-kuan) 浩官; head
of the I-ho (Ewo) firm 怡和行:
Wu Ping-chien (Wu Tun-
yuan) 伍秉鑑(伍敦元)

How-tow-san, Hu-t'ou shan
虎頭山

Hsi-ch'eng 西成

Hsi Li-kung 席立功

Hsia-meng. *See* Amoy.

hsiang-chuang 鄉莊

Hsiang-kang. *See* Hong Kong.

Hsieh Ch'ing-t'ai 謝慶泰

Hsu Shu-p'ing, Chu Sok Pin
    徐叔平

Hsu Tao-shen 許道身

Hsu Tzu-ching 徐子靜

Hsueh Huan 薛煥

Hu-chou 湖州

Hu Kuang-yung 胡光墉

Hu-t'ou shan. *See* How-tow-san.

Hua-an 華安

Hui-chou 徽州

hui-p'iao 會票

Hung-an kung-ssu 鴻安公司

Hung Hsiu-ch'uan 洪秀全

Jung Cho-sheng 容卓生

Jung Hung. *See* Yung Wing.

Khiqua, Li Kuang-hua 黎光華

Kiangnan, Chiang-nan 江南

Kiating, Chia-ting 嘉定

Kienning, Kinning, Chien-ning
    建寧

Kin-lee-yuen, Chin li yuan
    金利源

Kingqua, Liang Ching-kuo
    梁經國

Kinning. *See* Kienning.

Kingyong, Kinyang, Chien-yang
    建陽

Kinyang. *See* Kingyang.

Kiukee. *See* Koofunsing.

Kiukiang, Chiu-chiang 九江

Ko Yang-kao 葛仰高

Koofunsing, Kiukee, Ku Ch'un-
    ch'ih 顧春池, Ku Feng-sheng
    顧豐盛

Ku Ch'un-ch'ih. *See* Koofunsing.

Ku Feng-sheng. *See* Koofunsing.

k'uai-fa-ts'ai 快發財

Kuan Ch'eng-fa 關成發

kuan-tu shang-pan 官督商辦

kuan yin ch'ien hao 官銀錢號

Kuang-chou. *See* Canton.

Kuang-hsu 光緒

kung-hsi fa-ts'ai 恭喜發財

kung-ku 公估

Kuo Kan-chang. *See* Quok
    Acheong.

Kuo Sung-tao 郭嵩燾

Li Chao-min 黎召民

Li Cheng-yü 李振玉

Li Ch'ih-yao 李侍堯

Li Chin-yung 李金鏞

Li-ch'üan 麗泉

Li Hsieh-fa 李協發

Li Hu 李湖

Li Hung-chang 李鴻章

Li Kuan-chih 李貫之

Li Kuang-hua. *See* Khiqua.

Li Kuang-yuan 黎光遠

Li Sung-yun, Soong-yin 李松云

Liang Ching-kuo. *See* Kingqua.

Lien-yun-kang 連雲港

Lin Tse-hsu 林則徐

Lintin, Ling-ting 伶仃

Ling-hu 菱湖

Liu Ch'eng-shu 劉承澍

Liu Hsin-sheng 劉歆生, Liu Jen-hsiang 劉人祥

Liu Jen-hsiang. *See* Liu Hsin-sheng.

Liu K'un-i 劉坤一

Liu Shu-t'ing, Seating 劉述庭

Lo Shou-sung 羅壽嵩

Lu-lin yang-hang. *See* Renter, Brockelmann & Co.

Lu Wen-chin 盧文錦

Macao, Ao-meng 澳門

Mai Chin-t'ing 麥覲庭

Mu Shih-fang 沐士方

Namoa, Nan-ao 南澳

Nan-ao. *See* Namoa.

Nan-hsun. *See* Nantsin.

Nan-t'ung 南通

Nantsin, Nan-hsun 南潯

Newchwang, Niu-chuang 牛莊

Ni Wen-hung 倪文宏

Ningchow 寧州

Ningpo 寧波

Niu-chuang. *See* Newchwang.

Olyphant & Co., T'ung-fu yang-hang 同孚洋行

Pakhoi, Pei-hai 北海

P'an Ch'ang-yao 潘長耀

pao 包

pao-hsiao 報効

Pei-hai. *See* Pakhoi.

Peking 北京

pen-yang 本洋

p'iao-hao 票號

ping-chan 兵戰

P'ing-hu 平湖

P'ing-ch'üan 平泉

Pu-cheng-shih 布政使

Quok Acheong, Kuo Kan-chang 郭甘章

Renter, Brockelmann & Co., Lu-lin yang-hang 魯麟洋行

Seating. *See* Liu Shu-t'ing.

Sha-shih. *See* Shasi.

shang-chan 商戰

Shanghai 上海

Shasi, Sha-shih 沙市

Shen-p'iao 申票

Shen-tsun 深圳

Sheng Hsuan-huai 盛宣懷

Sheng-ta 升大

Shih Chung-ho 石中和

Shui-k'ou. *See* Sueykut.

Shun-ch'ang. *See* Sinchune.

Shung-oan, Ch'ung-an 崇安

Sinchune, Shun-ch'ang 順昌

Soong-yin. *See* Li Sung-yun.

ssu-p'iao 私票

Sueykut, Shui-k'ou 水口

sui-ju pu 歲入部

Sung-chiang 松江

Sung Ts'ai 宋彩

Swatow 汕頭

Ta-ch'ing 大慶

Ta-lien 大連

T'ai-chou 台州

T'ai-ts'ang 太倉

Takee, Yang Fang 楊坊

T'ang K'uei-sheng 湯癸生

T'ang Mao-chih. *See* Tong Mow-chee.

T'ang T'ing-shu. *See* Tong King-sing.

T'ang Ying-chai. *See* Akit.

Teng Chao-hsiang 鄧兆祥

Teng Chün-hsiang 鄧君翔

Tien-pai. *See* Tienpak.

Tienpak, Tien-pai 電白

Tientsin 天津

T'ien-pao 天寶

Ting Jih-ch'ang 丁日昌

Tong King-sing, T'ang T'ing-shu 唐廷樞

Tong Mow-chee, T'ang Mao-chih 唐茂枝

Tong-san, Tung-shan 東山

Ts'ai Shih-wen 蔡世文

ts'ao-liang 漕糧

Ts'en Yü-ying 岑毓英

Tsingtao 青島

Tso Tsung-t'ang 左宗棠

Tucksing, Te-sheng 德盛

Tung-shan. *See* Tong-san.

Tung-yü 東裕

T'ung-chih 同治

T'ung-fu yang-hang. *See* Olyphant & Co.

T'ung-t'ai 同泰

t'ung-yuan 銅元

Wan-yuan 萬源

Wang Shao-yun 汪少雲

Wei Lang-shan 韋朗山

Wei Lin-shih 韋麟石

Wenchow 溫州

Whampoa, Huang-p'u 黃埔

Whangpu, Huang-p'u 黃浦

Woochow, Wu-chou 梧州

Woosung, Wusung 吳淞

Wu Chao-p'ing 吳昭平

Wu Chien-chang 吳健彰

Wu-chou. *See* Woochow.

Wu Ch'ung-yueh 伍崇曜

Wu Han-t'ao 吳瀚濤

Wu-hu 蕪湖

Wu-i. *See* Bohea.

Wu Ping-chien. *See* Houqua.

Wu Shou-ch'ang 伍受昌

Wu Tun-yuan. *See* Houqua.

Wusung. *See* Woosung.

Yang-chou. *See* Yangchow.

Yang Fang. *See* Takee.

yang-hang 洋行

Yang Kuei-hsuan 楊桂軒

Yang-lou-tung. *See* Yong Low Toong.

Yangchow, Yang-chou 揚州

Yeh Ch'eng-chung 葉澄衷

Yen Shih-ying 顔時英

Yen-ta 衍大

Yentai. *See* Chefoo.

yin-hao 銀號

yin-p'iao 銀票

Ying-k'ou 營口

ying-yang 鷹洋

Yong Low Toong, Yang-lou-tung 羊樓洞

Yowloong, Yu-lung 又隆

yuan 元

Yu-lung. *See* Yowloong.

Yung Wing, Jung Hung 容閎

Yung-yuan 永源

Yü Hsia-ch'ing 虞洽卿

Bibliography

WORKS IN WESTERN LANGUAGES

Alcock, Rutherford. *The Capital of the Tycoon.* 2 vols. London, 1863.

Allen, G. C., and A. G. Donnithorne. *Western Enterprise in Far Eastern Economic Development: China and Japan.* London: Allen and Unwin, 1954.

Allen, Nathan. *The Opium Trade as Carried on in India and China.* 2d ed. Lowell, Mass., 1853.

American Neptune, The. Quarterly, 1941—.

Arnold, Julean. *Commercial Handbook of China.* 2 vols. Washington, D.C., Government Printing Office, 1919, 1920.

Atwell, William S. "Notes on Silver, Foreign Trade, and the Late Ming Economy," *Ch'ing-shih wen-t'i* 3:1–33 (Dec. 1977).

Barbour, Violet. *Capitalism in Amsterdam in the 17th Century.* Baltimore, Johns Hopkins Press, 1950.

Basu, Dilip K. "The Peripheralization of China: Notes on the Opium Connection," in W. Goldfrank, ed., *The World System of Capitalism.* Beverly Hills, Calif., 1979.

Bergère, Marie-Claire. *Une crise financière à Shanghai à la fin de l'ancien régime.* Paris, Mouton, 1964.

Black, C. E. *The Dynamics of Modernization.* New York, Harper & Row, 1966.

Bourne, F. S. A., et al. *Report of the Mission to China of the Blackburn Chamber of Commerce, 1896–1897.* London, 1898.

BPP: British Parliamentary Papers (Blue Books)

First and Second Report from the Select Committee of House of Commons on the Affairs of the East India Company. 1830.

Correspondence Relating to China. Vol. 36 (1840).

Report from the Select Committee on Commercial Relations with China, Minutes of Evidence. Vol. 5 (1847).

Returns of Trade. Vol. 40 (1847).

Returns of Trade. Vol. 39 (1849).

Commercial Reports of Her Majesty's Consuls in China. 1862–1885.

Reports from Her Majesty's Consuls in China, 1864. Vol. 71 (1866).

Commercial Reports from Her Majesty's Consuls in China, Japan, and Siam, 1865. Vol. 71 (1867).

Reports on Trade by the Foreign Commissioners at the Ports in China Open by Treaty to Foreign Trade for Year 1866. Vol. 69 (1867–1868).

Report of the Delegates of the Shanghai General Chamber of Commerce on the Trade of the Upper Yangtze River. Vol. 65 (1870).

Consular Report, Chinkiang. 1881–1884.

Braudel, Fernand. *Capitalism and Material Life, 1400–1800,* tr. Miriam Kochan. New York, Harper and Row, 1975.

———. *The Mediterranean and the Mediterranean World in the Age of Phillip II,* tr. Sian Reynolds. 2 vols. New York, 1975.

———. *Afterthoughts on Material Civilization and Capitalism,* tr. Patricia Ranum. Baltimore, Md., Johns Hopkins University Press, 1977.

Brown, Shannon R. "The Transfer of Technology to China in the Nineteenth Century: The Role of Direct Foreign Investment." *Journal of Economic History* 39.1:181–97 (March 1979).

Canton Register and Price Current, The. 1827–1843.

Cardoso, Fernando Henrique, and Enzo Faletto. *Dependency and Development in Latin America,* tr. Marjory Mattingly Urquidi. Berkeley and Los Angeles, Calif., University of California Press, 1979.

Carlson, Ellsworth C. *The Kaiping Mines, 1877–1912: A Case Study of Early Chinese Industrialization.* Rev. ed. Cambridge, Mass., East Asian Research Center, Harvard University, 1971.

Chan, Wellington K. K. *Merchants, Mandarins and Modern Enterprise in Late Ch'ing China.* Cambridge, Mass., East Asian Research Center, Harvard University, 1977.

Chang, Chung-li. *The Income of the Chinese Gentry.* Seattle, University of Washington Press, 1962.

Chang, Hsin-pao. *Commissioner Lin and the Opium War.* Cambridge, Mass., Harvard University Press, 1964.

Chang, T'ien-tse. *Sino-Portuguese Trade from 1514 to 1644: A Synthesis of Portuguese and Chinese Sources.* Leyden, E. J. Brill, 1934.

Chaudhuri, K. N. "The East India Company and the Export of Treasure in the Early Seventeenth Century," *Economic History Review,* 2d ser., 16:23–38 (Aug. 1963).

———. "Treasure and Trade Balances: The East India Company's Export Trade, 1660–1720," *Economic History Review,* 2d ser., 21: 480–502 (Dec. 1968).

———. "The Economic and Monetary Problem of European Trade with Asia during the Seventeenth and Eighteenth Centuries," *Journal of European Economic History* 4 (Fall 1975).

Cheng, Yu-kuei. *Foreign Trade and Industrial Development of China: An Historical and Integrated Analysis through 1948.* Washington, D.C., 1956.

Chinese Repository. Canton or Macao, 1832–1851.

Chu, Samuel C. *Reformer in Modern China: Chang Chien, 1853–1926.* New York, Columbia University Press, 1965.

Ch'üan, Han-sheng. "The Economic Crisis of 1883 as Seen in the Failure of Hsu Jun's Real Estate Business in Shanghai," in Chi-ming Hou and Tzong-shian Yu, eds., *Modern Chinese Economic History.* Taipei, Institute of Economics, Academia Sinica, 1979, pp. 493–498.

Clough, Samuél B., and Charles W. Cole. *Economic History of Europe.* Boston, 1952.

Coates, W. H. *The Old Country Trade.* New York, 1911.

Cochran, Sherman. *Big Business in China: Sino-Foreign Rivalry in the Cigarette Industry, 1890–1930.* Cambridge, Mass., Harvard University Press, 1980.

Cockcroft, James D., Andre Gunder Frank, and Dale L. Johnson, eds. *Dependence and Underdevelopment: Latin America's Political Economy.* Garden City, N.Y., Anchor Books, 1972.

Colquhoun, Archibald R. *Across Chryse: Being the Narrative of a Journey of Exploration through the South China Border Lands from Canton to Mandaley.* 2 vols. London, 1883.

Connolly, James B. *Canton Captain.* Garden City, N.Y., Doubleday, 1942.

Cooke, G. W. *China: Being "The Times" Special Correspondence from China in the Years 1857–1858.* London, 1858.

Cutler, Carl C. *Greyhound of the Sea.* New York, 1930.

Dennett, Tyler. *Americans in Eastern Asia.* New York, Barnes and Noble, 1963.

Dermigny, Louis. *La Chine et l'occident: Le commerce à Canton au XVIIIᵉ siècle, 1719–1833.* 3 vols. Paris, S.E.V.P.E.N., 1964.

Downs, Jacques M. "American Merchants and the China Opium Trade, 1800–1840," *Business History Review* 42:418–42 (Winter 1968).

Edwards, George William. *The Evolution of Finance Capitalism.* London, 1938.

Eisenstadt, S. N. *Modernization: Protest and Change.* Englewood, N.J., Prentice-Hall, 1966.

Eitel, E. J. *Europe in China: The History of Hongkong, From the Beginning to the Year 1882.* London, 1895.

Elvin, Mark, and G. William Skinner, eds. *The Chinese City Between Two Worlds.* Stanford, Calif., Stanford University Press, 1972.

Fairbank, John King. *Trade and Diplomacy on the Chinese Coast: The Opening of the Treaty Ports, 1842–1854.* 2 vols. Cambridge, Mass., Harvard University Press, 1953.

————. "Ewo In History," in Maggie Keswick, ed., *The Thistle and the Jade: A Celebration of 150 Years of Jardine, Matheson & Co.* London, Octopus Books, 1982.

Fairbank, John King, ed. *The Cambridge History of China,* Vol. 10, *Late Ch'ing, 1800–1911, Part 1.* Cambridge, England, Cambridge University Press, 1978.

Fairbank, John King, and Kwang-Ching Liu, eds. *The Cambridge History of China,* Vol. 11, *Late Ch'ing, 1800–1911, Part 2.* Cambridge, England, Cambridge University Press, 1980.

Fairbank, John King, Alexander Eckstein, and Lien-sheng Yang. "Economic Change in Early Modern China: An Analytical Framework," *Economic Development and Cultural Change* 9:1–26 (Oct. 1960).

Fairbank, John King, Edwin O. Reischauer, and Albert M. Craig. *East Asia: The Modern Transformation.* Boston, Mass., Houghton Mifflin, 1965.

Fay, Peter Ward. *The Opium War, 1840–1842.* Chapel Hill, N.C., University of North Carolina Press, 1975.

Feuerwerker, Albert. *China's Early Industrialization: Sheng Hsuan-huai (1844–1916) and Mandarin Enterprise.* Cambridge, Mass., Harvard University Press, 1958.

————. "Chinese History in Marxian Dress," *American Historical Review* 66: 327–30 (Jan. 1961).

————. *The Chinese Economy, ca. 1870–1911.* Ann Arbor, Mich., Center for

Chinese Studies, The University of Michigan, 1969.

Forbes, Frederick E. *Five Years in China, From 1842 to 1847.* London, 1848.

Forbes, Robert B. *Remarks on China and the China Trade.* Boston, 1844.

──── . *Personal Reminiscences.* 2d ed. Boston, 1882.

Fortune, Robert. *Three Years' Wanderings in the Northern Provinces of China.* London, 1847.

──── . *A Journey to the Tea Countries of China: Including Sung-lo and the Bohea Hills.* London, 1852.

Frank, Andre Gunder. *Capitalism and Underdevelopment in Latin America: Historical Studies of Chile and Brazil.* New York, Monthly Review Press, 1967.

──── . *Latin America: Underdevelopment or Revolution. Essays on the Development of Underdevelopment and the Immediate Enemy.* New York, Monthly Review Press, 1969.

──── . *Dependent Accumulation and Underdevelopment.* London, Macmillan, 1978.

Friedman, Edward. "Maoist Conceptualizations of the Capitalist World-System," in Terence K. Hopkins and Immanuel Wallerstein, eds., *Processes of the World-System.* Beverly Hills, Calif., Sage Publications, 1980.

Gras, Norman S. B. *Business and Capitalism.* New York, 1939.

Greenberg, Michael. *British Trade and the Opening of China, 1800–1842.* Cambridge, England, Cambridge University Press, 1951.

Gregor, A. James, with Maria Hsia Chang and Andrew B. Zimmerman. *Ideology and Development: Sun Yat-sen and the Economic History of Taiwan.* Berkeley, Calif., Institute of East Asian Studies, University of California, 1982.

Hao, Yen-p'ing. "Cheng Kuan-ying: The Comprador as Reformer," *Journal of Asian Studies* 29:15–22 (Nov. 1969).

──── . *The Comprador in Nineteenth Century China: Bridge between East and West.* Cambridge, Mass., Harvard University Press, 1970.

──── . "The Early Chinese-American Tea Trade," in John K. Fairbank, ed., *American-East Asian Economic Relations*, Harvard University Press, forthcoming.

Hao, Yen-p'ing, and Erh-min Wang. "Changing Chinese Views of Western Relations, 1840–1895," in John K. Fairbank and Kwang-Ching Liu, eds., *The Cambridge History of China*, vol. 11, *Late Ch'ing, 1800–1911, Part 2.* Cambridge, England, Cambridge University Press, 1980.

Hart, Robert. "Proposals for the Better Regulation of Commercial Relations," dated Jan. 23, 1876, in IMC, *Origin*, VI, 352–401.

Hilton, Rodney, ed. *The Transition from Feudalism to Capitalism.* London, New Left Books, 1976.

Hirschman, Albert O. *The Strategy of Economic Development.* New Haven, Conn., Yale University Press, 1958.

Ho, Ping-ti. "The Salt Merchants of Yang-chou: A Study of Commercial Capitalism in Eighteenth-Century China," *Harvard Journal of Asiatic Studies* 17:130–68 (June 1954).

————. *Studies on the Population of China, 1368–1953.* Cambridge, Mass., Harvard University Press, 1959.

————. *The Ladder of Success in Imperial China: Aspects of Social Mobility, 1368–1911.* New York, Columbia University Press, 1962.

Homan, J. Smith, comp. *A Historical and Statistical Account of the Foreign Commerce of the United States.* New York, Putman & Co., 1857.

Hong Kong Daily Press. Hong Kong High Court Library, Hong Kong.

Hopkins, Terence K., and Immanuel Wallerstein, eds. *Process of the World-System.* Beverly Hills, Calif., Sage Publications, 1980.

Hou, Chi-ming. *Foreign Investment and Economic Development in China, 1840–1937.* Cambridge, Mass., Harvard University Press, 1965.

Hsiao, Liang-lin. *China's Foreign Trade Statistics, 1864–1949.* Cambridge, Mass., Harvard University East Asian Research Center, 1974.

Hummel, Arthur W., ed. *Eminent Chinese of the Ch'ing Period, 1644–1912.* 2 vols. Washington D.C., Government Printing Office, 1943–1944.

Hunter, William C. *The "Fan Kwae" at Canton Before Treaty Days, 1825–1844.* London, 1882.

IMC: China, Imperial Maritime Customs. *Reports on Trade, 1864.* Shanghai, 1865.

————. *Reports on Trade, 1866.* Shanghai, 1867.

————. *Inspector General's Circulars.* 11 vols. Shanghai, 1879–1910.

————. *Reports on Trade at the Treaty Ports, 1879.* Shanghai, 1880.

————. *Decennial Report, 1882–1891.* Shanghai, 1892.

————. *Treaties, Conventions, etc. between China and Foreign States.* 2d ed. Shanghai, 1917.

————. *Documents Illustrative of the Origin, Development, and Activities of the Chinese Customs Service.* 7 vols. Shanghai, 1937.

Jardine, Matheson and Company. *An Outline of the History of a China House for a Hundred Years, 1832–1932.* Hong Kong, privately printed, 1934.

Jones, Susan Mann. "Finance in Ningpo: The 'Ch'ien-chuang,' 1780–

1880," in W. E. Willmott, ed., *Economic Organization in Chinese Society*. Stanford, Calif., Stanford University Press, 1972.

————. "The Ningpo *Pang* and Financial Power at Shanghai," in Mark Elvin and G. William Skinner, eds., *The Chinese City between Two Worlds*. Stanford, Calif., Stanford University Press, 1974.

Keswick, Maggie, ed. *The Thistle and the Jade: A Celebration of 150 Years of Jardine, Matheson & Co.* London, Octopus Books, 1982.

Keynes, John Maynard. *General Theory of Employment, Interest, and Money*. New York, Harcourt, Brace, 1936.

King, Frank H. H. *Money and Monetary Policy in China, 1845–1895*. Cambridge, Mass., Harvard University Press, 1965.

Knox, Thomas. "John Comprador," *Harper's New Monthly Magazine* 57: 427–34 (1878).

Landes, David S. "Some Thoughts on the Nature of Economic Imperialism," *Journal of Economic History* 21.4:499–500 (1961).

Larson, Henrietta M. "A China Trader Turns Investor: A Biographical Chapter in American Business History," *Harvard Business Review* 12:345–58 (1933–1934).

LeFevour, Edward. *Western Enterprise in Late Ch'ing China: A Selective Survey of Jardine, Matheson & Company's Operations, 1842–1895*. Cambridge, Mass., East Asian Research Center, Harvard University, 1968.

Levy, Marion J., Jr., and Shih Kuo-heng. *The Rise of the Modern Chinese Business Class: Two Introductory Essays*. New York, Institute of Pacific Relations, 1949.

Li, Lillian M. *China's Silk Trade: Traditional Industry in the Modern World, 1842–1937*. Cambridge, Mass., East Asian Research Center, Harvard University, 1981.

Lieu, D. K. *The Growth and Industrialization of Shanghai*. Shanghai, 1936.

Lindsay, H. H. *Report of Proceedings on a Voyage to the Northern Ports of China in the Ship Lord Amherst*. London, 1934.

————. *Is the War with China a Just One?* 2d ed., London, 1840.

Liu, Kwang-Ching. "Houqua: The Sources and Disposition of His Wealth." Ms., 1958.

————. "Steamship Enterprise in Nineteenth Century China," *Journal of Asian Studies* 18:435–55 (Aug. 1959).

————. *Anglo-American Steamship Rivalry in China, 1862–1874*. Cambridge, Mass., Harvard University Press, 1962.

————. "British-Chinese Steamship Rivalry in China, 1873–1885," in C. D. Cowan, ed., *The Economic Development of China and Japan*.

London, 1964.

———. "Credit Facilities in China's Early Industrialization: The Background and Implications of Hsu Jun's Bankruptcy in 1883," in Chi-ming Hou and Tzong-shian Yu, eds., *Modern Chinese Economic History*. Taipei, 1979.

Lockwood, Stephen C. *Augustine Heard and Company, 1858–1862: American Merchants in China*. Cambridge, Mass., East Asian Research Center, Harvard University, 1971.

Lopez, Robert S. *The Commercial Revolution of the Middle Ages, 950–1350*. Cambridge, England, Cambridge University Press, 1976.

Lubbock, Basil. *The Opium Clippers*. Boston, Lauriat Co., 1933.

McDonald, Angus, Jr. "Wallerstein's World Economy: How Seriously Should We Take It?" *Journal of Asian Studies* 38:535–40 (May 1979).

Mandel, Ernest. *Marxist Economic Theory*, tr. Brian Pearce, 2 vols. New York, Monthly Review Press, 1968.

Martin, R. Montgomery. *China; Political, Commercial, and Social; in an Official Report to Her Majesty's Government*. 2 vols. London, 1847.

Marx, Karl, and Friedrich Engels. *The Communist Manifesto*. New York, Monthly Review Press, 1964.

Matheson, James. *The Present Positions and Prospects of the British Trade with China*. London, 1836.

Mayers, William F., N. B. Dennys, and Charles King. *The Treaty Ports of China and Japan*. London, 1867.

Metzger, Thomas. "The State and Commerce in Imperial China," *Asian and African Studies* 6 (1970).

Morse, Hosea Ballou. *Currency, Weights, and Measures in China*. Shanghai, 1906.

———. *The International Relations of the Chinese Empire*, 3 vols.: vol. I, *The Period of Conflict, 1834–1860*. Shanghai, 1910.

———. *The International Relations of the Chinese Empire*, vol. II, *The Period of Submission, 1861–1893*. London, 1918.

———. *The International Relations of the Chinese Empire*, vol. III, *The Period of Subjection, 1894–1911*. London, 1918.

———. *The Trade and Administration of China*, 3rd ed. New York, Longmans, Green, 1921.

———. *The Chronicles of the East India Company Trading to China, 1635–1834*. 5 vols. Oxford, Oxford University Press, 1926–1929.

Moulder, Frances V. *Japan, China and the Modern World Economy: Toward a Reinterpretation of East Asian Development, ca. 1600 to ca. 1918*. Cambridge, England, Cambridge University Press, 1977.

Murphey, Rhoads. *Shanghai: Key to Modern China.* Cambridge, Mass., Harvard University Press, 1953.

———. *The Outsiders: The Western Experience in India and China.* Ann Arbor, Mich., University of Michigan Press, 1977.

Myers, Ramon H. *The Chinese Peasant Economy: Agricultural Development in Hopei and Shantung, 1890–1949.* Cambridge, Mass., Harvard University Press, 1970.

NCH: North-China Herald. Weekly, Shanghai, 1850–.

Owen, David Edward. *British Opium Policy in China and India.* New Haven, Conn., Yale University Press, 1934.

Packard, Laurence B. *The Commercial Revolution, 1400–1776.* New York, Holt, 1927.

Parkes, Sir Harry. "An Account of the Paper Currency and Banking System of Fuchowfoo," *Journal of the Royal Asiatic Society* 13:179–90 (1852).

Perkins, Dwight H. "Government as an Obstacle to Industrialization: The Case of Nineteenth-Century China," *Journal of Economic History* 27:478–92 (Dec. 1967).

———. *Agricultural Development in China, 1368–1968.* Chicago, Aldine, 1969.

Phipps, J. *A Practical Treatise on the China and Eastern Trade.* London, 1836.

———. *A Practical Treatise on the China Trade.* New York, 1895.

Pitcher, Philip Wilson. *In and About Amoy: Some Historical and Other Facts Connected with One of the First Open Ports in China.* 2d ed. Shanghai, 1912.

Pitkin, Timothy. *A Historical View of the Commerce of the United States of America.* New Haven, Conn., Currie and Peck, 1835.

Rostow, W. W. *The Process of Economic Growth.* New York, Norton, 1962.

Sayer, Geoffrey Robley. *Hong Kong: Birth, Adolescence, and Coming of Age.* London, Oxford University Press, 1937.

Shaw, Samuel. *The Journals of Major Samuel Shaw,* Josiah Quincy, ed., Boston, 1847.

Singh, S. B. *European Agency Houses in Bengal, 1783–1833.* Calcutta, Mukhopadhyay, 1966.

So, Alvin Yiu-cheong. "Development Inside the Capitalist World-System: A Study of the Chinese and Japanese Silk Industry," *Journal of Asian Culture* 5:33–56 (1981).

Spence, Jonathan. "Opium Smoking in Ch'ing China," in Frederic E. Wakeman, Jr., and Carolyn Grant, eds. *Conflict and Control in*

Late Imperial China. Berkeley and Los Angeles, Calif., University of California Press, 1975.

Stanley, C. John. *Late Ch'ing Finance: Hu Kuang-yung as an Innovator.* Cambridge, Mass., East Asian Research Center, Harvard University, 1961.

Tawney, R. H. *Land and Labour in China.* London, Allen and Unwin, 1932.

Teng, Ssu-yü, and John K. Fairbank. *China's Response to the West: A Documentary Survey, 1839–1923.* Cambridge, Mass., Harvard University Press, 1954.

Tiffany, Osmond, Jr. *The Canton Chinese; or the American's Sojourn in the Celestial Empire.* Boston, 1849.

Viraphol, Sarasin. *Sino-Siamese Trade, 1652–1853.* Cambridge, Mass., East Asian Research Center, Harvard University, 1976.

Wakeman, Frederic, Jr. "The Canton Trade and the Opium War," in John K. Fairbank, ed., *The Cambridge History of China,* vol. 10, *Late Ch'ing, 1800–1911, Part 1,* Cambridge, England, Cambridge University Press, 1978.

Wallerstein, Immanuel. *The Modern World-System: Capitalist Agriculture and the Origins of the European World-Economy in the Sixteenth Century.* New York, Academic Press, 1974.

———. "The Rise and Future Demise of the World Capitalist System: Concepts for Comparative Analysis," *Comparative Studies in Society and History* 16:387–415 (Sept. 1974). (Later included in his collection of essays, *The Capitalist World-Economy,* Cambridge, England, Cambridge University Press, 1979)

———. "From Feudalism to Capitalism: Transition or Transitions?" *Social Forces* 55:273–83 (Dec. 1976). (Later included in his collection of essays, *The Capitalist World-Economy*)

———. *The Capitalist World-Economy.* Cambridge, England, Cambridge University Press, 1979.

———. *The Modern World-System II: Mercantilism and the Consolidation of the European World-Economy, 1600–1750.* New York, Academic Press, 1980.

Wallerstein, Immanuel, ed. *World Inequality.* Montreal, Black Rose Books, 1975.

Wang, Yeh-chien. "The Secular Trend of Prices during the Ch'ing Period, 1644–1911," *Journal of the Institute of Chinese Studies of the University of Hong Kong* 5.2:347–71 (1972). (Later included in Yü Tsung-hsien et al., eds., *Chung-kuo ching-chi fa-chan shih lun-*

wen hsuan-chi [Selected essays on Chinese economic development], 2 vols., Taipei, 1980)

———. *Land Taxation in Imperial China, 1750–1911.* Cambridge, Mass., Harvard University Press, 1973.

———. "The Growth and Decline of Native Banks in Shanghai," *Ching-chi lun-wen* 6.1:111–42 (Mar. 1978).

———. "Evolution of the Chinese Monetary System, 1644–1850," in Chi-ming Hou and Tzong-shian Yu, eds., *Modern Chinese Economic History.* Taipei, Academia Sinica, 1979, pp. 425–52.

Williams, S. Wells. *The Chinese Commercial Guide.* 5th ed. Hong Kong, 1863.

Wright, Arnold, ed. *Twentieth Century Impressions of Hongkong, Shanghai, and Other Treaty Ports of China: Their History, People, Commerce, Industries, and Resources.* London, 1908.

Wright, Mary Clabaugh. *The Last Stand of Chinese Conservatism: The T'ung-chih Restoration, 1862–1874.* Stanford, Calif., Stanford University Press, 1957.

Yaggy, Duncan. "John M. Forbes: A Biography." Ph.D. dissertation, Brandeis University, 1972.

Yang, Lien-sheng. *Money and Credit in China: A Short History.* Cambridge, Mass., Harvard University Press, 1952.

WORKS IN CHINESE AND
JAPANESE LANGUAGES

Chang Che-lang 張哲郎. *Ch'ing-tai ti ts'ao-yun* 清代的漕運 (The transporting of tribute rice during the Ch'ing period). Taipei, 1969.

Chang Kuo-hui 張國輝. "Shih-chiu shih-chi hou-pan-ch'i Chung-kuo ch'ien-chuang ti mai-pan hua" 十九世紀後半期中国錢庄的買辦化 (The compradorization of China's native banks in the second half of the nineteenth century), *Li-shih yen-chiu* 歷史研究 (Historical studies) 6:85–98 (1963).

———. *Yang-wu yun-tung yü Chung-kuo chin-tai ch'i-yeh* 洋务运动与中国近代企业 (The foreign affair movement and China's modern enterprises). Peking, 1979.

Ch'en Chao-nan 陳昭南. *Yung-cheng Ch'ien-lung nien-chien ti yin-ch'ien pi-chia pien-tung* 雍正乾隆年間的銀錢比價變動 (Fluctuation in the silver-cash ratios during the Yung-cheng and Ch'ien-lung periods). Taipei, Chung-kuo hsueh-shu chu-tso chiang-chu wei-yuan-hui 中國學術著作獎助委員會, 1966.

Ch'en Chen 陳眞 and Yao Lo 姚洛, comps., *Chung-kuo chin-tai kung-yeh shih tzu-liao* 中國近代工業史資料 (Source materials on the history of modern industry in China). 6 vols. Peking, 1957–1961.

Ch'en Ch'i-t'ien 陳其田. *Shan-hsi p'iao-chuang k'ao-lueh* 山西票莊考略 (A brief study of the Shansi banks). Shanghai, 1937.

Ch'en Ts'an 陳燦. *Chung-kuo shang-yeh shih* 中國商業史 (A commercial history of China). 2 vols. Taipei, 1965.

Cheng Kuan-ying 鄭觀應. *Sheng-shih wei-yen* 盛世危言 (Warnings to a prosperous age). 6 chüan. 1893. Preface 1892.

————. *Sheng-shih wei-yen tseng-ting hsin-pien* 盛世危言增訂新編 (Warnings to a prosperous age, revised). 8 ts'e. Preface 1892.

————. *Sheng-shih wei-yen hou-pien* 盛世危言後編 (Warnings to a prosperous age, second part). 15 chüan. Shanghai, 1920. Preface 1910.

Chia Shih-i 賈士毅. *Min-kuo ts'ai-cheng shih* 民國財政史 (A history of finance in Republican China). 2 vols. Taipei, 1950.

Chiao-t'ung shih 交通史 (A history of communication), ed. Chiao-t'ung pu 交通部 (Ministry of Communication) and T'ieh-t'ao pu 鐵道部 (Ministry of Railroad). 37 vols. Nanking, 1930—.

Ch'üan Han-sheng 全漢昇. "Ming-Ch'ing chien Mei-chou pai-yin ti shu-ju Chung-kuo" 明清間美洲白銀的輸入中國 (The importation of American silver to China during the Ming-Ch'ing times), in his *Chung-kuo ching-chi shih lun-ts'ung* 中國經濟史論叢 (Collected essays on Chinese economic history). 2 vols. Hong Kong, 1972.

Chung-kuo chin-tai huo-pi shih tzu-liao 中國近代貨幣史資料 (Materials on the monetary history of modern China). Chung-kuo jen-min yin-hang 中國人民銀行, comp., Ti-yi chi 第一輯. Peking, Chung-hua, 1964.

Chung-kuo jen-min ta-hsueh Chung-kuo li-shih chiao-yen-shih 中國人民大學中國歷史教研室, ed., *Chung-kuo tzu-pen-chu-i meng-ya wen-t'i t'ao-lun chi* 中國資本主義萌芽問題討論集 (Collected papers on the problem of incipient capitalism in China). 3 vols. Peking, 1957–1960.

Fang T'eng 方騰. "Yü Hsia-ch'ing lun" 虞洽卿論 (On Yü Hsia-ch'ing), *Tsa-chih yueh-k'an* 雜誌月刊 (Monthly miscellany), 12.2:46–51 (Nov. 1943), 12.3:62–67 (Dec. 1943), 12.4:59–64 (Jan. 1944).

Feng Kuei-fen 馮桂芬. *Hsien-chih t'ang chi* 顯志堂集 (Collected essays of Feng Kuei-fen). 1876.

Fu I-ling 傅衣凌. *Ming-Ch'ing shih-tai shang-jen chi shang-yeh tzu-pen* 明清時代商人及商業資本 (Merchants and commercial capital during the Ming-Ch'ing times). Peking, 1956.

Hatano Yoshihiro 波多野善大, "Chūgoku yushutsucha no seisan kōzō" 中國輸出茶の生產構造 (Production structure of Chinese tea for export), *Nagoya daigaku bungakubu kenkyū ronshū, II, Shigaku* 名古屋大學文學部研究論集, II, 史學, 1:183–210 (1952). (Later included in his *Chūgoku kindai kōgyōshi no kenkyū* 中國近代工業史の研究 [Studies on early industrialization in China]. Kyoto, 1961, pp. 86–144).

Ho Lieh 何烈. *Li-chin chih-tu hsin-t'an* 厘金制度新探 (New inquiries into the likin system). Taipei, 1972.

Hsiang-kang Hua-tzu jih-pao 香港華字日報 (Hong Kong Chinese daily). Feng P'ing-shan Library, University of Hong Kong, Hong Kong.

Hsu Jun 徐潤. *Hsu Yü-chai tzu-hsu nien-p'u* 徐愚齋自敍年譜 (Chronological autobiography of Hsu Jun). 1 ts'e. 1927.

Hsu Jun et al. *Kuang-tung Hsiang-shan Hsu-shih tsung-p'u* 廣東香山徐氏宗譜 (The history of the Hsu clan in the Hsiang-shan district, Kwangtung). 8 ts'e. 1882.

Hsu K'o 徐珂. *Ch'ing pai lei-ch'ao* 清稗類鈔 (A classified collection of Ch'ing dynasty anecdotes). 48 ts'e. Shanghai, 1928.

Hua-tzu jih-pao. See *Hsiang-kang Hua-tzu jih-pao.*

Jen-min jih-pao 人民日報 (People's daily).

Ko Kung-chen 戈公振. *Chung-kuo pao-hsueh shih* 中國報學史 (A history of Chinese journalism). Shanghai, 1927.

Kuang-hsu ch'ao tung-hua hsu-lu 光緒朝東華續錄 (The Tung-hua records, continued: Kuang-hsu period), comp. Chu Shou-p'eng 朱壽朋. Shanghai, 1909.

Kuang-tung ts'ai-cheng shuo-ming shu 廣東財政說明書 (Descriptions of the financial administration of Kwangtung). 16 ts'e. 1910.

Kuo T'ing-i 郭廷以. *Chin-tai Chung-kuo shih-shih jih-chih* 近代中國史事日誌 (Daily historical events of modern China). 2 vols. Taipei, Cheng-chung, 1963.

Li Kuo-ch'i 李國祁, *Chung-kuo tsao-ch'i ti t'ieh-lu ching-ying* 中國早期的鐵路經營 (China's early railroad enterprises). Taipei, 1961.

Li Wen-chih 李文治, comp., *Chung-kuo chin-tai nung-yeh shih tzu-liao ti-i chi, 1840–1911* 中國近代農業史資料第一集, 1840–1911 (Source materials on the history of agriculture in modern China, 1st collection, 1840–1911). Peking, 1957.

Liang Chia-pin 梁嘉彬. *Kuang-tung shih-san hang k'ao* 廣東十三行考 (A study of the Canton thirteen hongs). Rev. ed. T'ai-chung,

Taiwan, 1960.

Lin Man-hung 林滿紅. "Ch'ing-mo pen-kuo ya-p'ien chih t'i-tai chin-k'ou ya-p'ien, 1858–1906" 清末本國鴉片之替代進口鴉片, 1858–1906 (The substitution of domestic opium for imported opium during the late Ch'ing period, 1858–1906), *Chung-yang yen-chiu yuan chin-tai shih yen-chiu so chi-k'an* 中央研究院近代史研究所集刊 (Bulletin of the Institute of Modern History, Academia Sinica) 9:385–432 (July 1980).

Liu Kuang-ching 劉廣京. "T'ang T'ing-shu chih mai-pan shih-tai" 唐廷樞之買辦時代 (Tong King-sing: His comprador years), *Ch'ing-hua hsueh-pao* 清華學報, n.s., 2:143–83 (June 1961).

———. "Cheng Kuan-ying *I-yen*: Kuang-hsu ch'u-nien chih pien-fa ssu-hsiang" 鄭觀應「易言」:光緒初年之變法思想 (Cheng Kuan-ying's *I-yen*: Reform proposals of the early Kuang-hsu period), *Ch'ing-hua hsueh-pao* 清華學報, n.s., 8.1–2:373–425 (1970).

———. "I-pa-pa-san nien Shang-hai chin-yung feng-ch'ao" 一八八三年上海金融風潮 (The financial crisis at Shanghai in 1883), *Fu-tan hsueh-pao* 复旦学报, She-hui ko-hsueh pan 社会科学版, 1983.3:94–102 (May 1983).

Liu Shih-chi 劉石吉. "Ch'ing-tai Chiang-nan shang-p'in ching-chi ti fa-chan yü shih-chen ti hsing-ch'i" 清代江南商品經濟的發展與市鎮的興起 (Commercial development and urbanization in Kiangnan during the Ch'ing period), M.A. thesis, National Taiwan University, 1975.

Liu Ta-chün 劉大鈞, ed. *Wu-hsing nung-ts'un ching-chi* 吳興農村經濟 (Rural economy of Wu-hsing). 1939.

Lo Yü-tung 羅玉東. *Chung-kuo li-chin shih* 中國釐金史 (History of likin in China). 2 vols. Shanghai, 1936.

Lü Shih-ch'iang 呂實強. *Ting Jih-ch'ang yü tzu-ch'iang yün-tung* 丁日昌與自強運動 (Ting Jih-ch'ang and the self-strengthening movement). Taipei, 1972.

Mao Tse-tung 毛澤東. *Mao Tse-tung hsuan-chi* 毛澤東選集 (Selected works of Mao Tse-tung). 6 vols. 10th printing. Peking, 1963.

Nieh Pao-chang 聶寶璋. "Ts'ung Mei-shang Ch'i-ch'ang lun-ch'uan kung-ssu ti ch'uang-pan yü fa-chan k'an mai-pan ti tso-yung" 從美商旗昌輪船公司的創辦與發展看買辦的作用 (The function of the comprador as viewed from the history of the American firm of Shanghai Steam Navigation Company), *Li-shih yen-chiu* 2:91–110 (1964).

Ou Pao-san 巫寶三, Feng Tse 馮澤, and Wu Ch'ao-lin 吳朝林, comps.,

Chung-kuo chin-tai ching-chi ssu-hsiang yü ching-chi cheng-ts'e tzu-liao hsuan-chi 中國近代經濟思想與經濟政策資料選輯, 1840–1864 (Selected materials of economic thought and economic policy in modern China, 1840–1864). Peking, 1959.

Pao Shih-ch'en 包世臣. *An Wu ssu-chung* 安吳四種 (Four works of Pao Shih-ch'en). 1872 preface.

P'eng Hsin-wei 彭信威. *Chung-kuo huo-pi shih* 中國貨幣史 (A history of Chinese currency). 2d ed. Shanghai, 1965.

P'eng Tse-i 彭澤益. "Shih-chiu shih-chi hou-ch'i Chung-kuo ch'eng-shih shou-kung-yeh shang-yeh hang-hui ti ch'ung-chien ho tso-yung" 十九世紀後期中國城市手工業商業行會的重建和作用 (Reconstruction and function of urban handicraft and commercial guilds in late nineteenth-century China), *Li-shih yen-chiu* 1:71–102 (1965).

P'eng Tse-i 彭澤益, comp. *Chung-kuo chin-tai shou-kung-yeh shih tzu-liao, 1840–1949* 中國近代手工業史資料, 1840–1949 (Source materials on the history of handicraft industry in modern China, 1840–1949). 4 vols. Peking, 1957.

P'eng Yü-hsin 彭雨新. "K'ang Jih chan-cheng ch'ien Han-k'ou ti yang-hang ho mai-pan" 抗日戰爭前漢口的洋行和買辦 (The foreign firms and compradors at Hankow before the resistance war against Japan). *Li-lun chan-hsien* 理論戰綫 (Theoretical war front) 11:28 (Feb. 1959).

Shang-hai ch'ien-chuang shih-liao 上海錢庄史料 (Historical materials of the native banks in Shanghai), comp. Chung-kuo jen-min yin-hang Shang-hai shih fen-hang 中國人民銀行上海市分行 (The Chinese People's Bank, Shanghai Branch). Shanghai, 1960.

Shang-hai hsien hsu-chih 上海縣續志 (Gazetteer of the Shanghai district, continued). 30 chüan. Shanghai, 1918.

Shang-hai shih mien-pu shang-yeh 上海市棉布商業 (The trade of cotton textiles in Shanghai city), ed. Chung-kuo she-hui k'e-hsueh yuan ching-chi yen-chiu so 中國社會科學院經濟研究所 (Economic Research Institute, Social Science Academy). Peking, 1979.

Shang-hai yen-chiu tzu-liao 上海研究資料 (Materials for research on Shanghai), ed. Shang-hai t'ung-she 上海通社. Shanghai, 1936.

Shen pao 申報 (Shanghai newspaper). Shanghai, 1872—.

Shen Pao-chen 沈葆楨. *Shen Wen-su-kung cheng-shu* 沈文肅公政書 (Administrative correspondence of Shen Pao-chen). 1880.

Shigeta Atsushi 重田德, "Shimmatsu ni okeru Konan cha no seisan kōzō, gokō kaikō igo o chūshin to shite" 清末における湖南

茶の生産構造——五港開港以後を中心として (The structure of tea production in Hunan in the late Ch'ing, especially after the opening of the five ports), *Jimbun kenkyū* 人文研究 (Studies on humanities) 16.4:369–418 (1962).

Sun Yü-t'ang 孫毓棠, comp., *Chung-kuo chin-tai kung-yeh shih tzu-liao ti-i chi, 1840–1895 nien* 中國近代工業史資料第一集, 1840–1895 年 (Source materials on the history of modern industry in China, 1st collection, 1840–1895). 2 vols. Peking, 1957.

Tōa Dōbunkai 東亞同文會. *Shina keizai zensho* 支那經濟全書 (Chinese economy series). 12 vols. Vols. 1–4, Osaka, 1907; vols. 5–12, Tokyo, 1908.

Toyama Gunji 外山軍治. "Shanhai no shinshō Yō Bō" 上海の紳商楊坊 (The Shanghai gentry-merchant Yang Fang), *Tōyōshi kenkyū* 東洋史研究, n.s., 1.4:17–34 (Nov. 1945).

Ts'ai-cheng shuo-ming-shu. See *Kuang-tung ts'ai-cheng shou-ming shu.*

Tseng Kuo-fan 曾國藩. *Tseng Wen-cheng kung shu-cha* 曾文正公書札 (Tseng Kuo-fan's letters). Shanghai, 1876.

Tung-hua hsu-lu. See *Kuang-hsu ch'ao tung-hua hsu-lu.*

Tzu-lin Hu-pao 字林滬報 (Shanghai newspaper).

Tz'u-yuan 辭源 (Dictionary of terms). Taipei, 1955.

Uchida Naosaku 內田直作, "Yōkō seido no kenkyū" 洋行制度の研究 (A study of the foreign firm system). *Shina kenkyū* 支那研究 50:187–211 (March 1939).

Wang Ching-yü 汪敬虞. "Shih-chiu shih-chi wai-kuo ch'in-Hua shih-yeh chung ti Hua-shang fu-ku huo-tung" 十九世紀外國侵華事業中的華商附股活動 (The activities of Chinese merchants in buying capital shares in the aggressive foreign enterprises in China during the nineteenth century). *Li-shih yen-chiu* 歷史研究, 4:39–74 (1965).

———, comp. *Chung-kuo chin-tai kung-yeh shih tzu-liao ti-erh chi, 1895–1914 nien* 中國近代工業史資料第二輯, 1895–1914 年 (Source materials on the history of modern industry in China, 2nd collection, 1895–1914). 2 vols. Peking, 1957.

Wang Erh-min 王爾敏, *Ch'ing-chi ping-kung-yeh ti hsing-ch'i* 清季兵工業的興起 (The rise of the armaments industry in the late Ch'ing period). Taipei, 1963.

Wang Yeh-chien 王業鍵. *Chung-kuo chin-tai huo-pi yü yin-hang ti yen-chin* 中國近代貨幣與銀行的演進, 1644–1937 (The development of money and banking in China, 1644–1937). Taipei, 1981.

Wu Hsing-lien 吳醒濂. *Hsiang-kang Hua-jen ming-jen shih-lueh* 香港華人名

人史略 (The prominent Chinese in Hong Kong). 2 vols. Hong Kong, 1937.

Yang Tuan-liu 楊端六. *Ch'ing-tai huo-pi chin-yung shih-kao* 清代貨幣金融史稿 (Draft history of money and currency in the Ch'ing period). Peking, 1962.

Yang Yin-p'u 楊蔭溥. *Yang-chu Chung-kuo chin-yung lun* 楊著中國金融論 (Money in China by Mr. Yang). Shanghai, 1932.

Yen Chung-p'ing 嚴中平. *Chung-kuo mien-fang-chih shih-kao* 中國棉紡織史稿 (A draft history of Chinese cotton spinning and weaving). Peking, 1955.

Yen Chung-p'ing et al., comp. *Chung-kuo chin-tai ching-chi shih t'ung-chi tzu-liao hsuan-chi* 中國近代經濟史統計資料選輯 (Selected statistical materials for China's modern economic history). Shanghai, 1961.

Yü Chieh-ch'iung 余捷瓊. *I-ch'i-ling-ling i-chiu-san-ch'i nien Chung-kuo yin-huo shu ch'u ju ti i-ko ku-chi* 一七〇〇—一九三七年中國銀貨輸出入的一個估計 (An estimate of the export and import of silver in China, 1700–1937). Changsha, 1940.

Yü Tsung-hsien 于宗先, et al., eds. *Chung-kuo ching-chi fa-chan shih lun-wen hsuan-chi* 中國經濟發展史論文選集 (Selected essays on Chinese economic development). 2 vols. Taipei, Lien-ching, 1980.

Index

Compositor: Asco Trade Typesetting Ltd.
Text: 10/13 Baskerville
Display: Baskerville
Printer: Braun-Brumfield, Inc.
Binder: Braun-Brumfield, Inc.